Appointments of Postmasters in Louisiana

12 January 1827–
28 December 1892

Harry F. Dill

HERITAGE BOOKS
2012

HERITAGE BOOKS
AN IMPRINT OF HERITAGE BOOKS, INC.

Books, CDs, and more—Worldwide

For our listing of thousands of titles see our website
at
www.HeritageBooks.com

Published 2012 by
HERITAGE BOOKS, INC.
Publishing Division
100 Railroad Ave. #104
Westminster, Maryland 21157

Copyright © 2002 Harry F. Dill

Other Heritage Books by the author:

African American Inhabitants of Rapides Parish, Louisiana: 15 June–4 Sept 1870

Appointments of Postmasters in Louisiana, 12 January 1827–28 December 1892

Louisiana Postmistress and Postmaster Appointments 20 June 1866–17 November 1931

Marriages and Deaths from The Caucasian, *Shreveport, Louisiana, 1903–1913*

Some Slaveholders and Their Slaves, Union Parish, Louisiana, 1839–1865
Harry F. Dill and William Simpson

The Underground Railroad and the Picayune *Connection*

All rights reserved. No part of this book may be reproduced or transmitted in any form or by any means, electronic or mechanical, including photocopying, recording or by any information storage and retrieval system without written permission from the author, except for the inclusion of brief quotations in a review.

International Standard Book Numbers
Paperbound: 978-0-7884-2090-0
Clothbound: 978-0-7884-9499-4

Table of Contents

Preface v

Records Group 28, Volume I 1

Records Group 28, Volume II 29

Records Group 28, Volume III 83

Records Group 28, Volume IV 155

Index 291

Preface

Appointments of postmasters in Louisiana (12 Jan 1827-28 Dec 1892) were extracted from a reel of microfilm produced by National Archives, Washington, DC, in 1968 from original, hand-written post office records.

The Postmaster General made appointments from 1775 when Congress named Benjamin Franklin as the first Postmaster General, until 1836, when Congress ruled that postmasters must be appointed by the President and confirmed by the Senate at post offices where annual compensation of a postmaster exceeded one thousand dollars. In smaller post offices, the Postmaster General continued to make appointments. (Identities of those appointed and confirmed are highlighted in this book, as (Pres) and (Pres & Sen).

In 1969 Congress removed the statutory requirement for presidential appointment and Senate confirmation. The Postal Reorganization Act of 1970 halted all appointments by the Postmaster General. Since then appointments have been made on merit alone, by selection boards.

When George Washington named Samuel Osgood as the first Postmaster General in 1789, under the Constitution, there were but 75 post offices in the United States. (The increase of post office locations in Louisiana, based upon population growth, can be seen from Volume II through Volume IV in this book)

It is hoped that a number of readers will experience the elation that arises upon discovery of an ancestor once considered lost! Added exhilaration could come in seeing both male and female forebears emerge as postmasters as well as members of family groups.

Records Group 28, Volume I

POST OFFICE LOCATIONS	POSTMASTER AND APPOINTMENT DATES
	ASCENSION PARISH
Donaldsonville	Francis Leford 24 Sep 1829 Richard Bond 17 Aug 1830 Andrew Gringoy 13 Sep 1838
New River	Henry B Sary 8 Mar 1836 Joseph D Blonin 28 Mar 1838 William Lees 23 Jul 1839 William R Booter 21 Mar 1840 Terince J Landry 20 Feb 1841 Horace G Whiting 1 Mar 1842 Shabael Tillotson 17 Apr 1844
	ASSUMPTION PARISH
Assumption	Pierre F Helluin 4 Feb 1831
Bedford	George C Bedford 23 Nov 1838 Philip B Key 18 Feb 1842 Philip Le Coy 13 Mar 1844
Paincourtville	Andre LeBlanc 23 Jul 1839 Elisee E Malhiot 6 May 1840
	AVOYELLES PARISH
Marksville Courthouse Discontinued 19 May 1844 Reestablished 3 Aug 1844	James Rey Jr 23 Dec 1828 A Durand 28 Apr 1843 Thomas B Tiller 3 Aug 1843 William H Duvall 17 Sep 1844
Bordino	Thomas H Kimball 11 May 1837

Bordeau

    Henry A Ford 23 Mar 1837
    Felix H Loze 16 Sep 1839
    Hylaire Gradnight 20 Oct 1839
    Evarist Rablais 15 Feb 1840
    Amboise Lecour 4 May 1840
    William L Voorhies 4 Sep 1840
    Robert A Cochran 26 Feb 1841

Holmesville
Disc 3 Jul 1838
Reest 21 Jul 1838

    Patrick H Glaze 23 Mar 1837

    Fabian Ricord 21 Jul 1838
    Shaw N Randon 27 Jul 1841
    Charles Kibbe 27 Jun 1842

Bayou Rouge

    Reuben Tousely 8 Jun 1837
    Daniel Clark Jr 27 Jun 1837
    Alonson G Pearce 28 Jul 1841

Bayou Ridge Prairie
Disc 15 May 1844

    Lovell Howell Snowden 29 Sep 1838

Borovina Mansura

    Nelson Durand 2 Feb 1839

Simmesport

    Samuel C Dunn 18 Mar 1840
    Daniel T Orr 22 Dec 1840
    J Kirk 27 Oct 1842
    Daniel T Orr 8 Jul 1843
    Ignatius Kirk 29 Mar 1844

Gorton's Landing
Disc 30 Jul 1844

    Lewis Gorton 13 Feb 1843

Borodino

    Abroise Lacour 2 Dec 1843

CARROLL PARISH

Milliken's Bend

Disc 14 May 1834
Reest 27 Nov 1835

    Edward Lee 17 Jul 1832
    A J Sowry 14 May 1833

    James B Rusk 27 Nov 1835

	James B Rusk 21 Jul 1838
	Philip O'Brien 19 Apr 1839
	Isaac Casmer 30 Sep 1839
Pecan Grove	Francis Y Thompkins 13 Feb 1835
	T M Prentice 18 Jul 1838
	James W Ledbetter 12 Aug 1839
	George R Newman 23 Nov 1839
Lake Providence	Thomas J Chambliss 26 Dec 1835
	William R Jones 1 Aug 1837
	James C Hollingsworth 15 Jul 1840
	Hercules Hillman 25 Jan 1844
Aston	Peter J Flynn 2 Oct 1844

CATAHOULA PARISH

Burshley Creek	James Ruggles 1 Mar 1832
	James Taliafero 1 Mar 1833
	John Galvin 15 May 1837
Disc 10 Jul 1839	
Reest 27 Aug 1839	Moses Wiggins 27 Aug 1839
Harrisonburg Courthouse	James M Daughters 10 Jan 1837
	Edom L Farris 27 Jun 1837
	George H Bell 30 Aug 1837
	Robert Fristas 1 Jun 1838
	Michael H Dosson 26 Feb 1839
	Allen D Ratcliff 13 May 1839
	Pleasant M Blakston 20 Apr 1840
	Rosemond Legrase 18 Jul 1841
	Edom L Farris 11 Oct 1842
	William W Tew 15 May 1843
	Stephen T Clark 28 Jul 1843
	Oren Mayo 9 Oct 1844
Lovelace	George W Lovelace 27 Jun 1832
Disc 15 Dec 1834	

New Kentucky	John H Meredith 25 Apr 1834
	John Lee 19 Feb 1835 Note: Moved away
Copenhagen	Henri Frellsen 18 Jul 1837
	J Bollenhagen 25 Feb 1840
Columbia	Fleming Noble 9 Aug 1837
	James L Stokes 18 May 1839
	J M Stuart 18 Mar 1840
Trinity	Felix Robb 7 Aug 1837
Disc 10 Jul 1839	
Reest 13 May 1842	E Hyde 13 May 1842
	Felix Robb 7 Jul 1842
	William H Turnley 19 Jan 1844
Doty's	Edward Doty 13 May 1842
Disc 29 Nov 1843	
Percy's	Robert D Percy 13 May 1842
Disc 29 Nov 1843	
Kirk's Ferry	David G Pickens 25 May 1844 (**Pres**)
Brown's Ferry	Coleman Brown 25 May 1844
Doty's	Silas Sillard 25 May 1844
Disc 24 May 1845	

CLAIBORNE PARISH

Allen's Settlement	John Murrell 20 Sep 1836
Russellville	Robert L Kilgore 26 May 1830
	David McMahon 14 May 1833
	James J Rogers 22 Jan 1834
	Isaac McMahon 18 Feb 1835
	Hiram Wilson 28 Oct 1835
	William B Hargis 17 Oct 1836

	Edmond King 1 Nov 1837
	Lazarus L Bard 14 Nov 1837
	James W Wright 20 Feb 1839
	Thomas H Jones 11 Feb 1841
Overton	David C Pratt 6 Sep 1837
	H L Newman 5 May 1838
	Philamon Rathbern 15 Oct 1839
	William C Copes 25 Oct 1842
Mount Lebanon	Reuben Drake 27 Dec 1837
	Landry A Key 17 Feb 1843
Darbone	Allen Bonner 26 Mar 1838
	Sack P Gee 18 Jul 1838
Disc 29 Nov 1838	
Manning's	Simon Manning 18 Jul 1838
Black Lake	Isaac Randolph 16 Jul 1842
	Allen Harris 23 Mar 1844
Minden	Miers Fisher 9 Feb 1839
	Nathaniel Moore 13 Jul 1841
	John Baker 13 Mar 1844
Madden's	William Madden 23 Oct 1839
Red Hill	Vincent Walker 9 Feb 1839
Flat Lick	Vincent Walker 11 Apr 1839
	Stephen Butler 15 Jan 1842
Quay	Jabezo Sanders 16 Jun 1841

CONCORDIA PARISH

New Carthage	William E Miner 28 Mar 1831
	David Starbrough 15 Feb 1835
	Joseph H D Bowman 30 Mar 1836

	John H Adkins 3 Aug 1836
Samoset Disc 19 Nov 1833	John Perkins 27 Jun 1832
Tomkinsville	Francis J Tomkins 26 Jul 1832 Fielding Fant 13 Feb 1835 Lewis Levy 22 Jun 1835
Disc 23 Nov 1837	
Waterproof Disc 26 Jul 1837	Abner Smalley 8 Nov 1836
Vidalia	Allen Whitlock 13 May 1842 Thomas B Thorpe 15 May 1844
St. Joseph	J Y Hollingsworth 8 Oct 1842

EAST BATON ROUGE PARISH

Baton Rouge Courthouse	Hugh Alexander 13 May 1829 Abel Waddill 14 Aug 1835 Moses L Meeker 22 Jun 1841 Hugh T Waddill 30 Dec 1843
Manchac	James J Neilson 2 Mar 1831 Samuel Peniston 24 Jul 1833 Fergus Duplantier and Gilbert Dagrie 10 Aug 1833 Francis Roberts 13 Dec 1834
Sandy Creek	P A Walker and D Hackett 1 Jul 1832 Amos Kent 26 Aug 1833 R H Burnett 20 Feb 1833
Ward's Creek	William Webb and B Haralson 10 Aug 1833 Joseph Heard 19 Nov 1833
Disc 28 Oct 1835	

Pine Grove

Disc 2 Nov 1835

Rovell Pearse 11 Nov 1833
Ananias Allen 9 Jul 1835

Burlington

Disc 19 Oct 1839

Amos Kent 19 Feb 1835
David W Ronnsville 20 Apr 1836

Redwood Grove

Disc 28 Jul 1842

John Talbott 1 Nov 1837
Robert W Newport 27 Sep 1838

Fontania
Disc 18 Nov 1841
Reest 8 Sep 1843
Disc 23 Oct 1844

James A Ronatoson 18 Mar 1840

James A Ronatoson 8 Sep 1843

Stony Point

James H Allison 9 Jul 1840
Michael Watson 15 Oct 1844

Salem
Disc 3 Feb 1842

Thomas W Gatlin 9 Aug 1841

EAST FELICIANA PARISH

Clinton Courthouse

John F Custman 10 Sep 1830
George W Munday 7 Mar 1833
William E Terrill 9 Jun 1834
George W Munday 23 Aug 1837

Jackson

Joseph Nichols 10 Nov 1832
Sandford Perry 2 Aug 1835

Mount Pleasant

Jess Hooper 24 Feb 1833

Richland Hill

Disc 28 Apr 1843
Reest 15 May 1843

William Silliman (No date)
John F Dickey 9 Mar 1835
Thomas C Black 21 Apr 1836

Angus McCarstle 15 May 1843

Woodward's Store	Abishai Woodward 28 Sep 1829
	Stephen Tildon 12 Mar 1834
Stony Point	John M Neell 26 Dec 1832
	Daniel Morgan and
	B J Chaney 11 Feb 1833
Disc 17 Sep 1835	
Port Hudson	Richard Roach 21 Feb 1833
	James B Bonner 8 Apr 1834
	James B Bonner and
	J D Barton 28 Sep 1834
	James H Row 31 Jan 1840
	Samuel H Row 3 Mar 1840
	Wallace Badger 12 Apr 1842
	James Hudson 15 May 1844
Mount Willing	A G Newport 22 Mar 1834
Disc 26 Jul 1838	
Woodland	Stephen Tildon 4 Jun 1834
	Benajah Dougherty and
	Samuel S Harrell 5 Aug 1842
	Alvert W Poole 29 Nov 1844
Mount Pleasant	Frederic M Kent 21 Apr 1836
	Guy B Willard 6 Apr 1837
	Jackson M Chaney 26 Oct 1838
Disc 23 Mar 1839	

IBERVILLE PARISH

Iberville Courthouse	Francis D Miller 27 Jul 1832
	Jean Eli Hebert 29 Nov 1834
	David T Ross 6 Jul 1838
	Jeremiah Pritchard 23 Oct 1839
	Joseph Walsh 29 Aug 1842
	Maxile LeBlanc 2 Nov 1843
Plaquemine	Louis DeSobry (No date) 1832

	John Burke 24 May 1836
	Joseph E Wilson 17 Oct 1837
	Thomas Chesnut 25 Mar 1839
	Archibald Block 2 Jul 1842
Claiborne Disc 19 Nov 1833	John Dominiques 24 Feb 1833
Dunboyne Disc 29 Jan 1834	Benjamin F Owen 21 Feb 1833
Khorasson Disc 1 Apr 1837	Eugene Breaux 8 Apr 1836 H G Doyle 21 Mar 1837
Bayou Goula	Joseph Breaux 26 Jul 1838 Henry G Doyle 19 Nov 1838 Valrey Roth 15 Jul 1839 Arvillien Breaux 7 Sep 1839 Henry Tennent 23 May 1842 P H Rivette 15 Mar 1843 Charles Fay 7 May 1844
Bayou Grosse Tete Disc 17 Oct 1839	James Crain 23 Apr 1838

LAFAYETTE PARISH

Perry's Bridge	Robert Perry 14 Aug 1830
Vermilionville	Emilie Chaix 21 Oct 1828 Allan Smith 20 Jan 1838 Daniel O'Bryan 23 Mar 1839 James M Moore 5 Aug 1840

LAFOURCHE PARISH

Thibodeauxville	James O'Connor 3 Nov 1832 Alexander Lawson 1 Dec 1832 Newcomb Hunt 20 Jan 1835

George W Squires 2 Apr 1835
Thibodeaux LaForest 23 May 1840

Thibodeaux Courthouse   Antoine LaForest 1 Jul 1840
Jonathan C White 26 Jan 1842

LIVINGSTON PARISH

Springfield   Abel Bartlett 17 Aug 1832
(Illegible entry)
Charles A Mix 23 Apr 1838
John H Wall 2 Feb 1839
Sylvester G Parsons 2 Jul 1842
William Westmoreland 20 Nov 1843

Port Vincent   John J Buck 28 Feb 1833

Van Buren   Young Settoon 1 Mar 1833

Beech Hill   David Felder 28 May 1835
Disc 20 Aug 1842

Banneyville   William Akins 7 Jun 1837
Disc 2 Oct 1838

NATCHITOCHES PARISH

Cantonment   Gordon H Irwin 14 Dec 1837

Cloutierville   Mayre Sanopaurae (no date)
Charles F Benoist 18 May 1837

Crow's Ferry   Acy Edwards 30 Mar 1832
Disc 15 May 1834

Isle Briville   J J Dumarest 8 Mar 1832
Charles Lewis and
          E Langlier 16 Jan 1834
Oscar Roubien 30 Apr 1834

Tarborough   W R D Speight 18 Apr 1840
                          Hosea Presley 18 Jun 1840

Disc 10 May 1842

Cadies (?)   Stephen M Sean 29 May 1841

Natchitoches Courthouse   Daniel R Hopkins 22 Jul 1831
                          James T Harrison 4 Dec 1833

                          D R Hopkins and
                                  John R Dunn 1 Jan 1834
                          William P Jones 16 Mar 1835
                          George W Reese 27 Apr 1840
                          John A Irvine 18 May 1841
                          Charles A Bullard 28 Jul 1841

Campti   Joseph T Robinson 2 Jan 1836
                          Remy Pirot 15 May 1837
                          Hilaire Bordelon 5 Jan 1841
                          A P Starring 11 Oct 1841

Disc 3 Jul 1842
Reest 15 Mar 1843   John Marcalle 15 Mar 1843

Fort Jessup   Gordon H Irvine 15 Apr 1833
                          A G Blanchard 3 Aug 1836
                          Willington A Mackie 29 Jul 1837
                          P H Barbour 5 Aug 1837
                          Presley H Craig 6 Jul 1838
                          Jeremiah H Cloud 14 Nov 1840
                          Henry J Lamb 3 Jun 1840

Negreet   John Boyce 18 Apr 1837
                          Asa A Reading 9 Oct 1837
                          Robert D Wright 29 Mar 1842

Thompson's Ferry   B J Thompson 15 Aug 1857

Sabine   Robert D Bogguss 4 Nov 1857
Disc 10 Jul 1839

Coushatta Chute	George Hammett 29 Sep 1843
	James K Belden 9 Oct 1844
Bayou Nichols Disc 17 Oct 1839	Stephen Pate 10 Apr 1838
Coate's Bluff	John G Green 10 Apr 1838
Temperance Hill	Robert McDonato 20 May 1843
Coushatta Disc 17 Oct 1839	John D Swain 10 Apr 1838
Grand Cane	William M Allen 10 Apr 1838
	Thomas D Hailes 10 Jul 1843
Loggy Bayou Disc 28 Jul 1842	Washington Bastion 10 Apr 1835
Shreveport	Charles A Sewall 15 May 1838
Manning's	Simon Manning 18 Jul 1838
Lowe's Ferry	John A McLanahan 23 Nov 1838
Randolph Disc 18 Mar 1842	Isaac Randolph 23 Jan 1840

ORLEANS PARISH

Coquille Disc (illegible date)	John Montfort 23 Jun 1828
New Orleans Courthouse	William H Reily 16 Jun 1829
	William H Ker 7 Jul 1836
	William H McQueen 27 Jul 1839
	Gabriel Montamat 9 Sep 1840
	(Illegible entry) 10 Jul 1841
	John B Dawson 18 Apr 1843

Alexander G Pinn 19 Dec 1843

Fort Pike   Francis Lee 30 Mar 1843

OPELOUSAS PARISH

Bayou Chicot   John B Isabell (no date)
                             Note: See St. Landry

Grand Coteau   Peter Doremus 29 Nov 1832

Washington   James Neyland 17 Jun 1834
Disc 31 Aug 1835

PLAQUEMINES PARISH

Fort Jackson   Michael M Clarke 9 Feb 1832
                             Jeremiah Badon 20 Feb 1833
                             A C Fowler 4 Apr 1834

Balize   James B Ross 19 Jan 1844
Disc 28 Jul 1842

POINT COUPEE PARISH

Pointe Coupee   Joseph Jewell 12 Jan 1827
                             (Illegible entry)
                             Washington Jewell 24 Mar 1838
                             Narcisse Beauvais 15 Jul 1840
                             Victor Moraine 18 Aug 1841

Red River Landing   John M Phillips 7 Apr 1836
                             Isaac S Phillips 25 Jun 1836
                             Charles Bishop 10 Apr 1838
                             William Brooks 30 Aug 1839
                             Joseph A May 27 Apr 1840
                             Francis Routh 15 May 1841
Disc 28 Jul 1841

Waterloo   Lavinien Pourcian 28 Oct 1840

Disc 29 Sep 1843 Reest 26 Feb 1844	Zenon Demorvello 7 Jun 1843 James M Bayley 26 Feb 1844
The Village	Jacob Fisher 20 Feb 1841
Atchafalaya	John T Brooks 13 Jun 1844
Williamsport	August M Shawl 3 Jul 1844

RAPIDES PARISH

Alexandria Courthouse	James Norment 24 Sep 1827 Vincent Page 23 Feb 1833 Archibald H Williams 5 Apr 1833 Charles Leckie 23 Sep 1837 Tilghman G Complin 23 Jan 1840 Thomas W Compton 7 Sep 1841 Lewis Zim 24 Jul 1843
Cheneyville	Thomas P Rich 21 May 1832 Leonidas A Robert 20 Feb 1833 Peter Randon 26 May 1835 A Robert and William H Cureton 1 Jul 1835 George W Smith 5 May 1838 James M Ardrey 24 Aug 1839 George W Smith 1 Mar 1842
Cotile	Daniel Robert 10 May 1830 (Illegible entry) Robert A Crane 16 Apr 1833 Thomas H Bonner 19 Feb 1835 D W Buckley 17 Oct 1836
Lamorie Bridge Disc 9 Jul 1835	John F C Henderson 27 Mar 1834
Plaisance	Marcelle Valery 21 Mar 1837 J M Bret LaCour 6 Oct 1841

Disc 18 Sep 1843

Spring Hill	Elisha Robinson 26 Apr 1839 Joseph R Eastbarn 28 Jul 1840 Thomas Rano 2 Aug 1841
Disc 8 Jul 1843	
Big Creek	Thomas Hooper 28 Apr 1843

ST. CHARLES PARISH

Ormand	(Illegible entry) Thomas Germain 26 Jul 1832
Disc 9 Mar 1835	
St. Charles Courthouse	Francois Chaix 9 Dec 1843 Onesime Touzanne 20 Oct 1844

ST. HELENA PARISH

Amite	William Collingsworth 12 Jul 1832 M Levy 27 Aug 1832 Peter A B Williams 24 Jun 1834 E Williams 25 Aug 1834 Robert Walker 24 Aug 1835
St. Helena Courthouse	John Holloway 20 Dec 1830 Paris Childress 12 Feb 1832 T G Davidson 3 Jul 1833
Mount Pleasant	Jesse W Hooper 24 Feb 1832 Mordacai Powell 22 May 1833 E Smith and W S Round 2 Jul 1833 Daniel Sharpe 23 Jun 1836 Frederick Starnes 4 Sep 1840 Blass Spiller 18 Sep 1841
Greensburgh	Maurice Cannon 26 Mar 1833 Elias H Murphy 21 Aug 1833

	James A Blount 27 Mar 1834
	D Addison and
	F C Kendrick 20 Apr 1834
	Gillian Wood 28 Jul 1834
	F C Kendrick and
	H F Kendrick 1 Nov 1834
	William H Dobbs 4 Nov 1836
	Sheppard B Draughan 20 Feb 1838
	Benjamin F Draughan 23 Apr 1838
	Henry Burd 22 Mar 1839
	Isaac H Wright 16 Sep 1839
	Isaac H Wright 22 Jul 1843
Amackersville	Harting P Howard 10 Jun 1836
	William Melton 6 Apr 1837
Disc 1 Apr 1840	
Darlington	William Collingsworth 16 Nov 1836
	Samuel B Hughes 15 Aug 1838
	William L Townsend 17 Feb 1844

ST. JAMES PARISH

Bringur's	Arc Chapdre (No date)
	Joseph Landry Sr 13 (No month) 1834
	Joseph Landry Jr 10 Feb 1835
Dubourg	Jean D Dubourg 11 Jun 1839
Disc 25 Jun 1842	

ST. JOHN THE BAPTIST PARISH

Bonnet Carrie	William H Barker 16 Dec 1830
	L McKay and
	J B Weltz 11 Nov 1832
	George Mackenzie 11 Oct 1833
	(No first name) De Lancieville 4 Dec 1834
	Pierre Burel 4 Apr 1836
	Thomas Norvell 29 Nov 1838
	Adolph Guyol 7 Jun 1843

ST. LANDRY PARISH

Calcasieu	Reed Perkins 4 Dec 1832 Isaac Applewhite 5 Jan 1837 Robert Neblett 13 Dec 1837
Cole's Settlement	Joseph T Calligan 6 Dec 1832 John T Heath 13 Jan 1833 Solomon Bonds 3 Oct 1833 William Forman and J Simmons 5 Apr 1834
Disc (Illegible date) Reest 24 Jan 1835 Disc 18 Nov 1840	Absolam Cole 24 Jan 1835
Opelousas	Edward W Taylor 11 Jan 1830 Guy H Bell 6 Aug 1834
Bayou Chicot	John B Isabell (No date) William Akenhead 28 Apr 1843
Grand Coteau	Peter Doremus 29 Nov 1832 Benjamin A Smith 26 Jan 1837 Charles B Smith 23 Oct 1839 Ferdinand L Muso 28 Oct 1840 Auguste Sambre 16 Jul 1842
Ville Platte	Daniel J Contini 23 Aug 1834 Marcellin Garand 16 Jul 1842
Washington Disc 18 Jul 1838 Reest 21 Jul 1838	Evariste Dijean 23 Mar 1837 Evariste Kijean 21 Jul 1838 William H Bassett 27 Nov 1839 Nathan Gilbert 10 Feb 1844
Buchanan's Ferry	James H Buchanan 29 Mar 1838
Ballew's Ferry	John Lyons Jr 11 May 1838

Plaquemine Brule Disc 1 Mar 1842 Reest 23 Sep 1842	John Cook 11 May 1838 Joseph Clark 23 Sep 1842 Jesse B Clark 23 May 1844
Big Woods Disc 18 Jul 1838	Robert C Neblett 11 May 1838
Richland Disc 8 Oct 1840	Edmund C Watson 27 Dec 1838 Eugene Egan 6 Mar 1839
Bayou Beouff	Edmund C Watson 28 Dec 1838

ST. MARTIN PARISH

St. Martinville Courthouse	Ransom Easton 19 Feb 1831 William L Stuart 30 May 1835 A Hamilton and H B Easton 1 Jul 1835 Adam Giffen 26 Dec 1835 Fergus Fusalier 5 May 1837 Valsin A Fournet 15 Jun 1838
New Iberia	Clarkson Edgar 20 Feb 1830 Achille Birard 14 Nov 1834 John Taylor 22 May 1837 Abner Milner 15 Jan 1839 John DeValcourt 5 Mar 1839
Breaux Bridge Disc 2 Jul 1838 Reest 18 Feb 1841	Jules Hardy 8 Mar 1837 F Genin 23 Nov 1837 Etienne Bulliard 18 Feb 1841 Edmund Bulliard 28 Apr 1843

ST. MARY PARISH

Dutch Settlement	Charles M Charpantier (No date)

	Arma Cornay and James Owen (No date)
Franklin Courthouse	Matthew Nimmo Jr 14 May 1830 Bennet A Curtis 30 Sep 1833 Judson Harmon 7 Jun 1836 Peter Picot 1 Apr 1837 Philip H Parrott 11 Jun 1838 Richard T Cocke 16 Oct 1838 Edward L Nimmo 8 Apr 1839 Timothy J Walker 1 Jun 1841
Jeanerett's	John W Jeanerett 25 Feb 1830 Charles Nettleton 18 May 1833 William Smith 15 Feb 1834 William H Bassett 7 Jun 1834 William Smith 11 May 1835 F D Richardson 14 Mar 1836 Nicholas L Prevost 24 Jul 1838 Aorian Virille 24 Feb 1841 Clet Provost 8 Apr 1842
Centreville	Joseph Bryan 1 Mar 1833 Charles Nettleton 23 Aug 1835 Bayliss L Wilcox 15 May 1837 Joshua B Cary 9 May 1838
Disc 23 May 1842 Reest 2 Nov 1843	Charles Nettleton 2 Nov 1843
Chauton	Victor Lataste 31 Mar 1841 Aristion Armelin 18 Aug 1841 Demary Nicholas 24 Jun 1842 Jules Guillard 27 Sep 1844
Pattersonville	John A Dwight 1 May 1844

ST. TAMMANY PARISH

Covington Courthouse	Elijah M Terrell 20 Apr 1829 Wesley Mallory 18 Jun 1833

	(Illegible entry)
	Thomas W Minton 6 May 1835
	Gilvary H Kennedy 7 Feb 1837
	(Illegible entry)
	Philip Keler 28 Oct 1840
Madisonville	M V Pinn and
	James Ruddock 29 Dec 1832
	William Battison 11 Jun 1833
	E Terel and Henry Boyd 30 Jun 1833
	D H Robertson and
	M Spring 15 Jan 1835
	Charles Y Kimball 10 Feb 1835
	Joseph Calmer 21 Mar 1837
	Henry Haynes 23 Dec 1839
	Matthew Dicks 23 Dec 1840
	Edward C Lehmanowsky 23 May 1844
Marburyville	Simeon C Blankston 16 Dec 1830
	Eli Headen 18 Dec 1838
	Milton Day 31 Jul 1839
	Eli Headen 7 Jul 1840
	Eli Headen 18 Dec 1843
Sweetwater	William Marbury 26 Dec 1832
	A T McNeil and
	Alen Rogers 2 Feb 1833
	B B Headen 30 Aug 1837
Disc 10 Jan 1838	
Reest 1 Jun 1840	William Marbury 1 Jun 1840
Tangipaho	Franklin L Warner 8 Apr 1834
	R McCarthy and
	G Rickinston 10 Mar 1834
Disc 10 Nov 1835	
Pine Grove	Thomas C Terry 25 Apr 1836
Cypress Grove	George Smith 17 Aug 1839
Disc 3 Jul 1842	

Mandeville   Antoine P Sanaux 29 Aug 1843

TERREBONNE PARISH

Cazeaux   Pierre Cazeaux 20 May 1831
Disc 18 Nov 1833

Williamsburgh   Caleb B Watkins 23 May 1831
Disc 18 Nov 1833

Houma Courthouse   Curtis Rockwood 1 Aug 1834
           John T Rockwood 25 Oct 1843

OUACHITA PARISH

Caldwell   (Illegible entry)
           Thomas B Rutland 8 Nov 1832

Lake Providence   James D Kerr 21 Jul 1831
           David R Richardson 16 Oct 1835
           Thomas J Chambliss 26 Dec 1835

Monroe Courthouse   Barnard Hemkin 1 Mar 1832
           Paul McEmery 11 Jun 1841
           John B Filhiol 28 Jan 1843

Pecan Grove   John L Buck 12 Mar 1831
           Francis Y Tomkins 12 Feb 1835

Pine Hill   Sheperd Wood 5 Jan 1833
Disc 14 May 1834

Point Pleasant   Eden G Garrett 27 Jul 1837
           James Garrett 25 Apr 1838
           John Temple 5 Mar 1842

Chadre   Haywood Alford 25 Mar 1838

Colvin's   Jeptha Colvin 24 Mar 1838

Mount Aerial   Haywood Alford 13 Jul 1838
                           James Grisham 18 Jul 1842
Disc 9 Feb 1843

Island De Liro   J L Brigham 24 Mar 1838
Disc 18 Jul 1838

Prairie Mer Rouge   Thomas C Lewis 24 Nov 1838
Disc 10 Jul 1839

WASHINGTON PARISH

Franklinton Courthouse   E P Ellis 22 Apr 1829
                           Jonathan Garrett 27 Jun 1833
                           Benjamin Hart Jr 1 May 1834
                           David Slocum 11 May 1835
                           Clabourn Hart 11 Feb 1836
                           Joshua Yarbrough 5 Apr 1838
                           William W Simmons 23 Sep 1838
                           Alexander Lea 16 Apr 1839
                           Stephen Gay 25 Feb 1840
                           David Gilchrist 11 Feb 1841
                           Richard A Sibley 23 May 1842
                           David G Lea 15 Oct 1842
                           Benjamin A Beason 15 May 1843
                           Presley Germain 27 Nov 1844

Goffsboro   John R Goff 29 Oct 1829
Disc 28 Oct 1835

Jacksonville Springs   David Ford 26 Jan 1832
                           John Landaman 19 Feb 1835

Cutrerville   Joseph Cutrer 21 Feb 1835

Siblia   Robert F Sibley 22 Nov 1834

Oak Grove   William Brumfield 30 May 1835

	Sherwood C Stratham 21 Mar 1838
	John Bickham 2 Jan 1839
	Elbert Clower 16 Apr 1839
	George Baumfield 1 Oct 1840
	Isaac A Myles 5 Oct 1842
Palestine Disc 28 Apr 1843	Martin G Penn 22 Apr 1840
Shady Grove Disc 19 Apr 1842 Reest 1 Jul 1844	Daniel R Warren 23 Nov 1840 Thomas Pearson 1 Jul 1844

WEST BATON ROUGE PARISH

West Baton Rouge	William Thomas 31 May 1836
Labdell's Store	James A Labdell 9 Sep 1839 Dexter Brooks 13 Feb 1841 Stephen Winters 18 Jan 1843 Hiram Noyes 15 Aug 1844
Bruly Landing	Ursin Aillet 15 Feb 1840 Eli LaJeune 7 Jun 1843

WEST FELICIANA PARISH

Laurel Hill	A T Simmons 24 Nov 1831 Stephen Windham 1 Aug 1832 William S Hamilton and John Wiley 15 Feb 1833 Nele N McCarstle 11 Aug 1834 (Illegible entry) Alexander Wilson 30 Aug 1841
St. Francisville	John M Bell 12 Mar 1831 William Cobb 13 Sep 1834 (Illegible entry) (Illegible entry) Lenfray T Landry 26 Jul 1838

	William A Sheldon 5 Jun 1839
	Rufus K Howell 29 Oct 1841
	Davis Austen 9 Feb 1842
	(Illegible entry)
Tunica Disc 23 Jun 1834	Charles H Davis 26 Jul 1833

JEFFERSON PARISH

Lafayette	Lawrence R Kenny 11 Nov 1835 Thomas Cook 28 Apr 1843
Carrollton	James Gilbert 31 Oct 1844

ST. BERNARD PARISH

Terre Aux Boeuffs Disc 12 Sep 1844 Reest 23 Jun 1852 Disc 29 Mar 1855	Vincent Nunez 10 Feb 1843 Vincent Nunez 23 Jun 1852 Francisco Ariste 19 Apr 1853

MADISON PARISH

McEachern's	Dan McEachern 11 Apr 1838
Walnut Bayou Disc 11 Apr 1840	Z H Rawlings 11 Apr 1838
New Carthage	John H Adkins 3 Aug 1836 William G Frasier 16 Aug 1842
Richmond Courthouse	Dan McEachern 14 Jun 1838 Isaac Casmer 14 May 1839 Jacob C Seale 12 Mar 1840 Richmond J Brashear 19 Sep 1840 Alfred Potter 23 May 1842 Nathaniel C Dortch 30 Dec 1843 Eli Ferry 23 Oct 1844

Milliken's Bend	Isaac Casmer 30 Sep 1839 Perry L Kennard 13 Jul 1841 Hector H McLeary 7 Jun 1843
Young's Point	Alfred M Young 23 May 1840
Chesterfield	Joseph W Williams 22 Jul 1841
Chickama Bend	John Seaton 9 Oct 1844

CADDO PARISH

Shreveport Courthouse	Charles L Sewall 15 May 1838 Seth Sheldon 25 Jun 1840 William Thatcher 30 Jul 1842
Summer Grove	Matthew Watson 17 Jul 1840 Richard A Catliff 18 Aug 1841 Jasper Powlis 29 Apr 1844 Robert V Marye 20 Jul 1844
Greenwood	William L Lewis 1 Jun 1840 James K Bayliss 3 Jul 1844
Tylerville	Ballard F Eppes 2 Nov 1844
Grand Cane	Thomas D Waites 10 Jul 1843
Spring Rogers	John L Rogers 7 Jun 1843 Dan Bozeman 15 May 1844

DE SOTO PARISH

Grand Cane	Thomas D Hailes 10 Feb 1843
Keatchie	William A Thorp 15 May 1844
Mansfield	Jacob D Wemple 30 Nov 1844

UNION PARISH

Farmerville   James H Seale 2 May 1840
                           Enoch B Whitson 7 Jul 1842

Enterprise   Wilson E Eubank 7 May 1840
                           Willoughby J H Dees 11 Nov 1840
Disc 1 May 1842

TENSAS PARISH

St. Joseph   J Y Hollingsworth 8 Oct 1842

Waterproof   Joseph Gorton 15 May 1844

Tensas Courthouse   J W Davenport 3 Jul 1844

Hard Times   J Y Hollingsworth 11 Jul 1844

Bellvue Landing   William T S Compton 3 Dec 1844

CALDWELL PARISH

Copenhagen   Jacob Bollenhagen 25 Jun 1840

Columbia Courthouse   James M Stuart 11 Mar 1840
                           Andrew J Grayson 3 Feb 1841

SABINE PARISH

Temperance Hill   Robert K McDonald 20 May 1843
Disc 6 Dec 1843

Many Courthouse   William L Rogers 11 Dec 1843
                           Chichester Chaplin Jr 9 Oct 1844

CALCASIEU

Big Woods   Thomas W Forsyth 16 Nov 1841
                           Hardy Coward 13 Apr 1842

Buchanan's Ferry Needham Coward 27 Sep 1844
Disc 15 May 1844

John C Ward 26 Feb 1844

FRANKLIN PARISH

Boeuff Prairie   Abram B Seay 2 Nov 1843

Hurricane   Ralph Price 15 May 1844

Oakley   Samuel G Cloud 13 Jun 1844

POST OFFICE LOCATIONS	POSTMASTER AND DATES OF APPOINTMENT
ASCENSION PARISH	
Donaldsonville	Andrew Gringoy 13 Sep 1838 Victor Marin 2 Sep 1850 Andrew Gringoy 20 Apr 1853
New River	Shabael Tillotson 17 Apr 1844 Horace G Whiting 22 Jul 1845 Henry Doval 11 Jun 1849
Live Oak	Honore V Laman 5 Oct 1848 Cyprien Bourgeois 29 Sep 1850 Honore V Laman 31 Mar 1854 Jules Landry 1 Sep 1854
Turead	Francois Jaumes 15 Apr 1842
ASSUMPTION PARISH	
Assumption Courthouse	Pierre F Helluin 4 Feb 1831 Adolphe Loret 6 Feb 1851 Edmund O Melancon 23 Jul 1851 Victorin Priche 23 Jun 1852 Louis A Dejarlais 22 Aug 1853 Charles A Besse 30 Jun 1854 Alphonse Charlet 2 Jan 1857 Francois X Gauthier 28 Sep 1857
Bedford Disc 22 Dec 1855	Philip S Cox 13 Mar 1844
Paincourtville	Elisee E Mailhiot 6 May 1840 Charles J E Gauthier 22 Dec 1845 Edward O Gagne 6 Oct 1851 Omer Rizan 12 Aug 1852

	Gustave Blanchard 16 Sep 1852
	Pierre Peignot 26 May 1853
	Jean Webre 25 Oct 1855
	Hargnin Hinkley 15 Jul 1856
	Eudaldo G Pintardo 18 Sep 1856
	Eudaldo G Pintardo 16 Feb 1857
Star	Amedre Dormas 8 Jul 1847
	L T Labadie 9 Apr 1849
	Aristedes Saulnier 26 Dec 1850
	F Barthet 23 Apr 1852
	Dominique Desbois 13 Jun 1856
	Edward Prout 9 Dec 1856
Crane's Forge	Thomas I Crane 10 Dec 1849
	Eugene Feray 11 Aug 1852
Albemarle	Marius Albadnao 7 Oct 1850
Disc 4 Feb 1852	
Reest 15 Jun 1855	Ferdinand Parilleaux 15 Jun 1855
Church	Claudius Linossier 15 Mar 1852

AVOYELLES PARISH

Bayou Rouge	Alonson G Pearce 28 Jul 1844
Bordeau	Robert A Cochran 26 Feb 1841
Disc 10 May 1848	
Borodino	Ambroise Lacour 2 Dec 1843
	Joseph Rebouche 21 Feb 1845
	Pierre J Normand 26 Jul 1848
	Joseph Cappell 18 Jun 1849
	Aurdie P Normand 25 Mar 1851
Holmesville	Charles Kibbe 27 Jun 1842
	Shaw N Randon 26 Aug 1849
	Miche McJilton 8 Jul 1850
	William H Bassett 7 Dec 1854

Mansura	Nelson Durand 2 Feb 1839
	Adolphe Lafargue 30 Oct 1850
	Pierre A Durand 27 Oct 1854
Marksville Courthouse	James R Rey Jr 23 Dec 1828
	Thomas B Tiller 3 Aug 1844
	William H Duvall 17 Sep 1844
	Archibald Ferinas 27 Sep 1845
	James McEnery 19 Feb 1849
	Francois B Barbin 1 Oct 1849
	Constant Guillebert 12 Sep 1850
	Valerien Gremillion 22 Jan 1856
Simmesport	Ignatius Kirk 29 Mar 1844
	James Brewster 4 Jul 1854
Big Bend	William Clopton 8 Mar 1847
	Benjamin W Kimball 5 Sep 1848
	William H Bassett 20 Jun 1850
	J Bonnett 21 Sep 1854
	Benjamin W Kimball 24 Apr 1855
	William Branch Marshall 5 Jan 1857
Snaggy Point	Bailey C Duke 8 Mar 1847
Disc 13 Oct 1847	
Florida Bend	Charles D Brashear 5 Jul 1848
	B W Ray 21 Aug 1850
Disc 1 Apr 1851	
Point Magre	Lewis White 5 Jul 1851
Disc 29 Jul 1855	
Moreauville Note:	Timothy C Ward 22 Jul 1852
Late Borodino	John H Boyes 30 Jul 1854
	John R Gremillion 27 Aug 1856
Evergreen	Alonson G Pearce 30 Jul 1854
	Joseph K Ewell 15 Aug 1857

CADDO PARISH

Greenwood	James K Bayliss 3 Jul 1844
	William Littlejohn 4 Jan 1847
	Francis J Murphy 10 Dec 1849
	William Flournoy 25 Mar 1851
	James M Duke 15 Sep 1851
	Asa H Rhodes 25 Apr 1854
	Sam J Greenhill 3 Oct 1856
	James W Orr 1 Jun 1857
Shreveport Courthouse	William Thatcher 30 Jul 1842
	Robert W Legrand 29 Apr 1847
	John C Barry 24 Mar 1849
	William R Douglass 5 Nov 1849
	John S Gooch 7 Apr 1852
	Peter Rush 16 May 1853
	Lewis E Carter 22 Nov 1853
	Henry Hunsicker 6 Dec 1855 (Pres & Sen)
Spring Ridge	Dan Bozeman 15 May 1844
Summer Grove	Robert V Marye 20 Jul 1844
	Robert Burnside 24 Dec 1845
	John T Foney 19 Jun 1848
Disc 22 Aug 1848	
Tylerville	Ballard F Eppes 2 Nov 1844
Disc 7 Jun 1847	
Willow Chute	Caesar Wallace 18 Feb 1847
	William Stinson 13 Sep 1847
Disc 15 Apr 1850	
Saline	Wiley P George 25 Apr 1848
Cookesville	William B Cooke 11 Feb 1849
	Charles H Stevens 6 Dec 1850

Blossom Hill	John Sempe 10 May 1849
	Isaac Hughes 15 Jul 1852
Albany	Wiley P George 2 Jun 1849
	Joseph R Betton 25 Jun 1850
	Wiley P George 24 Feb 1851
Disc 31 Oct 1851	
Caddo	William Stuckey 1 Sep 1849
Disc 30 Oct 1851	
Sentell's Store	Washington Sentell 19 Oct 1850
Cookville	Charles H Stevens 15 Apr 1852
Albany	John M McClelland 16 Mar 1854
Disc 17 Feb 1855	
Parker's Store	Stephen D Parker 15 Mar 1854
Disc 1 Sep 1854	
Spring Ridge	Albert G Scogin 15 May 1854
Disc 26 Feb 1855	
Reest 18 Apr 1855	Samuel Edmunds 18 Apr 1856
	William J Bony 31 Jan 1857
	Joshua Drailouse 23 Oct 1857
Mooringsport	Thomas S Syon 1 Aug 1854
	James M Christian 23 Oct 1857
Adam's	Howell C Adams 13 Dec 1855
Summer Grove	
Reest 12 Dec 1856	Mica P Stevens 12 Dec 1856
	Benjamin F Johnson 27 Oct 1857
Disc 1 Dec 1857	
Begusa Chute	Joseph H Beard 7 Sep 1857

CALCASIEU PARISH

Big Woods	Hardy Coward 13 Apr 1842
	Needham Coward 27 Sep 1844
	James Perkins 17 Mar 1846
	William Lyons 16 Mar 1848
	Jacob W Dunnam 16 Apr 1850
	Joseph E Moss 14 Jan 1851
Disc 15 Aug 1851	
Lake Charles	John Hagar 4 Oct 1850
	Charles A Hardy 12 Oct 1852
Bear Bone	Garrard M Wilbsaw 15 Mar 1852
	Eli A Perkins 18 Jul 1854
	David A Lyons 25 Nov 1854
Disc 5 Feb 1857	
Hamburgh	Josiah Johnson 11 Aug 1853
	Solomon Simmons 11 Dec 1857
Hickory Flat	William J Carnes 9 Oct 1854

CALDWELL PARISH

Columbia	Nathan S Chaffin 8 Sep 1843
	William J Hanna 31 Jul 1845
	Robert M Elkes 28 Sep 1847
	Dabney M Hundley 1 Feb 1850
	Robert A Blanks 2 Apr 1851
	James A Boyd 4 Oct 1852
	Frederick A Blanks 18 Feb 1854
	Isaac L Haas 3 May 1854
	Henry H Rice 27 Apr 1855
	James A Boyd 20 Dec 1856
Copenhagen	Jacob Bollenhagen 25 Feb 1840
	Emil Gouesen 17 Apr 1847
Disc 5 Jun 1848	
Reest 11 May 1849	William C Redditt 11 May 1849

Mount Pleasant	Thomas Meredith 19 Sep 1849
Castor	Asa Anderson 15 Jun 1850 Thomas B Butler 24 Apr 1857 Moses Wineberg 16 Sep 1857 George W Baygents 26 Oct 1857
Greenvield Disc 13 May 1854	Robert Richmond 7 Nov 1853
Sinope	Alfred Ferrand 16 Mar 1854
Corinth Disc 5 Feb 1856	Marcus S Routon 11 Jun 1855
Long Lake	John H Pinson 14 Aug 1855
Augusta	John J Meredith 19 Jun 1856
Columbia Courthouse	William J Hanna 7 Nov 1856 Henry Y Baughmann 19 Jan 1857
Alpha	Isaac C Jones 5 Jun 1857 Thomas J Humble 24 Jul 1857
Good Hope	Thomas McCormick 16 Jul 1857

CARROLL PARISH

Lake Providence	James C Hollingsworth 15 Jul 1840 Hercules Hillman 25 Jan 1844 Thomas V Davis 30 Dec 1845 James G Fitzgerald 2 Oct 1846

	Elihu Ferry 24 May 1847
	John M Miller 11 Apr 1849
	James M Perry 27 Oct 1853
	W Rudisill 28 Nov 1853
	Isaac N Kent 9 Mar 1855
	K Whitford 17 Sep 1855
	Alfred Kibbe 26 May 1856
	John Harvey 21 Jan 1957
Pecan Grove	George R Newman 23 Nov 1839
	Hugh Markham 23 Aug 1847
	Henry Goodrich 1 Oct 1849
Aston	Peter J Flynn 2 Oct 1844
Disc 10 Sep 1849	
Reest 12 Aug 1851	Anchel Harppe 12 Aug 1851
	J B Prescott 10 Mar 1852
	William Z Brown 1 Jul 1853
	William J Rule 2 Jul 1855
	James B Edington 20 Nov 1855
Disc 28 May 1856	
Deerfield	Peter G Oliver 4 Apr 1847
	William T Oliver 8 Nov 1848
	John M Murchisson 9 Dec 1852
	William C Purvis 16 Mar 1855
Wiggin's Ferry	Charles Richardson 5 Oct 1847
Monticello	Charles Richardson 3 Feb 1848
	John Bishop 11 Oct 1849
	John B Richardson 7 Jan 1850
	John Bishop 2 Mar 1852
	Richard H Dollehide 22 Jan 1855
	Robert M McCain 11 Dec 1857
Disc (No date)	
Lake Carraway	Jesse Kennedy 24 Oct 1849
Disc 3 Jun 1851	

Swan Lake   Lewis P Turner 5 Jan 1850
                                   Thomas J Couch 25 Feb 1851
Disc 3 Jun 1851

Vista Ridge   S C Floyd 11 Dec 1851
Disc 11 May 1852
Reest 23 Aug 1852   S C Floyd 23 Aug 1852
                                   William A Austen 19 Apr 1853
                                   John N Todd 21 May 1855
                                   David McCandless 29 Sep 1855
                                   James M Draughton 24 Dec 1856
                                   Thomas A Mann 28 Nov 1857

Joe's Bayou   Jackson B Tompkins 29 Jul 1852

Oak Bluffs   William W Owen 16 Mar 1854

Floyd   William C Pack 26 Aug 1854
                                   Harkwell H Harris 19 Jul 1855
                                   Robert J Herring 27 May 1856
                                   John S Gordon 15 Nov 1856
                                   James M Watson 28 Nov 1857

Caledonia   Amos Lawton 19 Oct 1854

Oak Grove   John M Steward 8 Aug 1857

CATAHOULA PARISH

Brown's Ferry   Coleman Brown 25 May 1844
Disc 24 May 1845

Burshley Creek   Moses Wiggins 27 Aug 1839
Disc 11 Nov 1845
Reest 11 Jul 1846   Samuel Glenn Jr 11 Jul 1846
Disc 21 May 1849

Doty's   Silas Sillard 25 May 1844
Disc 24 May 1845

Harrisonburgh Courthouse	Stephen T Clark 28 Jul 1843
	Oren Mayo 9 Oct 1844
	Rosemond Legrase 21 Feb 1845
	Thomas B Matthews 16 Feb 1846
	Charles Williams 15 Jan 1850
	Eleazer Fletcher 2 Apr 1851
Kirk's Ferry	David G Pickens 25 May 1844 (**Pres**)
Trinity	William H Ternley 19 Jan 1844
	Ransom W Collins 20 Jun 1844
	M C Rico 16 Oct 1849
	John A Newell 18 Jan 1850
	Philip Croocks 30 oct 1850
	Felix Robb 24 Feb 1851
	James W Martin 25 Jun 1852
	Tarleton W Graves 31 Jan 1854
	Harrison C Jones 12 Jul 1854
	John D Calvert 27 Dec 1854
	John R Woodridge 26 Oct 1855
Little Prarie	David H Stokes 27 Jan 1848
	Joseph N Colby 17 Jul 1849
	William B Buchanan 19 May 1854
Disc 10 Mar 1855	
White Sulphur Springs	Joseph P Ward 17 Apr 1848
	W C Aber 6 Jun 1854
	William M Slater 1 Nov 1854
	Joseph P Ward 12 Jun 1856
	A B Thompson 15 Jan 1857
Parkham's Landing	Peterson G Parkham 27 Jun 1848
	John Janney 21 Oct 1854
	John Thomas 22 Jan 1855
Disc 4 Jun 1855	
Haphazard	George W Miller 25 Jul 1848
	James D Cannon 13 Jan 1849
	Henry D Mandeville 4 Aug 1849

Disc 29 Jul 1852

Rosefield	John Stapleton 5 Mar 1850
	Fielding Reynolds 27 Oct 1851
Disc 17 Oct 1853	
Reest 16 Jan 1854	
Funny Louis	Allen J Davis 16 Apr 1852
	Edwin W Yancey 1 Nov 1853
Aimwell	Hardy Meacom 19 Oct 1852
	Elisha K Davis 30 Dec 1852
	Wiley M Squyres 27 Jan 1857
Ford's Creek	Jacob Lanius 8 Aug 1853
Sicily Island	Robert J Newsom 9 Sep 1853
Disc 12 Apr 1854	
Reest 14 may 1856	Henry L Green 14 May 1856
Green's Creek	Moses Collins 31 Mar 1854
Enterprise	Hugh Keenan 26 Aug 1854
Finlay's	Daniel Finlay 8 Aug 1857

CLAIBORNE PARISH

Allen's Settlement	John Murrell 22 Apr 1836
	John Murrell Jr 25 Jun 1846
	James W Miller 8 Mar 52
Black Lake	Allen Harris 23 Mar 1844
Disc 20 Jan 1848	
Reest 9 Feb 1848	Simon Manning 9 Feb 1848
Disc 28 Feb 1848	
Flat Lick	Stephen Butler 15 Jan 1842
	Dickson H Dyer 28 Jul 1851
	Rufus Phillips 7 May 1853

	Jesse C Godley 7 Nov 1853
	Stephen Butler 6 Apr 1855
	Green Culbertson 21 Sep 1857
Minden	John Baker 13 Mar 1844
	William A Drake 19 Aug 1845
	Edward Etler 27 Oct 1847
	Sarah Y Yost 7 Jan 1850
	Dickson H Dyer 19 Feb 1853
	John W Ross 30 Aug 1853
	George S Trott 31 Oct 1853
	Alexander Greene 17 Jun 1856
	Ryal L Lancaster 6 Oct 1856
Mount Lebanon	Landry A Key 17 Jan 1843
	Jasper Gibbs 12 Aug 1845
	C G Thurmand 12 Sep 1845
Overton Disc 17 Mar 1846	William C Copes 25 Oct 1842
Quay	Jabez Sanders 16 Jan 1841
	Littleton M Duty 11 Nov 1845
	Wiley Duty 8 Mar 1847
	Philip Payne 4 Nov 1856
	William B Smith 19 Apr 1857
Russellville	Thomas H Jones 11 Feb 1841
Athens	Francis Lyman 14 Jul 1846
	Sanders P Day 14 Oct 1846
	Arthur McFarland 18 Nov 1847
Walnut Creek	James Ward 22 Sep 1846
Wiseville	Benjamin J Lambright 8 Aug 1857
Homer Courthouse	Elijah Grooms 19 Jan 1849
	Zachariah Ragland 5 Aug 1850
	Michael Callahan 5 May 1851

	Jackson J Cooper 27 Jan 1852
	William C Crutcher 30 Jan 1854
	William B Gill 16 Dec 1854
	John H Cunningham 6 Dec 1856
	George W Price 4 Jan 1858
Franksville	Doctor Franks 5 Nov 1849
	James A Smith 3 Dec 1851
	L B Foster 11 Jun 1853
	William Beene 29 Dec 1853
	George A Gordan 6 May 1854
Disc 29 Mar 1855	
Scottsville	William L Burton 12 Nov 1849
	John C Milner 19 Mar 1851
	James S Bush 27 Jan 1853
	William L Burton 11 Jun 1853
	Robert Kilgore 8 May 1857
Dorcheat	David Hampton Courtney 10 Dec 1849
	Jackson Sikes 13 Jun 1855
Tiger Creek	John J Wise 15 Mar 1850
Disc 1 Sep 1856	
Reest 12 Feb 1857	J M Prestidge 12 Feb 1857
Lisbon	Seth Tatum 30 Sep 1857
	Thomas W Pool 23 May 1856
	Elias P Hester 10 Dec 1856
	Charles D Barrow 1 Jun 1857
Cane Ridge	Wash B Nicholson 30 Sep 1851
Disc 26 Aug 1853	
Reest 23 Feb 1856	George M Lowrey 23 Feb 1856
Haynesville	James C Taylor 9 Feb 1852
Forest Grove	Franklin Taylor 10 Nov 1850
Sugar Creek	John S Carlton 1 Oct 1853

Squier	William C Moreland 10 Feb 1857
Argus	Pool P Massy 15 Jan 1854

CONCORDIA PARISH

Vidalia	Thomas B Thorpe 15 May 1844
	Francis Marschalk 31 Jul 1845
	Thomas Cartwright 22 Aug 1848
	Hubbard F Robinson 12 Sep 1848
	Josias H McCornas 19 Feb 1849
	John H Tyson 28 Feb 1850
	Zebulon York 24 Jun 1851
Disc 15 Sep 1851	
Reest 13 Oct 1851	George B Wailes 13 Oct 1851
Vidalia	Benjamin F Dobyns 17 Sep 1857
Fairview	Jesse Guice 13 Jan 1845
	George W Green 2 Jun 1849
	R R Barker 18 Jun 1851
Disc 17 Feb 1852	
Reest 31 Jan 1855	William J Glasscock 31 Jan 1855
	Granville W Williams 19 Apr 1857
Rifle Point	Charles R Stewart 19 Aug 1846
	Ralph Butterfield 5 Jun 1848
Disc 19 Apr 1853	
Routh's Point	Jeremiah Powell 14 Jun 1846
	(No first name) Kirkland 27 May 1847
Disc 10 Aug 1848	
Grand Cutoff	Augustus T Welch 7 Jun 1847
Disc 8 Sep 1849	
Little Prairie	David H Stokes 27 Jan 1848
Howe's	A P Howe 27 Jan 1848

	Stephen McDonald 28 Dec 1848
Miller's	Joseph E Miller 27 Jun 1848
Parkham's Landing	P G Parkham 27 Jan 1848
Flowery Mound	Joseph E Miller 17 May 1848 Garrand W Miller 15 Jan 1850 Ezekiel Young 7 Feb 1854
Walker's Bluffs Disc 2 Jun 1849	Hiram Walker 5 Sep 1848
Monterey Landing	Samuel C Scott 18 May 1850 Cyrus S Magoun 6 Jul 1857
South Bend	Cyrus S Magoun 28 Sep 1857
Union Point	James S Richards 1 Nov 1850
Routh's Point Disc 5 Sep 1851	John Routh Williams 26 Dec 1850
Tooley's	Henry Tooley 8 May 1851 William Dale 31 Jan 1854
Black Hawk Point	Joshua Johns 23 Feb 1853 A T Welch 29 Jan 1857

DE SOTO PARISH

Grand Cane	Thomas D Hailes 10 Feb 1843 James Sumrall 15 Apr 1844 John B Gamble 16 Sep 1846 Hamilton Sloan 11 May 1852 John B Gamble 27 Sep 1852
Keatchie	William A Thorpe 15 May 1844
Mansfield Courthouse	Jacob D Wemple 30 Nov 1844

                        Warren J Massingale 24 May 1845
                        Samuel Quarles 14 Jul 1845
                        Joseph P Massingale 27 Sep 1845
                        James S Carr 24 Mar 1849
                        Micayah T J Alston 23 Aug 1849
                        Peter Shearer 30 Jun 1851
                        William Chalmers 27 Jul 1852

Pleasant Hill   John Gordon 21 Dec 1846
                        David A Blackshear 10 Jul 1851
                        John A Campbell 2 Aug 1852
                        George W Goss 11 Jun 1853
                        James C Whitten 30 Jan 1854

Logansport   Samuel Mather 29 Feb 1848
                        Stephen F Baker 4 Oct 1850
                        John F Simmons 30 Jun 1851
                        David J Laird 8 Jan 1852
                        John W Martin 10 Nov 1852
                        Moses Brown 14 Jul 1854
                        Henry E H Buck 6 Mar 1855
                        John W Martin 12 Sep 1855

Pleasant Grove   Garland S Hart 17 Aug 1849
                        Duncan B McMillan 12 Mar 1852

Ashland   William J Davis 19 Sep 1849
Disc 9 Sep 1850

Black Jack   Robert Hall 26 Dec 1850
                        John E Hall 12 Nov 1853

Bayou Pierre   Robert S Haden 30 Jun 1851
                        John F Ferguson 21 May 1852
Disc 19 Dec 1854

Red Bluff   Robert Stickney 6 Jun 1852
                        James A Beard 8 Apr 1854
                        Robert B Frierson 20 Jun 1854

Longstreet	William C Peyton 23 Sep 1854
Kingston	John M Prather 6 Aug 1856

EAST BATON ROUGE PARISH

Bayou Rouge Courthouse	Hugh T Waddill 30 Dec 1843 George A Pike 20 Dec 1846 John C LaNone 15 May 1850 Joseph McCormick 6 Apr 1853 John M McCormick 25 Nov 1857
Fontania Disc 23 Oct 1844	James D Ronaldson 8 Sep 1843
Manchac	Francis Roberts 13 Dec 1834 (Illegible entry) Daniel H Miller 19 Mar 1850 Gustave Lopez 30 Oct 1851 Daniel H Miller 27 Apr 1852 Aristides Daigre 15 Jun 1854 Joseph H Daigre 31 Jan 1856
Stony Point	Michael Watson 15 Oct 1844 (Illegible entry) John F Glover 24 Jul 1849 S F Blanchard 2 Feb 1854 William Stockwell 17 Jul 1854
Burlington	John Kerr 16 Aug 1849 L P Loflin 16 Aug 1851 Washington Greenwell 20 Apr 1853 James Jones 9 Aug 1854
Milford Disc 25 Nov 1851	William L Burnett 11 Oct 1849
Plain's Store	Luther R. Ronaldson 21 Oct 1853 Isaac Townsend 5 Dec 1853 Henry C Young 27 Jan 1857

Greenwell Springs   Robert S Stuart 29 Dec 1854
                       James R Kelley 11 Mar 1855
                       Robert W Greenwell 29 Sep 1856

EAST FELICIANA PARISH

Clinton Courthouse   Bythell Haynes 7 Jun 1842
                       F P Ellis 13 Sep 1847
                       J B P Poole 3 Feb 1849
                       August M Lacey 24 Apr 1851
                       Robert H Draughton 24 Feb 1852
                       James S Taylor 21 Apr 1852
                       Frederick W Ward 7 Jun 1853
                       John R Lemon 17 Feb 1854
                       Abraham Hagaman 2 Nov 1854
                       John M Bell 30 Jan 1855

Port Hudson   James Hudson 15 May 1844
                       Willim B Ranaldson 27 Nov 1848
                       Albert Wilson 14 Oct 1851
                       J Welch Jones 28 May 1852
                       S S Livingston 29 Feb 1854
                       Reuben Vansickle 24 Dec 1855
                       W H Haynes 23 Apr 1856
                       William Esmond 9 Dec 1856
                       Alexander C Greene 28 Apr 1857
                       Randolph Chick 15 Jun 1857

Richland Hill   Angus McCarstle 15 May 1843
                       James Keogh 15 Mar 1844
Disc 26 Aug 1845

Woodland   Stephen Tildon 4 Jun 1834
                       Albert W Poole 29 Nov 1848
                       Charles B Trask 11 Mar 1850
                       Solomon S Horton 26 May 1851
                       William A Carter 11 May 1852
                       Albert W Poole 20 Apr 1853

	William A Carter 31 Aug 1854
	Albert W Poole 17 Jan 1855
Mount Willing Disc 29 Mar 1850	A G Newport 19 Aug 1846
St Cloud Disc 29 Dec 1851	James S Peacock 10 Sep 1850
Peach Grove Disc 26 Dec 1854	Cullen M Carstle 12 Aug 1854

FRANKLIN PARISH

Boeuff Prairie	Abram B Seay 2 Nov 1843 Wiley B Grayson 2 Feb 1845 Edmond Nugent 26 Mar 1846 James Woodridge 4 Jan 1847 Thomas Bellew 20 Jan 1852 Thomas A Woodridge 31 Jul 1855 Thomas Wilkenson 28 Sep 1856 Thomas A Woodridge 20 Feb 1857
Hurricane	Ralph Price 15 May 1844 Benjamin K Hudgins 9 Feb 1846 Gabriel E Nash 21 Sep 1849 Daniel F Mauk 28 Jun 1854 William M Jennings 24 Mar 1857
Oakley	Samuel G Cloud 13 Jun 1844
Winnsborough	John C Chambers 23 Oct 1845 Daniel C Kiser 23 Feb 1847 A Hawthorn 28 Jan 1848 John R Nugent 8 Feb 1849 Henry H Heath 15 Jan 1850 Charles C Brown 29 Apr 1852 John W Willis 9 Dec 1852 J Bradley 20 May 1853 Henry T Earle 31 Mar 1854

	Joseph C Carter 22 Jun 1857
Oliver's Prairie Disc 23 Dec 1847	William T Oliver 5 Oct 1847
Coydoun Disc 8 Sep 1849	Levi Barfield 24 Mar 1848
Quitman Disc 10 Sep 1849	James Smith 24 Mar 1848
Buford Disc 14 Aug 1849	Daniel R McGahey 12 Aug 1848 James Buford 14 Dec 1848
Butler Disc 27 Jul 1849	Leroy S Ward 5 Sep 1848
Warsaw	George M Dorsey 5 Mar 1852 Jonathan Merrit 16 Oct 1853 George M Dorsey 15 Nov 1854
Pullaway	Isaac C Heath 22 Aug 1853
Red Mouth	Wesley T Griffin 17 Jun 1853 John Gurin 7 Dec 1855 William C Ilar 26 Aug 1856 Herman Rock 28 Oct 1857
Yellow Bluff	H S Thomason 17 Apr 1855 Theophilis Girod 4 Jun 1857 John D Thomason 24 Aug 1857

IBERVILLE PARISH

Bayou Goula	Charles Fay 7 May 1844 Charles LeBlanc 6 Jan 1846 (Illegible entry) Ernest E Cabry 30 Dec 1852 Pierre L Dufresne 30 May 1853

	Francis Marion 7 Jun 1855
	Elizer Landry 22 Jan 1850
	George I A Bush 27 May 1857
Iberville Courthouse	Maxile LeBlanc 2 Nov 1843
	Henry S Brown 23 Mar 1846
	Adolph Hebert 20 Jan 1854
	Henry S Brown 21 Jan 1857
St. Gabriel	Henry S Brown 16 May 1857
Plaquemine	Archibald Block 2 Jul 1842
	Theodore Johnston 29 May 1847
	Archibald Block 20 Apr 1853
	Peter E Jennings 25 Sep 1857
Bayou Gross Tete	Theodore Johnston 11 Aug 1848
	James H Johnston 9 Feb 1849
	Luis W Troxler 28 Jun 1851
	Charles H Gilbert 16 May 1853
	James P Langley 20 Jan 1854
	Joseph L Orillion 1 Nov 1854
	Joseph E Pargas 16 May 1856
	Joseph Pardos 11 Dec 1857
Rosedale	Charles F Dupuy 2 Sep 1857

JEFFERSON PARISH

Lafayette Courthouse	Thomas Cook 28 Apr 1843
Carrollton	James Gilbert 31 Oct 1844
	Chaunay Charles Porter 22 Apr 1852
	Harman H. Gogreve 16 Mar 1854
Lafayette City	Thomas Cook 28 Apr 1848
	Peter P Auvray 21 Sep 1849
	Fred Von Harten 12 Jan 1852
	John T Barrett 6 Feb 1852
	Fred Von Harten 7 May 1853

Jefferson   Wilmer H Zimmerman 3 Aug 1854

Kenner   Barney Gilcooly 31 Jul 1856

LAFAYETTE PARISH

Perry's Bridge   Robert Perry 14 Aug 1830
                            Elijah Ewing 21 Dec 1846

Vermillionville   James M Moore 5 Aug 1840
                            Joachim Revillion 14 Jan 1844
                            William P Thomas 23 Mar 1855
                            Enoch B Kemper 2 Sep 1856

Pare Perdue   Rosemond LeBlanc 21 Jun 1852
Disc 1 Oct 1852

Cote Gelee   Valsaint Broussard 13 Dec 1856

LAFOURCHE PARISH

Thibodeaux Courthouse   Jonathan C White 26 Jan 1842
                            Marcus P Zills 24 Jul 1844
                            George Whittmore 28 May 1846
                            John D Bioron 8 Dec 1846
                            Benjamin F Halsey Jr 26 Mar 1849
                            Henry L Karr 15 Sep 1851
                            Joseph R Niles 29 Dec 1852
                            J Yates Bennett 17 Apr 1853
                            Peter E Lorio 15 Mar 1856

Raceland   Charles G Thibodeaux 21 Aug 1855

LIVINGSTON PARISH

Springfield   William Westmoreland 20 Nov 1843
                            Hiram Carter 25 May 1844
                            Henry Duncan 14 Jul 1845
                            Jacob F Randolph 7 Oct 1845

Disc 7 Oct 1846
Reest 21 Jan 1847

Drury W Wall 21 Jan 1847
Lavis Alaucis 26 Mar 1848
P Harrison 22 Nov 1848
James P Elmore 20 Jun 1850
Robert Babington 1 May 1851

Coelk

Joseph F Lignon 28 Dec 1848
James W Stewart 9 Apr 1849
William J Gates 1 Nov 1850
Benjamin Singletary 19 Oct 1852
Otis Felder 8 Aug 1853
William J Gates 21 Apr 1854
Jesse J Felder 21 Mar 1856
Baxter Felder 16 Oct 1857

Wadeboro
Disc 28 Aug 1851

Charles Myers 4 Oct 1850

Bayou Barbary

William H Wilder 23 Jun 1852

Springfield

D Bleason 17 Jun 1853
C Impson 15 May 1854
W Read 8 Mar 1855
George Walker 21 Dec 1855

Wadeborough

Christian Grenes 11 Aug 1853

Ponchatoula

Robert P Guyard 11 Jun 1855
James Tucker 29 Jun 1857

Independence

James Soflin 18 Jul 1855
Sylvester D Simms 17 Apr 1856

Hollywood

Edwin B Starns 19 Jan 1856

Oldfield

Sandford R Terry 19 Jan 1856
Jefferson Lea 19 Apr 1857

Tickfaw

Jacob J Watts 19 Jan 1856

Disc 13 Feb 1857

Stony Point	John Margenis 21 Jan 1856
	John H Davidson 14 Apr 1857
	John Roughman 16 May 1857
Benton's Ferry	Robert Benton 25 Jan 1856
Cold Springs	Henry Wammach 25 Jan 1856
Disc 20 Oct 1856	
Reest 9 Dec 1856	James Turner 9 Dec 1856
Disc 9 Feb 1857	
French Settlement	Joseph Salassi 25 Jan 1856
Walker	John B Lockhart 25 Jan 1856

MADISON PARISH

Chesterfield	Joseph W Williams 22 Jul 1844
	William B Dunn 20 Mar 1847
	F Anderson 26 Sep 1850
	William H Bright 14 Feb 1851
Milliken's Bend	Hector H McLean 7 Jun 1843
	Thomas A Fitch 28 May 1844
	James T Pullen 15 Aug 1846
	Benjamin Campbell 26 Feb 1847
	James P Craig 17 Sep 1847
	Lewis Benedict 8 Jun 1849
	Nancy Craig 12 Dec 1851
Disc 7 Jul 1852	
Reest 13 Jul 1852	Nancy Craig 13 Jul 1852
	A Hawkins 7 Feb 1854
	Jacob Sartorias 5 Apr 1854
	Philip Sartorias 12 Apr 1855
New Carthage	William G Frazier 16 Aug 1842
	Mycajah Love 7 Jun 1847
	William Miller 23 Feb 1853

S E Love 31 Jan 1854

Richmond Courthouse	Nathaniel E Dortch 30 Dec 1843 Elihu Perry 23 Oct 1844 George A Morgan 2 Apr 1845 Temple C Coons 6 Jul 1846 Adrian E Adams 4 May 1855
Young's Point Disc 17 Jun 1842	Alfred M Young 23 May 1840
Chickama Bend Disc 2 Feb 1846 Reest 15 Apr 1846	John Seaton 9 Oct 1844 Benjamin F Hines 15 Apr 1846 James C Ross 19 Aug 1847 John W Andrews 28 Dec 1848 Thomas O Owings 18 Jul 1849 John Neely 27 Feb 1854
Dallas	Lafayette Jones 10 Aug 1846 William T Pugh 7 Feb 1848
Pugh's Disc 18 Aug 1853	James A Pugh 8 Sep 1852
Quebec	Samuel Barker 7 Oct 1853 Richmond J Brashear 31 Jan 1855 Thomas H W Baynard 19 Nov 1857

MOREHOUSE PARISH

Bastrop	Thomas S Simpson 26 May 1846 G W Enswiler 27 Jan 1847 Giles M Croxton 31 Jul 1848 Robert C Hendrick 9 Jul 1851 John W Mason 2 Jun 1855 Aaron Livingston 25 Jan 1856 Edmund B Pettis 21 Nov 1857

Point Jefferson   Grafton D Dorsey 5 Oct 1847
                               Hawkins Duvall 5 Jan 1848
                               Joseph Kelly 21 Jul 1849
                               Lucas Powell 28 Apr 1859
Disc 11 May 1857
Reest 18 Mar 1857   James C Cooper 18 Mar 1857
                               George T Malone 28 Apr 1859

Prairie Mer Rouge   Robert Knox 5 Oct 1847
Disc 12 Aug 1848
Reest 21 May 1856   William L Clark 21 May 1856

Des Glaize   Noah Ford 16 Aug 1848
                               Aaron H Brewer 26 Sep 1849
                               John M Hilliard 30 Oct 1850
                               Henry Curtis 4 Feb 1853
                               Aaron H Brewer 16 Jun 1853

Brooksville   James R Brooks 3 Apr 1852
                               William A Williams 21 Jun 1852
                               William Dyer 14 Jul 1853

Jones Ferry   John R B Jones 21 Jun 1852
                               John R B Jones 28 Dec 1854
                               Handsford Dean 9 Jan 1856
                               James Calwell 10 Apr 1857
Disc 29 Jun 1857

Plantersville   Aaron H Brewer 9 Sep 1853
                               John M Hilliard 23 May 1854

Hawkins Landing   Thomas M Jones 18 Feb 1854

Young's Bluff   James A Green 8 May 1855
                               George W Young 1 Apr 1856
                               William T Jordan 8 May 1857
                               Elijah Scott 21 Oct 1857

Lind Grove   Aaron H Brewer 19 Feb 1857
                               James E Warnock 2 Nov 1857

NATCHITOCHES PARISH

Adies
Disc 29 Aug 1845
Reest 5 Sep 1848

Stephen M Sean 29 May 1841

Solomon Smith 5 Sep 1848

Campti

John Marcalle 15 Mar 1843
Jacob A Wolfson 20 Dec 1847
Charles J Puckette 14 May 1850
Simon M Hart 20 May 1851
John W McDonald 29 Jul 1853
Jacob A Wolfson 21 Jan 1854

Cloutierville

Charles F Benoist 18 May 1837
Charles Sers 24 Jul 1845
Louis Gallien 30 May 1850
Charles Sers 16 Sep 1850
Samuel O Scruggs 6 May 1853
Belus Deslouches 29 Jan 1857
Abel C Sers 9 Dec 1857

Coushatta Chute

George Hammett 29 Sep 1843
James K Belden 9 Oct 1844
Bythol H Baird 30 May 1850
James C Pickett 8 Mar 1851
James R Bosley 14 Jul 1853

Fort Jessup

Henry S Lamb 3 Jun 1840
Nathan Darling 20 Jun 1843

Natchitoches Courthouse

Charles A Bullard 28 Jan 1843
Thomas H Airey 22 Aug 1845
B Carr 6 Mar 1851
Edward B Cook 21 Apr 1851
Francis H Arceaux 25 Feb 1852
Samuel J Wood 30 Aug 1852
(Illegible entry)

Negreet   Robert D Wright 29 Mar 1842
                              John D Tucker 24 Dec 1845
                              J Alford 10 Jun 1847
Disc 24 Oct 1849

Saline Mills   Reuben Drake 6 May 1846
Disc 19 Aug 1848
Reest 27 Nov 1849   Reuben Drake 27 Nov 1849
                              Milas H Wallace 16 Nov 1852
Disc 26 May 1854
Reest 6 Jul 1854   James C Weeks 6 Jul 1854

Lowe's Ferry   John A McLanahas 23 Nov 1838
                              Granberry McCook 20 Dec 1842

Grand Ecore   Charles H Alexander 5 Oct 1848
                              Samuel D Rutsell 9 Apr 1853
                              Charles H Alexander 16 Jul 1854
                              Willis Jenkins 21 Dec 1854
Disc 17 Aug 1854
Reest 29 Apr 1855   John H Stephens 29 Apr 1855
Disc 5 Dec 1857

Sonet   Joshua Dyess 10 Jun 1850
Disc 21 Apr 1852

Isle Breville   Peter Oscar Chaler 10 Sep 1850
Disc 26 Jul 1851

Kisatchie   William P Owings 9 Dec 1854

Louisville   William J Kidd 26 Aug 1855

ORLEANS PARISH

Fort Pike   William Bosworth 4 Apr 1846

New Orleans Courthouse   Alexander G Penn 19 Dec 1843
                              Michael Musson 18 Apr 1849
                              Robert W Adams 14 Apr 1855

	Arthur S Nevitt 3 May 1855
	Robert E McHatton 23 Mar 1857 (**Pres**)
Algiers	John O McLean 1 Aug 1854
	Selegman Simon 24 May 1856

PLAQUEMINES PARISH

English Turn	Jean Louis Marciacoje 16 Sep 1852
Point a La Hache	Armand Lartiges 16 Apr 1852
	Leon Martin 29 Jul 1853
	Claude F V Barbarot 10 Aug 1854
Balize	Joseph C Wilson 21 Sep 1854
Buras Settlement	Frederick G Schmidt 24 Nov 1854
Grand Prairie	Gorcham P Ayer 24 Nov 1854
Jesuit Bend	John S Titus 24 Nov 1854
	Alfred D Salvant 25 Nov 1855
Point Michael	Joseph Cathcart 24 Nov 1854

POINT COUPEE PARISH

Atchafalaya	John T Brooks 3 Jan 1844
	F Stilley 24 Feb 1846
	G Couedin 6 Mar 1850
	Hugh N Lindsey 1 Oct 1851
Disc 13 Jan 1852	
Point Coupee Courthouse	Victor Mourain 18 Aug 1841
	Joseph Jewell 27 Oct 1845
	Leon B Dayries 22 Sep 1846
	Henry A Aurst 21 Oct 1846
	Joseph Jewell 16 Dec 1847
	George Clauss 28 Apr 1848
	J Ellsworth 3 Feb 1849

	Charles Mix 5 Sep 1849
	C Van Dwingelow 25 Jun 1850
	Clement Enete 25 Jan 1851
Red River Landing	Francis Routh 15 May 1844
	E M Wells 31 Oct 1845
	N White 22 Dec 1845
	Joseph Tonas 5 Jan 1849
The Village	Jacob Fisher 20 Feb 1841
	Augustus Fisher 6 Jun 1843
Waterloo	James M Bayley 26 Feb 1844
	William Clemmans 2 Apr 1845
	E Colombo 23 Mar 1846
	John Lopez 21 Dec 1846
	Jules St. Germain 22 Jul 1854
Disc 15 Oct 1847	
Reest 18 Nov 1847	Lewis H Trudeau 18 Nov 1847
	Veronique Major 12 Apr 1848
	(Illegible entry)
	Veronegas Major 22 Jul 1852
	Lewis H Trudeau 8 Sep 1852
Williamsport	August M Shaul 3 Jul 1844
	John T Brame 11 Jul 1846
	Van Domingelo 28 Jan 1848
	John A Hamilton 9 Apr 1850
	William G Wilson 3 Jun 1852
Livonia	James B Johnson 22 May 1846
Routh's Point	Jeremiah Powell 4 Jun 1846
Morganzia	William S Batte 2 Jan 1847
	Simon Bissett 7 Feb 1848
	John W Swain 5 Feb 1850
Disc 1 Apr 1851	
Reest 2 Feb 1855	Charles Morgan 7 Feb 1855
	Joseph T Strother 19 Sep 1856

Hermitage	William G Bozeman Jr 8 Mar 1851
	Frederick J Munzesheimer 24 May 1854
	Lewis H Trudeau 16 Jul 1857
	George N Trudeau 10 Sep 1857
	Frederick J Munzesheimer 21 Sep 1857
Fordouche	Thomas G Farrar 18 Feb 1854
	Charles Morgan 15 Jul 1854
Disc 13 Jun 1855	
Marysville	Patrick H Toler 31 Mar 1854
Disc 30 Aug 1854	
Centerpoint	J R Herring 31 Dec 1857
Miller's Store	Joseph Miller 31 Dec 1857

RAPIDES PARISH

Alexandria Courthouse	Lewis Zim 24 Feb 1843
	Duncan C Goodwin 20 Jan (No year)
	Lewis Zim 6 Jul 1849
	Sam C W Hearick 26 Feb 1853
	Eugene R Biosatt 24 May 1853
	(Illegible entry)
	Eugene R Biosatt 21 May 1856
Big Creek	Thomas Hooper 28 Apr 1843
	Churchile A Hooper 27 Oct 1843
Cheneyville	George C Smith 1 Mar 1842
	William P G Hadley 17 Jul 1845
	Austin Tatum 28 Sep 1846
Disc 19 Aug 1847	
Reest 27 Sep 1847	W H Scott 27 Sep 1847
	Walter Bailey 7 Jun 1853
Cotile	Robert M Henderson 29 Sep 1843

Huddleston	Isaac Huddleston 22 Jan 1847
	Nathaniel Sanders 10 Jul (No year)
Hinestone	James Hines 22 Jan 1847
	Henry Levy 11 May (No year)
	(Illegible entry)
	Joseph T Hatch 27 Jan 1852
Walnut Hill	E H Garlande 8 Feb 1849
	William Burton 26 Mar 1849
	Leonard C Sweat 4 Dec 1849
Disc 30 Jul 1851	
Jatt	Thomas F Swafford 28 Feb 1850
Disc 15 Apr 1851	
Desrayauxville	Jules Desrayaux 21 Feb 1851
Hope	Tacitus G Calvit 20 Feb 1852
Disc 11 Aug 1853	
Liberty Creek	Wiley W Goynes 4 Oct 1852
	William B Shelton 3 Feb 1855
	John C Cavanaugh 10 Aug 1857
Lecompte	Joseph L Sharitt 26 Jul 1854
Ryland	Philip Ryland 15 Sep 1855
Disc 6 Jul (No year)	
Lucky Hit	William Randolph 8 Aug 1856
Rusqueville	Wade H Bynum 2 Jan 1857
Disc 25 Apr 1859	
Bear Creek	William Roe 2 Sep 1857

SABINE PARISH

Many Courthouse	William S Rogers 11 Dec 1843

	Chichester Chaplin Jr 9 Oct 1844
	William Taylor 16 Feb 1845
	John Waterhouse 30 Dec 1845
	John Baldwin 25 Jun 1846
	Henry McAllen 22 Sep 1846
	Robert B Stills 2 Dec 1853
	Robert H Campbell 5 Feb 1856
	Sterling G McLemore 27 Oct 1857
Fort Jessup	Nathan Darling 20 Jan 1845
	Ruluff W Peck 26 May 1846
	Charles Beck 30 Oct 1850
	C P Rogers 7 Aug 1852
Burr's Ferry	Gilman B Burr 2 Jan 1847
Mill Creek	Robert F Sibley 21 Jul 1849
	Elijah Self 26 Aug 1850
Toro	Samuel G Lucious 19 Sep 1849
	Charles Bennett 29 Dec 1855
Disc 26 Nov 1856	
Belmont	Lawrence E Stephens 8 Sep 1851
Disc 7 Dec 1851	
Anacoco	Isaiah Kirk 4 Feb 1852
Columbus	Augustus C A Godwin 2 Feb 1856
Disc 4 Mar 1856	
Negreet	Pleasant T Montgomery 19 Sep 1856
Disc 23 Jul 1857	
Nashboro	J Nash 26 Feb 1857
Disc 5 Nov 1857	

ST. BERNARD PARISH

Terre Aux Boeuffs	Vincent Nunez 10 Feb 1843
Disc 12 Sep 1844	

Reest 23 Jun 1845   Vincent Nunez 23 Jun 1845
                                     Francisco Artiste 19 Apr 1853
Disc 29 May 1855

Bienvu   Francisco Artiste 20 Feb 1857

ST. CHARLES PARISH

St. Charles Courthouse   Francois Chaix 9 Dec 1843
                                    Onesime Touzanne 20 Oct 1844
                                    Noel St. Martin 24 Apr 1856
                                    Marcus P Breckenridge 23 Mar 1857
                                    E Broadus 6 May 1857

St. Charles   Albert Hardonier 23 Dec 1837
Disc 25 Jul (no year)
Reest 8 Sep 1848   William Palso 8 Sep 1848
                                    Francois Chaix 24 Oct 1848
Disc 8 Jul 1850

Logan   Samuel W Logan 30 Dec 1844
Disc 8 Sep 1845

Taylor   William R Taylor 26 Apr 1848
                                    Birkett Stone 30 Nov 1848
                                    John C Colfield 19 Sep 1853

McCutcheon's   James W McCutcheon 25 Jun 1856
                                    Samuel McCutcheon 19 Aug 1856

Logan's Landing   Alberie Deplantier 31 Jan 1854
                                    Alcice LaBranch 31 Jan 1854
                                    Octave LaBranch 11 Jun 1857

ST. HELENA PARISH

Darlington   William S Townsend 14 Feb 1844

	William Barbury 23 Oct 1846
	M Smith 7 Jul 1847
	Thomas Price 9 Feb 1848
	Barnabus H Pipkin 17 Jul 1849
Greensburg	Isaac H Wright 27 Jul 1843
	Isaac H Wright 13 Sep (No year)
	(No first name) Packard 12 Mar 1846
	Archibald McIver 22 Jul 1846
	Gideon Darmond 16 Sep 1846
	Isaac H Wright 21 Dec 1846
	Harrison McKie 1 Feb 1848
	William M McKinney 11 Apr 1851
	William Pepper 9 Jun 1851
	Stanley N Veird 12 Mar 1852
	Wellington W Carter 19 Jul 1852
	D C Henson 30 Aug 1854
	R Strickland 18 Mar 1855
	Thomas S Smacker 21 Dec 1855
	Thomas Eubanks 19 Sep 1856
	James George Parker 29 Jan 1857
St. Helena	Blass Spiller 18 Aug 1841
	George Packwood 17 Mar 1850
	Joseph Killian 29 Sep 1853
Dennis Mills	Jacob Wiley Odom 15 May 1848
	William Dennis Jr 10 Feb 1850
	William Dennis 26 Apr 1853
	William Dennis Jr 18 Nov 1853
	Samuel J Chance 11 Apr 1857
Tangipahoa	James H George 19 Nov 1850
	Washington Wheat 28 Dec 1854
	H Hayden 5 May 1856
	Charles H Allen 2 Sep 1857
Amite City	Charles S Stewart 18 Jul 1855
Hog Branch	William J Bennett 19 Jan 1856

Prospect Hill   Benjamin Weil 6 Mar 1856

Roberts Mill   George S Roberts 9 Dec 1856

Kemp's Mill   Thomas D Kemp 17 Jul 1857

ST JAMES PARISH

St. James   Alphonse Bougeret 4 Jul 1846
Disc 4 Feb 1847

Convent   Joseph Landry 26 Jan 1847
                        (Illegible entry)
                        Joseph Landry 22 Sep 1847
                        Leon Blouin 8 Aug 1853
                        Marcellin Oubre 6 Jul 1857

Vacherie Road   John V Armant 29 May 1854

Cantrelle   Louis Decuiors 22 May 1854
                        Edouard Leboeuf 14 Aug 1855
                        Victor Melancon 6 Oct 1856

ST. JOHN THE BAPTIST PARISH

Bonnet Carre   Adolph Guyol 7 Jun 1843
                        Lazin Denoyer 3 Jul 1845
                        Lesin Ory 23 Dec 1845
                        Ezekial Fleming 19 Jun 1849
                        Leonidas Conrad 17 Jul 1849
                        Thomas S Edrington 4 Mar 1850
                        Onezime Bossier 4 Jul 1850
                        Edgard C Perret 7 Mar 1851

ST. LANDRY PARISH

Ballew's Ferry   John Lyons Jr 11 May 1838

Bayou Chicot   William Akenhead 28 Apr 1843

James Akenhead 23 May 1848

Grand Coteau	Auguste Sambre 16 Jul 1842
	John F Smith 23 Sep 1844
	Sylvester J Barry 5 Sep 1848
Opelousas	Guy H Bell 6 Aug 1834
	John I Hamilton 16 Dec (Year illegible)
	R Hawkins 2 Mar 1848
	John Posey 20 Jan 1852
	Andrew J Thompson 18 Apr 1853
	Theodore Chachere 25 Aug 1853
Plaquemine Brulie	Jesse B Clark 23 May 1844
Ville Platte	Marcellin Garand 16 Jul 1842
	Lemuel J B Shane 3 Feb (Year illegible)
	Marcel Daire 26 Mar 1849
	Yves Vidrine 4 Aug 1855
Washington	Nathan Gilbert 10 Feb 1844
	William I Perry 16 Dec 1846
	M Anderson 26 Mar 1848
	Thomas C Anderson 20 Jun 1850
	Robert S Wilkins 30 Dec 1852
	John Reed 16 Jun 1853
	Robert S Wilkins 25 Apr 1854
	George W Marsh 8 Aug 1854
	Abraham Millspaugh 14 Oct 1854
Big Cane	William A. Jackson 17 Feb 1848
	Hugh L Nelson 20 Jun 1849
	Isaac R Jackson 11 Nov 1850
Daniston	John Davis 15 Jun 1848
Disc 8 Sep 1849	
Bayou Boeuf	Thomas McCrory 25 May 1852
Midway	Constant Chachere 27 May 1852

Disc 29 Nov 1852

Arnaudville	Alphonse J Patin 7 Aug 1854
	Aristide Delahoussaye 17 Jun 1855
	(Illegible entry)
	John Chapman Mills 17 Feb 1857
Leonville	Michael Emonet 23 Feb 1856
Barry's Landing	Joseph M Canier Jr 18 Jun 1856
Disc 29 Oct 1856	
Mermenton	William Cottrell 2 Sep 1857
Couleur Blanc	James Mires 17 Sep 1857
Cataublan	Windsor Smith 31 Dec 1857

ST. MARTIN PARISH

St. Martinsville	Valsin A Fournet 15 Jun 1838
	Theodore Devalcourt 5 Aug 1845
	Theodore Devalcourt 29 Oct 1847
	Flavius Lebesque 4 Dec 1849
	Theodore Devalcourt 22 Jun 1850
	Francois M Dumartrait 27 Oct 1851
	Henry P Heard 12 May 1852
	Valsin A Fournet 21 Jun 1852
	Alexandre Thenet 30 Jul 1852
	Auguste Maraist 16 Jun 1853
Butte La Rose	J S Leonard 31 Dec 1857
Fausse Point	Francis O Dugas 19 Jul 1848
	Armand C Valet 6 Mar 1850
	Antoine A Picot 27 Oct 1851
Disc 24 Dec (No year)	
Breaux Bridge	Edmund Bulliard 28 Apr 1843
	Samuel Bell 24 Aug 1850

　　　　　　　　　　　Henry Rees 28 Dec 1855
　　　　　　　　　　　Thomas H Woodson 9 Dec 1856
　　　　　　　　　　　Valsai Bulliard 7 Jul 1857

New Iberia　　　　　John Devalcourt 5 Mar 1839
　　　　　　　　　　　Josiah French 22 Dec 1845
　　　　　　　　　　　John Devalcourt 6 Jul 1846
　　　　　　　　　　　Luther M Sugg 25 Jul 1856
　　　　　　　　　　　Robert J Epperson 24 Dec 1857

St. Mary Parish

Centreville　　　　　Charles Nettleton 2 Nov 1843
　　　　　　　　　　　Israel P Yancey 28 Jun 1845
　　　　　　　　　　　(Illegible entry)
　　　　　　　　　　　W S Cary 19 Feb 1849
　　　　　　　　　　　Julius Smith 21 Jun 1851
　　　　　　　　　　　Joshua B Cary 31 Mar 1854
　　　　　　　　　　　Theodore W Schockley 10 Jun 1857

Charenton　　　　　　Demary Nicholas 24 Jun 1842
　　　　　　　　　　　Jules Gaillard 27 Sep (No year)
　　　　　　　　　　　Charles Dutell 8 Apr 1851
　　　　　　　　　　　Philip Vogel 18 Mar 1852
Disc 10 Jan 1853
Reest 30 Jan 1854　　Elijah G Crowson 30 Jan 1854
　　　　　　　　　　　John Meynard 18 Nov 1856

Franklin　　　　　　Timothy J Walker 1 Jun 1841
　　　　　　　　　　　Emily Walker 24 Dec 1845
　　　　　　　　　　　Hubert Wilson 26 Aug 1846
　　　　　　　　　　　George N Seagrave 27 Jun 1848
　　　　　　　　　　　Daniel Doresiett 11 Jul 1849
　　　　　　　　　　　Thomas Pooley 1 Feb 1851
　　　　　　　　　　　Epaphedilius Howle 28 Feb 1854
　　　　　　　　　　　David R Muggah 8 Sep 1856

Jeanerette　　　　　Clet Provost 8 Apr 1842
　　　　　　　　　　　Thomas J McCarty 22 Aug (No year)
　　　　　　　　　　　(First name illegible) Prevost Jr 25 Jun 1846

	Paul Prevost 24 Jan 1848
Pattersonville	John A Dwight 1 May 1844
	Alexander G Brown 25 Jun 1846
	James Muggah 21 Dec 1846
Bayou Ramois	Thomas Stanberry 11 Nov 1847
	John A Bryant 14 Nov 1848
	James Collins 1 Feb 1850
Disc 1 Aug 1855	
Alligator	Stephen DeLucky 5 nov 1849
Penwick	Andrew J Forbes 24 May 1854
	James R Daly 8 Dec 1854
	A Todd 5 Sep 1855
	Moise Bloch 5 Jan 1857
	Andrew J Pyron 18 Aug 1857
Brashear	Robert B Brashear 8 Oct 1855
	William J Greenwood 8 Nov 1856
	P Gathright 16 May 1857
	Thomas T Brashear 10 Sep 1857

ST. TAMMANY PARISH

Covington	Philip Kellar 28 Oct 1840
	Ethan Colton 5 (No month or year)
	(Illegible entry)
	Ethan Colton 16 Apr 1853
	Jesse See 11 Jan 1856
Madisonville	Edward C Lehmanowsky 23 May 1844
	C G Martin 3 Jun (No year)
	(No first name) Dennison 8 Dec 1846
	C G Martin 5 Apr 1847
	Ethan Colton 9 Feb 1848
	C G Martin 25 Jun 148
	(No first name) Colorner 19 Nov 1850

Mandeville Disc 6 Jul 1845 Reest 30 Jul 1845	Antoine P Sanaux 29 Aug 1843 A Merle 31 Jul 1845 P Loutret 10 May 1849 Louis Cogullon 28 Nov 1850 Francois Drury 8 Feb 1855 Auguste Gubert 31 Jul 1855 Louis Cogullon 2 Dec 1855
Marburyville	Eli Headen 18 Aug 1843 William Spring 30 Dec 1844 John Gasoley 30 Aug 1845 William Spring 27 Feb 1849
Pine Grove Disc 10 Mar 1855	Thomas C Terry 25 Apr 1836 John L Robinson 14 Oct (No year)
Sweetwater Disc 16 May 1845	William Marbury 1 Jun 1840
Lima	Melchi Wadworth 28 Sep 1847 Enoch B Talley 6 Jan 1853
Parkerville	John Parker 28 Sep 1847 James M Ernest 2 Oct 1848
Sun	Matthew Richardson 29 May 1851 John Edes Smith 27 Oct (No year) James A Calhoun 14 Nov 1856
Pearl River Island Disc 11 Jan 1853	John G Coggins 23 Apr 1852
O'Rourke's	James O'Rourke 31 Dec 1853

TENSAS PARISH

Hard Times Disc 8 Sep 1845	J Y Hollingsworth 11 Jul 1844

Waterproof	Joseph Gorton 15 May 1844
	William F Lynch 14 Feb 1845
	R Miller 24 Sep 1845
	William F Lynch 19 Nov 1845
	Joseph Gorton 21 Dec 1846
	Francis A Gorton 15 Jun 1847
	Thomas H W Baynard 22 Nov 1848
	Thomas H W Baynard 16 Sep 1850
	John P Mason 18 Apr 1853
	David Wise 24 Oct 1855
St. Joseph Courthouse	James W Davenport 2 Sep 1844
	Charles H Forman 7 Oct 1847
	(Illegible entry)
	James W Davenport 8 May 1851
	Robert H Snyder 27 Dec 1855
Bellvue Landing	William T S Compton 3 Dec 1844
Ashwood	William T S Compton 9 Nov 1845
	Thomas O Moody 2 Apr 1850
Disc 28 Jun 1851	
Reest 15 Apr 1852	George C Nugent 15 Apr 1852
	James C Dougherty 27 Jan 1853
	Delos G Walker 5 May 1856
	James Stewart 1 Oct 1857
Mound Bayou	Thomas C Biller 19 Jun 1848
	Richard B Lynch 10 Sep 1850
	Haley J Inge 24 Feb 1851
Kirk's Ferry	William H Bowman 3 Jul 1849
Hollywood	John Routh 24 Jun 1854
Disc 25 Nov 1855	

TERREBONNE PARISH

Houma Courthouse	John T Rockwood 25 Oct 1843

	Richard Grinage 30 Apr 1845
	John T Rockwood 5 Apr 1848
	Joseph A Gague 1 May 1850
	James A Kelly 10 Jun 1850
	E Harrison 19 Jul 1852
	Aubin Bourg 11 May 1853
	Andrew W Lathrop 22 Apr 1854
	Thomas F Brooks 28 Jun 1856
Tigerville	F. W. Woodland 4 Nov 1847
	D D Mercer 23 May 1848
	William Bridgeford 3 Apr 1849
	James H Smith 16 Apr 1850
	Louisa C Price 25 May 1852
Terrebonne Disc 16 Apr 1857	Nicholas H Smith 12 May 1856

UNION PARISH

Farmerville Courthouse	Enoch B Whitson 7 Jul 1842
	John A Bayliss 30 Dec 1844
	James C Nygaard 8 Jun 1847
	James A Dozier 5 Sep 1849
	William A Darby 9 Feb 1852
	William B H Poer 18 Mar 1856
Colvin's	Zephaniah B Davis 13 Mar 1846
	Thomas Colvin 21 Dec 1848
Ouachita City	Vallen J Bird 13 Mar 1846
	David B Trousdale 16 Dec 1848
	James A Holliday 5 Nov 1849
	James L Jones 3 Nov 1851
	James C Brown 29 Dec 1853
	John G Hill 11 Jul 1854
	John Nosworthy 30 Aug 1854
	James M Lupe 28 Feb 1857
Shiloh	William A Milner 16 Apr 1851

	Wilson H Hammock 30 Dec 1852
	James F Wade 14 Jul 1853
	John C Knott 6 May 1854
	John D Cole 3 Sep 1856
	Jesse Trebb 6 Mar 1857
Downsville	Philemon Wilhite 9 Jun 1851
Lindville	John S Barr 8 Sep 1851
	Lewis Lanier 9 Sep 1853
Disc 1 May 1855	
D'Arbone	John B Wallis 8 Mar 1852
	Joseph H Morrow 25 Oct 1853
	Samuel W McClendon 5 Jun 1857
Spring Hill	James M Turner 1 May 1852
Disc 13 Jul 1854	
Reest 28 Aug 1855	James Edwards 28 Aug 1855
Disc 28 May 1857	
Union Cross Roads	George Everett 7 May 1853
	William D McBurton 4 Apr 1854

OUACHITA PARISH

Caldwell	Thomas B Rutland 8 Nov 1832
	John B Bres Jr 5 Apr 1838
Colvin's	Jeptha Colvin 24 Mar 1838
	Zephaniah P Davis 12 Nov 1840
Monroe Courthouse	John B Filhiol 28 Jan 1843
	Henry B Watkins 28 Jun 1846
	(Illegible entry)
	William Macouchy 8 Sep 1849
	James S Ray 1 May 1850
	Joseph F McGuire 5 Jun 1851
	Charles Delery 19 May 1853
	John E Larkin 28 Nov 1855

William H Gayle 9 Oct 1857

Point Pleasant	John Temple 5 Mar 1842
Forksville	William H Byron 20 Apr 1848 Mason Huey 7 Jan 1852 James H Milling 5 Sep 1854 Grove S Fitch 10 May 1856
Logtown Disc 20 May 1853	David Faulke 15 May 1848 Henry P Watkins 26 Aug 1850
Trenton	William Marburg 5 Jun 1848 Littleton A Phillips 25 Mar 1851 William H Rogers 11 Aug 1853 James C Richardson 8 Nov 1854 William H Rogers 20 Dec 1854 John Thacher 24 Feb 1855 Abraham Madden 18 Nov 1856 James S Grayson 10 Apr 1857
Indian Village	Edward Gilbert 10 May 1849 John T Bryan 8 Apr 1853 (Illegible entry) James Huey III 5 Dec 1854
Pine Hills Disc 8 Oct 1856	Jacob A Coon 18 Dec 1849 Duncan McVicker 8 Oct 1851 Fred C Newman 8 Jul 1852 West Parker 7 Oct 1854 Amos Clark 18 Sep 1855
Salamagundi	William McDonald 19 Mar 1851
Hamilton	Henry Beacham 11 Jul 1851 Alexander Hamilton 26 Aug 1852 Henry Bartlett 14 Jul 1853 Abram H Scribner 18 Feb 1854

Disc 30 Aug 1856

Red Mouth
Note: Late Salamagundi

Wesley T Griffin 17 Jun 1853

Sebastopol
Disc 28 Nov 1856

Durrett B Sandford 2 Jul 1855

Prevost

William D McDonald 25 Aug 1855
Samuel Allen 10 Dec 1856

WASHINGTON PARISH

Franklinton Courthouse

Benjamin A Beason 15 May 1843
Presley Germain 27 Nov 1844
Charles T Sherman 14 Jan 1846
Joseph Smith 11 Feb 1847
Stephen Ellis 17 Sep 1847
Benjamin F Impson 8 Feb 1849
David C Hewson 26 Feb 1850
Joseph M Simmons 10 Jun 1850
Benjamin F Impson 22 Oct 1851
Warren Rushing 27 Feb 1852
Stephen Ellis 18 May 1852
James M Burris 31 Jan 1853
Nicholas R Payne 15 Nov 1854
David Magee 23 Apr 1855
Michael W Shilling 21 Jul 1856
Mrs. Louise W Brooks 5 Jun 1857
Mrs. E A Magee 11 Dec 1857

Oak Grove

Isaac A Myles 5 Oct 1842
Jacob W Andrews 20 Dec 1844
William Brumfield 21 Dec 1846
John Carroll 11 Nov 1847
Boyd W Berson 27 Sep 1848
Pleasant B Stratham 29 Jan 1850
Henry Leach 3 Mar 1851
Samuel Wildblood 5 Jun 1851

Disc 4 Aug 1852

Shady Grove Disc 24 Oct 1850 Reest 29 Mar 1851	Thomas Pearson 1 Jul 1844 William A Harvey 29 Mar 1851 Joseph S Branon 20 Jul 1853 Seth Barnes 21 Mar 1855
Siblia Disc 5 Nov 1845 Reest 3 Jun 1846	Robert F Sibley 22 Nov 1834 Robert F Sibley 3 Jun 1846 Benjamin Bradshaw 11 Feb 1847 George W Dyson 22 Aug 1849 William Hogan 25 Sep 1850 Benjamin Bradshaw 19 Feb 1855
Disc 12 Mar 1857	
Palestine	John McGaha 25 Apr 1850 William Brumfield 12 May 1852
Davidson	James F Ard 28 Feb 1856
Roberts	John V Painter 7 Apr 1856

WEST BATON ROUGE PARISH

Bruly Landing	Eli LeJeune 7 Jun 1843 Onesime Doiron 13 Sep 1844
Labdell's Store	Hiram Noyes 15 Aug 1844 Henry R Graham 21 Feb 1846 Hiram Noyes 29 Jan 1847 William Markham 29 Jan 1847 Hiram Noyes 16 Dec 1847 Emeline Noyes 7 Nov 1855

WEST FELICIANA

Laurel Hill Disc 7 Dec 1848 Reest 4 May 1855	Alexander Wilson 30 Oct 1841 William H Semon 4 May 1855

St. Francisville Courthouse David Austen 7 Feb 1842

Tunica
                Oliver B Robinson 1 May 1851
                Benedict Wolfe 22 Jul 1852
Disc 27 Oct 1853

Bayou Tunica Nathaniel E Robinson 29 Apr 1856

LAFOURCHE INTERIOR PARISH

Lepine's Evariste A Lepine 23 Oct 1845
Disc 19 Jul 1846

JACKSON PARISH

Vernon Robert A Carson 4 Jun 1846
        Marion W Ashley 24 Dec 1852
        John C Jones 10 Dec 1854
        John W Arnold 15 May 1856
        James M Smith 29 Jan 1857

Dugdemona John Gibson 28 Sep 1846
        William F Bond 24 Jan 1849

Grove Hill William A ONeal 2 Dec 1846
        Nathaniel Miscon 29 Jan 1855
Disc 30 Oct 1855

Colvin's Thomas Colvin 21 Dec 1846
        James Grisham 26 Nov 1848
        Willis B Otts 15 Jan 1850

Vienna John Huey Jr 9 Apr 1850
        J A Phillips 14 Feb 1852
        J H Stevens 6 Oct 1853
        Micajah P Quinn 7 Jul 1857

Rochester William B McDonald 20 Jun 1850
Disc 20 May 1851

Brookline	Dawson W Kennedy 25 Jun 1850
Carter's Disc 30 Dec 1851	Henry Carter 1 Nov 1850
Woodville	Henry W Shenard 22 Jun 1854 William F Bond 27 Sep 1855
Plankville	Robert E Davis 2 Jun 1855
Wyatt's Roads	Reuben Hargrove 23 Aug 1855 James H Hargrove 21 Nov 1856
Ebenezer Disc 4 Mar 1857	Joel P Otts 4 Apr 1856
Mount Morian Disc 19 Apr 1857	William B Warren 4 Apr 1856
Douglas	Moses Spivey 5 Jun 1857
Timberville	Joel Embrey 5 Jun 1857

BOSSIER PARISH

Red Land Disc 14 Oct 1853	Jerome B Mading 2 Nov 1846 Daniel H Pettery 23 Jan 1848
Pineville	Francis W Armour 18 Feb 1847
Bellvue	Nathaniel S Currier 5 Apr 1847 John O Westbury 28 Feb 1848 Robert J Looney 11 Nov 1850 Samuel N Furniss 31 Mar 1852 David J Elder 19 Jun 1852 Lysander Rathburn 7 Feb 1854 William Chevalier 5 Oct 1855 Albert W Spurlin 25 Jan 1856

Willow Chute	Cezaire Wallace 18 Feb 1847
	William Stinson 13 Sep 1848
Pine Flat	John M Holloway 17 Jul 1849
	Augustus Martin 8 Mar 1851
	F Linn 7 Apr 1852
	John F Gambill 10 May 1856
	Asa H Hearne 9 Nov 1857
Cypress	Michael W Larkin 11 Oct 1849
Disc 10 Jan 1851	
Bossier Point	Richard Coombs 20 Jul 1850
	Paschal P Bates 10 Sep 1850
	James H Brown 31 Dec 1851
Connell's Cross Roads	George W Sentell 19 Jul 1850
	William V Brown 12 Jan 1852
	(Illegible entry)
	Ezekial F Sockard 4 Nov 1855
	William N Chevalier 26 Jul 1856
	James H Jones 13 Dec 1856
	Benjamin F Looney 5 Dec 1857
Yarborough	Arthur Yarborough 22 Jul 1851
	Richard S Sandidge 11 Jan 1852
Disc 22 Sep 1854	
Fillmore	William E Hamilton 28 May 1852
Bisteneau	Simeon R Doyle 21 Jun 1852
	Claiborn S Love 18 Apr 1853
	Simeon R Doyle 21 Sep 1854
	William F Boon 24 Jun 1856
Rocky Mount	Charles Kaisser 31 Aug 1853
	Noah Phillips 21 Sep 1854
	John J Thomas 29 May 1855
	James T Talbert 22 Aug 1856

Deck's	Burton P Deck 27 May 1856 John Holley 29 Jun 1857
Orchard Grove	George B Sligh 27 May 1856 Charles S Greene 5 Dec 1857
Collinsburg	Francis W Armour 28 Jun 1856
Knox Point	Sam E McKenley 24 Nov 1857

VERMILION PARISH

Perry's Bridge	Elijah Ewing 21 Dec 1846 William Kibbs 29 Jan 1850 Rosemand LeBlanc 9 Feb 1852 Robert H Mills 25 Apr 1855
Abbeville Disc 18 Dec 1848 Reest 19 Mar 1850	Nicholas Demary 4 Nov 1847 Valsin Veasey 19 Mar 1850 Alanson Spaulding 14 Jul 1853
Pare Perdue	Rosemand LeBlanc 21 Jun 1852

BIENVILLE PARISH

Salt Spring	Burrell H Matthews 4 Jan 1849 Alfred P King 25 Nov 1851
Sparta	James M Denson 4 Jan 1849 David Carr 31 Mar 1852 James M Denson 30 Aug 1854 James P Dyess 1 Sep 1854 Elbert N Warren 11 Jul 1855 Lewis Eldridge 1 Sep 1855
Ringgold	James Fudge 3 Aug 1849 Jesse Mobley 18 May 1850

	(Illegible entry)
	Hilliard J Bankston 5 Nov 1851
	John Henry Scheens 26 Aug 1852
	Lewis Eldridge 29 Dec 1853
	Benjamin S Allums 22 Jun 1854
	H Sheppard 8 Jan 1856
	James B Booth 30 Aug 1856
	William D Griffin 6 May 1857
Saline	James R Heard 11 Oct 1849
	Samuel Sprawls 14 Dec 1851
Buckhorn	James D Mims 10 Jul 1850
Disc 2 Feb 1854	
Reest 19 Jun 1857	James D Mims 19 Jun 1857
Disc 18 Aug 1857	
Arcadia	Shadrack P Sutton 19 Mar 1851
	Edward J Beard 29 Dec 1854
	James Ruys 5 Jan 1856
	William A Lucas 22 Aug 1856
	John F Gray 5 Dec 1857
Everson	John McDowell 17 Nov 1851
	James Monroe 21 Feb 1853
Montcalm	Tilman Hemphill 16 Mar 1854
Disc 30 Aug 1855	
Mount Lebanon	Catlet G Thurmond 12 Sep 1848
	Hiram Gibbs 24 Jun 1850
Boon's Landing	Curtis Boon 29 Apr 1854
Disc 30 Dec 1855	
Mud Branch	Meredith Buckner 10 Jun 1856
	Eli T Buckner 18 Aug 1857
Soggy Bayou	Whitfield Williams 7 Sep 1857

WINN PARISH

Tanock Prairie	Robert M Rogers 31 Aug 1852 James Gray 7 Dec 1853
St. Maurice Disc 22 Sep 1853	William B Prothro 8 Sep 1852
Reest 27 Dec 1854	William B Prothro 27 Dec 1854 David H Boulet 26 Aug 1856
Bertrand Prairie	Thomas Harvey 3 Feb 1853 Elisha K Davis 6 Feb 1857
Pine Ridge	George H Walker 19 Feb 1853 Josiah H Lacey 31 Dec 1854
Winnfield	Asbury C Sewell 24 Mar 1854 Quincy A Hargis 2 Aug 1854 C Banks 19 Nov 1855 Edmund W Edwards 27 Dec 1856
Goodwater	Adam Riser 2 Aug 1854
Saline Mills	James C Weeks 6 Jul 1854
Wheeling	Jeremiah J Wilder 12 Nov 1855 Aaron C Rugan 15 Dec 1856
Louisville	William J Kidd 23 Aug 1853 Elisha K McGinty 1 Nov 1854

POST OFFICE LOCATIONS	POSTMASTER AND DATES OF APPOINTMENT

ASCENSION PARISH

Donaldsonville Courthouse	Andrew Gringoy 20 Apr 1853 Henry W Miller 12 Jun 1863 Emilie Collins 10 Apr 1869 Pierre Landry 1 May 1871
Live Oak Disc 22 Jun 1866	Jules Landry 1 Sep 1857 Deminie LeBlanc 21 May 1860
New River	Henry Doyal 11 Jun 1849 John S Minor 24 Feb 1859 Thomas E Hills 26 Dec 1865
Turead	Francois Jaumes 15 Apr 1852 Auguste Gantran 2 Apr 1866
Dominique's Store Disc 26 Sep 1859	A Dominique 25 Feb 1859
White Houmas Disc 28 Jun 1866	Vincent Paul Landry 27 Aug 1864

ASSUMPTION PARISH

Albemarle	Ferdinand Barilleaux 15 Jun 1853 Sulia Blanchard 2 Mar 1859 Magloire Bourgeois 29 Mar 1860
Disc 22 Jun 1866 Reest 19 Dec 1866	Magloire Bourgeois 19 Dec 1866 Miss Artemise G Fonteley 12 Apr 1867
Disc 13 Sep 1870 Reest 14 Mar 1871	Pierre Carmouche 14 Mar 1871 Frank Loret 13 May 1872 William Himel 31 Jan 1873

Assumption Courthouse	Pierre H Besse 28 Sep 1857
	T Caver 14 Jan 1861
	Joseph D Ford 11 Apr 1866
	Henry L Swords 29 May 1869
	A T Bushee 3 Jan 1870
	Eudaldo G Pinatado 9 May 1870
	Elisha Eastwood 31 Mar 1871
	William C Cramer 19 May 1872
	Facunda E Pintado 3 Jul 1873
Church	Claudius Linossier 5 Mar 1852
Disc 2 Jan 1860	
Reest 19 Jan 1861	Arthur D Blanchard 19 Jan 1861
Disc 26 Jun 1867	
Crane's Forge	Eugene Feray 4 Aug 1852
	Joseph D Guidry 25 Jul 1860
Disc 22 Jun 1866	
Reest 3 Sep 1867	S C Mollere 3 Sep 1867
	Theodore Lear 23 Mar 1868
Disc 24 Jan 1870	
Paincourtville	Eudaldo G Pintado 16 Feb 1857
	Vincent T Pintado 12 Oct 1860
Disc 12 Oct 1864	
Reest 19 Jun 1866	Joseph T Hebert 19 Jun 1866
	Geolfide Trahan 7 Apr 1868
	Narcisse Alleman 24 Sep 1868
	Louis Weil 21 Jul 1871
	Charles Aubery 14 Apr 1873
Star	Edward Prout 9 Dec 1856
Disc 28 Jun 1866	
Reest 19 Dec 1866	Hubert Arsenaux 19 Dec 1866
Belle River	Hilaire Bourg 13 Sep 1860
Disc 22 Jun 1861	
Labadieville	Spicer Jones 18 Jun 1867

AVOYELLES PARISH

Big Bend William Branch Marshall 5 Jan 1857
Disc 17 Nov 1858
Reest 30 Dec 1858 William Clopton 30 Dec 1858
Benjamin W Bond 5 Mar 1859
Gisard F Sancier 4 Jan 1860

Disc 22 Jun 1866
Reest 11 Oct 1866 Zachariah Kimball 11 Oct 1866
John Everett 25 Oct 1867

Evergreen Joseph K Ewell 15 Aug 1857
William T Fuqua 31 Oct 1859
Nelson Kenyon 19 oct 1866
William E Ewell 17 Oct 1867
Joseph Cappel 3 Jan 1870

Holmesville William H Bassett Jr 7 Dec 1854
John W McDonald 16 Apr 1864
M Ferrin 6 Feb 1866
Samuel Hass 16 Jul 1866
H O Tubre 1 Jul 1867

Disc 4 Apr 1868
Reest 14 Dec 1868 Walter Arkenhead 14 Dec 1868

Mansura Pierre A Durand 27 Oct 1856
Jean J Guerineau 5 May 1860
Pierre A Durand 12 Jul 1860
Jean J Guerineau 23 Oct 1860

Disc 28 Jun 1866
Reest 21 Jul 1866 David Siess 20 Jul 1866

Marksville Courthouse Constant Guillebert 12 Sep 1856
Emile Chaze 7 Oct 1858
Henry Dupuy 1 Jan 1861
Henry Dupuy 3 Oct 1865
Jules A Dalsuet 15 Jun 1869
George L Mayer 11 Apr 1871

Moreauville	John R Gremillion 27 Aug 1856 Alonzo L Boyer 26 Jan 1858 John R Gremillion 23 May 1864 James A Boyer 30 Jul 1866
Simmesport	James Brewster 4 Jul 1854 Jerome B Robinson 3 May 1859
Disc 28 Jun 1866 Reest 3 Oct 1867	Michael Loeb 3 Oct 1867
Disc 2 Sep 1868 Reest 23 Jun 1871	Mrs. Azema Leigh 23 Jun 1871
Cassandria	Montillion J Ryland 22 Nov 1871
Cottonport	Gervais A Bordelon 7 Mar 1872
Heuffpower	Thomas J Heard 3 Jun 1873

BIENVILLE PARISH

Arcadia	William A Lucas 22 Aug 1856 John F Gray 5 Dec 1857 Micajah C Pace 27 Apr 1859 John N Ryant 2 Apr 1866 A Holland 30 Sep 1872 Allen Barksdale 21 Oct 1872 John T Winfield 24 Jun 1873
Brush Valley	James E Cook 11 May 1855 Isaac Coleman 20 Mar 1858 W H Gray 11 Jan 1861
Disc 22 Jun 1866	
Iverson	James Monroe 21 Feb 1855 Allen S B Pior 27 Sep 1858 Matilda A Monroe 2 Aug 1859 Bettie A Monroe 8 Dec 1865
Disc 26 mar 1867	
Soggy Bayou	Whitfield Williams 7 Sep 1857

Wiley W Williams 24 Jan 1860

Mount Lebanon	Hiram Gibbs 24 Jun 1854
Thomas B Tompkins 9 Dec 1858
Hanson Lee 21 Dec 1858
William F Wells 23 Jul 1859
James C Rogers 39 Nov 1865
Benjamin F Parnell 20 Feb 1866
Peter G Thompson 15 Jul 1869
Robert Hardy 20 May 1872

Mud Branch	Eli T Buckner 18 Aug 1857
William E Collins 19 Jan 1859
Disc 26 Jan 1867

Ringgold	William D Griffin 6 May 1857
Daniel H Sheppard 19 Feb 1858
Richard C Whitted 7 Feb 1859
Disc 28 Jun 1866
Reest 17 Oct 1866	Miss Mary A Wilkinson 13 Oct 1866
Marshall H Twitchell 15 May 1867
John C Mosley 19 Aug 1869

Saline	Samuel Sprawls 14 Dec 1855
Alfred B Prothro 26 Sep 1859
Disc 28 Jun 1866
Reest 7 Dec 1866	Hiram Shaw 7 Dec 1866
George C Lewis 17 Mar 1873
Jackson S Corbette 20 Oct 1873

Salt Spring	Alfred P King 2 Nov 1854
Disc 28 Jun 1866

Sparta	Lewis Eldridge 1 Sep 1855
W W Upshaw 13 Mar 1866
Hodge Rabun 15 Nov 1866
John H Scheen 30 Sep 1872

Buckhorn	Mrs. Martha A Mims 26 Jun 1858
Disc 4 Mar 1864

Reest 15 Feb 1867					John James Mims 15 Feb 1867

Walnut Creek					Josiah F Allen 3 Jun 1858
						Thomas Davenport 7 Jun 1860
						Thomas Davenport 2 Apr 1866
Disc 26 Mar 1867

Simsborough					John A Casey 22 Jul 1867

Liberty Hill					John S Vernon 7 Mar 1872
						E A Crawford 28 Apr 1873
						Thomas Crawford 16 Jun 1873

Bear Creek					William Price 3 Jun 1872
Disc 11 Jul 1873

BOSSIER PARISH

Belllvue					Albert W Spurlin 25 Jan 1856
						James W Jones 31 Mar 1859
						John C Lofton 15 Sep 1859
						James Chandler 8 Jan 1866
						Michael W Hodgeon 14 Mar 1866
						Miss Marg V Long 11 Oct 1866
						F B Haynes 20 May 1873
						John A Turner 3 Jul 1873

Bisteneau					William F Boon 24 Jun 1856
Disc 11 Oct 1859

Bossier Point					James H Brown 3 Dec 1857
						Isaac F Sibley 28 Jan 1861
Disc 22 Jun 1866

Collinsburgh					Francis W Armour 28 Jun 1856
						George W Sentell 21 Oct 1858
						William M Sentell 5 Jun 1861
						Oliver Richardson 18 Jul 1866

Deck's						John Holley 20 Jun 1857

Disc 27 Jan 1859	Joseph Raborn 27 Apr 1858
Fillmore Disc 26 Jun 1867 Reest 12 Jun 1870	William E Hamilton 28 May 1852 David B Platt 12 Dec 1870 A H Burns 12 Mar 1872 Elias F Connell 26 Jun 1873
Orchard Grove Disc 26 Jun 1866	Charles S Greene 5 Dec 1856 James L Taylor 4 Oct 1858 Thomas Nettles 3 Jan 1859 Henry J Taylor 6 Dec 1859
Pine Flat	John F Gambill 10 May 1856 Asa H Hearne 9 Nov 1857
Rocky Mount Disc 26 Jun 1867 Reest 21 Mar 1871	James J Talbert 22 Aug 1856 Benjamin W Stewman 7 Feb 1860 William J Hughes 21 Mar 1871 William A Martin 23 Oct 1871
Sentell's Store	James M Jones 13 Dec 1856 Benjamin F Looney 5 Dec 1857 Knowles D Taylor 2 Aug 1859 William W Healy 22 Mar 1866 Alonzo P Haywood 14 Jul 1866
Benton	Elias O Neil 1 Mar 1870 Thomas W Woodruff 17 Jul 1871 John J Scott 15 Oct 1872
Dixie Disc 1 Sep 1871	Alvin N Rounsevelt 7 Aug 1871
Dickson's Cross Roads	Alvin N Rounsevelt 22 Nov 1871

CADDO PARISH

Adams
Disc 5 Nov 1859

Howell C Adams 13 Dec 1855

Begusa Chute
Disc 4 Feb 1867
Reest 1 Jul 1872

Joseph H Beard 7 Sep 1857

Joseph H Beard 1 Jul 1872

Blossom Hill
Disc 22 Jun 1858

Isaac Hughes 15 Jan 1852

Cooke's Store

Disc 16 May 1860

William B Cooke 28 Apr 1852
Amaziah R Miller 24 Oct 1859

Greenwood

James W Orr 1 Jun 1857
E G Smith 17 Jul 1860
Edward H Baugh 11 Sep 1860

Disc 22 Jun 1866
Reest 5 Jan 1867

Mrs. Maria Moore 5 Jan 1867
James D Jenkins 11 Apr 1871

Disc 19 Apr 1872
Reest 1 Aug 1872

Michael Roth 1 Aug 1872

Mooringsport

James M Christian 23 Oct 1857
Calvin S Croom 25 Jun 1860
Mrs. Margaret A Croom 25 Apr 1870
William H B Croom 9 Mar 1876

Disc 4 Feb 1861
Reest 25 Apr 1870

Shreveport Courthouse

Henry Hunsicker 6 Dec 1855 (Pres & Sen)
T G Compton 31 Aug 1865
Joseph Howell 27 Dec 1865 (Pres & Sen)
Charles H Thompson 29 Aug 1867 (Pres & Sen)
William Heffner 26 Sep 1867 (Pres)
Charles W Keating 5 Apg 1869 (Pres & Sen)

	Frank T Hatch 1 Oct 1871 (Pres)
	William McKenna 1 Apr 1873 (Pres)
Spring Ridge Disc 4 Nov 1867	Joshua Draifouse 24 Oct 1847
Reest 4 Oct 1869	Leonidas H Wightman 4 Oct 1869 William W Sebastian 20 Dec 1871
Summer Grove Disc 1 Dec 1857	Benjamin F Johnson 27 Oct 1857
Reest 31 Jul 1858	Arthur S Moore 31 Jul 1858 Wiley B Adams 8 Sep 1859
Disc 3 Sep 1860	
Sunny Side Disc 22 Feb 1860	John G Christian 2 Feb 1858
Albany	Peter H Crocker 30 Jul 1858 Thomas W Hull 7 Feb 1859 Peter H Crocker 15 Jul 1859 John A Hawkins 5 Nov 1859
Disc 22 Jun 1866	
Bethany Disc 22 Jun 1866	Gidon Owens 2 May 1864
Currie's Store Disc 9 Nov 1871	David F McClure 24 May 1870
Bridgeport	A F Tucker 3 Jul 1872
Longwood	James H Parnell 19 Nov 1872
Woodlawn	T L Flemming 12 Aug 1874

CALCASIEU PARISH

Hamburg	Josiah Johnson 1 Aug 1853 Solomon Simmons 11 Dec 1857

Hickory Flat   William J Carnes 9 Oct 1854
                            John R Cole 30 Dec 1858
                            William J Carnes 28 Jun 1859
Disc 22 Jun 1866
Reest 18 Oct 1872   James Cole 18 Oct 1872

Lake Charles Courthouse   Charles A Hardy 12 Oct 1852
                            John A Spence 19 May 1858
                            W C Underwood 24 Nov 1865
                            Charles Barbe 21 Mar 1866
                            Charles Glasspool 11 Jul 1866
                            Chancy Barbe 17 Aug 1869

Lake Arthur   Michael Valditaro 5 Aug 1858
                            Placido Hebert 20 Dec 1858
Disc 22 Jun 1866
Reest 24 May 1870   Delino Derouen 24 May 1870

Beckwith   Benjamin Parker 19 May 1859
                            William Meers 27 Sep 1860

West Fork   Adolphe Escoubas 14 Apr 1860
Disc 28 Jun 1866
Reest 26 Oct 1866   Adolphe Derosier 26 Oct 1866
Disc 20 Sep 1869

Gum Springs   Robert Elliston 4 Oct 1860
Disc 22 Jun 1866

Niblett's Bluff   Samuel A Fairchild 21 Apr 1873

Rose Bluff   Oliver R Moss 7 Jun 1873

Woods Bluff   Jerisan Broussard 12 Jun 1873

CALDWELL PARISH

Alpha   Thomas J Humble 24 Jun 1857
                            Nathan M Davis 24 Dec 1860
Disc 22 Jun 1866

Reest 19 Dec 1872					Alexander Morrison 19 Dec 1872

Augusta						John J Meredith 19 Jun 1856
						John E Wright 17 Feb 1859
Disc 11 Sep 1860

Castor						Jeorge W Baygents 26 Oct 1857
						Moses Wineburg 29 May 1858
Disc 4 Feb 1867

Columbia Courthouse				Henry Y Baughmann 19 Jan 1857
						William J Hanna 14 Jan 1858
						Henry M Guffey 27 Jan 1858
						Sanders B Cook 30 Apr 1860
						James A Boyd 20 Nov 1865
						D P Gibson 2 Jan 1866
						Alexander Duchesne 14 May 1866
						Jarret Harris 11 Oct 1866
						William F Roberts 8 Feb 1869
						Emanuel Preifus 23 Aug 1872

Copenhagen					William C Redditt 11 May 1849
Disc 22 Jun 1866
Reest 16 Sep 1867				John A Edgeworth 16 Sep 1867
						Lizzie T Edgeworth 24 Dec 1867
						Francis F Mitchell 23 Jan 1868
						John S Davis 9 Aug 1871

Good Hope					Thomas McCormick 16 Jul 1857
Disc 24 Jul 1858

Long Lake					John H Pinson 14 Aug 1855
						John B Neal 20 Mar 1858
Disc 22 Jun 1866

Mount Pleasant					Thomas Meredith 19 Sep 1849
Disc 4 Feb 1867
Reest 26 Jan 1872				Simon Thomas 26 Jan 1872
						Malachi B Thomas 13 Jan 1873

Sinope
Disc 13 Jan 1859

Alfred Ferraud 16 Mar 1854

Oakville
Disc 18 Oct 1858

L W McCallum 8 Jun 1858

Waverly

Mrs. Emeline D Perkins 5 Aug 1870

Pine Bluff

Edwin Lawrence Hill 12 Oct 1871
Stephen Williams 26 Nov 1872

Cotton Plant

Aurelius S Hundley 17 Apr 1873

Eureka

James M Bennett 10 Aug 1874

EAST CARROLL PARISH

Aston

James B Edington 20 Nov 1855
Major J Grace 15 Mar 1858
William F Brown 26 Mar 1858
Bonhome Cuhn 2 Mar 1860

Disc 26 Jun 1867

Caledonia

Amos Lawton 19 Oct 1854
Thomas R Willcox 15 May 1858
Simon Witkouski 20 Sep 1859

Disc 26 Jun 1866
Reest 5 Dec 1871

Simon Witkouski 5 Dec 1871

Deerfield

William C Purvis 16 Mar 1855

Floyd

John L Gordon 15 Nov 1856
James M Watson 28 Nov 1857
John S Herring 3 Feb 1858
J M Langford 15 May 1858
Duncan A McCrae 26 Jun 1858
David Hall 8 Jan 1857

Disc 23 May 1869
Reest 18 Dec 1871

Andrew Donnam 18 Dec 1871

Joe's Bayou
Disc 22 Jun 1866

Jackson B Tompkins 29 Jul 1852

Lake Providence	John Harvey 21 Jan 1857
	Frank H Harvey 19 Mar 1858
	George W McCarroll 5 Feb 1859
	Edward Matthews 20 Nov 1865
	(Illegible entry)
	George C Benham 21 Feb 1868
	William H Schneider 13 Oct 1869
	Charles E Moss Jr 28 Feb 1870
	George Van Kirk 15 Nov 1871
	Charles H Nash 15 Jan 1872
Monticello	Richard H Dollehide 22 Jan 1855
	Robert McCain 11 Dec 1857
Disc 26 Jun 1867	
Oak Bluffs	William W Owen 16 Mar 1854
Disc 28 Jun 1866	
Pecan Grove	John M Stewart 8 Aug 1857
	D F Ratcliff 9 Sep 1859
	John H Onley 9 Apr 1860
Disc 28 Jun 1866	
Reest 1 Jul 1872	Enoch Farmer 1 Jul 1872
Vista Ridge	James W Draughn 24 Dec 1856
	Thomas M Mann 28 Nov 1857
	David McCandless 7 Feb 1859
Disc 28 Jun 1866	
Reest 29 Aug 1870	John Miller 29 Aug 1870
Delhi	John Bishop 23 Jun 1859
Note: Late Deerfield	David S McKelvy 6 Aug 1860
	W J Caldwell 12 Mar 1866
	William D Davis 9 Jul 1866
	Robert H Brumby 1 Apr 1870
	Simon Fox 31 Oct 1871
	Thomas Hogan 20 Aug 1872
	Calvin H Moore 15 Jan 1873
Goodrich Landing	Henry Goodrich 27 Oct 1865
	John Polansky 10 Apr 1866

Illawara	John Polansky 10 May 1866 John Lynch 24 Oct 1867 Thomas B Rhodes 12 May 1868 Henry Hinson 9 Dec 1870
India	Sterling T Austen 18 Jan 1872 Rolla W Wyatt 11 Mar 1873
Melville	Henry Hinson 22 Oct 1872 George Rhodes 9 Jun 1873
Transylvania	Richard T Keene 31 Oct 1872
Henderson	Albert C Rhoton 15 Apr 1873

CATAHOULA PARISH

Aimwell	Wiley M Squyres 27 Jan 1857 Chapman Hood 15 May 1858 Andrew J Davis 17 Dec 1858
Disc 22 Jun 1866 Reest 13 Oct 1871	Carter Thompson 13 Oct 1871 Wiley M Squyres 4 Mar 1872 M C Thompson 19 Jan 1873
Enterprise	Hugh Keenan 26 Aug 1854 DeWitt Davis 4 Feb 1861
Disc 22 Jun 1866 Reest 7 Aug 1871	Patrick H Carter 7 Aug 1871
Finlay's	Daniel Finlay 8 Aug 1857
Disc 22 Jun 1866 Reest 20 Jul 1866 Disc 26 Mar 1867	John P Blake 20 Jul 1866
Funny Louis	Edwin W Yancey 1 Nov 1853 William B Wilbanks 3 Feb 1859 Edwin W Yancey 28 May 1860 James M Adair 28 Jan 1861 William C Aber 8 Jan 1866 Samuel Paul 2 Aug 1866

	Martha Cockerham 9 Apr 1867
	James M Adair 20 Oct 1873
Green's Creek	Moses Collins 31 Mar 1854
Disc 22 Jun 1866	
Reest 2 May 1872	Thomas B Prichard 2 May 1872
Harrisonburgh Courthouse	Eleazer Fletcher 2 Apr 1857
	Drury M Prichard 14 Oct 1865
	Henry T Spann 21 Mar 1866
	Kent M Dowden 18 Jul 1866
	Miss Mary J Rhodes 11 Oct 1866
	Mrs. Sarah E Dowden 7 May 1867
	Miss R Allen 22 Oct 1869
	Mrs. Sarah E Dowden 27 oct 1871
	William E Robb 27 Jan 1873
Sicily Island	Henry L Green 10 May 1856
	John Buie 11 Jan 1859
	Henry L Green 31 Aug 1860
Disc 28 Jun 1866	
Reest 17 Jun 1867	Miss Amelia K Doniphan 17 Jun 1867
	Albert L Hopkins 14 Jan 1868
Disc 19 Feb 1869	
Reest 2 May 1872	Sarah Carter 2 May 1872
	Miss Sallie E Lovelace 26 May 1872
Trinity	John D Calvert 23 Dec 1854
	Thomas M Morris 22 Jan 1859
	William D Spann 26 Jan 1860
	John D Calvert 2 Feb 1861
	William R Cherry 13 Mar 1866
	Schuyler Marvin 6 Jul 1866
	Mrs. Ruth A Marvin 22 Jun 1867
Disc 12 Oct 1871	
Reest 27 Oct 1871	Isaac Shlenker 27 Oct 1871
	Leopold Maritz 29 Jan 1873
White Sulphur Springs	A B Thompson 15 Jan 1857

                              James F Newton 23 Jun 1858
                              J J Greer 13 Apr 1859
                              Benjamin Robison 4 Aug 1859
                              James W Sheppard 16 Jul 1866
Disc 19 Mar 1867
Reest 24 Jun 1867   John Frazer 24 Jun 1867
                              P H Orwell 9 Oct 1867
                              Henry Johnson 1 Apr 1868
                              William Griffith 17 Jul 1868

Castle Springs   Benjamin F Anderson 30 Jan 1858
Disc 22 Jun 1866

Hemp's Creek   Isaac L Baker 10 Dec 1860
Disc 22 Jun 1866
Reest 31 Jul 1867   Miss Lucy J Baker 31 Jul 1867
                              Leroy Brown 14 Nov 1870

Jena   James Clay White 29 Mar 1871
                              James Forsythe 19 Dec 1872

Little Prarie   Michael Beard 3 Jun 1872

Parkham's   (Illegible entry)
                              James B Wigginton 29 Jan 1873

Kirk's Ferry   Ransom Hall 26 Jan 1872

Wildwood   Frank J Bowman 26 Jul 1872

Pisgah   Joseph W Thomas 26 Mar 1873

Eden   Phineas Whatley 7 Jul 1873

CLAIBORNE PARISH

Allen's Settlement   James W Miller 8 Mar 52
                              Temple W Crow 27 Aug 1858
Disc 22 Jun 1866

Argus

Disc 22 Jun 1866
Reest 8 May 1868

Disc 8 Jul 1870

Athens Courthouse
Disc 22 Jun 1866
Reest 23 Jul 1866

Cane Ridge
Disc 22 Jun 1866
Reest 20 May 1868

Dorcheat

Disc 26 Jun 1867

Flat Lick

Disc 22 Jun 1866

Forest Grove
Disc 22 Jun 1866

Gordon

Disc 7 Mar 1868
Reest 2 Dec 1872

Haynesville

Disc 26 Jun 1867

Pool P Massy 15 Jan 1854
Joseph F G Hargis 1 Dec 1858

William Alexander 8 May 1868
William T Thompson 22 Jun 1868

Arthur McFarland 18 Nov 1847

Mrs. Elizabeth A Wise 23 Jul 1866
Barney W Bridges 6 Dec 1872
Thomas A Wilborn 13 May 1873

George W Lowrey 23 Feb 1856

George B Bevan 20 May 1868
George W Lowrey 15 Jun 1872

Jackson Sikes 13 Jun 1855
Samuel S McDaniel 5 Nov 1859
Jackson Sikes 3 Feb 1860

Green Culbertson 21 Sep 1857
Francis O Krouse 6 Dec 1860
Robert A Crow 16 Jan 1861

Franklin Taylor 10 Nov 1852

James G Robinson 23 Nov 1855
Jesse D Proctor 27 Feb 1866

William D Anderson 2 Dec 1872

James C Taylor 9 Feb 1852
Samuel Kirkpatrick 25 Feb 1859
James C Taylor 21 Mar 1860

Reest 8 Feb 1870	Mrs. Martha Kirkpatrick 8 Feb 1870
	James B Kenico 21 Oct 1872
	R F Hardaway 21 Jan 1873
	James C Taylor 20 Oct 1873
Homer Courthouse	John H Cunningham 6 Dec 1856
	George W Price 4 Jan 1858
	William C Crutcher 8 Feb 1859
	Cornelius E Carr 16 Mar 1860
	William L Phillips 5 Jan 1861
	Jesse P Smith 25 Sep 1865
	Jasper Blackburn 11 Oct 1866
	Robert T Vaughn 27 May 1867
	Augustus P Lovellette 3 Sep 1867
	James A Witter 28 Feb 1868
	Miss Lou Martin 1 Apr 1870
	Datus W Harris 15 Jan 1872
Lanier	William C Moreland 10 Sep 1857
Lisbon	Charles D Barrow 1 Jun 1857
	Americanus Willis 20 Dec 1858
Disc 22 Jun 1866	
Reest 23 Jul 1867	John B Williams 23 Jul 1867
	J J Robinett 27 Mar 1868
	David A Carathers 30 Sep 1872
Minden	Ryal A Lancaster 6 Oct 1856
	John E Loey 6 Oct 1865
Quay	William B Smith 19 Apr 1857
	James J Browning 26 Sep 1859
	William Mitcham 21 Feb 1860
Disc 4 Feb 1867	
Rose Hill	Leander M Hall 2 Jun 1855
Disc 28 Jun 1866	
Scottville	Robert Killgore 8 May 1857
	Robert E Thompson 7 Feb 1859

Disc 28 Jun 1866

Sugar Creek   John S Carlton 1 Oct 1853
                           William A Sherrard 29 Dec 1857
                           R Raven 14 Jan 1861
Disc 28 Jun 1866
Reest 24 Jul 1868   James A Enlow 24 Jul 1868
                           M J Beckhaur 26 Jun 1871

Disc 19 oct 1872

Tiger Creek   J M Prestridge 12 Feb 1857
Disc 16 Mar 1859

Wiseville   Benjamin F Lambright 8 Aug 1857
                           Giles L Wise 23 Nov 1858
                           Burkett B Lindsey 22 Jun 1860
Disc 26 Jun 1867

Shongaloo   James M Burns 1 Nov 1858
                           John M Fuller 2 Sep 1859
                           Isaac L Lennard 20 Feb 1860

Disc 20 May 1867

Griffin   William P Mitchell 17 Apr 1860
Disc 22 Jun 1866

Knoxville   Miss Georgia Knox 21 Nov 1866

Arizona   William Manley 2 Mar 1868
                           Frank Wilson 8 Apr 1869
                           Thomas C Monroe 1 Mar 1872
                           James F Barnett 30 Sep 1872
                           Joel S Morris 7 Jan 1873

Coleman   James F Ford 18 Jan 1872

Summerfield   Albert L Harper 19 Nov 1872

Scottville   Edward F Williams 20 Nov 1872

CONCORDIA PARISH

Black Hawk Point   A T Welch 29 Jan 1857
Disc 22 Jun 1866
Reest 18 Jan 1867   Louis Trager 18 Jan 1857
Disc 13 Oct 1869
Reest 6 Feb 1871   Leon Moyse 6 Feb 1871
                                James Pullin 27 Aug 1872

Fairview   Granville W Williams 19 Apr 1857
                                D F Miller 30 Dec 1858
                                William B Ulrich 5 Feb 1859
                                Wesley Conner 8 Jan 1866
                                William T Lewis 9 Feb 1873

Flowery Mound   Ezekial Young 7 Feb 1854
                                Joseph E Miller 23 Dec 1858
                                Ezekial Young 27 Apr 1859

Disc 22 Jun 1866

South Bend   Cyrus S Magoun 28 Sep 1857
                                Samuel C Scott 11 Dec 1858

Disc 26 Jun 1867

Tooley's   William Dale 31 Jan 1854
Disc 26 Jun 1867
Reest 3 Jun 1872   John F Tooley 3 Jun 1872

Vidalia Courthouse   Benjamin F Dobyns 17 Sep 1857
Disc 26 Feb 1859
Reest 31 Aug 1866   William P Gallian 31 Aug 1866
                                Christian Rush 5 Nov 1866
Disc 29 Feb 1868
Reest 27 Jan 1870   Clinton F Seaman 27 Jan 1870
                                Robert Hough 31 Oct 1871
                                J P Drake 30 Apr 1872
                                Walter G Kalord 12 Aug 1872
                                John A Washington 20 Oct 1873

Rifle Point   Henry V Barringer 22 Oct 1866

Disc 7 Apr 1868

Packard
Disc 7 Apr 1868

James B Packard 22 Feb 1867

Frogmore
Disc 4 Feb 1868
Reest 28 Jul 1872

John Hill 23 Apr 1867

Charles H Hester 28 Feb 1872
William D Scofield 17 Mar 1873

Good Hope Landing

Disc 10 Jun 1872

Benjamin C Mosby 1 Mar 1872
William B Mosby 26 Mar 1872

Bullitt's Bayou

John C Seaman 26 Feb 1872

Shamrock

Patrick Quinlan 3 Jun 1872
John F Damerson 3 Feb 1873

River's Landing

Hugh G Sneed 22 Aug 1873

DE SOTO PARISH

Black Jack

Disc 22 Jun 1866

John E Hall 12 Nov 1856
Augustus Conway 15 Nov 1859

Grand Cane
Disc 22 Jun 1866
Reest 30 Nov 1866

Disc 19 Mar 1872

John B Gamble 27 Sep 1852

John Davidson 30 Nov 1866
B F Spearman 11 Apr 1871

Keatchie

Disc 26 Nov 1866
Reest 28 Mar 1867
Disc 6 Feb 1868
Reest 9 Mar 1868

William A Thorpe 15 May 1844
Miss Helen H Schroeder 3 May 1866

B A Holmes 28 Mar 1867

William B Peyton 9 Mar 1868
Thomas S Cole 7 Jul 1871

                            William G Spilker 11 Mar 1873

Kingston   John M Prather 6 Aug 1856
                            Mitchell J Scott 25 Feb 1860
Disc 22 Jun 1866

Logansport   John W Martin 12 Sep 1853
                            John Culbertson 23 Oct 1860
Disc 22 Jun 1866
Reest 11 Oct 1866   A Rainey 11 Oct 1866
                            Robert H Alston 26 Mar 1867

Longstreet   William C Peyton 23 Sep 1854
Disc 22 Jun 1866
Reest 11 Oct 1866   Sterling Ansley 11 Oct 1866
Disc 9 Oct 1867
Reest 29 Jan 1868   Matthew M Moore 18 Jun 1869

Mansfield Courthouse   Henry E H Buck 6 Mar 1855
                            Albert H Thomas 22 Jun 1858
                            Henry E H Buck 15 Feb 1860
                            George R Draghon 7 Jun 1861
                            Philip Allen 30 Mar 1866
                            William M Allen 12 Dec 1870

Pleasant Grove   Duncan B McMillan 12 Mar 1852
                            John H Linkins 19 Jul 1859
                            William McIntosh 26 Jul 1860
Disc 28 Jun 1860

Pleasant Hill   James C Whitten 30 Jan 1854
                            William H Jordan 24 Jun 1859
                            Thomas S Sims 3 May 1866
                            James Osery Jr 19 Jul 1866
Disc 26 Mar 1867
Reest 1 Jul 1867   William Fanly 1 Jul 1867
Dics 13 Apr 1868
Reest 15 Jun 1871   Zachariah Blackmon 15 Jun 1871

Hart's Bluff   John P Nall 21 Jul 1860

Disc 22 Jun 1866

Wallace Lake   John B Pugh 17 Oct 1860
Disc 28 Jun 1866

EAST BATON ROUGE PARISH

Bayou Rouge Courthouse   Joseph McCormick 25 Mar 1857 (Pres & Sen)
Christopher G Breckenridge 28 Jul 1860 (Pres & Sen)
Orton Hackett 8 Sep 1868 (Pres)
John O'Connor 5 Apr 1869 (Pres & Sen)

Greenwell Springs   Robert W Greenwell 29 Sep 1856
Disc 22 Jun 1866

Manchac   Joseph A Daigre 31 Jan 1857
Disc 22 Jun 1866
Reest 3 Jul 1872   Amedee C Brugier 3 Jul 1872
Disc 20 Feb 1872

Plain's Store   Henry C Young 22 Jan 1857
Disc 28 Jun 1866

Stony Point   William Roberson 9 Oct 1858
John B Powers 24 Jan 1860
Disc 22 Jun 1866
Reest 4 Dec 1866   Philip Spiller 4 Dec 1866
John B Easterly 21 Oct 1869
Solomon Montgomery 6 Feb 1871
Ezra J Stillman 23 Oct 1871

Magnolia Springs   Randolph DeSarodeire 18 Jan 1859
Disc 28 Jun 1866

Burlington   James Carl 20 May 1869

Magnolia   Daniel Morgan 8 Nov 1872

Hope Villa   Andrew B Booth 17 Mar 1873

Ambrosia	Robert John Kennard 25 Aug 1873

EAST FELICIANA PARISH

Clinton Courthouse	John M Bell 30 Jan 1855 J G Darmond 29 Oct 1865 Bruce Smith 3 Jan 1866 Mrs. Bruce Smith 25 Nov 1867 Joseph Israel 29 Sep 1871
Jackson	Abraham Hagaman 2 Nov 1854 John E Courlay 10 Jan 1859 Elijah C Kiblinger 25 Feb 1860 John M Conway 21 Mar 1866 Arthion McKenna 10 Aug 1866 Mrs. Sarah McKenna 17 Jan 1867 Mrs. Sarah McKenna 22 Mar 1867 John O'Callaghan 10 Sep 1867 Mrs. Susan J Hunster 2 Aug 1870 John Calligan 18 Feb 1871
Port Hudson	Randolph Chick 15 Jun 1857 Benjamin P Crane 30 Apr 1866 Mrs. Sussanne Bear 15 Apr 1867 John T Brown 1 May 1868 Abraham Levy 29 Jun 1869 Aaron Steeg 1 Mar 1871 Louis Wolf 2 Aug 1871 Abraham Levy 8 May 1872 Albert Rayburn 21 Jul 1873
Woodland Disc 26 Apr 1867 Reest 23 Sep 1867	Albert W Poole 17 Jan 1855 Miss Maria Ann Woodward 23 Sep 1867 Maria R Poole 19 Feb 1869
Oakland Disc 4 Feb 1867	James B Prewitt 16 Jun 1858

Bluff Creek Disc 23 Sep 1858 Reest 13 Nov 1871	William F Chaney 5 Aug 1858 John W Veers 13 Nov 1871 Leslie A Cooper 17 Feb 1873
Darlington Disc 22 Jun 1866 Reest 19 Apr 1867	Hezekiah Thompson 14 Dec 1859 John H Welden 19 Apr 1867
Kent's Store	Lemuel T Ligon 1 Jul 1872

FRANKLIN PARISH

Boeuff Prairie Disc 10 Nov 1860 Reest 8 Jan 1861 Disc 10 Apr 1861	Thomas A Woodridge 20 Feb 1857 Thomas W Word 26 May 1858 Thomas A Woodridge 8 Jan 1861
Hurricane Disc 28 Sep 1859	William M Jennings 24 Mar 1857 F A Henry 12 Jul 1859
Oakley Disc 22 Jun 1867 Reest 3 Sep 1867	Samuel G Cloud 13 Jun 1854 Charles A Phelps 3 Sep 1867 Miss Josephine R Gilbert 27 May 1868 Chauncey Lewis 1 Apr 1870
Pullaway Disc 9 Feb 1860	Isaac C Heath 22 Aug 1853
Red Mouth Disc 26 Jul 1867	James A Greenlee 21 Feb 1856 George A Gwin 4 Oct 1858 John W Cazey 21 Sep 1859 James M Crook 25 Oct 1859 John W Cazey 15 Nov 1860
Warsaw	George W Dorsey 15 Nov 1854

Disc 26 Jun 1867 Reest 25 Nov 1867 Disc 28 Feb 1868 Reest 20 May 1868	John House 25 Oct 1858 William Bailey 21 Mar 1860 Mrs. Frances Kilbourn 25 Nov 1867 Obadiah D Gibson 20 May 1868 Amedis J Pennybaker 16 Jul 1872
Winnsborough Courthouse Disc 28 Jun 1866 Reest 27 Mar 1867	Herman Block 28 Oct 1857 Martin L Haggard 13 Mar 1858 Jesse J Holder 15 May 1858 James Barry 21 Jun 1859 H W Lee 27 Mar 1867 Thomas C Cottingham 3 Apr 1867 Mrs. Bridget Meyer 27 Nov 1868 Armstrong Osborn 14 Jul 1870 Edward Parker 21 Nov 1872 Lewis Zim Jr 2 Jul 1873
Yellow Bluff Disc 26 Jun 1867	John D Thomason 24 Aug 1857 John Tegard 18 Nov 1858 John Sanderneau 25 Jun 1860
Crockett's Point Disc 15 Feb 1861	Charles T Hatch 10 May 1860
Louisville Disc 11 Mar 1872	E G Fay 14 Oct 1869
Crowville	James W Rainey 4 Feb 1873

IBERVILLE PARISH

Bayou Goula	George I A Bush 27 May 1857 James Crowell 8 Dec 1865 Miss Rosanna Crowell 19 May 1867 Jeremiah Supple 14 May 1868 Emile S Allain 15 Jul 1869

	Ernest Callery 17 Aug 1871
Gross Tete	James E Bargas 16 May 1857
	Joseph Pardos 11 Dec 1857
Disc 20 Oct 1859	
Plaquemine	Peter E Jennings 25 Sep 1857
	Joseph St. Dizine 22 Jan 1861
	Oliver A Pierce 20 Sep 1865
	Mrs. A Merrill 26 Mar 1869
	Orlando H Hempstead 29 Dec 1869
	George B Loud 13 May 1870
	John H Jackson 28 Feb 1871
	James S Roche 7 Apr 1873
Rosedale	Charles E Dupuy 2 Sep 1857
	John Larrasan 24 Jan 1867
	Charles W Slack 2 Nov 1869
	William Page 3 Jun 1870
	Charles W Slack 22 Mar 1871
	James O Larose 29 Sep 1873
St. Gabriel Courthouse	Henry S Brown 16 May 1857
	Louis S Babin 8 Sep 1859
	Louis S Babin 27 Dec 1865
	Henry Stingel 2 Apr 1866
Musson	Richard C Richardson 7 Feb 1870
Disc 21 May 1872	
Sandford	Levi Pennington 6 May 1872
St. Gabriel	Levi Pennington 29 May 1872
	Joseph Jolesaint Jr 4 May 1873
Raphael	Dorselie Landry 10 Jun 1873

JACKSON PARISH

Brookline	Dawson W Kennedy 25 Jun 1850

Disc 22 Jun 1866 Reest 3 Jun 1867	James Williams 24 Mar 1858 Wilson Williams 3 Jun 1867
Douglas	Moses Spivey 5 Jun 1857 Randle D Sholars 28 Oct 1858 Oriel R Milner 21 Aug 1860 Miss Mary E Powell 30 Mar 1866 James S Davis 19 Mar 1868 Uriah C Pipes 11 Mar 1872 John T McDowell 16 Oct 1872
Ebenezer Disc 22 Jan 1858 Reest 7 Apr 1858 Disc 9 Jun 1858	John P Shows 30 oct 1855 John G Hargrave 7 Apr 1858
Plankville	Robert E Davis 2 Jun 1855 Francis M McLeroy 18 Jan 1859
Timberville Disc 17 Jun 1859	Joel Embrey 5 Jun 1857
Vernon Courthouse	James M Smith 29 Jan 1857 J T Allen 26 Dec 1865 John H Tatum 3 Feb 1866 William L Smith 9 May 1871
Vienna	Micajah P Quinn 7 Jul 1857 William P Otts 22 Jan 1858 Micajah P Quinn 23 Feb 1859 William B Otts 1 Sep 1859 Thomas C Coker 17 Apr 1860 William B Morgan 26 Jan 1861 Mrs. Maria Van Cook 2 Apr 1866 Mrs. Missouri Cox 13 Oct 1866 Zackariah M Jackson 11 Feb 1867 Thomas B Colvin 30 Oct 1867 Mrs. Lydia Cullen 1 Apr 1870 Mrs. Mary A B C Winfrey 9 Dec 1870

	Mrs. Mary A B C Winfrey 12 Dec 1871
	H C Slaton 22 May 1872
	Eugene Howard 6 Jan 1873
	Joseph M Goff 29 Jan 1873
Woodville	William E Bond 27 Sep 1855
	Mrs. C Stamper 19 Jan 1866
	Miss Minerva Hinton 27 Mar 1866
	Jonathan Brown 18 Jun 1867
	William A McKee 29 Aug 1872
Wyatt's Cross Roads Disc 6 Jul 1860	James A Hargrove 21 Nov 1855
Bonner Disc 22 Jun 1866	Francis M McLeroy 28 Sep 1860
Reest 11 Oct 1866	James H Fuller 11 Oct 1866
	Miss Laura Stathing 8 Mar 1867
	Adam Riser 26 Apr 1872
Caneville	Irvin Mixon 22 Oct 1866
	Sarah A Thompson 21 Mar 1867
Disc 14 Apr 1868	
Greensborough	Allen Green 12 Oct 1871
Rochester	William C McDonald 20 Jan 1873

JEFFERSON PARISH

Carrollton	Harman H Gogreve 16 Mar 1854
	E F Schmidt 31 Aug 1860
	John Henry Tebbe 4 Sep 1865
	Mrs. Mary Robinson 4 May 1869
	Stewart L Henry 24 May 1869
	Conrad Henchert 16 Aug 1872
	Henry Tebbe 4 Sep 1872
	Langdon C Tebbe 27 Nov 1872
Jefferson	Wilmer H Zimmerman 3 Aug 1854

Disc 13 Oct 1862 Reest 6 Nov 1866	Julius Ennesmoser 17 Jan 1860 Julius Ennesmoser 24 Jul 1862 Robert H Brown 6 Nov 1866 J L Andre 28 Sep 1868 John Moylan 24 May 1869
Disc 22 Dec 1870	
Kenner	Barney Gilloly 31 Jul 1856 John J Greenwood 18 Jan 1860 Minor Kenner 9 Apr 1860
Disc 22 Jun 1866 Reest 5 Nov 1866	Mrs. Mary Long 5 Nov 1866
Lafayette City	Frederick B Von Karsten 7 May 1853 Herman F C Pressler 23 Oct 1860
Disc 27 Mar 1867	
Gretna	John E Sutton 21 Dec 1869 Henry Vering 21 Apr 1870 Frank Hardardt 6 Jun 1870 Henry Faber 27 Aug 1871 E Tournier 2 Jun 1873
Grand Isle	Ami M Joly 9 Jun 1873

LAFAYETTE PARISH

Cote Gelee Disc 22 Jun 1866 Reest 1 Jul 1867 Disc 2 Apr 1868 Reest 15 Oct 1868	Valsaint Broussard 13 Dec 1856 J G St. Julien 1 Jul 1867 Jean B S Melancon 15 Oct 1868 Marcel Melancon 25 Apr 1872 Francis P Paseut 8 Nov 1872 Oliver Saunier 24 Jun 1873
Vermillionville	Enoch B Kemper 2 Sep 1856 John Rykoski 20 Dec 1858 Louis A Roussel 2 Feb 1866

	John H Chargois 8 Jun 1866
	Alphonse Neven 8 Jul 1867
	Jean J Neven 8 Aug 1867
	Alponse Neven 12 May 1871
Bertrandville Disc 28 Jul 1871	Gustave Bertrand 4 Oct 1869
Carencro	August Melchoir 11 Jan 1872
Youngsville	Albert S Dyer 18 Feb 1873 Jacques Bonnemaison 8 Nov 1872

LAFOURCHE PARISH

Raceland	Charles G Thibodeaux 21 Aug 1855 Evariste A Lepine 6 Jun 1866
Disc 12 Oct 1866 Reest 28 Dec 1866	Edward Cross 28 Dec 1866
Disc 29 Oct 1868 Reest 19 Nov 1869	Mrs. Selina J Cross 19 Nov 1869
Disc 22 May 1872 Reest 3 Jul 1872	Joachim Gaude 3 Jul 1872
Thibodeaux Courthouse	Peter E Lorio 15 Mar 1856 Ely R Bourg 2 May 1863 F Adolph Knobloch 3 Dec 1863 Henry H Hitchcock 25 May 1865 Alvan N Gardner 21 Oct 1865 Daniel H Reese 10 Apr 1867 Louis Boudreaux 30 Sep 1867 Gustave Boudreaux 17 May 1870 Mrs. Mary King Fullford 16 Dec 1870 Gustave Boudreaux 11 Apr 1871
LaFourche Crossing Disc 6 Jul 1860	Charles C Williams 29 Apr 1859
Reest 7 Mar 1872	Charles C Williams 7 Mar 1872
Orange City	S F Gard 4 Apr 1873

LIVINGSTON PARISH

Bayou Barbary
Disc 22 Jun 1866
Reest 6 Nov 1866

William H Wilder 23 Jun 1852

William C Opdenweyer 6 Nov 1866
E M Davidson 25 Nov 1867
S H Shroder 24 Feb 1868

Disc 24 Jan 1870
Reest 21 Apr 1870

Benton's Ferry
Disc 22 Jun 1866
Reest 6 Nov 1866

Robert Benton 25 Jan 1856

James L Harris 7 Nov 1856

Goelk

Baxter Felder 16 Oct 1867
Lewis Watson 7 Jun 1858
Rufus K Felder 11 Jun 1866
Joseph Scivieque 16 Jul 1866
Levi Spiller 27 Jul 1871

French Settlement
Disc 22 Jun 1866
Reest 3 Sep 1867
Disc 15 Jul 1869
Reest 13 oct 1871

Joseph Salassi 25 Jan 1856

Denis F Salassi 3 Sep 1867

Henry Brignac 13 Dec 1871

Hollywood
Disc 22 Jun 1866

Edward B Starns 19 Jan 1857

Independence

William D Wilson 9 Oct 1857
William D Wilson 27 Oct 1865
Charles H George 9 Apr 1866

Oldfield

Jefferson Lea 10 Apr 1857
Gabriel G Sibley 12 Mar 1858
Miss Martha Ann Lea 23 Jun 1858

Disc 8 Apr 1859
Reest 21 Nov 1859

John W Courtney 21 Nov 1859
Charles Brumfield 9 Jul 1866

Disc 26 Mar 1867
Reest 29 Mar 1871   Lafayette W Odom 29 Mar 1871

Ponchatoula   James Tucker 29 Jun 1857
                                     Thomas M Akers 27 Oct 1865
                                     James W Frost 27 Dec 1865
                                     Levi Arnold 25 Jun 1866
                                     Michael Bugel 19 Dec 1866

Springfield   George Walker Jr 21 Dec 1855
                                     Purnell F Starnes 12 Jun 1858
Disc 28 Jun 1866
Reest 16 Jan 1867   Henry Leach 16 Jan 1867
                                     Joseph Alois Schenk 4 Nov 1867
                                     Joseph Alois Schenk 5 Mar 1872

Strong Point   John Roughman 16 May 1857
                                     William Robertson 9 Oct 1858

Walker   John B Lockhart 4 Apr 1856
                                     Michael Milton 14 Jan 1858
Disc 6 Jul 1860

Tickfaw   Jacob J Watts 26 Sep 1859
Disc 28 Jun 1866
Reest 17 Feb 1868   Oren M Kincher 17 Feb 1868
Disc 2 Oct 1868

Hammond   Melzar Waterman 4 Apr 1866
                                     Miss Hattie V A Waterman 4 Oct 1867
                                     Henry C Mooney 11 Sep 1868

Pass Manchac   William Tennent 31 Jul 1866
Disc 28 Jan 1868

Live Oak Store   James Turner 4 Oct 1869
                                     Frederick Weiss 19 Jan 1872

Clio   Thomas H Jones 2 May 1872

MADISON PARISH

Chickama Bend
Disc 8 May 1860

John Neely 7 Feb 1854
Charles R Slider 5 Sep 1859

Dallas
Disc 6 Feb 1861

William T Pugh 7 Feb 1854

Milliken's Bend

Philip Sartorius 12 Feb 1856
John A Woodry 6 Dec 1865
E M Joel 21 Mar 1866
George Watt 7 Mar 1871

New Carthage

Leander E Love 31 Jan 1854
John M Carr 24 Apr 1858
Micajah H Love 24 May 1860
L L Leonard 27 Nov 1865
Henry R Smith 13 Feb 1866
Edward S Jeffrey 29 Jan 1867
William Alling 24 Feb 1868

Disc 24 Jan 1870
Reest 14 August 1871

Scott Bettis 14 Aug 1871

Delta

S Prentiss Dangerfield 29 Sep 1869
Henry M Floyd 21 Nov 1872

Duck Port

David Mayer 12 Nov 1869
Green L Boney 26 Feb 1873

Tallulah

Jacob P Kiernan 27 Mar 1871
F H Fowler 19 Sep 1871

Mound

J A Mercer 7 Aug 1871
Charles E Nichols 12 Mar 1873

Carrville

Jeff T Beasley 2 May 1872
Jeff T Beasley 10 Aug 1874

Quebec

Richmond J Brashear 31 Jan 1855

	Thomas H W Baynard 19 Nov 1857
	Francis P Watkins 19 Aug 1860
Disc 28 Jun 1866	
Reest 10 Jun 1867	William H Tanner 10 Jan 1867
Disc 14 Dec 1868	
Richmond Courthouse	Adrian E Adams 4 May 1855
	Belitha Powell 7 Feb 1860
Disc 4 Apr 1868	
Reest 22 Sep 1868	Jacob P McKiernan 22 Sep 1868
	John T Mason 10 Jun 1869
	Mrs. A M Tanner 3 Jul 1869
	Jacob P McKiernan 27 Sep 1869
De Soto	John N Nolly 30 Jun 1858
Disc 23 Jul 1859	
Reest 9 Dec 1867	John E Fell 9 Dec 1867
Disc 14 Jan 1870	
Omega	John J Owen 19 Jul 1859
	James Cavileer 6 Dec 1865
	George P Deweese 19 Feb 1866
Disc 25 Oct 1869	

MOREHOUSE PARISH

Bastrop Courthouse	Edmund B Pettis 21 May 1857
	Miss Abigail Condon 2 May 1861
	Michael Ball 5 Jun 1866
	Andrew Meuer 13 Feb 1867
	William A Moulton 6 May 1869
	R A Phelps 28 Feb 1870
	John Temple 14 Mar 1870
	William McCallson 2 Mar 1871
	Andrew Meuer 6 May 1871
Ion	William Dyer 14 Jul 1853
	Wiley D Whittington 3 Feb 1859
	Pervis Brooks 15 Jun 1860
	William J Cowart 3 Sep 1860

Disc 26 Jun 1867
Reest 4 Nov 1867   Benjamin Myrick 4 Nov 1867
                          Jeremiah J Baldwin 17 Apr 1868
Disc 10 Jun 1870

Line   Thomas M Jones 18 Feb 1854
Disc 22 Jun 1866
Reest 29 Oct 1868   Jesse A Peterkin 29 Oct 1868

Plantersville   John M Hilliard 23 May 1854
                          Newton S Greenwood 26 Feb 1860
Disc 26 Jun 1867
Reest 16 Nov 1872   Thomas O Leavel 26 Nov 1872

Point Jefferson   George T Malone 28 Apr 1859
                          Bennett W Wright 10 Jun 1859
Disc 28 Jun 1866
Reest 31 Jul 1868   James H L Duval 31 Jul 1868
                          Edward P Harrison 21 Jul 1869
                          Roger Whetstone 15 Mar 1871
                          Ambrose O McCord 16 Jul 1872

Mer Rouge   William L Clark 21 May 1856
Disc 28 Jun 1866

Young's Bluff   Elijah Scott 21 Oct 1857
Disc 20 Apr 1858

Lind Grove   James E Warnock 2 Nov 1857
Disc 22 Jun 1866
Reest 29 Oct 1868   George M Harrison 29 Oct 1868

Rashville   Willis P Rash 30 Jun 1858
Disc 4 Oct 1858

Tipton   Henry M Naff 8 Dec 1858
Disc 26 Jun 1867

Jones Ferry   Calvin Mason Jr 25 Jun 1860
Disc 26 Jun 1867

Raysville	James S Ray 11 Jul 1867
	I E Hibbler 25 Jan 1869
	William W Compton 28 May 1869
Disc 3 Oct 1871	
De Gallion	S Boozman 19 Mar 1872

NATCHITOCHES PARISH

Adies	William Smith 5 Sep 1848
	John C Brooke 3 Feb 1859
Disc 22 Jun 1866	
Campti	Jacob A Wolfson 21 Jan 1854
	Ramy Sambre 23 Nov 1857
	Ramy Sambre 5 Feb 1866
	Morris Rashiet 20 Nov 1867
	John W McDaniel 21 Apr 1868
	Adolphus Dupre 4 Aug 1868
	Samuel Cohn 23 Sep 1868
	Solon B Perot 1 Mar 1872
Cloutierville	Belus Deslouches 29 Jan 1857
	Abel C Sers 9 Dec 1857
Disc 22 Jun 1866	
Reest 18 Jul 1866	Oliver Brosset 18 Jul 1866
	Louis F Titus 12 Dec 1867
Disc 2 Feb 1869	
Reest 19 Feb 1869	Victor L Benoist 19 Feb 1869
	(Illegible entry)
	S O Scruggs 5 Jun 1872
	S O Scruggs 18 Jun 1873
	J A Sampite 24 Feb 1876
Coushatta Chute	James R Bosley 14 Jul 1853
Disc 4 Feb 1857	
Kisatchie	William P Owens 9 Dec 1854
Disc 4 Feb 1867	

Natchitoches Courthouse	Terence Wakefield 18 Sep 1855 (Pres & Sen) Terence Wakefield 21 Jun 1860 (Reappointed) John W Taber 2 Oct 1860 (Pres & Sen) F E Fitzgerald 31 Aug 1865 John W Taber 27 Feb 1866 George Monroe 5 Jun 1866 Charles Leroy 29 Apr 1869 W B Carr 26 Jul 1872 Joseph F Vargas 18 Sep 1872
Bethel Disc 20 Jun 1859	Pleasant Barnes 30 Jun 1858 Noah V Scarborough 6 Sep 1858
Marthaville Disc 28 Jun 1866 Reest 11 Oct 1866 Disc 17 Aug 1871	John J Rains 5 Aug 1858 Nathaniel J Lilly 11 Oct 1866
Loggy Bayou Disc 26 Jun 1867 Reest 26 Apr 1870	Wiley W Williams 21 Jan 1860 Benjamin G Kenney 26 Apr 1870 William H Treadwell 20 May 1873
Grand Ecore Disc 22 Jun 1866	Benjamin T Atkins 10 Dec 1860
Springville	James McAllister 8 May 1868
Coushatta Chute	Samuel Clark 28 Feb 1870 Montezuma L Pickens 21 Apr 1870
DeLoche's Landing	Alexander Boston 9 Aug 1870 L P Bridges 14 Aug 1871
Marthaville Disc 11 Mar 1872	Nathaniel J Lilly 18 Oct 1871

Reest 5 Nov 1872   John J Rains 8 Nov 1872

ORLEANS PARISH

Algiers   Selegman Simon 24 Mar 1856
                          Henry Schrote 14 Oct 1865
                          Lawford Johnson 2 Jan 1868
                          Mrs. Matilda Johnson 22 Nov 1869
                          John N Riley 21 Feb 1872
                          James Foster 8 Apr 1872
                          Joseph Lyons 13 Sep 1872

Fort Pike   William Bosworth 21 Jun 1856
Disc 22 Jun 1866
Reest 6 May 1867   Henry Walker 6 Sep 1867

New Orleans Courthouse   Robert E McHatton 23 Mar 1857 (Pres)
                          John L Riddell 16 Jan 1860 (Pres & Sen)
                          John M G Parker 19 Feb 1863 (Pres & Sen)
                          Robert W Talliaferro 20 Mar 1865 (Pres & Sen)
                          Walter W Smallwood 30 Jul 1868
                          Charles W Lowell 5 Apr 1869 (Pres & Sen)
                          B P Blanchard 2 Dec 1870
                          Charles W Ringgold 1 May 1873 (Pres & Sen)

PLAQUEMINES PARISH

Balize   Joseph C Wilson 21 Sep 1854
Disc 22 Jun 1866

Buras   Frederick G Schmidt 25 Nov 1854
                          Richard Westfield 3 Jul 1860
                          William A Brainerd 3 May 1866
                          William A Brainerd 11 Jan 1869
                          Richard Westfield 28 Feb 1872

Grand Prairie Disc 22 Jun 1866	Gorcham P Ayer 24 Nov 1854
Jesuit Bend Disc 22 Jun 1866 Reest 6 Jul 1866 Disc 26 Feb 1867 Reest 17 Jun 1867	Alfred D Salvant 25 Jun 1855 William L Stewart 6 Jul 1866 James W Mead 17 Jun 1867 Christopher C Packard 17 May 1870 Oscar B Sarpy 29 Jun 1871
Point a la Heche	Claude F V Barbarot 10 Aug 1854 Jean Bourdells 3 May 1866 Claude F V Barbarot 12 Dec 1866
Point Michael Disc 22 Jun 1866 Reest 29 Oct 1870	Joseph Cathcart 24 Nov 1854 Victor M Solis 15 May 1860 L Haspie 29 Jun 1870 Paschal Encolade 29 Jun 1871
South West Pass Disc 28 Jun 1866	Charles Dennis 19 Jan 1859
Moss Grove Disc 23 Jan 1867	John B Halley 16 May 1866
Home Place	Patrick Lyons 4 May 1871
Bel Air	Edward Smith 15 Jun 1871
Grand Prairie	Diedrich Wischusen 15 Jun 1857
St. Sophie	Rufin J B Morand 26 Jun 1871
Beau Sejour	Leon C Courcelli 29 Jun 1871
Pilot Town	William F Smith 14 Jun 1873

POINT COUPEE PARISH

Hermitage   Frederick J Munzesheimer 21 Sep 1857
                             D Brady 30 Jun 1859
                             Leonard P Day 15 Aug 1859
                             John Landreau 10 Jun 1867

Livonia   James B Johnson 28 May 1846
Disc 4 Jul 1867
Reest 2 Feb 1869   James M Bailey 4 Feb 1869

Morganza   Joseph T Strother 19 Sep 1855
                             Eugene Oubre 27 Dec 1865
                             George W Brown 28 May 1869
                             Leon Oubre 11 Mar 1872

Point Coupee Courthouse   Clement Enete 24 Jan 1857
                             Clement Enete 27 Dec 1865
                             John J Plantevignes 11 Feb 1867
                             Clement Enete 11 Mar 1868
                             Clementine Enete 26 Apr 1872

Red River Landing   Joseph Torras 5 Jan 1849
                             Joseph Torras 30 Jan 1866
                             J B Leggett 13 Oct 1866
Disc 3 Jan 1870   Samuel M Kingsburg 8 Nov 1866
Reest 24 Jan 1870   M Ferris 2 Dec 1868
Disc 31 Jan 1870
Reest 24 Jan 1870   Ruffin Piper 27 Jan 1870
                             John L Kingsburg 25 Aug 1871

The Village   Augustus Fisher 6 Jun 1854
                             Louis V Porche 19 Sep 1859
Disc 22 Oct 1866

Waterloo   Jules St. Germain 22 Jun 1854
                             Jules St. Germain 3 Oct 1865
                             Paul Melancon 13 Oct 1866
                             James M Hurst 23 Sep 1867
                             Arthur Porche 25 Nov 1867

Williamsport   John A Hamilton 29 Jul 1853
                           Daniel Levy 26 1858
                           Charles Duvall 16 Sep 1859
Disc 4 Feb 1867

Centerpoint   John R Herring 31 Dec 1857
Disc 6 Sep 1860

Miller's Store   Joseph A Miller 31 Dec 1857

Cypress Point   Joseph A Miller 16 Feb 1858
                           J T Brooks 9 Dec 1858
                           J J B Kirk 22 Oct 1859
                           T C Kirk 28 Jan 1861
Disc 22 Jun 1866

False River   Veronique Major 20 Feb 1858
                           Pierre A Roy 17 Oct 1859
Disc 22 Jan 1861

Alabama Bayou   Aleck C Carruth 5 Oct 1858
Disc 20 Feb 1859

New Texas   Leon Oubre 1 Aug 1873

RAPIDES PARISH

Alexandria Courthouse   Eugene R Biosat 21 May 1856 (Pres & Sen)
                           Eugene R Biossat 30 Jan 1860 (Pres & Sen)
                           Levi Wells 31 Aug 1865
                           John Rodgers 21 Nov 1865 (Pres)
                           Thomas S Bacon 15 Feb 1866 (Pres & Sen)
                           Mrs. Hamoline B Ringgold 16 Dec 1867
                           William Mills Jr 12 Mar 1873 (Pres & Sen)

Bear Creek Disc 22 Jun 1866	William Roe 2 Sep 1857
Big Creek	Churchill A Hooper 22 Oct 1852 Joseph Hopkins 21 May 1859
Disc 22 Jun 1866 Reest 27 Mar 1867	D J Kitterlin 27 Mar 1867
Disc 2 Sep 1868 Reest 13 Nov 1871 Disc (No date)	Lavenia Jane Lovell 13 Nov 1871
Cheneyville	Walter Bailey 7 Jun 1853 George C Smith 5 Jul 1860 Charles Simpson 21 Dec 1860 George B Marshall 20 Nov 1865
Disc 23 Mar 1866 Reest 29 Oct 1866	Orestis K Hawley 19 Oct 1866 John H Reynolds 2 Oct 1867 D T Safford 18 May 1868 Robert Luckner 28 May 1869 Samuel Blum 11 Feb 1870 Clovis Lemoin 22 Apr 1870 Francis W Marshall 16 May 1871
Cotile	Robert M Henderson 29 Sep 1843 William C James 5 Jan 1861 Henry A Boyce 6 Sep 1865 John N Taylor 20 Dec 1865 Leon Dufilno 28 Dec 1866 Miss Ann L Henderson 21 Feb 1868 William C James 16 Dec 1868 Hyman Bath 3 Mar 1873
Hineston Disc 22 Jun 1866	Joseph T Hatch 27 Jan 1852
Lecompte Disc 23 Mar 1866	Joseph L Sharitt 26 Jul 1854

Liberty Creek   John C Cavanaugh 10 Aug 1857
Disc 22 Jun 1866

Lucky Hit   William Randolph 8 Aug 1856
Disc 4 Feb 1867

Barnwell   William P Wales 30 Jun 1858
Disc 23 May 1860

Spring Creek   John J Swann 30 Jun 1858
                             Andrew J Wells 28 Dec 1858
                             Michael Paul 20 Oct 1859
Disc 28 Jun 1866
Reest 13 oct 1871   Lewis Barnidge 13 Oct 1871

Samothe   Moses Rosenthal 20 May 1859
Disc 22 Jun 1866

Jatt   Robert S Hester 13 Apr 1860
Disc 22 Jun 1866
Reest 15 Feb 1867   William Stevens 15 Feb 1867
                             Thomas T Swafford 11 Apr 1868

Cotile Landing   Gus Rose 8 Mar 1871
                             H A Thompson 7 Jul 1971
Disc 11 Mar 1872

Pineville   Edward J Barrett 9 Jun 1871

Wellswood   Alexander Glucksman 29 Apr 1871
                             Edward L Watkins 23 Jan 1873

Quantico   Levi Wells 15 Jan 1873

Sullivan's Landing   John H Sullivan 19 May 1873

SABINE PARISH

Anacoco   Isaiah Kirk 4 Feb 1852
Disc 22 Jun 1866

Burr's Ferry　　　　　　　　Gilman B Burr 2 Jan 1847
Disc 26 Jun 1867

Fort Jessup　　　　　　　　Charles Beck 1 Oct 1855
Disc 22 Jun 1866
Reest 11 Oct 1866　　　　　John A Gould 11 Oct 1866
　　　　　　　　　　　　　　Theodore Beck 15 Jun 1869
　　　　　　　　　　　　　　William H Barbee 14 Mar 1872
　　　　　　　　　　　　　　Theordore Beck 19 Mar 1872

Many Courthouse　　　　　　Sterling G McLemore 27 Oct 1857
　　　　　　　　　　　　　　Jeptha Weeks 19 Jun 1858
Disc 26 Jun 1867
Reest 31 Oct 1867　　　　　William B Stille 31 Oct 1867
　　　　　　　　　　　　　　L Barbee 9 Feb 1870
　　　　　　　　　　　　　　William B Stille 22 Apr 1870

Mill Creek　　　　　　　　　Elijah Self 26 Aug 1852
Disc 26 Jul 1867

Nashborough　　　　　　　　J Nash 26 Feb 1857
Disc 5 Nov 1857
Reest 17 Sep 1858　　　　　Joseph C Truly 17 Sep 1858
　　　　　　　　　　　　　　Valentine Nash 3 Sep 1860

Dillonsburgh　　　　　　　　Moses K Speight 23 Jun 1858
Disc 22 Jun 1866

Negreet　　　　　　　　　　Jesse Morris 31 Jul 1858
Disc 28 Jun 1866

Columbus　　　　　　　　　John J M Godwin 15 Nov 1858
Disc 22 Jun 1866

Toro　　　　　　　　　　　Solomon Arthur 15 Nov 1858
　　　　　　　　　　　　　　Isham N McCollister 3 Feb 1860
Disc 28 Jun 1866

San Patrice　　　　　　　　John Branch 4 Jun 1859

Disc 28 Jun 1866
Reest 10 Mar 1868   Miss Beneta Presler 10 Mar 1868
Disc 23 Jul 1869

Justice   Allen Holland 9 Sep 1859
Disc 22 Jun 1866

Darnell's Gin   John Honeycutt 15 Feb 1875

ST. BERNARD PARISH

Bienvenu   Francisco Artiste 19 Sep 1856
                       Augustus Armstrong 17 Mar 1858
Disc 22 Jun 1866

Ducros Station   Francisco Arista 17 Sep 1866
Disc 21 Jan 1869

St. Bernard Courthouse Daniel Van Ruff 13 Nov 1866
                        Mrs. Martha A Van Ruff 27 Jul 1871

Drew's Station   Francisco Artiste 15 Jun 1871

ST. CHARLES PARISH

McCutcheon's Landing   James W McCutcheon 25 Jun 1856
                       Jules B Tripaquier 5 Feb 1866
                       Joseph Walker 22 Sep 1867
Disc 4 Sep 1868

St. Charles Courthouse Thomas E Broadus 6 May 1857
                        George E Payne 19 Jul 1859
                        Lewis Jolessaint 24 Dec 1865
                        Lawrence Wachter 19 Apr 1866
                        Forbes Cuthbert 19 Dec 1866
                        James Condon 8 May 1867
                        E E Tilly 9 Sep 1867
                        A J Numa Brou 22 Jan 1869
                        Louis D Broussard 19 Aug 1869

	O J Flagg 10 Feb 1871
	Alexander Morales 20 Apr 1871
	William J Moffitt 24 Feb 1873
	Jacob A Burbank 20 Apr 1873
Taylor	John C Cofield 19 Sep 1855
	Francis Webb 21 Dec 1858
Gassins' Landing	John Ridge 3 Oct 1865
	Antoine Gassin 21 Jan 1867
Disc 24 Jan 1870	
Boutte	Edward B Tinney 29 Jun 1866
	Robert Scott 23 Jul 1868
	Joseph C Koranson 19 Oct 1870
	Joseph B Friedman 6 Aug 1872
Allemands	William Kussman 19 Aug 1868
Disc 10 Aug 1869	
Reest 13 Dec 1872	Junius F Williams 13 Dec 1872

ST. HELENA PARISH

Amite City	Charles S Stewart 18 Jul 1853
	James S Rivers 31 Aug 1865
	William H Wilder 15 Jan 1866
Darlington	Barnabus H Pipkin 17 Jul 1849
	Hezekiah Thompson 14 Dec 1859
Disc 27 jun 1866	
Reest 19 Apr 1867	John H Welden 19 Apr 1867
	Samuel D Heap 8 Feb 1869
	Mrs. Sarah C Reiting 7 Mar 1871
	Samuel D Heap 13 May 1872
Dennis Mills	Samuel J Chance 11 Apr 1857
	Thomas D Bridges 31 May 1859
	George H Gause 13 Mar 1866
	Daniel Cortez 14 Feb 1867

Disc 11 Feb 1870	Soloman Lewis 30 Jun 1868
Reest 12 May 1871	Thomas R Craft 12 May 1871
	John P Merrick 4 Jan 1872
Greensburg Courthouse	James George Parker 29 Jan 1857
	William J Bennett 26 Mar 1858
	Hezekiah Wheat 3 Feb 1859
	Davis A Morgan 14 Nov 1859
	Seth Decker 5 Jan 1860
	James George Parker 27 Jan 1860
	Elijah S Eady 1 Mar 1860
	Robert Cole 6 Aug 1860
	Robert Y Burton 13 Sep 1865
	Mrs. M Purley 8 Jul 1867
	James W Cole 17 Mar 1871
	James H George 27 Apr 1871
Hog Branch	William J Bennett 19 Jan 1856
	Robert O Pennington 22 Feb 1858
	Miss Mahala Mullins 9 May 1866
	Miss E J Jackson 13 Aug 1866
	Edward G Brown 4 Dec 1866
	Miss Easther Carter 10 Jun 1867
	Robert Jackson 20 Jan 1868
	Mrs. Lydia Underwood 25 Jan 1869
Kemp's Mil	Thomas D Kemp 17 Jul 1857
	Hillery Kemp 9 Feb 1860
Disc 22 Jun 1866	
Prospect Hill	Benjamin Weil 6 Mar 1856
	George Kraemer 6 May 1858
	Mary Ann Weil 9 Nov 1858
	Caleb O Gayle 9 Sep 1859
	Richard M Ellis 1 Jun 1861
Roberts Mill	George S Roberts 9 Dec 1856
Disc 4 Jul 1866	
Reest 4 Feb 1867	John Ryan 4 Feb 1867

Disc 16 Dec 1868

St. Helena Disc 20 Jan 1859	Joseph Killian 29 Sep 1853
Tangipahoa	Charles H Allen 2 Sep 1857 John P Wall 6 Jun 1859 Julius Wusthoff 30 Oct 1865 Johnson E Yerkes 25 Oct 1869
Black Walnut Disc 4 Feb 1867	Jonathan K Gorman 15 Jul 1859
Arcola	John W Leonard 20 Nov 1865
Sunny Hill	Peter Brumfield 23 Nov 1871
Pine Grove	William Fletcher 1 Dec 1872

ST. JAMES PARISH

Cantrelle	Victor Melancon 6 Oct 1856 Theobold Bruno 21 Mar 1866 Jean B E Theriot 11 Jul 1866 Pierre Richard 10 Jun 1867 John J Clayton 21 Apr 1870
Convent Courthouse	Marcellin Oubre 6 Jul 1857 Marcellin Oubre 27 Dec 1865 James F Oubre 20 May 1867 Mrs. Mary Trust 22 Apr 1869 Joseph W Shade 1 Feb 1873
Vacherie Road Disc 28 Jun 1866 Reest 20 Dec 1869 Disc 11 Jun 1872 Reest 21 Oct 1872	John V Armant 29 May 1854 Frank E Smith 20 Dec 1869 (Illegible entry) (Illegible entry) Elphege Poche 21 Oct 1872

Grand Pointe Disc 22 Jun 1866	Charles Parent 26 Feb 1868
Turead Disc 7 Oct 1868	Auguste G Autrau 22 Apr 1866
Long View	Alice Melancon 12 May 1871
St. James	Euphemon Hebert 11 Mar 1872 Louis F Fazinde 9 Apr 1873
Welcome	B Henry Elfer 14 May 1872
St. Patrick's	Elphege Poche 5 Dec 1872

ST. JOHN THE BAPTIST PARISH

Bonnet Carre	Adolphe Madere 31 Mar 1854 Gustave Dupuy 5 Sep 1860 Ovide Trigre 9 Apr 1866 Celestin Vickner 17 Jun 1869 Charles Lasseigne 10 Nov 1870
Edgard	E Edgard Perrot 7 Mar 1857 Armand Perrilliat 17 Jan 1860 Maxmillian Becnel 16 Jan 1861 Sosthene Becnel 26 Mar 1866 Maxmillian Becnel 28 Feb 1872
Desair Station	Fred K Bredemeier 25 Mar 1872

ST. MARTIN PARISH

Breaux Bridge Disc 22 Jun 1866 Reest 9 Dec 1867	Stephen DeLucky 7 Jul 1857 Cyprian Melancon 9 Dec 1867 Charles Berbin 20 Sep 1869 Edgar Richard 2 Nov 1869
Disc 14 Sep 1870	

Reest 5 Oct 1870	Cyprian Melancon 5 Oct 1870
New Iberia	Luther M Sugg 25 Jul 1856
	Robert J Epperson 24 Dec 1857
	Abner D Miner 17 Jan 1860
	William G Daunt 31 Aug 1865
	Pierre L Renoudet 21 Mar 1867
	J R Esnard 15 Jun 1869
	William A Riggs 13 Aug 1869
	William A Riggs 13 Aug 1870 (Pres & Sen)
St. Martinville Courthouse	Auguste Marnist 16 Jun 1855
	Henry Blanc 31 Aug 1865
	Gideon B Vinson 22 Jun 1866
	John F Heard 15 Nov 1866
	Ernest Fontenette 15 Jun 1869
	Pierre Dupre 13 Feb 1871
	Charles Neven 28 Jul 1873
Butte La Rose	J S Leonard 31 Dec 1857
Disc 25 Jun 1858	
Bayou Chene	Nicholas Verrel 12 Jun 1858
	Jacob Roth 25 Jan 1859
Disc 22 Jun 1866	
Chicot Pass	Nathaniel P Millard 17 Jan 1858
Disc 26 Jun 1867	
Grande Riviere	Robert McGunnegle 12 Jun 1858
	H W Hart 18 Aug 1858
Laplace	Rudolphe Beer 30 Jun 1858
Disc 7 Jun 1859	
Reest 17 Aug 1859	Alphonse Landry 17 Aug 1859
Disc 17 Jul 1860	
Reest 17 Jul 1860	Francois Bradon 19 Jul 1860
	John D Thorne 17 Oct 1867
	John Roussaue 29 Dec 1868

Disc 28 Aug 1871
Reest 14 Jul 1873

Alfred H Lastrapes 8 Feb 1869

Fred Thus 14 Jul 1873

Fausse Point
Disc 22 Jun 1866

Francis O Dugas 5 Aug 1858

Myrtle Grove
Disc 14 Mar 1860

Marcelin Landry 7 Feb 1859

ST. LANDRY PARISH

Arnaudville

Disc 4 Jul 1867
Reest 24 Feb 1868

John Chapman Mills 17 Feb 1857
Samuel F Simpson 27 Oct 1860

Mrs. Azilie Durie 24 Feb 1868
Thomas K Wouton 18 May 1869
Adeline Durio 13 May 1870

Ballew's Ferry
Disc 22 Jun 1866

John Lyons Jr 11 May 1838

Bayou Boeuf
Disc 4 May 1867
Reest 23 May 1868
Disc (No date)

Thomas McCrory 25 May 1852

Barney S Gary 23 May 1868

Bayou Chicot

James Akenhead 23 May 1848
Terance L Scott 2 Apr 1858
Terance L Scott 6 Feb 1866
Mrs. Martha A Haas 22 Mar 1871

Big Cane
Disc 22 Jun 1866
Reest 8 Jul 1868

Isaac R Jackson 11 Nov 1850

John Morris 8 Jul 1868
Warren F Jackson 31 Aug 1868
H W Decuir 8 Jul 1872
Leopold Goudchaux 12 May 1873

Couleur Blanc

James Mires 17 Sep 1857

Disc 28 Feb 1859

Grand Coteau	Sylvester J Barry 5 Sep 1848
	Henry S Dunbar 2 Feb 1866
	Alexander H Castille 22 Mar 1871
Leonville	Michael Emonet 23 Feb 1856
Disc 22 Jun 1866	
Reest 24 Mar 1868	Mrs. Mary F Emonet 24 Mar 1868
Disc 24 Jan 1870	
Reest 3 Jun 1872	Jules D Allfrey 3 Jun 1872
Mermenton	William Cottrell 2 Sep 1857
	William Wallis 25 Jan 1858
	William Cottrell 8 May 1858
	Helaire Desessants 13 Mar 1866
	John A Powell 17 Jun 1867
	John O Wright 24 Oct 1867
	John Castel 8 May 1868
	Victor Magamaud 12 May 1871
	Jules Castel 7 Apr 1873
	Paul Castel 10 Jun 1873
Opelousas	Theodore Chachere 25 Aug 1855
	Tilghman G Compton 18 Oct 1865
	Alexander B Chacher 20 Aug 1868
	Paul J Lefebure 30 Jan 1872
Plaquemine Brule	Jesse B Clark 23 May 1844
	Orasamus Hays 19 May 1859
	(Illegible entry)
	Dallas B Hayes 18 Jan 1872
	George J Rose 18 Jun 1873
Ville Platte	Yves Vidrine 4 Aug 1855
	Marcel Daire 25 Jun 1858
	Laclair P Davidson 20 Aug 1860
	Yves Vidrine 6 Feb 1866
	Thomas Reed 9 Aug 1871
	Oscar Dardean 28 Feb 1872

Washington	Abraham Millspaugh 14 Oct 1854
	Abraham Millspaugh 15 Dec 1865
	Abraham Millspaugh 15 Jul 1870 (Pres & Sen)
	Edward W Goodwin 21 Mar 1872
	Edward W Goodwin 6 May 1872 (Pres & Sen)
Cataublan	Windsor Smith 31 Dec 1857
Atchafalaya	Franklin C Robertson 11 Jul 1858
	Thomas W Woodruff 15 Mar 1859
Disc 22 Jun 1866	
Pouppeville	Octave P Bonnin 5 Aug 1858
	Joseph D Bernard 26 Apr 1856
	John H Puffpower 21 May 1866
	Mrs. Scolastie Sitting 31 Jul 1866
Disc 24 Jun 1870	
Dunbarton	Henry S Dunbar 17 Sep 1858
	John W Daniel 10 Nov 1859
Disc 22 Jun 1866	
Reest 17 Mar 1873	John W Harvey 17 Mar 1873
Gum Spring	Robert Ellison 4 Oct 1860
Disc 22 Jun 1866	
St. Peter's	John Ewell 31 Jul 1868
Disc 31 Aug 1866	
Reest 3 Jul 1869	Frederick Millspaugh 3 Feb 1869
Churchville	William M Nelson 28 Feb 1873
Prudhomme	Spotswood H Sanders 15 Apr 1873
Faquetique	Joseph Chemier 5 May 1873
Fabacher	Joseph Fabacher 11 Jun 1873

ST. MARY PARISH

Alligator
Disc 22 Jun 1866

Stephen DeLucky 5 Nov 1849

Berwick

Andrew J Pyron 18 Aug 1857
Alfred B Vail 23 Aug 1858
Auguste Cashie 25 Aug 1859
William C Sickels 2 Jan 1860
Michael H Mooney 11 Oct 1866

Disc 5 Sep 1867

Brashear

Thomas T Brashear 10 Sep 1857
Samuel E Lawes 11 Nov 1858
Onezipher Landry 20 Jan 1860
Charles P Simmons 17 Dec 1860
Abiel Rosengrants 31 Aug 1865
Isaac Lehmann 25 Jun 1866
Valentine Chase 15 may 1867
Percy O'Brien 4 Feb 1868
Thomas W Nelson 18 Nov 1868
Charles Miller 12 Apr 1871

Centreville

Theodore F Schockley 10 Jun 1857
John Laspeyre 4 Oct 1865
N J Wooster 4 Dec 1865
Shakespeare Allen 2 Feb 1866
Joseph S Whitworth 23 Jul 1866
Paul Cheval 9 Aug 1871

Charenton

Edward Teray 20 Jun 1857
Octave A Picot 27 Aug 1858
Ernest Gigleux 20 Sep 1858
Josiah G Washington 23 Oct 1865

Disc 13 Aug 1866
Reest 23 Mar 1868

Emile Perret 23 Mar 1868
August Mora 20 Apr 1868

Disc 5 Jun 1869

Franklin Courthouse	Epaphedilius Howle 28 Feb 1854 William Ray 3 Oct 1865 Mrs. Sidonie Delahoussaye 18 Jan 1866 James Fourny 3 Sep 1867 John Migeat 9 Feb 1870 Abraham Davis 3 Jun 1872
Jeanerette	Paul Prevost 24 Jan 1848 William F Hudson 19 Oct 1865
Pattersonville	David R Muggah 8 Sep 1856 William Ager 6 Dec 1865 Miss Lizzie Rogers 7 Jul 1870 George W Kern 9 Sep 1870
Cypre Mort	D Kobleur 8 Apr 1868 O Pecot 29 Apr 1872
Baldwin	Mrs. Jane S Roberts 27 Jan 1870
Clarenton	Mrs. Marguerite C Bienvenu 9 Jun 1873

ST. TAMMANY PARISH

Covington Courthouse	Jesse Lee 11 Jan 1856 John E Smith 23 Nov 1865 Jesse Lee 27 Mar 1868 John S Prichard 13 Jul 1868 Thomas H Magee 5 Oct 1869 Mrs. Anna M Duniai 15 Nov 1872
Lima	Enoch B Talley 6 Jan 1853 Benjamin F Sadler 21 Feb 1859 Jones B Turner 4 Nov 1859
Disc 22 Jun 1866 Reest 11 Oct 1866 Disc 4 Sep 1868	Mrs. Emilia Talley 11 Oct 1866
Madisonville	Josi Colomer 19 Nov 1850 Theodore M Hurst 15 Dec 1860

Disc 28 Jun 1866	
Reest 11 Oct 1866	Frederick Perrin Jr 11 Oct 1866
Disc 7 Apr 1867	
Reest 13 Dec 1869	Charles L Dutch 13 Dec 1869
	Washington H R Haugen 8 Jan 1872
Mandeville	Louis Cogullin Jr 21 Dec 1853
Disc 21 Oct 1858	
Reest 23 Feb 1859	Charles Morgan 23 Feb 1859
	John L Morgan 9 Mar 1860
	Isaac Black 10 Oct 1860
Disc 28 Jun 1866	
Reest 2 Jul 1866	Louis Cogullin Jr 2 Jul 1866
	Wyndham R Nixon 26 May 1871
Parkerville	Joseph W Ernest 2 Oct 1857
Disc 28 Jun 1866	
Sun	James A Calhoun 14 Nov 1856
Disc 28 Jun 1866	
Reest 10 Aug 1866	Mrs. Eliza S Calhoun 10 Aug 1866
Disc 28 Aug 1871	
O'Rourke's	James O'Rourke 11 Jan 1858
	John O'Rourke 4 May 1859
Disc 28 Jun 1866	

TENSAS PARISH

Ashwood	James Stewart 7 Oct 1857
	Samuel E Chamberlain 21 Apr 1858
	William A L Potts 29 May 1860
	Henry Pennill 1 Jan 1862
Disc 22 Jun 1866	
Reest 26 Jan 1869	William D Miller 26 Jan 1869
	William Watson 26 Oct 1869
Disc 6 Mar 1872	
Kirk's Ferry	William H Bowman 3 Jul 1849
Disc 26 Jun 1867	

Mound Bayou   William W Walker 21 Apr 1852
Disc 4 Feb 1867

St. Joseph Courthouse   Robert H Snyder 27 Dec 1855
                           Robert Murdock 27 Nov 1865
                           A Pearcy Marshall 22 Jan 1866
                           Albert R Whitney 7 Mar 1866
                           Arthur L Post 22 Mar 1867
                           George G Gilson 29 Jul 1867
                           Alonzo L Alley 5 Jun 1868
                           Andrew S Graham 29 Mar 1869
                           Frederic W Matthews 4 Feb 1870
                           Charles E Bowman 16 Jan 1871

Waterproof   David Wise 24 Oct 1853
                           Sylvester York 24 Oct 1865
                           Mrs. S Woodward 29 May 1871
                           Benjamin F Bonney 19 Oct 1871

Hard Times Landing   Charles J Bourgoin 14 Sep 1870
                           Charles H Fenwick 22 Oct 1870
                           Henry P Bell 14 Apr 1873

Buck Ridge   Joseph S Douglass 8 May 1871
                           Edward Lake 22 Jan 1872

TERREBONNE PARISH

Houma Courthouse   Thomas F Brooks 25 Jun 1856
                           Howard B Bond 23 Jan 1860
                           George A Calhoun 2 Mar 1860
                           Alfred Rongelot 31 Aug 1865
                           Richard W Francis 4 Oct 1865
                           James L Belden 18 May 1870

Tigerville   Louisa C Price 25 May 1852
                           William K Hornsby 24 Oct 1859
                           H M Wallis 2 Mar 1863
                           Mrs. Emma V Summers 25 Jun 1866

Disc 19 Dec 1866	Zachary T Knight 15 Nov 1866
Reest 15 Jan 1867	Mrs. Anne Casey 15 Jan 1867
Disc 17 Feb 1868	
Reest 8 Jun 1869	Mrs. Jane E Nash 8 Jun 1869
	William M Moody 11 Mar 1870
	William Price 13 Nov 1871
Laurence	Ulysse Bru 1 Nov 1858
Disc 22 Jun 1866	
Chachahoula	Charles North 11 Oct 1866
	Pierre Portier 24 Dec 1866
Disc 7 Apr 1868	
Reest 13 Oct 1870	Charles B Matthews 13 Oct 1870
	Amede Boudreaux 20 Nov 1871
	Leonard P Lasseigne 7 Apr 1873
Live Oak	Monarch Littman 13 May 1872
Ardoyne	Henry V J Cooke 3 Jun 1872

UNION PARISH

Cherry Ridge	William C Carr 20 Jan 1848
	George W Joiner 25 Jun 1858
	Sylvanus Shepherd 24 Aug 1858
	James R Shepherd 5 Nov 1858
	John Ramsey 18 Sep 1860
D'Arbonne	Samuel W McClendon 5 Jun 1857
	John Autrey 24 Mar 1859
Downsville	Philemon Wilhite 9 Jun 1857
	John E Woodward 4 Dec 1865
	Abel Dixon 26 Mar 1866
	Austin Martin 17 Oct 1867
	Wesley B Anderson 31 Mar 1873
Farmerville Courthouse	William B H Poer 18 Mar 1856

                        Henry Archer 15 Mar 1858
                        T J Cann 18 Aug 1858
                        Campbell Lassiter 31 Dec 1859
                        Mrs. Harriett R Dozier 1 Mar 1866
                        James A Dozier 13 Mar 1866
                        Edward Bronson 12 Dec 1866
                        James C Trimble 17 Oct 1867

Marion   William L Rowland 19 Jun 1857
                        John Traylor 23 Nov 1857
                        Herman Meyer 16 Mar 1859
Disc 26 Jun 1867
Reest 4 Oct 1869   John J Loper 4 Oct 1869

Ouachita City   James M Lupe 28 Feb 1857
                        Claiborne M Smith 25 Oct 1858
                        James L Jones 18 Jan 1860
Disc 28 Jun 1866
Reest 6 Nov 1867   Edward G Cashell 6 Nov 1867
Disc 24 Nov 1869
Reest 13 Apr 1871   William Parks 13 Apr 1871
Disc 2 Dec 1871
Reest 2 May 1872   William Parks 2 May 1872

Shiloh   Jesse Trebb 6 Mar 1857
                        Robert G Pleasants 31 Mar 1858
Disc 28 Jun 1866
Reest 17 Jun 1867   Lewis Henderson 17 Jun 1867
                        W W Payer 6 Feb 1869
                        Mrs. Mary J Hopkins 12 Nov 1869
Disc 21 Dec 1859
Reest 12 Oct 1871   Thomas Lowery 12 Oct 1871
                        John D Hamilton 27 Oct 1871
                        William G Simmons 4 Feb 1873

Spears Store   Joseph R Goyne 14 Mar 1856
                        James M Post 17 Mar 1858

Union Cross Roads   Washington J Pickell 10 Mar 1857
Disc 26 Jun 1867

Reest 11 Mar 1868	Miss Nancy Pickell 11 Mar 1868 Henry Rogers 6 Jul 1868 Mrs. Dettie A Goldsby 5 Oct 1868
Pipesville Disc 27 Jun 1867	William Pipes 24 Aug 1858
Lindeville Disc 20 Jul 1860	Samuel E Barr 11 Nov 1858
Midway Disc 28 Jun 1866	James T White 13 Feb 1860 D P Cook 19 Jan 1861
Spearsville Disc 28 Jun 1866 Reest 3 Jun 1872	James M Post 13 Mar 1860 James W Hayes 13 Jun 1872 James M Post 6 Jan 1873
Mineral Spring Disc 28 Jun 1866	John B Wright 25 Oct 1860
Mount Olive Disc 28 Jun 1866	James E Haynie 22 Jan 1860
Lone Well	James H McBroom 2 Nov 1867
Cherry Ridge Disc 15 Jan 1872	William C Carr 29 Jun 1871
Meridian	Thornton D Manning 3 Jun 1872 John B Robinson 2 Jun 1873

VERMILION PARISH

Abbeville Courthouse	Alanson Spaulding 14 Jul 1855 James W Bradley 17 Dec 1859 David Frank 3 Nov 1865 Manuel de Llano 13 Aug 1869

	Eugene J Addison 19 Apr 1871
	George E Lyons 4 Feb 1873
Perry's Bridge	Robert H Mills 25 Apr 1855
	Robert H Mills 30 Mar 1866
Disc 29 Jan 1869	
Reest 1 Mar 1869	Robert H Mills 1 Mar 1869
Disc 13 Mar 1871	
Grand Chenier	Abel A Alexander 3 Sep 1858
Disc 22 Jun 1866	
Reest 10 Jul 1866	Miss Doxia A Wood 18 Jun 1866
Disc 7 Apr 1868	
Reest 13 Apr 1868	Lorenzo Sturlise 13 Apr 1868
	James B Rodgers 1 Mar 1871

OUACHITA PARISH

Forksville	Grove S Fitch 10 May 1856
Disc 12 Mar 1858	
Reest 17 Aug 1860	George W Brady 17 Aug 1860
Disc 17 Jan 1861	
Reest 19 Jun 1866	Mrs. Catherine Huey 19 Jun 1866
Disc 26 Mar 1867	
Reest 4 Dec 1867	James E Butler 4 Dec 1867
Indian Village	James Huey III 5 Dec 1854
	Joel Tatum Jr 11 Jun 1858
	Nicholas L Zeigler 23 Dec 1859
	William Thompson 31 Jul 1860
Disc 22 Jun 1866	
Reest 27 Nov 1872	James B Landers 27 Nov 1872
	John L Bryan 20 Oct 1873
Monroe Courthouse	William H Gayle 9 Oct 1857
	Nero S Hardy 15 Feb 1858
	Henry B Holmes 13 Oct 1860
	Miss Nicettie M Dinkgrave 14 Oct 1865
	Miss Nicettie M Dinkgrave 15 Apr 1869
	(Pres & Sen)

                                Miss Nicettie M Dinkgrave 13 May 1873
                                (Pres & Sen)

Prevost   Samuel Allen 10 Dec 1856
                                Aaron S Wood 6 Mar 1858
                                William H Raiford 6 Sep 1869
                                Rosanner P Adams 2 Nov 1860
Disc 2 Feb 1867

Spring Place   Francis M Grant 24 Mar 1857
                                Jacob B Hollingsworth 26 Jun 1858
                                Gustavus A Puckett 21 Jan 1860
Disc 16 Feb 1861

Trenton   James S Grayson 10 Apr 1857
                                John Thacker 5 Apr 1858
                                Abram Madden 20 Mar 1860
                                William Lucas 2 Apr 1866
Disc 29 Jan 1867
Reest 11 Jun 1867   Theodore C Sachise 11 Jun 1867
                                Jethro Moore 22 Jun 1868
                                Richard J Wheaton 5 Jan 1869
                                John James 19 Aug 1869
                                Isaac T Bowers 28 Sep 1869
                                John E Morris 27 Mar 1871
                                Richard J Wheaton 29 May 1871
                                T M Leatherman 2 Jun 1873
                                Miah Millsaps 2 Jul 1873

Frenchville   Paul Prudhomme 13 Nov 1858
Disc 22 Dec 1858

Hamilton   James B Caldwell 12 Apr 1860
Disc 22 Jun 1866

Log Town   John B Kirkwood 30 May 1866
Disc 26 Mar 1867
Reest 19 Apr 1867   John C Wiseman 19 Apr 1867
                                James A Cheatham 14 Oct 1867

Cuba	Warren G Kennedy 29 Aug 1870
	W W Butler 22 Aug 1871
	A B Wood 17 Apr 1872
	David C Brown 20 Jul 1872
	William L Graffenreid 16 Jun 1873
Loch Arbor	Samuel M Pickett 6 Oct 1870
	Leon Lange 20 Oct 1873
Sterlington	Frank May 15 Jun 1871
	James O Barr 21 Jul 1871
Cheniere	Alexander Myatt 30 Jul 1872
Mill Haven	Joseph H Walker 8 Nov 1872
Hamilton	Augustus D Russell 26 Nov 1872
Toll Bridge	Michael Perry 3 Mar 1873
Cadeville	John W Cade 9 Jun 1873

WASHINGTON PARISH

Davidson Disc 22 Jun 1866	James F Ard 28 Feb 1856
Franklinton	Mrs. Louise W Brooks 8 Jun 1857
	Mrs. E A Magee 17 Dec 1857
	Samuel E Slocum 21 Jun 1858
	Ellen J Babington 23 Dec 1858
	John R Wood 14 Feb 1866
	Jacob W Andrews 10 Apr 1866
	Kenneth McLain 9 Jan 1867
	Robert Babington 15 Mar 1871
	William H Jones 4 Dec 1872
Palestine Disc 28 Jun 1866	William Brumfield 12 May 1854
	Alexander C Bickham 25 Feb 1859

Reest 25 Aug 1871	Young P Bankston 25 Aug 1871
Roberts Disc 28 Jun 1866	John V Painter 7 Apr 1856
Shady Grove Disc 28 Jun 1866	Seth Barnes 21 Mar 1855
Reest 18 Feb 1867	Seth Barnes 21 Feb 1867 Joseph M Simmons 19 Mar 1868 William A Daniel 18 Dec 1871
Stubbs' Mill Disc 22 Jun 1866	Franklin Stubbs 12 Mar 1858
Bailey's Mill Disc 22 Jun 1866	Champion P Bailey 11 Dec 1858

WEST BATON ROUGE PARISH

Bruly Landing	Trasimond Bourg 28 Jul 1848 Charles Quenu Jr 30 Mar 1866 Doiron Joinville 30 Jul 1867
Disc 7 Apr 1868 Reest 22 Jul 1872	J Caire 22 Jul 1872
Hermitage	Lemuel P Day 15 Aug 1859 Louis H Trudeau 2 Nov 1860 John Landreau 10 Jul 1867
Belle Vale	Matthew Lawless 7 Mar 1870
West Baton Rouge Courthouse	Juan Pages 7 Jun 1871 Philip Bauer 19 Apr 1872
Lobdell's Store	Archibald H Lamon 20 Nov 1871

WEST FELICIANA PARISH

Bayou Tunica	Benedict Wolf 9 Dec 1856 Gustave Wolf 6 Sep 1865

	Lemuel P Day 23 Jan 1866
	Micajah Row Jr 24 Jul 1868
	William A Williams 2 Feb 1869
Laurel Hill Disc 22 Jun 1866 Reest 23 Apr 1867 Disc 4 Sep 1868	William H Lemon 4 May 1855 M Wicker 27 Apr 1867
St. Francisville	David Austen 7 Feb 1842 Archibald H Pillet 30 Jan 1861 Charles Farrelly 19 Aug 1865 John T Trice 21 Dec 1865 Charles Farrelly 30 Jan 1866 Bernard Farrelly 30 Oct 1867 Susan H Hunster 12 Jul 1870 (Order rescinded 29 Jul 1870) Bernard Farrelly 29 Jul 1870 Mrs. Mary E Riley 23 Mar 1871 James H Stephens 1 Apr 1872

WINN PARISH

Bertrand Prairie Disc 22 Jun 1866 Reest 11 Oct 1866 Disc 2 Sep 1868	Elisha K Davis 6 Feb 1857 Mrs. Rebecca Hall 11 Oct 1866 Miss D A Jones 22 Jul 1867
Good Water Disc 29 Jan 1867	Adam Riser 2 Aug 1854 Samuel C Bullock 20 Dec 1860 Mrs. Sibby A Smith 19 Oct 1866
Louisville Disc 22 Jun 1866	Elisha K McGinty 1 Nov 1856 John S Lewis 16 Mar 1859
Pine Ridge	Josiah H Lacey 31 Dec 1853 Absolom E Lard 27 Feb 1860

Disc 28 Jun 1866
Reest 23 Jul 1866   John B Low 23 Jul 1866
Disc 13 Mar 1871
Reest 23 Jun 1871   James P Readheimer 23 Jul 1871
         William D Hadwin 21 Jun 1875

St. Maurice   David H Boulet 26 Aug 1856
Disc 28 Jun 1866
Reest 16 Oct 1866   David H Boulet 16 Oct 1866
Disc 7 Apr 1868
Reest 12 May 1868   Thomas J Boulet 12 May 1868
         Marion E Evans 21 Mar 1870

Disc 7 Nov 1870
Reest 12 Jun 1871   Conrad Starks 12 Jun 1871

Saline Mills   James C Weeks 6 Jul 1854
Disc 19 Oct 1859

Tancock Prairie   James Gray 7 Dec 1854
Disc 4 Oct 1858

Wheeling   Jeremiah J Wilder 12 Nov 1855
         Aaron V Ragan 15 Dec 1857
         William H Goode 12 Mar 1859
         William Y Moore 10 Apr 1860
         D S Kuntrel 16 Oct 1866
         Clem Wilson 5 Feb 1867
         Julius Shean 8 Apr 1867
         James M Rummell 21 Dec 1868

Disc 7 Oct 1870

Winnfield   Edmund H Edwards 27 Dec 1856
         John L Walker 25 Jan 1858
         James M Houston 25 Jun 1858
         Philip Bernstein 9 Sep 1858
         R B Williams 10 Mar 1860
         David Pierson 14 May 1860
         Absolom Wade 13 Feb 1866
         E A Lucas 31 Jul 1867
         William A Smith 24 Mar 1868

	Maurice Bernstein 9 Feb 1870
	Dennis E Haynes 30 Mar 1871
	Elisha W Gillcrease 11 Apr 1871
	Austin C Banks 14 Mar 1872
Montgomery	Samuel H Wilder 30 Jun 1858
	Jeremiah J Wilder 23 Nov 1858
	John A Smith 7 Oct 1859
Disc 28 Jun 1866	
Reest 24 Jul 1867	George A Matthews 24 Jul 1867
Kyishe	Guion J L Brown 1 Nov 1858
Disc 4 Feb 1867	
Lanark	William R Bingham 12 Dec 1859
Disc 22 Jun 1866	
Buckoo	Squire E Hart 24 Sep 1860
Disc 22 Jun 1866	
Atlanta	F S Collier 3 Sep 1867
	Lorense George 9 Feb 1870
	Mrs. Emily Peace 20 May 1873
Newport	Richard Cole 31 Mar 1868
	James Rentz 13 May 1870
	Levi Banks 11 Apr 1871
Disc 19 Apr 1872	
Reest 3 Jun 1872	Levi Banks 3 Jun 1872
Flat Creek	Samuel J Harper 3 Jul 1872
Gansville	William M Moffett 20 Jan 1873
	James E Bain 21 Jun 1875

TANGIPAHOA PARISH

Hammond	Henry C Mooney 11 Sep 1868
Independence	Charles H George 9 Apr 1866

	Charles J Venable 2 Aug 1871
	Hillary K George 14 Dec 1871
Ponchatoula	Michael Biegel 19 Dec 1866
Tickfaw	Henry Watts 7 Aug 1871
Amite City	William H Wilder 15 Jan 1866
Welch's Bridge	James D Welch 5 Aug 1872
Pass Manchac	James M Alexander 9 Jun 1873
Sunny Hill	George W Dyson 5 Mar 1875
Arcola	Aldred Rhody 22 Dec 1874

GRANT PARISH

Colfax Courthouse	William B Phillips 24 Jun 1869
	William F Shackleford 6 May 1870
	Samuel E Cuney 15 Mar 1872
	Peter Boreland 20 May 1873
Jatt	Mary M Smith 20 Jul 1871
Fairmount	George W Hickman 8 May 1872

RICHLAND PARISH

Girard	Jeremiah J Baldwin 16 Jul 1871
	D Killingsworth 19 Sep 1871
	Julian P Gay 30 Apr 1872
Red Mouth	Aldolphe A Gilly 6 Feb 1871
Alto	W G Bulger 6 Feb 1871
	Josiah Bruce 4 Apr 1871
	H F Vickers 31 Mar 1873

	Obediah W Williams 2 Jun 1873
Rayville	Joe W Simmons 9 Feb 1872
Midway	Parke W DeFrance 1 Jul 1872

WEBSTER PARISH

Minden	James D Harper 3 Jun 1870
Cotton Valley	George W Martin 13 Oct 1871

RED RIVER PARISH

Coushatta Chute	William W Upshaw 7 Jul 1871 Julius Snead 3 Oct 1871 John T Yates 7 Oct 1873
Iverson	G B Thomas 22 Aug 1873
Love's Lake	M L Bryan 20 Jan 1876

IBERIA PARISH

New Iberia	Samuel Wakefield 22 Jul 1871 (Pres) Samuel Wakefield 11 Dec 1871 (Pres & Sen) Charles DeCuir 12 May 1873 (Pres & Sen)
Loreauville	Adrien Gonsoulin 24 Sep 1873

CAMERON PARISH

Cameron	J D McFall 24 Nov 1871 Samuel P Henry 31 Jan 1873
Leesburg	James M Lacy 9 Jun 1873

VERNON PARISH

Burr's Ferry	John M Liles 1 Jul 1873

Leesville	Isaac O Winfree 22 Aug 1873

Records Group 28, Volume IV

POST OFFICE LOCATIONS	POSTMASTER AND DATES OF APPOINTMENT
	ASCENSION PARISH
Donaldsonville	Pierre Landry 1 Mar 1871
	Frederick Robb 25 May 1875
	Henry Loeb 2 Apr 1877
	William G Wilkinson 1 May 1877
	William G Wilkinson 3 Mar 1880 (Pres & Sen)
	Louis Lefort 31 Oct 1881 (Pres)
	Louis Lefort 20 Dec 1881 (Pres & Sen)
	Camille Mollere 13 Jan 1886 (Pres & Sen)
	Richard T Hanson 19 Nov 1888 (Pres)
	Richard T Hanson 28 Feb 1889 (Pres & Sen)
	John Cecile Legare 28 Feb 1896 (Pres & Sen)
	Emile L Weber 13 Apr 1891 (Pres)
	William D Park 21 May 1891
	Gustave Israel 10 Jun 1891 (Pres & Sen)
New River	Thomas C Hills 26 Dec 1865
	Enoch G Jordan 24 Mar 1874
	Randall Cole 1 Feb 1875
	Hampton D Percy 8 Apr 1884
Allemania	Henry E Duffell 25 Aug 1875
	W Frank Thelcok 29 Sep 1876
Disc 3 Apr 1877	
Hohen	William A Little 11 Sep 1877
	John C Kilos 18 Sep 1878
	Joseph LaFreyre 26 Jun 1882
	Rudolph Landiman 8 Apr 1884
	Joseph G Joly 15 May 1888
	George B Reuss 30 Jan 1889
Vickner Bayou	Charles F Salassi 6 Nov 1879
	Amidie Frederic 21 Jun 1888

Riverside   Joseph Pecard 26 Nov 1877
Disc 8 Mar 1878
Rest 6 May 1878   Lott Mansfield 6 May 1878
Disc 12 Nov 1878

Turead   Benjamin Turead 13 Feb 1875
                       Louis A Bringier Jr 21 Sep 1880
Disc 10 Jan 1881

Dutch Town   Leon Piccard 29 Mar 1878
                       Henry D Miner 11 Jun 1878
Disc 11 Dec 1878
Reest 3 Nov 1879   Leon Piccard 3 Nov 1879

Lane   Thomas C Hills 28 May 1878
                       Thomas H Davis 29 May 1879
                       Enoch G Jordan 30 Oct 1879
                       Thomas C Hills 8 Jul 1880
                       Benjamin Palmer 19 Jul 1885
                       Barnabas M Hobby 20 Apr 1888

Darrow   Albert C Love 27 Dec 1881
                       Oliver S Duncan 6 Aug 1884
                       Frederick Higguson 18 Aug 1885
                       L W Armitage 31 Mar 1890

Galvez   Franklin S Lyons 6 Sep 1882

Burnside   Henry C Brand 9 Jul 1884

Prairieville   Hercule Landry 21 Jul 1884

St. Amant   Joseph St. Amant 23 Jul 1884

Cofield   William H Davis 7 Jun 1886
                       Joseph L Rolling 9 May 1888
                       William V Davis 8 Jun 1891

Gonzales   P Alcide Gautreaux 21 May 1887

	Joseph Bonzales Jr 9 May 1888
McCall	Henry McCall 26 Apr 1888
Geismer	Willis Beauais 26 May 1888 Charles Geismer 2 Oct 1889
Southwood	Barnabas M Hobby 30 Jan 1889 Alexander C Gordan 17 Nov 1890
Belle Hellene	Hampton D Percy 19 Nov 1889 Joseph Goudrau 29 Dec 1890
Ellis	Alexander C Gordon 14 Nov 1891
Barton	Leon Levy 19 Aug 1892
Cornerview	Octave S Broussard 15 Oct 1892

ASSUMPTION PARISH

Albemarle	F B Cinnel 31 Jan 1873 Jean B Landry 7 Jan 1874 Desire N Carmouche 10 May 1875 Anatole B Bourgeois 22 May 1876 Angus C Littlejohn 3 Apr 1878 Magloire Bourgeois 22 Jul 1878
Assumption Courthouse	William C Cramer 19 May 1872 Facuna E Pintado 3 Jun 1873 Eudaldo G Pintado 3 Sep 1874 Mrs. Johanna W R Pintado 31 Jan 1877
Sabadieville Disc 28 Oct 1874 Reest 14 Dec 1874	Spicer Jones 10 Jun 1867 Jules Bassett 31 Aug 1874 Oscar F Hebert 14 Dec 1874 Mrs. Johanna W R Pintado 14 Feb 1877 Delphan Bienvenu Jr 8 Dec 1881

	Anatole A Achee 15 Mar 1888
Paincourtville	Charles Aubry 14 Apr 1873
	Oscar Dugas 14 Feb 1879
	Clairville J Savoy 6 Jun 1881
Crane's Forge	Silveste C Mollere 7 Jan 1875
	Pierre E Durand 25 Jan 1876
	Nicholas LeBlanc 21 May 1881
Bertie	P Emile Juge Jr 21 May 1879
	Joseph G R Ganthreaux 16 Feb 1881
	Angus C Littlejohn 11 Jan 1882
	Rudolph H Dossat 2 Nov 1886
Napoleonville	Mrs. Johanna W R Pintado 1 Apr 1879
	Pascal E Thibodeaux 16 Jun 1884
	Edgar P Helluin 2 Sep 1887
	Edward Vives 23 Jan 1889
	Louis Corde 18 Oct 1889
Belle Rose	Nicholas LeBlanc 21 May 1881
Amelia	Felix Thibodeaux 22 Jul 1885
	Thomas S DeLucky 10 Jun 1889
Valenzuela	W D Dalferes 25 Jan 1886
	Elie Baccarat 28 Sep 1886
Plaitenville	Mrs. Theresa M Marks 18 Nov 1886
Tallien	George A Meunet 2 Dec 1889
Klotzville	Joseph A Brand 23 Mar 1892

AVOYELLES PARISH

Big Bend	John Everett 25 Oct 1867
	James T Griffin 7 Nov 1881
	William Branch Marshall 15 Nov 1882

	Mary P Spurlock 12 Nov 1883
	James T Griffin 3 Oct 1888
	Mrs. Effa S Griffin 21 Aug 1889
	Clint Pearce 11 Jun 1891
Cassandra	Montillion J Ryland 22 Nov 1871
Disc 6 Jun 1879	
Cottonport	Gervais A Bordelon 7 Mar 1872
	John T Nelson 17 Mar 1875
Disc 23 Jun 1875	
Reest 17 Dec 1878	Avit Lemoine 17 Dec 1878
	Firmin Serenne 12 May 1880
	Serge Callegory 25 Oct 1880
	Oscar Lemoine 23 Jan 1884
	Louis F Callegari 30 Apr 1886
Evergreen	Joseph Cappel 3 Jan 1870
	Isaac C Johnson 27 Dec 1879
	John D Earnest 31 Jan 1887
	Isaac C Johnson 23 Dec 1888
	Clara Toon 15 Jun 1890
Holmesville	Walker Arkenhead 14 Dec 1868
	Gertrude A Arkenhead 8 May 1877
	Daniel B Hudson 3 May 1880
Mansura	David Siess 20 Jun 1866
	Jean Pride Dormas 30 Dec 1881
	Pierre A Durand 5 Oct 1883
Marksville	George L Mayer 11 Apr 1871
	Henry Dupuy 1 Jun 1874
	Charles F Huesman 2 Feb 1881
	Henry Dupuy 15 Aug 1883
	George L Mayer 18 Feb 1887
	James M Edwards 22 May 1889
	Oscar B DeBellvue 16 Apr 1891
	Benjamin F Edwards 1 Jul 1891

Moreauville	James A Boyer 30 Jul 1866
	Alonzo L Boyer 1 Jul 1874
	Jacques A Boyer 12 Mar 1875
	Alonzo L Boyer 2 Aug 1882
	Alphonse J Escude 2 Feb 1888
	Gervais A Bordelon 3 Oct 1888
	Alonzo L Boyer 22 May 1889
Simmesport	Mrs. Azema Leigh 23 Jun 1871
	John S Hosea 18 Sep 1873
	Walter T Lansdell 22 Jun 1883
	Thomas L Berand 30 Nov 1883
	William H Thompson 10 Apr 1884
	Thomas S Denson 22 Oct 1890
Heuffpower Disc 22 Feb 1875	Thomas J Heard 3 Jun 1873
Bordelonville	Remie Bordelon 20 Jun 1870
Woodside	William J Bentley 13 Mar 1878
	Victor J Oplalek 18 May 1870
	William J Bently 27 Jan 1882
Egg Bend	Archibald D Derivas 21 May 1878
	Francois M Joffrion 8 Feb 1881
	Jules E Didier 11 Apr 1888
	Mrs. Clara Frank Didier 31 Jul 1888
Tiger Bend	Alexander M Haas 18 Dec 1879
Plaucheville Disc 23 Jun 1880	F M Gremillion 10 May 1880
Couvillon	Gregory O Couvillon 30 Sep 1880
	L L Gauthier 7 Jul 1882
Tilden	Jefferson D Robinson 16 Dec 1880
	Walter F Coyle 30 Dec 1881
	Charles Smith 18 Dec 1882

	Robert H Baker 20 Feb 1883
	James O E Cain 14 Jan 1884
	James K Bond 30 Apr 1886
	Mrs. Mary A Bond 2 May 1888
Eola	Daniel B Hudson 14 Nov 1881
	William C Scott 24 May 1884
	Mrs. Laura F Hudson 21 Jan 1885
	Daniel B Hudson 26 Jul 1888
	M A Wade 18 Nov 1889
	(Rescinded 24 Dec 1889)
Bunkie	Thomas B Kimbro 26 Jan 1883
	Louis W Anderson 16 Apr 1884
	John D Earnest 30 Aug 1889
Odenburg	Clarence Hetherwick 14 Apr 1885
	Jefferson Hetherwick 27 Apr 1885
	John D Oden 15 Feb 1890
Corner	Augustin F Bonnett 7 Apr 1886
Red Fish	William R Howard 11 May 1888
	Henry C Perkins 11 Sep 1888
Meyersville	Mrs. Esther Alexander 2 Jun 1888
Hamburg	Edward D Coco 15 Aug 1888
	Francis M Pavey 19 Dec 1890
Mordoc	Winburn L Chafin 3 Oct 1888
	Traville E Jeansonne 21 Mar 1892
Milburn	William C Townsend 23 Nov 1889
Green Stone	Eugene C Hayes 4 Feb 1890
Plaucheville	Jean V Plauche 4 Jun 1890
	Richard H Cox 24 Jan 1891
	Richard H Cox 9 Mar 1892

Centerpoint	Alexander S Baker 14 Dec 1891

BIENVILLE PARISH

Arcadia	Allen Barksdale 21 Oct 1872 John T Winfield 24 Jun 1873 Allen Holland 8 Dec 1873 John T Winfield 9 Oct 1874 John C Brice 7 Feb 1876 John H Givens 11 Nov 1878 John C Brice 4 Sep 1883 William T Huested 17 Apr 1889
Bear Creek Disc 11 Jul 1873	William Brice 3 Jun 1872
Buckhorn	John James Hines 15 Feb 1867
Liberty Hill	E A Crawford 28 Apr 1873 Thomas Crawford 16 Jun 1873 William L Davis 10 Apr 1888 Clarence E Whitley 19 Mar 1891
Montcalm	William A Jones 12 Oct 1871 Robert T Goff 2 Aug 1875 James C Goff 6 Feb 1882 Mrs. Carrie Goff 5 May 1885 P Harrison 1 Mar 1890
Mount Lebanon	Robert Hardy 20 May 1872 William B Colbert 10 Nov 1873 William L King 18 Feb 1888
Ringgold	John C Moseley 19 Aug 1869 A B Shehee 1 May 1874 James M Lockett 19 Oct 1874 James Booth 31 Jul 1876 James H Jones 18 Sep 1876 James M Lockett 31 Jul 1877

	John A Sledge 24 Aug 1881
	George W Lawhon 20 Mar 1886
	William P B Tucker 21 Dec 1891
Saline	George C Lewis 17 Mar 1873
	Jackson S Corbette 20 Oct 1873
	Blake W Braswell 3 May 1877
	Lewis J Lucky 26 Nov 1880
	Miss Martha Dorman 11 Jan 1887
	M A Harris 20 Jan 1887
	Wiley M Dorman 9 Jan 1888
Sparta Courthouse	John H Scheen 30 Sep 1872
	Herman F Scheen 13 Jul 1877
	Moses A Cockerham 17 Jul 1877
	E Herbert Hightower 24 Aug 1877
	Herman F Scheen 26 Mar 1884
	James B Heard 10 Jul 1888
Friendship	Lawrence Readenheimer 9 Jun 1875
	James L Barron 3 Jan 1879
	V Z Mixon 23 Dec 1880
	Grindy C Whitlow 28 Jan 1886
	James T Carson 20 Jul 1887
	James L Barron 6 Jan 1888
	Thomas M Blackwood 24 Sep 1890
Burk Place	John P Harrell 19 Jul 1880
	A J Harrell 24 Aug 1880
	William L Sprawls 9 Nov 1883
Mulberry	Elbert H Warren 19 Jul 1880
	Govener B Crawford 27 Jan 1881
	John H Blume 17 Nov 1882
	John H Blume 7 Dec 1882
	William H Brown 21 Apr 1890
	Napoleon B Williams 21 Nov 1891
Gibsland	Eliza J Reed 15 Jan 1883
	Thinalder F Parnell 19 May 1884

Taylor	Lawrence A Taylor 18 Sep 1883
Bulah	Lorenzo P Hamner 11 Feb 1884
	Charlie W Hamner 13 Apr 1886
	James C Christian 14 Apr 1891
	Bernhard H Stall 11 Jun 1891
Sandtree	John J Bridger 15 Aug 1884
	Elias Murphy 27 oct 1888
	John H Griffith 29 Apr 1892
Rabon	Hodge Rabon 29 Aug 1884
Nutmeg	David R Norman 3 Sep 1885
Armistead	William W Armistead 17 Jan 1886
Henry	Henry A Raborn 21 Apr 1887
	Mrs. Rebecca E Blume 6 Apr 1888
Grigsby	Joseph Grigsby 3 Aug 1887
	Theodore A Carson 6 Jan 1888
	Frank D Vernon 5 Oct 1888
Mount Olivet	A B Alexander 9 Feb 1888
	Mrs. Mary E Tait 14 Apr 1888
Disc 22 Aug 1889	
Sugar Creek	George W Sims 14 Jun 1888
Blume	Mrs. Rebecca E Blume 28 Jul 1888
Bienville	John A Nelson 17 Jul 1890
	Jesse Murphy 8 Sep 1890
Edna	John P Abel 30 Jun 1890
Disc 28 Sep 1891	
Brice	Martha V Brice 6 Mar 1891

	Charles W Hamner 30 Jul 1891
Mobley	John W Averett 23 Jan 1892
Moore	Robert B Moore 14 Mar 1892
Bear Creek	Judge R Clegg 6 Dec 1892

BOSSIER PARISH

Belllvue	F B Haynes 20 May 1873 John A Turner 3 Jul 1873 Thomas J Moore 10 Feb 1876 Percy Baker 5 Jun 1876 John C Lofton 21 Aug 1877 James H Cabeen 26 Apr 1886 Addie Head 15 Apr 1890 Sue Steele 8 Mar 1892
Benton	John J Scott 15 Oct 1872 Adam Simon 16 Aug 1875 William J McCray 25 Jul 1876 Thomas W Woodruff 23 Feb 1877 James B Woodruff Jr 4 Sep 1878 William R Prather 20 Jan 1880 Joseph E Adger 2 Mar 1880
Disc 19 Sep 1881 Reest 28 Nov 1881	George T Flemming 28 Nov 1881 Charles Kingsley 2 Jun 1884 Thomas M Vaughan 24 Jul 1892
Colesville	M J Cox 9 Feb 1872 (Illegible entry)
Dickson's Cross Roads	Alvin N Rounsevelt 22 Nov 1871 Joseph J B Kirk 1 Jul 1874 William A Martin 18 Jul 1882
Fillmore	A H Burns 17 Mar 1872 Elias F Connell 6 Jun 1873

	Elias F Connell 18 Nov 1873
	Edwin M Platt 19 Feb 1879
Disc 10 Jul 1881	
Knox Point	Thomas S Flemming 20 May 1873
	John R Moss 23 Sep 1874
	Samuel M Furniss 3 May 1875
	Joseph D Atkins 16 Apr 1877
	James W Atkins 24 Jul 1891
Rocky Mount	William A Martin 26 Apr 1871
	Rufus Sibley 2 Apr 1880
	William A Martin 26 Apr 1880
	Joseph B Kirk 18 Jul 1882
Red Chute	Joseph B Oneal 26 May 1879
Disc 27 Jan 1880	
Ash Point	Elaine S Dortch 22 Jul 1879
Red Land	William B Boggs 3 Nov 1879
	Lucy Baird 3 Sep 1890
	William C Rogers 2 Mar 1891
Mount Ebon	Rufus Sibley 31 May 1880
Disc 4 May 1881	
New Kansas	John W Rains 20 oct 1881
Disc 3 Jul 1882	
Midway	William E Farley 8 May 1882
	Thomas Lyles 10 Aug 1887
Ansel	Lucy Baird 3 Jul 1882
	Miss Katie E Stroud 3 Jul 1888
	Emma S McClellan 18 Jul 1890
	Lucy Baird 20 Jan 1891
Pickett	John Pickett 27 Jul 1882
Disc 30 Jan 1888	

Lawrenceville	Luther E McDade 3 Jul 1884
	Milus W Haughton 11 Sep 1884
Haughton	Milus W Haughton 6 Oct 1884
	James W Elston 17 Nov 1885
	Joseph W Elston 2 Dec 1885
Oak Hill	William J Linson 4 Jun 1886
Pandora	Hugh C Quarles 21 Jun 1886
Dixie	William A Martin 9 Jul 1886
Love's Mill	Thomas M Love 20 Apr 1887
Vanceville	Govan D Grayden 23 May 1887
	Robert L Carstarphen 2 Jul 1890
	Clinton O Gayle 8 Apr 1891
	George E Gilmer 27 Oct 1891
Hank's Mill	William R Sibley 11 May 1888
	William B Brooks 17 Dec 1888
	Cyrus H Gates 20 Jul 1890
Cottage Grove	John Pickett 2 Jul 1888
Plain Dealing	Miss Mary M McClenagham 7 Jul 1888
	Cunningham McClenagham 25 Sep 1889
Curtis	Antonio Curtis 10 Jul 1888
Brownlee	Charles B Wimbish 11 Mar 1880
Arkana	James B O'Neill 16 Apr 1890
Alden's Bridge	John Pickett 30 Jul 1890
	Irvin F Elder 18 Jul 1890
	(Rescinded per order 3 Sep 1890)

Carterville	William B Boggs 30 Jun 1890 Henry J Boggs 18 Jul 1890 William N Carter 7 oct 1891
Hughes' Spur	William C Hughes 15 Apr 1890
Mack's Bayou	John L Holmes 7 Jan 1891
Bossier City	Charles T Smith 7 May 1891
Ivan	Jasper B Whittington 4 Jul 1891
Bodeau	Frederick T Grounds 5 Oct 1891 Frederick T Grounds 14 Nov 1891
Roberta	Robert H Davis 25 Apr 1892

CADDO PARISH

Bayou La Chute	Joseph H Beard 1 Jul 1872 J S Webster 16 Jun 1880 Emma M Hanes 28 Jan 1886 John Nelson 2 Nov 1888 Mrs. Mary L Riggs 23 Jan 2889
Bridgeport Disc 9 Mar 1874	A F Tucker 3 Jul 1872
Greenwood	Michael Roth 1 Aug 1872 Samuel Bryson 12 Feb 1874 Mrs. Ellen Donley 25 Jul 1876 Miss Henrietta Herbeg 16 Dec 1879 Josephine Herbeg 10 May 1880 Eugene F Horton 7 Nov 1881 J G Jones 12 Feb 1891
Longwood	James H Parnell 19 Nov 1872 Andrew J Parnell 10 Sep 1878 W D Noel 9 Dec 1880 Thomas J Hearne 4 Aug 1881

	Elvin C Hearne 22 Oct 1883
Mooringsport	Mrs. Margaret A Croom 25 Apr 1870 Ransom T Cole 12 Dec 1873 William H B Croom 9 Mar 1876
Reisor	Andrew L Reisor 29 Sep 1889
Shreveport Courthouse	William McKenna 1 Apr 1873 (Pres & Sen) William McKenna 7 Apr 1874 (Pres & Sen) William McKenna 4 Aug 1882 (Pres & Sen) James C Soape 25 Sep 1886 (Pres) James C Soape 20 Dec 1886 (Pres & Sen) Thornton F Jacobs 13 Mar 1890 (Pres & Sen) Pinckney B Weaks 8 Feb 1892 (Pres & Sen)
Spring Ridge Disc 27 Sep 1881 Reest 17 Oct 1881	William W Sebastian 20 Dec 1871 William W Sebastian 17 Oct 1881
Jones Bayou Disc 2 Mar 1880	John P Painter 30 Jul 1874
Rose Hill Disc 27 Sep 1881	Wesley G Prather 3 Aug 1874 John S Gamblin 8 Mar 1875
Black Bayou	John R R Harrison 17 Aug 1874 John W Stallcup 18 Aug 1879 Charles C Hale 26 Sep 1879 Laura Stallcup 24 Mar 1880 S P Harrell 27 Apr 1885 Joseph Jernigan 15 Dec 1885 John Hardin 24 Apr 1886 Sallie S Hobbs 27 Apr 1891
Woodlawn Disc 18 Jun 1876 Reest 22 Aug 1877	Thomas S Flemming 12 Aug 1874 Milus W Haughton 29 Dec 1874 E R Connell 22 Aug 1877

Cross Lake   General L Lucar 10 Jul 1876
Disc 24 Oct 1878

Bethany   James M Trospher 22 Aug 1876
                          Vinklen H Gill 15 Apr 1884

River Dale   Josiah D Cawthon 3 May 1878
                          Charles D Jones 19 Nov 1878
                          Josiah D Cawthon 19 Jul 1881
Disc 16 Jul 1886

Frog Level   William C Spearman 11 Apr 1879
                          John B Spearman 10 Oct 1879
                          William C Spearman 10 Oct 1883
                          George H Harp 27 Dec 1888
                          Thomas R Simmons 27 Sep 1890
                          Benjamin F Nugent 27 Jul 1891
                          Benjamin F Nugent 24 Mar 1892

Villa Vista   William M Aiken 26 Sep 1879

Lawn Wood   Thomas D Elder 8 Mar 1880
Disc 8 Nov 1880
Reest 9 Dec 1880   W. L Bell 9 Dec 1880

Robson   William V Robson 13 May 1881

Garfield   George W Huckabay 16 Jan 1882
                          Harold H Huckabay 11 Jan 1886
                          Joseph T Ivins 2 May 1890

Flournoy   Patrick Carmody 12 Jun 1883

Hearrington   John C Hearrington 18 Mar 1884
Disc 23 Sep 1884

Jewella   Alva W Jewell 19 mar 1884

Cole's Store   Ransom T Cole 4 Sep 1884

Keithville	Perry P Keith 27 May 1885 Henry T Keith 16 Jun 1886
Dooley	Palmer Dickson 4 Aug 1885 Edward R Mooring 24 Sep 1885 Thomas R Gladney 7 Jun 1888 E O Watker 10 Mar 1890
Rush Point	Michael A Dickson 5 Aug 1885 James W Dickson 15 Mar 1890
Erwin	Thomas L House 15 Jun 1886 John L Gardner 17 Mar 1890
Danville	Donald Monroe 6 Jun 1887
Howard	John Nelson 14 Dec 1888
Hale	James M Hale 16 May 1890
Wild Lucia	William C Campbell 25 May 1890
Beach Disc 3 Sep 1891	Frank Bicknell 12 Sep 1890
Missionary	Walter E Ivey 22 Dec 1890
Latex	William C Blocker 27 Dec 1890

CALCASIEU PARISH

Hickory Flat Disc 6 Feb 1880 Reest 12 Apr 1880	James Cole 18 Oct 1872 Abner Cole 12 Sep 1880 Louis Doucet 14 Sep 1880 Seth B Singleton 29 Jun 1883 Joseph Chenier 6 Feb 1884 Milton L Bihm 11 Jun 1884

Lake Arthur	Delino Derouen 24 May 1870
	Felix Laurents 13 Aug 1887
	Alexander P Hebert 16 Apr 1888
	Joseph H Shively 18 Nov 1889
	Maria Agnes Lee 5 Mar 1891
	Clement W Gorman 10 Oct 1891
	Henry B Wright 5 Oct 1892
Lake Charles Courthouse	Charvey Barbe 13 Aug 1869
	William meyer 13 Apr 1872
	Daniel H Reese 16 Nov 1876
	William D Mearns 4 Jun 1879
	W H Haskell 24 Feb 1881
	J B Kirkman 29 Aug 1881 (Declined)
	Thomas B Ferren 12 Sep 1881
	William D Mearns 26 Feb 1883 (Pres & Sen)
	Mary J Leveque 12 jan 1886 (Pres & Sen)
	Dennis M Foster 11 Feb 1890 (Pres & Sen)
Nibbet's Bluff	Samuel A Fairchild 21 Apr 1873
	Jacob Humble 28 Apr 1882
Disc 3 Jan 1884	
Rose Bluff	Oliver R Moss 7 Jun 1873
Disc 5 Mar 1883	
Wood's Bluff	Jerisan Broussard 12 Jun 1873
Disc 12 Sep 1873	
Sugartown	Henry C Farquhar 28 Oct 1873
	George W Richardson 10 Jul 1885
Big Woods	Benjamin B Saxon 22 Jun 1874
	David A Lyons 27 Jun 1876
	George W Roberts 14 Feb 1877
Disc 5 Aug 1878	
West Fork	Allen J Perkins 21 Sep 1874
	James K Perkins 4 May 1875
Disc 19 Jul 1876	

Barnes Creek Disc 19 Jun 1876	Hiram C Lyles 29 oct 1874 Henry A Williams 4 May 1875
Dry Creek	Levi A Miller 3 Nov 1874 George W Heard 4 Jan 1883 Norman J Perry 25 Aug 1891 Joseph T Kent 29 Apr 1892
Lakassine Disc 24 Aug 1877	Pierre A Hebert 7 Dec 1874
Philip's Bluff Disc 21 Jan 1878 Reest 16 Jul 1878	Henry F Myers 26 Jul 1876 Edgar L Riddick 11 Jun 1877 Eych Clement 16 Jul 1878 Martha A E Moore 9 Oct 1884
The Bay	Hugh B Thompson 9 oct 1876 William T Dunn 27 Dec 1890
Lyons Disc 3 Sep 1878	John F Davidson 8 Aug 1877
Meadows	Isaac S Meadows 11 Dec 1879 Laban Wingate 29 Feb 1884 Henry A Knight 9 Feb 1885
Lacasine Note: Late Lakassine	Coleman D Welsh 31 Mar 1880 Louis Lorrain 9 Feb 1885
China	William Jackson 6 Jul 1880 Miss Lucinda Jackson 18 Aug 1880 Benjamin F Carr 30 Jan 1888 Isaac Griffith 5 May 1888 Frank McVey 26 Feb 1892
Pinchburg	Louis E Mazilly 26 Aug 1880 Shivene S Andues 4 Feb 1886

	Edward B Wright 29 Jul 1886
	Edward B Wright 1 Sep 1886
Soileau	James Cole 5 Oct 1880
	Joseph D Lafleur 7 My 1888
	William L Davis 22 Aug 1888
	Jethro Thompson 16 oct 1889
	Charles W Staneart 6 Aug 1890
Edgerly	John F Davidson 2 Oct 1880
	Edward J Fairchild 23 Mar 1888
Calcasieu	August Johnson 8 Nov 1880
Jennings	Andrew D McFarlain 29 Nov 1880
	Delino Derouen 11 Aug 1885
	Andrew D McFarlain 17 May 1889
	John H Roberts 17 Jun 1889
Merryville	Moses E Frazar 30 Nov 1881
	James E McMahon 14 Feb 1889
Hardy Disc 7 Jan 1884	Hardy C Gill 24 Oct 1882
Pearl	Joseph J Kingrey 4 May 1883
	Samson R Kingrey 21 Aug 1891
Loretta	Ethelbert L Cannon 1 Feb 1883
Welsh	Coleman D Welsh 18 Sep 1883
	Lee E Robinson 23 Aug 1889
Sabine Station	Joseph H Jackson 7 Nov 1883
	Edwin F M Fairchild 24 May 1887
	James H Jackson 30 Sep 1889
Sulphur City Disc 31 Jul 1884	Frederick W Schinkoth 15 Feb 1884
Reest 2 Feb 1885	John A Vincent 2 Feb 1885

	John T Henning 1 Feb 1886
	Eli A Perkins 2 Dec 1880
Bryan	William F Perkins 11 Aug 1885
	Fredericka G Perkins 4 Dec 1888
Oaklin Spring	George Wilcocks 12 jan 1886
	Joseph Chenier 8 Jun 1888
	Samuel C Poole 25 Nov 1891
Serpent	Sevrin Langley 18 May 1886
	Octave Gaidry 13 Oct 1891
Hellinger Disc 20 Sep 1887	Joseph Hellinger 2 Jul 1886
Ten Mile	Archey C R Turner 21 Sep 1886
	James I Hamilton 12 Mar 1891
Canton	James N Strother 30 Sep 1886
	Ernest Lafleur 2 Apr 1891
Bear	Joseph W Barrow 18 Feb 1887
	John Hill 24 Jan 1891
	William M Young 14 Sep 1891
Beckworth	William R Davis 18 Feb 1887
Gay	William F Fargue 18 Feb 1887
Iola	Thomas E Wingate 26 Feb 1887
	Samuel Biven 17 Apr 1888
Burissa	George W Ford 7 Jun 1887
Vincent	Nathaniel Vincent 12 Aug 1887
Iowa	Mrs. Eliza A Williamson 24 Mar 1888
	Elmer J Johnson 22 Aug 1888
	James Storer 22 Oct 1889

Ledoux Disc 5 Nov 1890	Ozette Ledoux 25 Apr 1888
Thompson	Ignace Redriques 10 Jul 1888
Cleveland Disc 18 Nov 1889	Harry S Bridges 21 Aug 1888
Vinton	Ezekial P Melwick 10 Sep 1888
West Lake Note: Late Bryan	Fredericka A Perkins 31 Jan 1889 Fredericka A Perkins 23 Nov 1889
Pine Vill	James D Standfield 4 Feb 1889 Larkin M Mims 1 Apr 1890
Easterly	Michael Funk 17 Jun 1889
Pickett	Christianna L Pickett 2 Aug 1889
Jacksonville	James H Jackson 3 Apr 1890
Simmons	Albert Burnett 24 Mar 1890
Oberlin	Charles Powers 16 Apr 1890 Harvey L Rice 22 Sep 1890 Lula M Evans 25 oct 1890 Harvey L Rice 22 Dec 1890 Elizabeth A Paul 24 Jul 1891
Mystic	John T Davidson 15 May 1890
Breland	William G Breland 6 Sep 1890
Crown Point	James Ellis 6 Sep 1890 Ivan A Perkins 21 Mar 1891
Edgerly	Edward J Fairchild 14 May 1891

Raymond	Henry M Brown 27 Jun 1891
Johnson	William C Johnson 13 Jul 1891

CALDWELL PARISH

Alpha	Alexander Morrison 19 Dec 1872 John B Hargrove 26 Jan 1874 Washington Harrington 17 Jan 1876 Nathan M Davis 3 Apr 1876 James W Dunn 23 Jun 1880
Disc 21 Jul 1880	
Columbia Courthouse	Emanuel Dreyfus 23 Aug 1872 Marquis L Meredith 25 Nov 1880 John A Dowden 27 mar 1874 Mrs. Rebecca S Lombard 13 Oct 1874 R Smith Slemons 8 Dec 1874 F M Thornhill 11 oct 1875 John M Bagley 8 Nov 1875 Thomas R Verbois 10 May 1876 Archibald J McKeithen 26 Feb 1879 William A Bozone 14 May 1883 Epoline Sizemore 13 Jun 1890
Copenhagen	John S Davis 9 Aug 1871 Benjamin N Humphries 11 Sep 1877 Mrs. Elizabeth Wade 28 Dec 1884 Miss Lilly Seiler 21 Jan 1885 Mrs. Mary F Smith 10 Mar 1887
Disc 27 Feb 1892	
Cotton Plant	Aurelius S Hundley 17 Apr 1873 Thomas B Butler 3 jan 1878 James Estess 14 Mar 1878
Disc 16 oct 1882 Reest 31 Mar 1884	William H Hines 31 Mar 1884 Mattie A Hines 24 Oct 1884 Sallie E Bolton 24 Apr 1890 Asa M Meredith 29 Feb 1892

Mount Pleasant
Disc 11 Dec 1873
Reest 9 Jan 1875

Malachi B Thomas 13 Jan 1873

Stephen M Cade 9 Jun 1875
Samuel Gregory 31 Jan 1876
Levy Banks 4 Feb 1880

Pine Bluff
Disc 28 Oct 1874

Stephen Williams 26 Nov 1872

Waverly

Mrs. Emeline D Perkins 5 Aug 1870
F A Glass 27 Mar 1874
James M Bennett 28 Jul 1874

Eureka

James M Bennett 10 Aug 1874
Jeptha R Collins 3 Jan 1878
Mary D Bennett 16 Jun 1879

Castor

James A Webb 17 Mar 1873
Emile V Ferrand 21 Aug 1877

Disc 10 Sep 1879

Callton

Orrin Call 6 Jun 1876

Boeuf River

Louis F Turner 6 Nov 1877
Sarah E Turner 3 Jan 1878

Disc 9 May 1878
Reest 20 Jun 1878

Peter Recoulley 20 Jun 1878
Leopold P Brandin 3 Feb 1880

Hogan's Landing

Henry Haas 25 Jun 1878
Leona Drake 29 Jan 1881

Maud

Thomas J Webb 1 Dec 1880
Stephen M Cade 15 Jan 1884
Joseph p Coates 6 Dec 1888

Marshall
Disc 13 Sep 1881

Thomas J Brodway 15 Nov 1880

Andalusia	Lewis C Prickard 4 Apr 1881
	Columbus C Myers 5 Mar 1883
Disc 29 Dec 1886	
Holum	Mary A Lowe 20 Feb 1881
Disc 26 Jul 1883	
Reest 18 Jun 1886	William Hanchey 18 Jun 1886
	Henry Hays 12 Feb 1889
	Lucie K Babcock 13 Aug 1890
Sinope	Horace B Powell 17 Nov 1881
Rodolph	Charles R Benson 20 Dec 1883
	Albert Mixon 14 Mar 1888
Glenn Ella	James M Adair 9 Jul 1886
Fredericksburg	Lycurgus H Wooten 14 May 1890
Emory	Archibald J McKeithen 3 oct 1890
Blankston	Joe S Swift 30 Jun 1891
	William J Webb 27 Nov 1891
Grayson	John G Keller 25 Nov 1891
Armston	Nathan H Hester 17 Oct 1892

CAMERON PARISH

Cameron	Samuel P Henry 31 Jan 1873
	Harriet I Henry 16 Jan 1880
Leesburg	James M Lacy 9 Jun 1873
Disc 15 Dec 1873	
Grand Chenier	James C Suttles 22 Oct 1875
Disc 21 Apr 1879	
Reest 2 Jun 1879	Emanuel Sturlese 2 Jun 1879
	Alcide Miller 4 Dec 1890

Johnson's Bayou	Joseph B Pevoto 5 Dec 1877
	John J Eddleman 9 Dec 1878
Disc 3 Nov 1886	
Reest 15 Jan 1887	Frederick Erbelding 15 Jan 1887
Radford	William H Eddleman 20 Nov 1885
Disc 12 Jul 1887	
Reest 10 Dec 1890	August Pavell 10 Dec 1890
Grand Lake	Fenelon Dreuen 28 Jan 1888
	Josephina Poughel 29 Feb 1892
Hackberry	Jacob A Elender 28 Jan 1888
	Mary A Elender 5 Oct 1888
Ledoux	Osite Ledoux 25 Apr 1888
Shell Bank	Ferdinand Pavell 19 Nov 1889
Creole	Norbert LeBoeuf 24 Mar 1890
	Benoni Weber 19 Jun 1891
Lakeside	Peter K Miller 24 Jul 1880

EAST CARROLL PARISH

Caledonia	Simon Witkouski 23 Jan 1873
Delhi	Calvin H Moore 15 Jan 1873
Floyd	Andrew Donnan 18 Dec 1871
	William H Stroube 2 Feb 1874
	F H Taylor 12 Jan 1876
	William A Hedrick 29 Aug 1879
	J Taylor Jackson 19 Jun 1882

Illawana	Henry Hinson 22 Oct 1872 George Rhodes 9 Jun 1873 Felix R Bartholemy 25 Nov 1873 Emanuel Mouser 10 Apr 1877 Richard N Rea 14 Apr 1881 Joseph Block 12 Nov 1885 S C Brown 21 Dec 1888 Samuel H Mobberly 29 Aug 1889
India	Rolla W Wyatt 11 Mar 1873 George S Owen 25 Nov 1873
Lake Providence	Charles H Nash 15 Jan 1872 M Shelby Powell 10 May 1875 Charles E Shearer 6 Jan 1876 Isaac L Lewis 10 Jul 1876 Isaac L Lewis 28 Jun 1877 Sterling C Austin 5 Aug 1878 Robert L Jones 16 Jul 1879 Thomas J Galbert 6 Apr 1881 Robert L Jones 14 Feb 1882 F H G Taylor 28 Apr 1885
Oak Grove	Enoch Farmer 1 Jul 1872 H J Cheatham 20 Aug 1878 Leon C Massingill 29 Oct 1878
Transylvania Disc 29 oct 1874	Richard T Keene 31 Oct 1872
Vista Ridge Disc 6 May 1879	John Miller 29 Aug 1870 Thomas W Mann 22 Aug 1877
Henderson	Albert C Rhoton 15 Apr 1873 William M Aiken 14 Nov 1878

Wilson's Point	M Dreyfus 14 Aug 1874
	Frederick R Holbrook 21 Feb 1876
	Albert Dreyfus 12 Jul 1876
	James F Redmond 19 Jul 1877
	William M McCullough 25 Nov 1878
	James F Redmond 4 Aug 1882
	George A Palmer 7 Jan 1884
	William Lewis 24 Jan 1884
	John S Greenwood 26 May 1884
	Richard M McIlie 21 Jul 1886
	James J Robinson 2 Mar 1891
Pilcher's Point	George S Owen 17 Aug 1875
India	James Andrews 14 Aug 1876
	George S Owen 4 Apr 1879
	Charles F Hall 10 May 1883
	George S Owen 5 Nov 1885
Villa Vista	William M Aiken 26 Sep 1879
	George R Aiken 25 Jun 1883
	Joseph A Craig 14 Dec 1883
	Robert Nicholson 19 Apr 1886
Aston	Henry L Newcomb 11 Jul 1881
	Burton L Settoon 7 Mar 1884
	Julius Witkouski 21 Aug 1884
	A Judson Thompson 4 Dec 1884
	James Imboden 27 May 1885
	Henry L Newcomb 1 Mar 1887
	James S Semple 19 Oct 1889
	Albert W Bivens 10 Feb 1892
Brunett	Edward Jackson 13 Jun 1882
	Robert H Hamlin 11 Jun 1884
	Robert H Hamlin 9 Mar 1885
	Philip D Quays 30 Jul 1890
Benham	William G Benham 19 Jan 1889
	Mrs. Carrie F Benham 19 Jan 1890

	John F Graves 8 May 1891
	Andrew M Nelson 3 Mar 1892
Robertdale	Philip D Quays 22 Dec 1884
	Robert H Hamlin 30 Jul 1890
Temple	Andrew J Thompson 17 Apr 1886
Disc 3 Nov 1886	
Epps	Thad Lindsey 10 Jul 1888
	Stouton E McMichael 4 Dec 1888
Shelborn	Flournoy B Davis 29 May 1891

CATAHOULA PARISH

Aimwell	M H Thompson 9 Jan 1873
Disc 11 May 1874	
Reest 2 Jul 1878	Stephen S Ford 2 Jul 1878
Disc 20 Feb 1886	
Reest 29 Jan 1887	Reubin M Beasley 29 Apr 1887
	Reubin M Beasley 22 Dec 1891
Enterprise	Patrick H Carter 7 Aug 1871
	Henry G Baughman 15 Jul 1880
	Patrick H Carter 10 Sep 1880
Funny Louis	Martha Cockerham 9 Apr 1867
	James M Adair 20 Oct 1873
	Edwin W Yancey 27 Mar 1874
	Uriah T Whatley 22 Oct 1877
Disc 6 Feb 1878	
Reest 15 May 1878	William V Taylor 15 May 1878
	John S Paul 19 Mar 1880
	Isaac R Adams 29 Aug 1881
Green's Creek	Thomas E Richard 2 May 1872
Disc 1 Apr 1874	
Harrisonburg Courthouse	William E Robb 27 Jan 1873

	James C White 22 Jan 1877
	Edward Dosher 31 May 1877
	John H Carter 11 Sep 1879
Jena	James Forsythe 19 Dec 1872
	Harmon Browning 3 Sep 1874
	Jacob H Ringgold 4 Jun 1877
	William C Coleman 6 Aug 1887
	Charles R W Brown 30 Aug 1888
	Shep B Hanes 1 Nov 1889
Kirk's Ferry	Ransom Hall 26 Jun 1872
	John D Usher 29 Jan 1878
	Nathan Fass 3 Mar 1879
	(Illegible entry)
	Stephen N Sojourner 19 Dec 1887
	F A Jones Jr 7 Nov 1890
	Benjamin E Carter 13 Dec 1890
	Warren W Gilbert 5 Dec 1891
Little Prarie	Michael Beard 3 Jun 1872
Disc 6 Apr 1874	
Parkham's	
Disc 3 May 1875	James B Wiggington 29 Jan 1873
Reest 18 Jun 1875	Howard J Moreland 18 Jun 1875
Disc 13 Nov 1876	
Reest 5 May 1878	William G Bruce 5 May 1878
	William F Miller 7 Apr 1879
	Joseph E Montgomery 6 Jan 1882
	Alonzo F Mardis 19 Dec 1882
	Abner R Mardis 19 Jul 1886
	William F Miller 26 May 1888
	Joseph N Thomas 20 Mar 1873
Pisgah	Joseph N Thomas 20 Mar 1873
Rosefield	H C Parker 22 Apr 1873
	(Illegible entry)
	Robert W Flowers 1 Nov 1885

Sicily Island	Miss Sallie E Lovelace 26 Aug 1872
	Mrs. Sallie E Stone 4 Jan 1877
	Mrs. Florence Curry 3 Mar 1877
	Richard H Harris 14 May 1877
	Mrs. Laura R Enright 12 May 1879
	John G Kostmayer 15 Dec 1880
	Amy L Peck 20 Feb 1883
	John Higgins 4 Sep 1883
	R E Holstein 11 Sep 1883
	Mary A Holstein 30 Oct 1883
	Elizabeth Smith 22 Apr 1884
White Sulphur Springs	Mrs. Sallie E Lovelace 5 Nov 1872
	William E Spence 10 Feb 1879
	George W Bethard 6 Apr 1880
	John Enright 29 Jul 1886
	Mary V Bethard 12 Nov 1887
Wildwood	Frank J Bowman 26 Jul 1872
	Henrietta E Bowman 17 Jan 1877
	Charles O Bowman 16 Feb 1888
	Henrietta E Bowman 22 Jan 1891
Trinity	Leopold Moritz 29 Jan 1873
	Bernard Moritz 17 Feb 1879
	John H McCabe 11 May 1883
	Emile Enete 6 Jun 1883
	Caspar H Fulgaar 31 Jul 1884
	Hugh Watson 14 Sep 1886
	Philip Crooks 9 Nov 1886
	Frank O Worster 22 May 1891
	Emma E Snyder 16 Mar 1892
Eden	Phineas Whatley 7 Jul 1873
Disc 1 Apr 1874	
Reest 15 Feb 1882	William R Whatley 15 Feb 1882
Manifest	Joseph N Thomas 19 Jan 1874
	Benjamin Huffman Jr 1 Dec 1874

	Francis M Taylor 21 Jan 1878
	John W Heard 30 Jan 1878
	William N Cooper 22 Oct 1879
	William R Webb 17 Feb 1880
	Marion C Blackman 14 Apr 1882
	Joseph N Thomas 24 Jun 1883
	John W Heard 25 Sep 1883
Disc 30 Jan 1888	
Reest 24 May 1888	Ruben N Streagall 24 May 1888
	Jacob G Womack 17 Aug 1889
Castor Sulphur Springs	Joseph J McQuatters 3 Mar 1875
	George Jackson 14 Jun 1875
	Joseph J McQuatters 19 Jul 1875
	Robert S Slemons 11 Oct 1875
	Commodore P Keith 16 Jun 1876
	John M Kees 24 Mar 1884
	Frank M Mills 25 Aug 1884
Security	James Smith 20 Dec 1875
	Charles J Montgomery 17 Jun 1878
	James Cook Jr 24 Nov 1880
	Benjamin Campbell 17 Jun 1881
	James Cook Jr 26 Mar 1883
	Emanuel Livingston 18 Feb 1887
	Whitlock Norment 16 May 1888
Stark's Landing	Mrs. A E Allen 15 Feb 1876
Disc 21 Feb 1877	
Stafford Point	David Stafford 16 Jul 1877
Gludo?	Michael J Beard 22 Aug 1877
Disc 21 Apr 1879	
Reest 5 Jun 1879	(Illegible entry)
	Noah Reddick 31 May 1881
	Michael J Beard 22 Jun 1886
	Mrs. Effie M Beard 19 Nov 1888
Troyville	Robert B Walters 17 Jun 1878

	William P Cherry 21 Oct 1881
	William P Cherry 11 Sep 1883
Davis	John Randolph Binow 5 Mar 1879
	Thomas M Butler 8 Jul 1884
	William V Taylor 10 Jul 1886
Leland	James E Kipes 23 Jun 1879
	Elizabeth P Smith 9 Jan 1882
	Ann E Smith 23 Feb 1882
Disc 19 Jan 1883	
Reest 4 Sep 1888	Edward F Keenan 4 Sep 1888
	Pleasant L Miles 11 Mar 1890
	Conrad Weilenman 29 Jan 1892
Cades	Aladan Broussard 25 Jul 1881
Rhinehart	S T Yancey 4 Aug 1881
	Jonathan N Luce 31 May 1882
	Langston Yancey 26 Mar 1886
Lavacca	Mary E Bannerman 26 Oct 1881
Routon	Robert W Crews 28 Sep 1883
Tooleys	Matilda C Frisler 27 Mar 1884
Simmons	John W Simmons 7 May 1886
Disc 10 Jun 1887	
Utility	Samuel L Dale 20 Aug 1876
	William H Waters 7 May 1890
Prohibition	Marquis D L Andrews 29 Sep 1886
Jack	Jackson E Cockerham 2 Aug 1888
Disc 5 Nov 1890	
Jonesville	William P Cherry 3 Aug 1888

Summerville	Isaac R Adams 25 Sep 1891
Tullos	Cornelius G Dempsey 7 May 1891

CLAIBORNE PARISH

Arizona	Joel S Morris 7 Jan 1873 James W Corry 8 Dec 1873 Benjamin F Beard 26 Oct 1874
Athens	Thomas A Wilborn 13 May 1873 Francis Henry 27 Dec 1873 Albert L Atkins 10 Aug 1875 George W Beck 18 May 1876 Albert L Atkins 25 Sep 1877 Thomas W Brooks 30 Dec 1878 Thomas B Wallace 1 Mar 1880 Francis Henry 4 Apr 1881 Albert L Atkins 11 Sep 1881 James T Baker 15 Jan 1883
Cane Ridge Disc 11 Dec 1873 Reest 1 Sep 1876	George W Lowrey 15 Jan 1872 Andrew J Williams 1 Sep 1876 George W Lowrey 9 Jul 1890
Coleman Disc 7 Jul 1874	James F Ford 18 Jan 1872
Gordon	William D Anderson 2 Dec 1872 Jesse A Anderson 13 Sep 1880 William R Manning 8 Jul 1886
Haynesville	R F Hardaway 21 Jan 1873 James C Taylor 20 Oct 1873 William L Phillips 1 Sep 1876 Joseph Taylor 27 Jun 1877 John A Brooks 1 Apr 1878 Joseph Taylor 20 May 1878 John G Warren 19 Jan 1880

	William Y Dawson 12 Nov 1888
	John M Henry 12 May 1891
Homer Courthouse	Datus W Harris 15 Jan 1872
	William W Brown 2 Feb 1887
	Mrs. Etta V Boring 15 Jun 1889
Knoxville Disc 28 Aug 1874	Miss Georgia Knox 21 Nov 1866
Lisbon	David A J Carruthers 30 Sep 1872
	Olney W Meadows 17 Jan 1876
	A B Boykin 29 Aug 1877
	Olney W Meadows 8 Oct 1877
Scottville	Edward F Williams 20 Nov 1872
	George W Eskew 15 Apr 1874
	Robert E Thompson 14 Apr 1875
	Atlas M Thornton 1 Jun 1875
Disc 22 Aug 1877	
Summerfield	Albert L Harper 19 Nov 1872
	Paul T Talbot 18 Aug 1879
	N Wise 23 Aug 1880
	John W Harper 21 Oct 1881
	Albert L Harper 7 Nov 1881
	John W Harper 29 Jul 1886
	Milton A Talbot 2 Aug 1888
Holly Springs	William H Maxey 29 Aug 1876
Ward's Mills	Alfred J Ward 4 Jun 1879
Blackburn	Washington W King 21 Oct 1879
	John H King 25 Nov 1891
Aycock	Elias G Thomas 27 Apr 1881
	Walton Wilson 10 Mar 1887
Tulip	Benjamin F Marsalis 22 Jun 1884

Disc 1 May 1888

Dykesville	Alexander N Garland 30 Apr 1886
	William J Garland 8 Aug 1889
Dawson	Alonzo H Dawson 22 Sep 1886
Disc 10 Jan 1887	
Millerton	Hugh Miller 26 Sep 1886
Langston	Robert Langston 4 Apr 1887
Sugar Creek	George W Sims 14 Jun 1888
	Frank T Taylor 12 Apr 1890
Marsalis	James T Barnette 6 Jul 1888
Weldon	Charles A Wade 30 Aug 1888
Antioch	John B Williams 15 Feb 1889
Max	John W McFarland 28 May 1890
State Line	James Thomas Waller 3 Jun 1890
	James W Beckett 11 Dec 1890
Orono	John W McFarland 2 Aug 1890
Owens	Daniel P Owens 19 Sep 1890
Relief	Leonidas C Bolin 21 Aug 1891
Bethlehem	James H Maddry 30 Oct 1891
Gilgal	James M Norman 12 Feb 1892

CONCORDIA PARISH

Black Hawk	James Pullin 27 Aug 1872
	William L Shaw 12 Jul 1877

	Edward Pullin 9 Feb 1880
	Berthold Lehmann 15 May 1882
	Edward Pullin 28 Jan 1884
	Edgar F Pipes 15 Jun 1888
	Albert F Collins 18 Apr 1890
	William O Bunch 27 Jan 1891
Bullitt's Bayou	John C Seaman 26 Feb 1872
	John D Usher 29 Dec 1887
	Vinton F Seaman 11 May 1888
	John D Hart 21 Jun 1888
Fairview	William T Lewis 19 Feb 1873
	M T Tolbert 10 Nov 1873
Disc 16 Jan 1874	
Reest 7 Jan 1875	Joseph M Craig 7 Jan 1875
	William G Walton 14 Dec 1883
	Joseph D Miller 18 Jun 1887
Frogmore	William D Scofield 17 Mar 1873
	Ralph P Miller 27 Mar 1874
	Manuel Guiu 25 Jun 1874
	Robert Oakman 30 Oct 1874
	Jonas Marx 13 Sep 1875
	(Illegible entry)
	Benjamin T Wade 5 Jun 1886
Shamrock	John F Dameron 3 Feb 1873
Tooley's	John F Tooley 3 Jun 1872
	Mrs. Matilda Tusler 27 Mar 1874
Vidalia Courthouse	Walter G Kalow 12 Aug 1872
	John A Washington 20 Oct 1873
	Justus H Schauf 15 May 1876
	Jacob Schiele 4 Dec 1879
	Harry G Meng 16 Jul 1882
	Bettie W Evans 17 Oct 1883
	Bettie W E Vernon 12 Jun 1884
	Thomas Brady 10 Nov 1885

	Isadore Lemle 18 May 1889
River's Landing	Hugh G Snead 22 Aug 1873
	Raphael Rosenthal 1 Jun 1876
	G H Green 8 Oct 1880
	Karl Lehmann 24 Nov 1880
Lake St. John	John F Damerson 10 Jan 1876
	John Spires 29 Mar 1876
Bougere	Frank Bougere 18 Sep 1876
Disc 6 Oct 1877	
Reest 6 Feb 1878	William G Walton 6 Feb 1878
	Polk Smith 8 Jan 1880
Disc 13 Oct 1881	
Reest 3 Mar 1882	George L Walton 3 May 1882
	George L Walton 30 Oct 1883
	Chris Stevens 4 Nov 1889
	John K Skipworth 12 Mar 1890
Sisemore	Jonathan C Taylor 16 Jul 1877
	Nancy E Taylor 9 Nov 1877
	Thomas S Hooper 8 Mar 1879
	George C Burrill 11 Aug 1882
	Mrs. Eugenia Phillips 14 Jul 1888
	Albert G Campbell 1 Sep 1890
Flowery Mount	Thomas H Ester 16 Jul 1877
	Fountain L Campbell 12 Feb 1878
	Seaborn M Campbell 13 Jan 1880
New Era	Solomon Harris 21 Oct 1877
Union Point	Isaac Lemle 21 May 1878
Disc 19 Aug 1879	
Gibson's Landing	Aaron Stanton 28 May 1878
	James H Scott 7 Aug 1883
	Beverly B Parham 13 Jan 1885
	J Oscar Bailey 14 Jun 1888

	James T Welch 23 May 1890
Bowie's Point Disc 3 Jan 1879	Philip Wesler 8 Jun 1878
Acme Disc 20 Jul 1880 Reest 15 Oct 1890	Mrs. Elizabeth Pecanty 18 Nov 1878 Mrs. Elizabeth Pecanty 15 Oct 1890
Lemargris	Peter H O'Ferrell 16 Jun 1880
Lemarque	Peter H O'Ferrell 3 Sep 1880 Thomas O Green 21 Oct 1886
Trivia	Peter H O'Ferrell 1 Dec 1880 John M Clayton 11 May 1888
Buie Disc 17 Feb 1885	Sigmon Zuzak 28 Jan 1884
Lehmann	Karl Lehmann 1 Aug 1884
Moreville	Samuel B Yeager 20 Nov 1885 Michael Beyusdorfer 8 May 1888 John C Lindsay 8 Mar 1890 James O Bailey 16 Feb 1891
Rivers	Frank H Smith 26 May 1886 John D Hart 15 Feb 1887
Morton Disc 29 Dec 1888	Frank Morton 10 Jul 1886 Mrs. Kettie Morton 26 Mar 1886 Louis Marks 18 May 1887
Eva	Nathan Calhoun 21 Jun 1886
Nock's Disc 14 Jun 1889	William J Nock 29 Jun 1888

Monterey	Louis F Broussard 27 May 1889 Samuel P Crane 27 Dec 1890
Rosenthal	Douglas L Rivers 28 May 1889 Henrietta Rosenthal 12 May 1890
Serena	Susie S Jackson 18 Sep 1889
Cross	John S Cross 1 Nov 1889 Frederick Schleicher 25 Jan 1891 Adolph Schleicher 20 Feb 1892
Morton Station	J M Dixon 16 Apr 1890

DE SOTO PARISH

Keatchie	William G Spilker 11 Mar 1873
Logansport	Robert H Alston 26 Mar 1867 Alfred M Garrett 26 Apr 1875 R J Alexander 12 Mar 1890 Cunningham C Chatham 4 Apr 1890
Longstreet	Matthew M Moore 18 Jun 1869 William J Headrick 19 Apr 1875 C W Cater 22 Nov 1875 John F Norris 8 Feb 1876 A W Jordan 29 Oct 1877 Wiley E Carter 11 Feb 1878 Victoria L White 31 Mar 1886 James E Cagburn 5 Mar 1887 William A Smith 6 Mar 1888 T Lafayette Aycock 17 Sep 1888 R J Aycock 9 Jun 1890 Elbert Bishop 13 Jan 1891
Mansfield Courthouse	William M Allen 12 Dec 1870 Mrs. Harriet Dewess 28 Sep 1874 R T Carr 8 May 1875 William B Taylor 27 Aug 1875

Pleasant Hill	Zachariah Blackmon 15 Jun 1871
	Henry J Davis 12 Dec 1873
	William D Gooch 29 Dec 1881
	Irwin T Harrell 30 Nov 1882
Sunny South	Nathaniel A Stamper 14 Jan 1874
Disc 17 May 1875	
Reest 13 Oct 1879	Sterling E Russ 13 Oct 1879
Disc 16 Sep 1880	
Lula	James Jackson 29 May 1878
	Robert L Pollard 15 Jun 1881
Fierson's Mill	David J Frierson 21 Aug 1878
Kingston	Mitchell J Scott 29 Oct 1878
	Robert B Frierson 23 Aug 1881
Disc 27 Sep 1881	
Reest 28 Oct 1881	Robert B Frierson 28 Oct 1881
	Robert E Scott 25 Feb 1884
Stonewall	Matt A Murphy 6 Nov 1878
	John M Nelson 26 Jul 1880
	E L Ford 20 Mar 1883
	Nellie E Ford 9 Apr 1883
	James P Ratliff 30 Mar 1885
Tulip	Petty H Ricks 8 Jun 1880
Disc 15 Apr 1881	
Grand Cane	John B Poston 19 Sep 1881
	James B Walker 23 Mar 1885
	Jeptha F Walker 25 Nov 1890
Cook	John T Prude 30 Nov 1881
Gloster	James L Sheridan 4 Nov 1881
	Charles D Perry 19 Dec 1882
	Thomas E McWhiney 5 Apr 1886

Lassiter	Wiley D Lassiter 27 Mar 1882
	Susan A Murphy 13 Mar 1884
Oxford	Susan A Murphy 24 Nov 1885
	Thomas Steele 20 Jun 1886
Naborton	Mrs. Mary L Nabors 3 Nov 1886
	John H Nabors 11 Jan 1887
Pelican	William R Carroll 11 Dec 1876
	Eugene L Joyner 25 Feb 1891
Blanchard	John A Hunter 18 Nov 1886
	Richard C Ettredge 28 Jan 1889
Hewitt	J E Hewitt 10 Apr 1888
	J G Glover 17 Apr 1888
Waddill	John D Mahaffy 11 May 1888
	Mollie A Mahaffy 10 Apr 1891
Carmel	Anastase Peters 6 Feb 1890
Grace	Isadore A Tucker 2 May 1890
	Willis G Sikes 31 Jul 1891
	William L Parker 1 Mar 1892
Butler	Thomas F Butler 16 Jun 1890
Pottsville	Paul M Potts 30 Jun 1890
Sayers	William M Sayers 22 Jul 1891

EAST BATON ROUGE PARISH

Baton Rouge Courthouse	John O'Connor 5 Apr 1869 (Pres & Sen)
	John O'Connor 17 Mar 1873 (Pres & Sen)
	S H Schoonmaker 20 Dec 1881 (Pres & Sen)

	Alexander Smith 18 Dec 1884 (Pres & Sen) E L D Conrad 26 Feb 1887 (Pres & Sen) Oscar H Forman 29 Oct 1889 (Pres) Alexander J McGregor 12 May 1890 (Pres & Sen) Charles G Pages 10 Apr 1876 (Pres & Sen) John O'Connor 27 Aug 1877 (Pres & Sen) Alexander Smith 22 Oct 1890 (Pres & Sen) Alexander Smith 27 Jan 1891 (Pres & Sen)
Hope Villa	Andrew B Booth 17 Mar 1873 James D Kenton 6 Jun 1881 James S Webster 30 Jun 1884 Joseph D Kenton 27 Jan 1886 Winnie Booth 18 Nov 1889
Magnolia	Daniel Morgan 8 Nov 1872 George W Dearing 21 Aug 1877 Robert H Pruyn 8 Aug 1881 Robert E Ambrose 21 Dec 1882 John S Powers 18 Sep 1888 Joseph A Impson 1 Jun 1891
Strong Point	Ezra J Stillman 23 Oct 1871 Fred Weiss 23 Jul 1890
Ambrosia Disc 18 Oct 1888	Robert John Kennard 25 Aug 1873 William H Heath 20 Dec 1877 James W Eccles 18 May 1888
New St. Louis Disc 16 Jul 1883 Reest 15 Sep 1886 Disc 28 Dec 1888	Wilson L Laremore 2 May 1876 George A Pike 18 May 1881 Henry Zinco 5 Sep 1886
Manchac	Henry Blouk 1 Apr 1878 Herman H Cohn 7 Apr 1879 Julian J Cohn 20 Jun 1884

	Hyppolite L Cohn 27 Apr 1885
	Andrew Matta 20 Jan 1889
Port Hudson	Joseph Baehl 4 Jun 1879
	Lewis Doyle 12 Apr 1881
	Richard J Hummell 15 Feb 1882
	Theresa M Hummell 28 May 1884
Pike	Edwin R Griffin 3 Jul 1879
Disc 26 Jan 1881	
Deer Ford	Jesse Eaton Roberts 21 Nov 1879
	L J Kelly 12 Jan 1881
	Jesse Eaton Roberts 12 Dec 1882
Disc 4 Jan 1883	
Fridge's Store	Benjamin F Fridge 8 Mar 1880
	Robert W Tucker 27 Apr 1885
Brown's	F B Brown 3 May 1881
Disc 4 oct 1883	
Cottonville	Jerome Merritt 25 Apr 1884
Comite	Franklin F Puckett 3 Jun 1884
	J Johnson David 30 Apr 1886
Disc 23 Feb 1887	
Zachary	Ewell H Skillman 20 Jan 1885
	James M Loudon 30 Apr 1886
Ward's Creek	Sebastian L Kleinpeter 10 Mar 1886
Indian Mound	Franklin F Puckett 27 May 1886
	Louis F Dear 27 Dec 1890
Pride	William A Craig 23 Jun 1886
Disc 2 Dec 1889	
Baker	John B Merritt 3 May 1888

Irene	Stephen O Beauchamp 7 Jun 1888
Camp Harvey	Isaac J David 28 May 1889
Foreman	Annie Foreman 3 Jul 1890
Foster's Hedge	Mary L Johnson 11 Apr 1891
Baywood	Margaret M Stringer 27 Jun 1892
Burtville	Joseph Byrne 25 Mar 1892
Scotland	Robert O Munson 25 Mar 1892

EAST FELICIANA PARISH

Bluff Creek
Leslie A Hooper 17 Feb 1873
Judson D Naul 7 Feb 1876
Thomas G Edwards 8 Oct 1877
Mrs. Mary L Causey 20 Nov 1877
C R Chaney 20 Aug 1879
John L McManus 16 Oct 1879
James M Watson 22 Jul 1886
Disc 30 Apr 1887

Clinton Courthouse
Joseph Israel 29 Sep 1871
Samuel D Chapman 12 Dec 1876
Samuel D Chapman 16 Jan 1877
Joseph Israel 24 Jun 1877
James D Grey 16 Jan 1882
John A White Jr 22 May 1885
Henry Skipworth Sr 1 Jun 1887
Thomas M Green 22 May 1889
George J Reilly 11 Jun 1889

Jackson
John Calligan 18 Feb 1871
James Oscar Howell 27 Apr 1874
James Law 3 Mar 1876
Joseph H Flunacher 23 Oct 1876

	Elijah C Kiblinger 21 Oct 1884
	A E Kiblinger 21 Oct 1884
Kent's Store	Seaborn B Kent 2 May 1872
	Giles W Kent 11 Oct 1882
	Wyndham R Skipworth 13 Oct 1884
	Xanthus D Hays 5 Jan 1886
Port Hudson	Abraham Levy 8 May 1872
	Albert Rayburn 21 Jul 1873
	Joseph Baehl 9 Sep 1874
Woodland	Maria R Poole 19 Feb 1869
	Charles G Steadman 14 Aug 1878
	Howard M Poole 5 Jan 1886
Young's Station	Lemuel T Ligon 1 Jul 1872
	Marshall W Courtney 12 Jan 1875
Bell's Store	Clarence Bell 6 Oct 1879
Olive Branch	A G Roberts 12 May 1880
	Joseph A Stott 26 Feb 1884
Fluker	Stephen M Powell 15 Sep 1884
Wilson's Station	Warren J Taylor 20 Oct 1884
	William S Scott 30 Apr 1886
	Mary S Steadman 26 May 1886
Ethel	Willis W Worthy 11 Nov 1884
	David A Simpson 21 May 1886
	George D Simpson 17 Aug 1886
	Corydon C Brown 26 Feb 1889
	Mary Pond 14 Oct 1890
	Olivia A Pond 24 Oct 1890
Gayden	Iverson G Gayden 24 Nov 1884
Belzora	Robert D Anderson 24 Dec 1884

Norwood	James A Ramsey 9 Jul 1885 R C Ramsey 4 Dec 1890 Charles W Sebastian 29 Dec 1890
Slaughter	Mrs. Flora F Lothrop 13 Jul 1886 Mrs. Flora F Bledsoe 28 Nov 1887 Sarah K Howell 22 Mar 1890
Blairstown	Eugene Adler 24 May 1887 Thomas D Lipscomb 22 Aug 1889
Lindsey	Henry Skipworth Jr 16 Jan 1888
Felixville	Felix Dreyfous 12 Jun 1888
Wilson	Mary S Steadman 18 Sep 1888
Farley	Thomas H Madden 14 Sep 1889
Orville	Orville H Cline 7 Jun 1890

FRANKLIN PARISH

Crowville Disc 20 May 1875 Reest 23 Jun 1876 Disc 6 Jan 1879 Disc 27 Dec 1888 Reest 8 Feb 1881	James W Rainey 4 Feb 1873 Ruben H Simms 23 Jun 1876 Henry A Fetche 24 Aug 1879 William Ralph Price 8 Feb 1881 Edward C Abell 26 Sep 1883 James C Copeland 8 Mar 1887
Oakley	Chauncey Lewis 1 Apr 1870 Clemens Schreiner 6 Jul 1874 Mrs. Kate L Campbell 19 Mar 1879 Jacob H Richardson 25 Oct 1880 Louis M Griffin 13 Sep 1881 Daniel C Gilbert 5 Jun 1891

Warsaw	Amides J Pennybaker 16 Jun 1872
	Josephine J Jassap 2 Jun 1879
Winnsborough	Edward Parker 21 Apr 1872
Courthouse	Lewis W Zim Jr 2 Jul 1873
	Aaron Laudoner 8 Aug 1877
	Lewis W Zim Jr 4 Mar 1879
	John L Murphy 7 May 1881
	Henry M Scott 7 Feb 1883
	Stuart Wiley 15 Mar 1883
	Willis H McVey 31 Mar 1891
Highland	Caleb H Snyder 22 Jun 1874
	Joseph Cordilt 3 Sep 1874
Disc 27 Sep 1875	
Baskinton	P C Baskin 7 Feb 1876
	James C Baskin 11 Feb 1876
	Adolphus D Baskin 5 Oct 1883
Prairie Landing	William O Parker 15 Feb 1876
	William B Winkler 14 Apr 1879
Disc 5 Jan 1880	
Reest 13 Nov 1886	A Jeffries 13 Nov 1886
Disc 9 Aug 1887	
Reest 2 Feb 1889	William G Disch 2 Feb 1889
Disc 2 Apr 1890	
Boeuf Prairie	Thomas W Word 15 Feb 1876
	Mrs. Cymantha Word 14 Mar 1876
	Mrs. Sallie Bonner 10 Jul 1876
Disc 22 Jan 1879	
Fort Necessity	William T Moore 9 Jul 1877
Holly Grove	Frederick N Abell 3 Jul 1879
Liddieville	George W Humble 14 Sep 1880
Disc 13 Sep 1881	

Como	Caleb H Snyder 19 Mar 1882
Lamar	Martha J Barker 31 Mar 1886 Martha J Jones 7 May 1890
Gilbert	Samuel L Richardson 12 Sep 1890 Stephen T Yancey 15 Dec 1891

GRANT PARISH

Colfax Courthouse	Peter Boreland 20 May 1873 Charles H Mumford 16 Apr 1875 Arthur F Lemonin 13 Jun 1882 Miss Mary I Grow 27 Apr 1885
Iatt	Mary M Smith 20 Jul 1871 Burrell Williams 18 Jan 1875 Rufus M Dean 17 Apr 1879 Mrs. Nancy H Corbitt 6 Mar 1880 William B Buckelew 9 Mar 1883 Nathan D Morris 9 Mar 1886 James A Harvey 26 Sep 1886 William B Buckelew 13 Jan 1888
Montgomery	George A Matthews 24 Jul 1867 Christopher C Dunn 6 Apr 1875 Henry A McCain 16 Apr 1879 John J McCain 19 Dec 1881 H D Walters 28 Jun 1882 Jules Lamereaux 23 Mar 1885 George L Ethridge 16 Jan 1891
Big Creek	Lavenia J Lovell 27 Oct 1873 J A Hamilton 27 Oct 1884
Black Creek	Oliver C Watson 12 Nov 1877 Thomas C Custis 17 Oct 1882 James E Collins 24 Jun 1884 William H Hodnett 9 Jan 1885

	William N Creed 18 Feb 1886
	B B Arrington 9 Apr 1890
	Jesse Baxley 24 Nov 1891
Fairmount	George W Hickman 14 Apr 1879
	James M Rhorer 31 May 1886
Nantaches	Joseph Billes 28 Nov 1879
	Milton A Dunn 19 Jan 1881
	E Grandchamp 26 Apr 1881
	Emma Waddell 15 Aug 1881
	Milton A Dunn 10 Feb 1886
	John L Chellete 11 Mar 1890
Cottonburg	Michael Hennigan 24 Aug 1880
	Shelby D Cooper 2 Nov 1880
Ada	George W Bruce 6 Apr 1881
	J W Baldridge 19 Jan 1885
	George H Harvill 7 Jan 1886
	Poas A Grant 8 Jun 1888
	Mary E Irwin 3 Oct 1888
	William Fuller 1 Mar 1890
	George H Harvill 21 Apr 1890
	Thomas J Chandler 30 Dec 1890
Solar	Hiram P Stephens 6 Oct 1885
	Sarah J Richardson 14 Nov 1891
Action	William B Stallings 25 Oct 1885
	William Walker 15 Jul 1886
Shaw	Wesley B Richardson 15 Oct 1885
	Mrs. Iowa T Richardson 19 Jul 1887
	Mrs. Iowa T Richardson 12 Nov 1887
Fishville	Henry B Thompson 21 May 1886
	Miss Virginia Hamilton 4 Oct 1887
Dunns' Ferry	Milton A Dunn 19 Jul 1886

Disc 18 Aug 1886

Prairie Home	Iley M Brian 20 Aug 1886 James W Ray 1 Dec 1888 Edward H Hagan 27 Feb 1890 Edward H Hagan 9 Jul 1890
Hadnot	Mrs. Lavina A Hadnot 6 Dec 1886
Vilas	Samuel Johnson 10 Apr 1888
Dunn's Gin	A J Dunn 19 Aug 1889
Guy	Thomas A Moses 27 Apr 1891
Barrett	John M Barrett 21 Jan 1892
Georgetown	Wyatt S Miles 5 Feb 1892
Howcott	James T Burke 12 Feb 1892
Antonia	Amanda Snodgrass 17 Sep 1892

IBERIA PARISH

New Iberia	Charles Decuir 12 Mar 1873 (Pres & Sen) Charles Decuir 6 Apr 1877 (Pres & Sen) Charles Decuir 29 Jan 1878 (Pres & Sen) Charles Decuir 6 Feb 1882 (Pres & Sen) Carmelite C Guilfoux 7 Oct 1885 (Pres) Carmelite C Guilfoux 13 Jan 1886 (Pres & Sen) Robert Brantley 21 Dec 1889 (Pres & Sen)
Raphael	Dorvill A Landry 18 Jun 1873
Loreauville	Adrien Gonsoulin 24 Sep 1873 St. Clair Dugas 27 Apr 1885
Jeanerette	Alexander W Edgar 23 Sep 1873 James J Lemon 23 Aug 1875

	Aristede T Monno 11 Apr 1877
	(Illegible entry)
	Moses L Frazier 29 May 1882
	Theodore Minvielle 8 Mar 1883
	George H Ring 3 Aug 1885
	Mrs. Alice Bowman 22 Jan 1889
	Fulgence P Schexnayder 17 Mar 1890
Belle Place	Eugene H Walet 9 Jul 1879
Oasis Disc 3 Apr 1879	Charles T Cade 30 Dec 1878
Potonville Disc 9 May 1881 Reest 19 May 1884	Octave Louviere 11 Jan 1881 Ernest H Darby 19 May 1884 William McNamar 7 May 1892
Olivier	Elias Boutte 30 Jan 1882 Edward E Soulier 28 Jul 1885 Henry J Walker 11 Aug 1886 Mary O Olivier 18 May 1887
Grand Cote	William T Weeks 11 Jul 1882
Burke Station	Pierre Couvillon 17 May 1883 Robert C Callaway 15 May 1885 Felix Jacquet 18 Nov 1890 Paul Nelson 30 Dec 1890
Derouen	Theodore A Derouen 10 Aug 1883 Michael Delcambre 6 May 1890
Cades Note: In St. Martin's Parish 1 Jul 1890	Aladin Broussard 25 Jul 1881 Henri Cientat 29 Oct 1883 Aladin Broussard 28 Jul 1885
Avery	J A Haskell 25 Jan 1886 Joseph C Haskell 10 Feb 1886 John H Hamilton 5 Mar 1890

IBERVILLE PARISH

Bayou Goula

Ernest Callery 17 Aug 1871
Joseph Richard Jr 26 Apr 1875
Paul A Viallon 2 Jul 1878

Plaquemine

James S Roche 7 Apr 1873
Albert Verret 14 Feb 1877
E P Durand 3 Aug 1877 (Pres)
E P Durand 13 Nov 1877 (Pres & Sen)
P G Deslonde 13 Dec 1877 (Pres & Sen)
William L Roche 25 Mar 1878 (Pres & Sen)
A St. Dezier 11 Apr 1882 (Pres & Sen)
Charles E Dupuy 26 Apr 1886 (Pres & Sen)
Charles E Dupuy 30 Apr 1890 (Pres & Sen)

Rosedale

Charles W Stack 22 Mar 1871
J O Larose 29 Sep 1873
Joseph L Orellon 28 Aug 1874
Anthony W Hutchins 9 Jan 1875
Charles W Cox 30 Jan 1878

Disc 6 Jun 1878

St. Gabriel

Joseph Jolesaint Jr 4 May 1873
Remistine Brunet 30 Mar 1874
Joseph Jolesaint Jr 27 May 1874
Peter Brunet 18 Feb 1875
Auguste Dehon 13 Aug 1878
Frank M Posey 25 Feb 1884
Benoni Maes 25 Sep 1884
Frank E Posey 23 May 1885

Raphael

Thomas Hebert 18 Jan 1875
Dorselie Landry 10 Jun 1873
Alfred H Clement 12 Apr 1876
Joseph A Barthet 9 Aug 1880
Thomas L McCoy 6 Dec 1880
Joseph D Continent 27 Jun 1881

Musson	Daniel H Miller 4 Feb 1875
	Alphonse Babin 2 Aug 1876
	Emile D Verbois 15 Mar 1880
	Alphonse Ennes 25 Feb 1881
	Oscar A Druz 1 May 1883
	Edward Taylor 24 Sep 1884
	Anthony W Tufts 27 Apr 1885
Island	Auguste Dehon 7 Jun 1875
	Jules Dehon 13 Aug 1878
	Louis Dehon 16 Sep 1879
	Octavia Carrville 1 Mar 1883
Brooksville Disc 7 May 1878	Joseph K Brooks 28 Sep 1876
Rosedale Reest 5 Aug 1878	T R Fauntleroy 5 Aug 1878
	James B Bennett 21 Aug 1878
	John H Matta Jr 16 Dec 1878
	James B Bennett 8 Sep 1880
	Andrew Jackson 12 Sep 1882
	George J A Bush 26 Dec 1882
	Harry J Slack 16 Apr 1891
Forlorn Hope	Thomas W Nichol 9 Mar 1879
Cannon's Store	Joseph J Thompson 16 Oct 1879
	James T Larase 2 Mar 1883
Soulougue	Leon Hebert 26 Aug 1881
	Charles Hebert 15 Jan 1883
	Joseph D Berrett 18 Jul 1890
Doreyville	Leonce M Louiat 14 Nov 1881

Sunnyside	Johnson Davis 11 May 1883
	Lillian Peterson 15 Jan 1884
Woolfolk Disc 9 Nov 1885	Harry J Slack 27 Jul 1885
Sunshine	Oscar Richard 17 Apr 1886
White Castle	Zachariah T Earle Jr 18 Oct 1887
Wheelock	Mrs. Kate F Nelson 14 Jun 1888
Regina	Joseph E Bargas 20 Oct 1890
Knowlton	Jacob W Altemus 13 Sep 1889
Dreyfus	Emile Dreyfus 28 Nov 1881
Seymourville	Frank M Seymour 19 Dec 1891

JACKSON PARISH

Bonner	Adam Riser 26 Apr 1872
	Joseph Berstein 19 Mar 1879
Brookline Disc 20 Mar 1876	Wilson Williams 3 Jun 1867
Douglas	John T McDowell 16 Oct 1872
	Wesley W Hinton 21 Nov 1873
	Mrs. L E Colbert 16 Apr 1877
	Wesley W Hinton 14 Oct 1878
Greensborough	Allen Greene 12 Oct 1871
	William L Greene 12 Jan 1875
Rochester	William C McDonald 2 Jun 1873
	Fadra A McDonald 26 Dec 1875
	William C McDonald 7 May 1883
	William C McDonald 14 May 1891

Vernon Courthouse	Hiram S Smith 19 May 1870
	Mrs. Mary M Slover 1 Dec 1873
	Ferdinand M McCormick 21 Jan 1878
	Dennis M Pyborn 9 Jan 1879
	William H Squyres 27 Feb 1879
	Edward L Hill 28 Mar 1881
Vienna	Joseph M Goff 29 Jan 1873
	Charles G Allen 24 Jun 1874
	E C Fulford 2 Jun 1874
Woodville	William A McKee 29 Mar 1872
	William Gullatt 22 May 1874
Hood's Mill	Whitfield Hood 26 Jan 1874
	Mrs. Martha A Hood 7 Sep 1880
	Stephen M Hearn 19 Apr 1882
	James K Head 2 Jan 1892
Redwine	Benjamin F Smith 5 Aug 1878
Craney Creek Disc 19 Aug 1884	James P McKaskle 2 Dec 1881
Dalley	Titus J Smart 8 Jul 1884
Indian Village	James L Bryan 4 Nov 1878
	Waid A Bryan 18 Feb 1887
	James M Griggs 19 Nov 1888
Weston	Sophia Walker 4 Nov 1885
	William F Walsworth 18 Feb 1887
Nash	Mary J Collins 11 Dec 1886
Macedonia	William S Jones 21 Jun 1886
Terral Disc 28 May 1887	Henry C Walsworth 29 Dec 1886

Kiddton	William E Kidd 1 Jun 1888
Hebron	Stephen J Shows 25 Sep 1890
Brooklyn	Thomas J Anders 29 Sep 1891
Stovall	Jeremiah J Stovall 23 Jan 1892

JEFFERSON PARISH

Carrollton Courthouse Disc 26 Jun 1882	Langdon C Tebbe 27 Nov 1872 Alfred H Pascoe 15 Dec 1875
Gretna	E Tournier 2 Jun 1873 Amos Morrison 17 Nov 1873 Mrs. Mary L Heminis 30 Nov 1874 Henry B Reddick 5 Sep 1881 Ava H Hildenbrand 8 Apr 1884 Henry B Reddick 16 Nov 1886 (Rescinded 20 Jan 1887) Ava H Hildenbrand 8 Sep 1886 Mrs. Ava H Snypp 15 Aug 1888 Virginia C Jacquin 19 Apr 1890
Kenner	Mrs. Mary Lang 5 Nov 1866 John D Fawcett 18 May 1889 Elizabeth Lecomte 31 Mar 1890
Grand Isle	Ami M Joly 9 Jun 1873 Benjamin Margot 8 Sep 1880 John Krantz Jr 10 Jul 1886
Bartaria	Ignace Perrin 3 Nov 1879 William B Berthoud 25 Nov 1886 Ignace Perrin 12 Mar 1888
Fort Livingston Disc 17 Nov 1881	Eugene Walsh 28 Apr 1880

Waggaman	Francis Lecler 9 Jun 1882
	Joseph Trahan 6 Aug 1883
	Eugene J Fortier 29 Jan 1884
Disc 11 Jul 1884	
Reest 26 Sep 1884	Nevil Lebeuf 26 Sep 1884
Camp Parapet	Paul Koerber 5 Jan 1885
	Charles Labarre 5 May 1890
	John Shillings 9 Jun 1890
	W L Geiseler 13 Aug 1890
Amesville	C H Mareno 22 Jul 1888
	Louis H Marrero 8 Aug 1888
Harvey	Charlotte Thompson 13 May 1890
Camindville	Thomas S Valence 5 Feb 1891

LAFAYETTE PARISH

Carencro	August Melchior 11 Jan 1872
	Viviana Melchoir 27 Aug 1877
	Ignace Bernard 18 Sep 1882
	Jacintha Chassaugnac 5 Mar 1883
	Viviana Melchoir 27 Apr 1885
	Henry Crouchet 30 Apr 1887
	Gustave Schmulen 29 May 1890
	Henry Crouchet 22 Aug 1890
Vermillionville	Alphonse Neven 12 May 1871
Courthouse	Auguste Monnier 17 Oct 1881
Youngsville	Albert S Dyer 18 Feb 1873
	Harrison Hall 17 Jun 1879
	Dominique Bonnemaison 18 Nov 1889
Broussard	Jacques Bonnemaison 19 Sep 1881
	Lognerd Malagarie 7 Oct 1881
	Pierre D Comeau 7 Feb 1882

	Felix Haas 28 Feb 1883
	Romain U Bernard 11 Jun 1883
	J B Fournet 28 Jul 1885
	Edmond St. Julien 11 Aug 1885
	Albert Extorge 21 Apr 1891
	Felix C Latiolais 21 Jan 1892
Scott	Alcide Judice 21 May 1883
	Jules Guidry 4 Jun 1889
Lafayette	M T Martin 2 Jun 1884
	S F Simpson 29 Jun 1885
	Paul Demanade 18 Nov 1889
	Paul Demanade 12 Mar 1890 (Pres & Sen)
Ridge	Elijah Hoffpauir 31 Oct 1887
	Alice Clark 4 Feb 1891
Duson	Joseph G Bertrand 24 Oct 1887
	Jack R Davis 15 Nov 1892

LAFOURCHE PARISH

Lafourche Crossing	Charles C Williams 7 Mar 1872
	Louis Lacroix 26 Apr 1875
Disc 23 Jun 1875	
Reest 13 Feb 1878	Louis Lacroix 13 Feb 1878
	Jacob Goldenberg 14 May 1881
Orange City	S F Gard 4 Apr 1873
Disc 23 May 1874	
Reest 16 Dec 1874	Charles Dugan 16 Dec 1874
	Rene Brilliot 1 Mar 1875
	William R Williams 22 Nov 1875
	Sheldon Guthrie Jr 21 Feb 1876
	B Eymard 26 Dec 1878
Disc 20 Jul 1881	
Reest 18 Apr 1882	James M Bollinger 18 Apr 1882
	Sheldon Guthrie Jr 29 Jun 1883

Raceland Disc 27 Jan 1875 Reest 26 Feb 1875	Joachim Gaude 3 Jul 1872 Auguste C Landreut 26 Feb 1875 Amades Lesesune 11 Dec 1878 Simon Abraham 29 Jan 1889
Thibodeaux	Gustave Bondreaux 11 Apr 1871 Gustave Bondreaux 29 Jan 1878 (Pres & Sen) Gustave Bondreaux 6 Feb 1882 (Pres & Sen) Robert W McBride 16 Apr 1886 (Pres & Sen) Robert W McBride 11 Apr 1890 (Pres & Sen) Gustave Bondreaux 11 Apr 1891 (Pres & Sen) Mrs. Jennie Curtis 8 Feb 1892 (Pres & Sen)
Lockport	Onesime Falgout 16 Dec 1874 Alexander Barker 16 Aug 1875 Gustave Abribat Jr 22 Nov 1880
Cut Off Disc 2 Nov 1886 Reest 16 Feb 1888	Auguste Claudet 9 Jun 1875 Octave W Adam 14 Jan 1876 Theophile Ducas 2 Dec 1890 Elie Ducas 2 Dec 1890
Guidry's Disc 27 Aug 1887	Auguste Cretini 12 Nov 1877
Harang Disc 20 Aug 1884	M Kantrowitz 18 Nov 1879 Thophile Harang 7 Sep 1880 M Kantrowitz 2 Dec 1881 Marcellin LeBlanc 9 Aug 1883 Octave W Adam 6 Jun 1884
Pugh	Emile Angelloz 2 Feb 1886 Oscar Angelloz 3 Sep 1890
Gheens	Joseph P Gheens 4 Mar 1886
Malagay	E Kraemer 17 Apr 1886

	Clovis Nicholas 15 Jul 1886
	Mrs. Margaret Kraemer 24 Sep 1887
Ariel	Filebert Bourgeois 24 Aug 1888
Lacroix	Eugene H Lacroix 6 Oct 1890

LIVINGSTON PARISH

Bayou Barbary	William C Opdenweyer 21 Apr 1870
	Robert K W Bennefield 12 Feb 1874
	Leonard Z T Gowers 3 Sep 1874
	Hillery S Glasscock 16 Jul 1891
Benton's Ferry	James L Harris 26 Mar 1867
	Mrs. Jane F Allen 2 Mar 1874
	Frederick F Miller 20 Apr 1887
	Charles F Miller 15 Feb 1890
Clio	Thomas H Jones 2 May 1872
	Z T Freeman 13 Apr 1874
	Andrew M Davidson 8 Mar 1875
	James A Davidson 21 Mar 1882
	Dudley H Weaver 15 Jul 1884
	John E Hudson Sr 1 Oct 1885
	John E Hudson Jr 9 Apr 1887
	Pinkney A Pennington 6 Jun 1887
Coelk	Levi Spiller 27 Jul 1871
French Settlement	Henry Brignac 13 Dec 1871
	Calvin D Bowman Jr 12 Feb 1874
	Joseph S Hebert 27 Jan 1880
Live Oak Store	Frederick Weiss 19 Jan 1872
	Warren H Carter 24 Nov 1879
	G W Watson 20 Dec 1880
	William T Hill 3 Sep 1884
	John B Easterley Jr 11 May 1886

Old Field	Lafayette W Odom 29 Mar 1871
	Andrew B Robertson 2 Mar 1874
	Jacob W Odom 12 May 1875
Disc 4 Aug 1875	
Reest 6 Apr 1888	Thomas G Anderson 6 Sep 1888
	Andrew Jones 10 Oct 1890
Springfield Courthouse	Alois Schenk 5 Mar 1872
	Alexander W Hinchen 28 Mar 1876
	Andrew F Hinchen 9 Jan 1879
	Annie T Hinchen 27 Sep 1889
Port Vincent	Levi Spiller 27 Jan 1874
	William H Merritt 27 Sep 1881
	Delimer C Leftwich 8 Jun 1886
	Bernice Singletary 19 Oct 1890
Maurepas	John H Ellis 9 Jun 1875
	J H Bailey 3 Aug 1876
Disc 22 Jan 1877	
Reest 26 Feb 1877	Robert K W Bennefield 26 Feb 1877
	John O Hutchison 24 Apr 1878
	Miss Hattie L Dear 3 Sep 1879
	Benjamin B Cleneary 2 Jul 1880
	Benjamin B Cleneary 11 Dec 1880
	Hardy Little 7 Jan 1886
	Sanford Webber 21 Jul 1886
	Lena Mascaline 28 May 1887
	Lena Mascaline 14 Jun 1887
Bourgeois Landing	John A Porter 22 Sep 1875
Disc 11 Apr 1878	
Melton Old Field	J J Martin 25 Sep 1876
	L L Martin 8 Nov 1886
	Nathan D Castle 15 Oct 1887
Disc 21 Feb 1888	
Otts Mills	William McDonald 25 Sep 1876

	Isaac A Minton 14 Feb 1881
	Levi Durbin 25 Nov 1884
	Burlin Starr 12 Apr 1887
Sand Hill	Urene Desouge 7 May 1887
	F D Herring 8 Sep 1880
Disc 25 Aug 1881	
Head of Island	John Hougham 25 Jul 1878
	William Salles 21 Nov 1882
	Octave Lebourgeois 15 Aug 1888
Hills Springs	John Sullivan 2 Jun 1880
	John R Allen 6 Oct 1884
Ralley Hill	Thomas L Leftwich 22 Jun 1880
	Thomas M Moseley 20 Jan 1882
Starns	Adolphus Starns 13 Apr 1882
Springville	Christopher W Gayle 2 Jul 1883
Disc 19 Sep 1883	
Reest 14 Mar 1884	Martin B Coates 14 Mar 1884
	Jesse C Tate 23 Apr 1884
	George W Spiller 19 Jun 1884
	George B Lavigne 13 May 1887
	Emily S Clayton 27 Dec 1890
Hudson	John E Hudson Jr 9 Apr 1884
Disc 3 Nov 1884	
Plain View	John R Fridge 11 Nov 1884
Disc 8 Feb 1887	
Colyell	Drew M Easeley 20 Mar 1885
Reid's	Francis M Reid 5 Oct 1888
Walker	Major J Germany 13 May 1890
	William H Bridges 9 Dec 1890

Killan   Robert J Dunwoody 19 Jun 1891

MADISON PARISH

Carrville   Jeff T Beasley 2 May 1872
                                Adam Kellogg 10 Jan 1874
                                Jeff T Beasley 10 May 1874
                                Robert L Carpenter 5 Apr 1875

Delta Courthouse   Henry M Floyd 21 Nov 1872
                                W H McVey 16 Jan 1882
                                Henry M Floyd 10 Feb 1882
                                James J Dundas 9 Aug 1889

Duckport   Green L Boney 26 Feb 1873

Milliken's Bend   George Watt 7 Mar 1871
                                Thomas M Jackson 10 Jul 1876
                                Charles K Dancy 29 Jul 1877
                                Nicholas Kahn 10 Jul 1879
                                Joseph Witherow 22 Apr 1891

Mound   Charles E Nicols 12 Mar 1863
                                Friend S Maxwell 14 Feb 1876
                                Thomas J Majors 8 May 1882
                                Coleman H Lucas 13 Mar 1883
                                Maximillian Fischel 13 Feb 1892

New Carthage   Scott Bettis 14 Aug 1871
Disc 17 Nov 1873

Tallulah   F H Fowler 19 Sep 1871
                                Richmond W Brown 27 Mar 1874
                                Harry F Fell 8 Nov 1874
                                Joseph A Hebert 4 Oct 1878
                                Julia M Hebert 15 Nov 1880

Waverly   Francis M Dunvern 25 Aug 1874
                                Louis M Alston 14 Jun 1875

	Henry Hanley 22 Nov 1875
	Red Reichman 9 Oct 1877
	Louis M Alston 24 Aug 1888
	John W Dunn 10 Feb 1889
	Joseph S Agee 7 Apr 1892
Kellogg's Landing	Robert L Carpenter 17 Jun 1875
	Adams Kellogg 16 May 1881
Omega	James A Stone 5 Jun 1879
	Alice James 18 Dec 1882
	Gabriella Woodland 15 Mar 1883
	James B Galloway 9 Aug 1883
Islington Disc 23 Dec 1879	Charles L Gelphin 14 Dec 1879
Dallas	Roger C Weightman 19 Dec 1879
	William D Postlethwaite 5 Sep 1881
	Ira Jones 3 May 1889
	James S Richardson 22 Mar 1890
Cape	R Albert Inge 7 Jul 1880
	Alfred L Fischel 11 Jul 1882
	John G Lucas 22 Jan 1883
	Alfred L Fischel 15 Jan 1884
	Alfred L Fischel 19 Nov 1885
	Jeff D Attlesey 19 Jul 1887
	Alfred L Fischel 2 Mar 1888
King	William Jose W Smith 8 Nov 1880
	John L Wilson 11 Mar 1890
	Thomas P Kett 29 Dec 1890
Bank Disc 26 Dec 1882	George W Levier 10 Aug 1882
Thomaston	William K Alston 20 Mar 1884
	Isadore Kaufmann 13 May 1887
	Nathaniel W Thomas 4 Feb 1889

	Jasper G Bolls 17 Jul 1890
	Zack Griffing 22 Apr 1892
Dalkeith	William E McKain 6 Aug 1884
	David George Humphreys 7 Jun 1890
Ashley	George A Waddill 24 Jun 1886
	William H Ward 7 Apr 1892
Florence	Stonewall J Prevatt 23 Feb 1888
Altoona	Silas W Boswell 19 Jan 1888
	William P Richardson 9 Oct 1889
Barnes	Stonewall J Prevatt 6 Mar 1888
	John W Yoste 5 May 1888
Griffin	Madison Bedford 14 Aug 1889
Quebec	F Silas Catchings 4 Feb 1890
Afton	Thomas A Hyland 3 Apr 1890
Eldorado	Thomas P Ellis 7 Jun 1890
Albordon	Edward M Fischel 24 Nov 1891
	William F Long 14 Jan 1892

MOREHOUSE PARISH

Bastrop	Andrew Miner 22 Aug 1871
	Jacob S Schardt 19 Aug 1874
	James M Turpin 22 Jan 1877
	S T Mickosson 1 Jun 1881
	Henry C Wright 31 Aug 1881
	James M Turpin 22 Jun 1882
	Benjamin H Gray 19 Dec 1883
	A C McMeans 9 Aug 1885
	John W Brown 30 Sep 1885
	Benjamin H Gray 18 May 1889

DeGallion Disc 6 Apr 1874	S Boozman 19 Mar 1872
Lind Grove	George M Harrison 29 Oct 1868 William F Watt 1 Jun 1875 Robert M Hardy 29 May 1881 Thomas Leavel 4 Mar 1886 Julius A Williams 12 Apr 1886
Line	Jesse A Peterkin 29 Oct 1868 George A Peterkin 8 Sep 1874 Henry C Lawrence 10 May 1878 David Kimpel 7 Mar 1881 Joseph J Daniel 24 Oct 1882 William F Beard 30 Jul 1886
Plantersville Disc 2 Feb 1874	Thomas O Leavel 26 Nov 1872
Point Jefferson	Ambrose O McCord 16 Jul 1872 Bennett W Wright 5 Jan 1874 Miss Mary E McCord 6 Jul 1874 Mary E Baker 10 Sep 1877
Woodburn Disc 22 Nov 1877	Mrs. Sarah A Bell 22 Jun 1874
Oak Ridge	Mary E Baker 13 Oct 1879
Bonada Disc 23 Aug 1882	F W Turpin 4 Nov 1881
Brodnax	Benjamin H Brodnax 2 Oct 1882
Tipton	Joseph A McGowen 1 Sep 1884
Mer Rouge	Josiah Davenport 10 Aug 1886
Pratt's Mill	Frank B Pratt 30 Jun 1888

Disc 16 Aug 1890

DeGallion
Reest 19 Jul 1890   Samuel W Handy 19 Jul 1890

Collins   John B Higman 24 Jul 1890
                                 Frank B Pratt 30 Mar 1891
                                 James C Reily 11 Feb 1892

Bonita   William W Denham 6 Aug 1890

Jones   William H Hadley 27 Aug 1890
                                 George M Kimbrough 16 Jun 1891

Pass   Alexander N Keller 5 Sep 1890

Causey   John P Causey 11 Nov 1890

Tillou   George W Westbrook 24 Apr 1891

Doss   James C Reily 12 Jun 1891

Turpin   Lewis L Davidson 25 Jul 1891

NATCHITOCHES PARISH

Campti   Solon B Perot 1 Mar 1872
                                 Martin Hirsch 1 Jul 1874
                                 James P Reathinner 25 oct 1875
                                 Leopold Perot 9 Apr 1884
                                 Elizabeth McDaniel 27 Jul 1885

Cloutierville   Victor S Benoist 18 Jan 1863
                                 Ernest Sers 12 Feb 1874
                                 Antoine Marinovich 8 Feb 1875

Disc 17 apr 1876
Reest 24 Feb 1876   Joseph A Lampite 24 Feb 1876
                                 Denis Deblanc 31 Mar 1879
                                 Numa Desloriches 12 Sep 1879

	Gilbert W Rachal 13 Sep 1880
	Amelia Sanches 17 Mar 1889
Soggy Bayou	William H Treadwell 20 May 1873
	William B Stewart 18 Sep 1873
Marthaville	John J Rains 8 Nov 1872
Natchitoches Courthouse	Joseph F Vargas 18 Sep 1872
	William B Harkins 11 Feb 1876
	Mary A Burke 3 Mar 1883 (Pres & Sen)
	Edwina Suddath 29 Dec 1884
	J Emile Breda 2 Jul 1889 (Pres)
	J Emile Breda 11 Feb 1890 (Pres & Sen)
Planter's Landing	L P Bridges 17 Aug 1871
Disc 11 Dec 1873	
Isle Brevelle	Charles Dupre 24 Dec 1873
	Ananias Neal 8 Feb 1875
Disc 6 May 1875	
Grappe's Bluff	Joseph N Wolfson 21 Dec 1875
	Francis L Grappe 12 Jan 1883
	Robert B Roubreu 25 Oct 1883
	Henry P Bower 3 Aug 1887
Cote Janense	J J A Plauche 25 Sep 1875
Disc 23 Dec 1875	
Lake Village	Leonard W Stephens 12 Jul 1877
Disc 23 Oct 1877	
Reest 29 Oct 1877	Leonard W Stephens 29 oct 1877
	Llewellyn G Barron 1 Feb 1882
	Marion R Joyner 1 Feb 1883
Bermuda	Alain L Metoyer 28 Dec 1877
Disc 5 Feb 1879	
Reest 12 Jan 1883	John D W Sero 12 Jan 1883

Broadwell's Station	A N Timon 4 Mar 1878
	Omer Trichell 22 Apr 1878
	Jacob B Broadwell 13 Nov 1880
	Henry M Hyams 20 Dec 1882
	Wilford A Oliphant 6 Oct 1885
Allen	Richard W Freeman 30 Oct 1878
	E E Jordan 8 Jun 1880
	James Bonds Sr 24 Jan 1882
	William H Jordan 5 Jun 1882
	Willliam H Bonds 28 Feb 1883
	John A Sledge 18 Jun 1888
	William R Hollingsworth 18 Sep 1890
	John E Knott 16 Feb 1892
Monette's Ferry Disc 20 Aug 1879	Samuel B Newman 5 Jun 1879
Kisatchie	Jacob Kile 18 Nov 1879
	Abraham R Dowden 3 Jun 1884
	S G Dowden 27 Apr 1885
	Abraham R Dowden 2 Jun 1885
	John Clark 28 Jan 1886
	Abraham R Dowden 16 Apr 1886
	Berry Boswell 18 Sep 1889
Willow	Bernardin L Devlicux 13 May 1880
Ecore Disc 19 Sep 1881	Heyman Manheim 28 Jun 1880
Leolia	Nathaniel Stamper 24 Jan 1880
	A V Carter 10 Nov 1881
	James M H McCook 8 Dec 1881
Warnack	Thomas Gregory 18 Nov 1881
Leland Note: In Catahoula Parish 24 Feb 1882	Ann E Smith 22 Feb 1882

Provence	Thomas Gregory 30 Mar 1882
	Joseph H Stephens 6 May 1891
Robeline	James M H McCook 5 Jul 1882
	Hickson Capers 17 May 1889
	James M H McCook 16 Jul 1891
Chopin	Edmond Delacerde 5 Jul 1882
	T T Snead 16 Dec 1884
	Lamay Chopin 16 Jan 1885
Alpha	James M Corley 12 Oct 1882
Derbonne	John T Jordan 2 Jul 1883
Disc 9 Jan 1884	
Weaver	Henry W Weaver 18 Feb 1884
	Eliza J Weaver 26 Mar 1886
Bellwood	John D Addison 3 Jun 1884
Tiger Island	William M Clark 13 Oct 1884
	James T Clark 19 Nov 1884
	Mollie Airey 12 Feb 1886
	W Tucker 18 Aug 1886
Disc 20 oct 1886	
Trichell	Septime Trichell 9 Nov 1885
Victoria	William L Gilmer 3 Nov 1886
Melrose	Belesaire Storens 11 Dec 1886
	John T Jordan 17 Sep 1888
Robertsville	George A Roberts 17 Mar 1887
	Don G Petty 9 Apr 1890
Oliphant	Wilford A Oliphant 21 Dec 1887
Mora	Joseph S Kingrey 28 Nov 1887

	William L George 27 Sep 1888
	Charles W Ausley 18 Dec 1888
Richardville	Richard B Williams 16 Apr 1888
Bayou Pierre	Sterling E Russ Jr 21 Apr 1888
Egypt	Jared S Dixon 10 May 1888
Marston	Henry M Johnson 9 Jul 1888
	G A Killgore 9 Apr 1890
	James M Jones 2 May 1890
	Robert C Murphy 31 Oct 1891
Derry	John H Henry 9 Jan 1887
Newton	Roseaner T Burnside 28 May 1889
	Janie C Burnside 31 May 1890
Harris Disc 8 Dec 1890	Edward J Harris 3 Jun 1889
Pecan	Thomas J Flanner 12 Feb 1890
Roy	Angelo P Cockfield 11 Mar 1890
Jamba Disc 7 Jan 1891	William D Stewart 27 Mar 1890
Chestnut	James Y Wallace 10 Oct 1890
Gorum	Joseph M Gorum 21 Nov 1890
Mallett Disc 24 Feb 1892	Isaac W Mallett Jr 20 Oct 1890
Starlight	Victorin Prudhomme 27 Apr 1891
Clarence	Matthew M Fisher 15 Jul 1891

Clear Lake	John R Sanders 3 Mar 1892
Vowell's Mill	Hamilton G Vowell 30 Jan 1890 Benjamin C Campbell 8 Mar 1892
Waco	John W Self 22 Mar 1892

ORLEANS PARISH

Algiers Disc 26 Jun 1882	Joseph Lyons 13 Sep 1872
Fort Pike	Henry Walker 6 May 1867 David Porter 4 Dec 1883
New Orleans Courthouse	Charles W Ringgold 10 Mar 1873 (Pres & Sen) John M G Parker 6 Apr 1875 (Pres) John M G Parker 14 Dec 1875 (Pres & Sen) Algernon Badger 10 Dec 1878 (Pres & Sen) Washington B Merchant 27 Mar 1883 (Pres & Sen) Samuel H Buck 23 Jul 1885 (Pres) Samuel H Buck 29 Mar 1886 (Pres & Sen) George W Nott 10 May 1887 (Pres) George W Nott 9 Jan 1888 (Pres & Sen) Stephen M Eaton 13 Aug 1890 (Pres & Sen)
Rigolets	Edward K Russ 9 Sep 1875 John A Otway 15 Nov 1875 George L Walker 9 Jul 1877 Mary A Green 5 May 1879 Maggie E Green 18 Aug 1880 Mamie K Gray 7 Jan 1884 C A Flinn 5 May 1885 John Borzant 22 Dec 1885 C A Bullard 27 Sep 1889 Georgiana Cree 31 Mar 1890
Chef Menteut	F A St. Amant 17 Feb 1879 William Daniels 18 Mar 1879

Disc 19 Nov 1880	W H Kinsey 4 Nov 1880
Lee	David W Eames 7 Sep 1883

OUACHITA PARISH

Cheniere Disc 6 Apr 1874 Reest 26 Feb 1879 Disc 9 Apr 1880 Reest 23 Jan 1884 Disc 25 Apr 1890	Alexander Myatt 30 Jul 1873 Alexander Myatt 26 Feb 1879 Charles C Harris 23 Jan 1884 Thomas J Humble 8 Dec 1884 Alexander Myatt 14 Feb 1889
Cuba	David C Brown 30 Jul 1872 William L Graffenreid 16 Jun 1873 William E Redditt 27 May 1874 William L Graffenreid 9 Dec 1877 William L Graffenreid 9 Dec 1884 Abraham A Carr 5 Sep 1890
Forksville	James E Butler 4 Dec 1867 John A Covington 8 Dec 1873 W W Patrick 16 Apr 1874 Willia H Sanders 4 Jun 1874 James Harris 17 May 1875 John A Covington 3 Jun 1875 Willis H Sanders 27 Feb 1878 Mrs. Annie C Hamilton 23 Jun 1888 Israel l Grant 23 Nov 1888 Annie Head 6 May 1892
Hamilton Disc 23 May 1878	Augustus D Russell 26 Nov 1872 Alexander G Hamilton 1 Jun 1876
Indian Village	James B Sanders 27 Nov 1872

	John L Bryan 26 Oct 1873
	Francis J McClendon 27 May 1874
	Stephen M Cade 14 Jan 1877
	James L Bryan 4 Nov 1878
	James M Griggs 19 Nov 1888
	A J Campbell 1 Nov 1889
	William Fuller 3 Jul 1890
	James M Griggs 18 Nov 1890
Loch Arbor	Samuel M Puckett 6 Oct 1870
	Leon Lange 20 Oct 1873
	Bartold B Schuster 27 Mar 1874
	Francis M Grant 30 Dec 1879
	F S Menes 9 Feb 1881
	(Illegible entry)
	Joseph Thompson 18 Nov 1889
Log Town	James A Cheatham 14 Oct 1867
	Roland M Filhiol 25 Jun 1874
Mill Haven	Joseph H Walker 8 Nov 1872
Disc 1 Apr 1874	
Reest 19 May 1879	Samuel Whited 19 May 1879
	William Spearman 9 Nov 1885
	Prosper Trouard 2 Dec 1889
Monroe Courthouse	Mrs. Nicettie M Dinkgrave 13 May 1873 (Pres)
	Mrs. Nicettie M Dinkgrave 10 Dec 1873 (Pres & Sen)
	Robert Ray Jr 18 Jul 1876 (Pres & Sen)
	Julius Ennemoser 4 Aug 1882 (Pres & Sen)
	Isaiah Garrett 2 Sep 1885 (Pres)
	Isaiah Garrett 13 Jan 1886 (Pres & Sen)
	Robert Ray Jr 2 Jun 1890 (Pres & Sen)
Trenton	F M Leatherman 2 Jun 1873
	Uriah Millsaps 2 Jul 1873
	George W Roberson 20 Jul 1881
	Thomas F Millsaps 7 Oct 1881
	Jethro Moore 10 Jan 1883

	Joseph R Herron 19 Feb 1883
	Jethro Moore 26 Sep 1884
	Josie Wilder 25 Jan 1886
Toll Bridge Disc 20 Oct 1874	Michael Perry 3 Mar 1873
Cadeville	John W Cade 7 Jun 1873 George M Young 12 Jan 1875 Chapel H Rogers 24 Oct 1878 Eli S Parker 19 Nov 1878 Chapel H Rogers 10 Dec 1879 William R Mitchell 2 Feb 1881
Fairfield Disc 11 Aug 1876	George W McCormick 28 May 1873
Okaloosa	Chapel H Rogers 20 Jan 1874 James Brewster 3 Mar 1875 William R Young 19 Nov 1883 Samuel E Reagan 13 Mar 1890 John C Nixon 15 May 1890 Levis A Coon 27 Jun 1892
Lapine	(Illegible entry) Henry M Bryan 24 Feb 1880 Henry M Bryan 16 Dec 1880 Richard A Rymer 5 Apr 1881 Anderson M Stuckey 18 Feb 1886 James T Dean 22 Oct 1891
Deliard	James C Steele 12 Dec 1881 Alexander L Helmich 19 Sep 1882 Moses Elder 23 Apr 1883
Fouche	Nettie L Johnson 3 Apr 1882
Calhoun	Lucius M Calhoun 20 Dec 1883 Charles A Peevy 5 Jun 1886 Larche C Drew 19 Nov 1888

	Thomas J Humble 24 Dec 1890
Puckett	William M Etheridge 12 May 1884 J William Puckett 4 Jun 1884 James O Harrell 16 Jan 1885
Disc 19 Aug 1885	
West Monroe	Joseph R Herron 18 Aug 1885 William L Morris 12 Sep 1887 Loretta A Moore 11 May 1891
Seale	Willis H McCormick 2 Jul 1888 George W Herrick 28 Jul 1888
Head	Walter A Head 22 Jul 1891
Myatt	Alexander Myatt 22 Jul 1891
Drew	Heloise L Pugh 13 Oct 1892
Swartz	Edward G Swartz 22 Oct 1892

PLAQUEMINES PARISH

Beau Sejour Disc 17 Apr 1874	Leon C Courcelle 29 Jun 1871
Buras	Richard Westfield 28 Feb 1872 Bernard Fasterling 2 Nov 1885 Anna Fasterling 21 May 1886
Grand Prairie	Diedrich Wischusen 15 Jul 1871 Mrs. Abigail H Hingle 12 Feb 1874 Peter Ochiglevich 27 Aug 1875 Mrs. Mary Ochiglevich 31 Jul 1886 Diedrich Wischusen 8 Aug 1888 Mrs. Mary Ochiglevich 4 Nov 1889 Robert Bowes 22 Mar 1890
Home Place	Patrick Lyons 4 May 1871

	Joseph Cathcart 10 Jan 1881
	Thomas Lyons 14 Jun 1884
	Frank Gordano 2 Mar 1892
Jesuit Bend	Oscar B Sarpy 29 Jun 1871
	Michael Haleran 16 Apr 1875
Disc 28 Sep 1875	
Reest 28 oct 1875	G Raymond Fox 25 Oct 1875
	Robert Levy 8 Apr 1878
	Mrs. Sue Levy 30 Nov 1886
	Thomas C Dennis 25 Jul 1891
Point a la Hache	Claude V F Barberot 12 Dec 1866
	Bernard Mevers 22 Apr 1874
Point Michael	Pascal Encolade 29 Jun 1871
St. Sophie	Rufin J B Morand 26 Jun 1871
	Charles Goffaly 3 May 1875
	George H Crowther 6 Jan 1880
	Olivia Crowther 16 Nov 1891
Pilot Town	William F Smith 14 Jun 1873
	Albert Schlesenger 20 Oct 1879
	Sophie R Dunning 29 Nov 1880
	Joseph Cathcart 18 Feb 1886
	Bradford J Williams 3 Oct 1891
Happy Jack	John G Grant 20 Oct 1874
	Thomas Dennesse 22 Mar 1881
	Bernard Potash 23 Dec 1881
	David G Wire 20 Feb 1886
Wood Park	Henry J Fettus 26 Oct 1874
	J B Wire 20 Dec 1877
	Thomas H Ballow 21 Jun 1878
The Forts	Henry E Gilmore 4 Feb 1875
Disc 29 Dec 1886	

Port Eades	William J Karner 16 Jul 1875
	Joseph H Stockley 3 Jun 1876
	William L Wright 13 Jun 1876
	Mrs. Cecelia L Kleinpeter 13 May 1887
	Mrs. Cecelia L Merritt 23 Jun 1889
Bel Air	Alfred G Brady 22 May 1870
	Charles S Kay 21 Aug 1876
	William E McKnight 2 Apr 1879
	John Dymond 22 Mar 1881
Diamond	Jochim Wiese 3 Apr 1878
	Simon Abraham 11 Jun 1883
	John W Booth 28 Oct 1885
Lawrence	Lawrence Effingham 19 Apr 1878
	Alvin T Allen 13 Jun 1879
	Luther H Whittlesby 9 Mar 1880
	Herman Dustmann 27 Apr 1884
	Albert Werner 17 Feb 1890
Empire	John B Pignido 1 Jul 1878
Red Stone Disc 19 Apr 1880	Simon Lederer 17 Feb 1879
Concession	Ernest Voizin 15 Jun 1879
	Edward J Engman 8 Mar 1882
	Lemuel Sandborn 12 Feb 1889
	George P Anderton 14 Sep 1891
City Price	
	Fidel N Tagliaferro 22 Sep 1879
	Paul V Bordes 27 Feb 1883
	Aristides Pinard 26 Sep 1884
	Anatole Maury 20 Jan 1885
	David Withan 3 Jul 1890
Jump	Louis P Buras 3 Nov 1879

Nichols	George F Preusch 24 Mar 1880
Nero	Edward F Smith 10 June 1880
	Jules B Savoie 4 Apr 1884
English Town	Julius Strack 10 Jun 1880
Dalcour	Lazard D Dalcour 30 Sep 1880
	Leonard Dalcour 13 May 1886
	Darestan D Daunoy 11 Jun 1886
Dime	William Boyle 15 May 1881
	N Aristides Pinaud 4 Nov 1889
Junior	Mannsell White Jr 27 Feb 1882
	A Sidney White 25 May 1885
	Daniel Bradford 2 Mar 1887
	Fidel N Tagliaferro 5 Jan 1888
	Victor Adema 27 Aug 1889
	A B Fortier 12 Apr 1890
	Charles Kelly 19 Apr 1890
	A F Jeanfreaux 12 Feb 1891
	Ethel Conrad 5 Jun 1891
Myrtle Grove	John C J Rivers 28 Mar 1882
Sunrise	Antoine P Albert 29 May 1882
Neptune	John Butler 4 Dec 1883
	Sarah A Butler 30 Oct 1889
Daisy	Thomas Willis 3 Mar 1884
Vandyke Disc 15 Dec 1884	Vandice Johnson 16 May 1884
Olga Disc 30 Nov 1887	Raduslav G Abramovich 4 Sep 1884

Potash	Joseph Potash 5 Jul 1888
Quarantine	Harry Hayward 26 Aug 1889 James Christianson 5 May 1891 Ludger M Finney 29 Dec 1891
Martin	Leonard Schayot 25 Oct 1889 Joseph Fontenelle 26 Jan 1891
Nairn	Edward Dosher 13 Jul 1891

POINT COUPEE PARISH

Hermitage	John Landreau 10 Jun 1867 F C Trudeau 26 Feb 1877
Livonia	James M Bailey 4 Feb 1869 Abram A Alford 29 Dec 1874 M S Michael 14 Feb 1878 Max Mayer 14 Mar 1878 Millard F White 3 Apr 1878 Thomas C Bailey 13 Mar 1879 August Heller 3 Apr 1879 Mrs. Lucy E Stockett 13 Apr 1879 Thomas C Bailey 5 Mar 1880
Disc 6 Oct 1879 Reest 31 Jul 1888	Bell Simrall 31 Jul 1888 Albin Major 16 Oct 1890
Morganza	Leon Oubre 11 Mar 1872 F Eugene Hubert 16 Jan 1885
Point Coupee Courthouse	Clementine Enete 26 Apr 1872 Joseph G Vignes 8 Feb 1875 Leon B Dayries 26 Feb 1877 Justin Plantevignes 15 Apr 1878 Celeste Dayries 10 Oct 1878
Red River Landing	John S Kingsbury 25 Aug 1871 Warren S Gay 18 Jan 1882

	Ewen Mortimer 14 Nov 1882
	William C Nelson 15 Jan 1889
	George W Reagan 22 Nov 1889
Waterloo	Arthur Porche 25 Nov 1867
	Alphonse Pourcian 29 Apr 1875
	Mrs. Mathilde Pourcian 17 Jan 1879
	Cyrille Pourcian 1 Jul 1881
New Texas	Leon Oubre 1 Aug 1873
	James Eugene Tirquit 7 Oct 1875
	Leon Oubre 26 Jan 1876
	James Eugene Tirquit Jr 12 Dec 1876
	Numa Tirquit 10 Apr 1890
Belair Disc 20 Apr 1875	Zadock Casey 9 Jun 1875
Bayou Alabama	William W Daily 13 Mar 1878
Lakeland	Edward F Phillips 15 Apr 1878
	Marshall P Phillips 27 Feb 1886
Merrick's Station	William E Satterfield 21 May 1878
	David T Merrick 25 Mar 1881
St. Mary	Joseph Richy 4 Jun 1878
	Robert Arlington 21 Jun 1878
Smithland	Archie D Smith 20 Aug 1878
	Benjamin G Cornwell 8 Feb 1881
	Walter T Bell 13 Mar 1882
	Benjamin G Cornwell 28 Nov 1883
	Archie D Smith 11 Apr 1890
	Walter T Coyle 23 Oct 1890
New Roads	Robert Arlington 12 Nov 1879
	Joseph P Gosserand 2 Dec 1887
Sherman Mills	Windsor Row 15 Dec 1879

Merrick	David T Merrick 13 Dec 1882
Fordoche Disc 13 Jun 1884 Reest 5 Jan 1886	William B McNeeley 26 Dec 1883 William B McNeeley 5 Jan 1886
Raccourci	Edward P Shaw 16 Jun 1885 Joseph W Comstock 4 Mar 1890
Ventress	Arcade Major 19 Nov 1885
Legonier	Edward W Hanlon 22 May 1888
Anchor	Joseph D Major 10 Oct 1888
Lafanache	W W Mains 17 Mar 1890
Lettsworth	Robert S Bienvenu 30 Sep 1890
Chenal	Francis J Guerin 14 Sep 1892

RAPIDES PARISH

Alexandria Courthouse	William Mills Jr 12 Mar 1873 (Pres & Sen) Calcott F Burges 26 Feb 1874 (Pres & Sen) John D Lacy 13 May 1875 (Pres) John D Lacy 21 Jan 1878 (Pres & Sen) Frank Connelly 15 Jan 1880 (Pres) Jefferson W Gordon 24 Jan 1881 (Pres & Sen) Thomas B French 2 Apr 1885 (Pres & Sen) Edward J Barrett 21 Dec 1889 (Pres & Sen)
Big Creek Disc 10 Oct 1873 Reest 27 oct 1873	Lavenia Jane Lovell 13 Nov 1871 Lavenia Jane Lovell 27 Oct 1873
Cheneyville	Francis W Marshall 16 May 1871 Norton R Roberts 17 May 1875 Miss Eunice Bailey 20 Aug 1877

	Eunice B Roberts 3 Mar 1880
Cotile	Hyman Bath 3 Mar 1873
	Joseph Malachowsky 18 Sep 1873
	Francis B Amsden 10 Mar 1875
	Mary Amsden 28 Nov 1879
	Rufus R Robinson 3 Jan 1882
	William H Simons 14 Jul 1882
Pineville	Edward J Barrett 9 Jun 1871
	Mary A Barrett 3 Apr 1884
	Andrew Davis 27 Jul 1884
	Edith A Houston 20 Aug 1890
Quantico Disc 7 Jul 1874	Levi Wells 15 Jan 1873
Spring Creek Disc 25 Aug 1875	Lewis Q Barnidge 13 Oct 1871
Sullivan's Landing	John H Sullivan 19 May 1873
	Rodin C Peterson 2 Feb 1874
Wellswood	Edward L Watkins 23 Jan 1873
	Montfort Wells 16 Nov 1874
Disc 4 May 1876	
Reest 22 Aug 1877	John R Grogan 22 Aug 1877
Disc 11 Jan 1878	
Kanomie	Reuben H Carnal 2 Dec 1874
	Whitmet P Norfleet 6 Aug 1875
	Bernard D Meyer 6 May 1878
Bertrand	William J Koehn 2 Jun 1874
	Miss Fanny C Smith 21 May 1875
	Mrs. Fanny C Stevens 8 Jun 1875
	Lewis Richardson 24 Feb 1876
	Thomas P Dakin 23 Mar 1876
	Lewis Richardson 22 Sep 1876
	Jordan Gibson 7 Mar 1877

	Henry A Biossat 3 Dec 1877 Jordan Gibson 2 Sep 1878 Arthur C Watson 24 Sep 1878 M M Marner 3 Mar 1879
Hineston	Moses Rosenthal 1 Jul 1873 Stephen D William 1 Apr 1878 Mrs. Mary M Williams 12 Jan 1885
Millford	John Cordukes 22 Jul 1875 Mrs. R D Cordukes 19 Sep 1881 James H Sorelle 27 Nov 1883 (Illegible entry) Cordelia Lyles 8 Jan 1891
Babb's Bridge	Henry A Biossat 1 Oct 1877
Lecompte Disc 5 May 1880 Reest 30 Aug 1880	Kenneth M Clark 21 Jun 1878 S Bluestein 30 Aug 1880 Joseph H Meeker 27 Jun 1881 J R Williams 8 Jul 1881 Benjamin Pressburg 6 Dec 1883 Miss Bessie G Wells 16 Nov 1889
Booneville Disc 27 Sep 1881	Augustus D Harard 27 Jul 1878 John T Rhodes 4 Nov 1879
Lamourie	Bernhardt Mayer 26 Jul 1876 David S Ferris 11 Apr 1890
Midway Disc 2 Mar 1880	Mayo S Duke 31 Mar 1879
Loyd	Thomas C Wheadon 21 Apr 1879 Lindsey L Brown 24 May 1883 G V Wilson 29 Sep 1884 Morris Weinburg 21 Oct 1884

Bayou Rapides   Daniel D Arden 19 May 1879
Disc 16 Jan 1880

Bismarck   Benjamin H Randolph 13 Jun 1879
Disc 15 Jan 1889

Westport   John A Hamilton 27 Sep 1881
                       Robert Sweat 29 Jan 1882
Disc 25 Jun 1883

Moorland   Charles C Weems 4 Apr 1882
                       J Eugene Johnson 30 Apr 1883
                       Bernard M Hayes 28 Jan 1886
                       Thomas C Wheadon 12 Mar 1890

Crane   Caroline C Roberts 24 Jul 1882
                       Miss Iva H McKinney 23 Oct 1886

Poland   Joseph T Hatch 27 Jul 1882

Pacific   David A Smith 7 Sep 1882
                       Henry A Biossat 22 Sep 1882
Disc 29 Dec 1892

Boyce   William M Simons 18 May 1883

Gum   William R Hargrove 4 Dec 1883
                       William Odum 14 Sep 1880
                       Obey Johnson 11 Nov 1886

Melder   Felix Van Melder 21 Aug 1884
                       Henry L Melder 16 Feb 1887
                       Daniel B Horgan 7 Dec 1891

Godwin   William R Eldred 9 Nov 1885

Lena Station   Charles C Cleveland 3 Nov 1886

Welchton   Louis V Mallett 21 Apr 1887
                       Adolph Hartiens 5 Jan 1892

Weil	Simon Weil 3 Aug 1887
Holloway	Thomas C Barron 7 Sep 1887
Mora	Joseph S Kingsley 28 Nov 1887 W L George 27 Sep 1888
Elmer	Charles M Shaw 15 May 1888
Bennettville	Edward S Soulier 2 Aug 1888 George M Bennett 1 Oct 1890
Dyer	William Dyer Sr 13 Jun 1889 John A Dixon 24 Apr 1890 William Winegeart 17 Dec 1890
Rapides	James T Dezendorf 15 Jul 1889
Asher	Archibald Smith 2 May 1890
Quadrate	Joseph W Swann 17 Feb 1892
Hemphill	Bettie Owens 12 Sep 1890 Jesse E Collins 27 Feb 1891
Lamothe	James C Cooper 11 Apr 1891
Levin	Anger Siess 2 Apr 1892
Ryland	John E Ryland 2 Apr 1892
Morris	William J Morris 28 Sep 1892

RED RIVER PARISH

Coushatta Chute	John T Yates 7 Oct 1873 Andy Bosley 24 Feb 1874 Henry A Scott 12 Oct 1874 John R Hayes 16 Apr 1875

	John W Harrison 19 May 1875
	Zachary Wester 31 Jul 1876
	George G Winder 20 Aug 1877
	Samuel Lisso 20 Dec 1877
	Thomas B Selby 21 Jul 1880
	John R McGoldrick 9 Sep 1881
	Oren L Penny 10 Mar 1882
Iverson	G B Thomas 22 Aug 1873
	Newport Thomas 13 Nov 1874
	Matthew Ratcliff 8 Feb 1875
	Thomas G McGraw 13 Nov 1883
Soggy Bayou	William B Stewart 18 Sep 1873
	Eugene A Terry 31 Aug 1876
	Stanislau F Spencer 11 Oct 1877
Love's Lake	M L Bryan 20 Jan 1876
	John A Sledge 22 Aug 1876
	Henry R McGinty 25 Nov 1879
	Thomas L Page 12 Feb 1883
East Point	Stanislau F Spencer 17 Jan 1879
	William H Treadwell 24 Mar 1881
	Walter E Hawkins 13 May 1888
Esperanza	Joseph C Brown 17 Jul 1882
Collins Disc 16 May 1883	Philip L Collins 3 Nov 1882
Coushatta	John R McGoldrick 10 May 1883
Fortson Disc 2 Oct 1888	Presley Watkins 18 Feb 1884
Williams	William P Scarborough 11 Nov 1884
Lake End	Will S Atkins 15 Jun 1886

Bedford	Archibald A Farmer 13 Nov 1886 Frank J Pierson 15 Feb 1890 William S Mudgett 16 Jan 1891 William Hutchinson 17 Dec 1891
Blanchard	John A Hunter 18 Nov 1886
Oliphant	Wilford A Oliphant 21 Dec 1887 Lucious O C Grappe 3 Mar 1891
Howard	John Nelson 14 Dec 1888 John C Elstner 18 Nov 1890 Leonard C Russell 11 Nov 1891 Henry J Buvens 13 Apr 1892
Chloie	Oliver C Jones 13 Jun 1889
Andora	Mignet Manti 26 Oct 1889
Lamothe	Salathies S Paul 10 May 1890
Timon	Alonzo N Timon 24 Jul 1891
Buffalo	Benjamin F Britain 28 Dec 1892

RICHLAND PARISH

Alto	Obediah W Williams 2 Jun 1873 William T Ivy 13 Apr 1874 George M Moseley 4 Jun 1874 Peter W Ivy 14 Dec 1874 Leonidas B Duff 2 Aug 1875 William T Ivy 13 Sep 1875 John A Hemler Jr 2 Oct 1882 Robert L Binion 27 Mar 1886
Girard	Julian P Gay 30 Apr 1872 Julian P Gay 19 Aug 1875 J R Brown 25 Apr 1890 Dempsey D Morgan 13 May 1890

Midway   Parke W DeFrance 15 May 1873
Disc 14 Sep 1874
Reest 7 Nov 1874   Albert C Brock 3 Nov 1874
Disc 3 Dec 1875

Rayville   Joe W Simmons 9 Feb 1872
                        Henry B Newhall 16 Jan 1878
                        Lucius E Tisdale 13 Oct 1879
                        George W Wright 21 Aug 1884
                        John H Abraugh 19 Nov 1884
                        J R Brown 27 Apr 1885
                        Robert H Brown 12 May 1885
                        Mrs. Annie C Liddell 29 Mar 1887
                        Mrs. Emma P Hatch 1 Sep 1890

Red Mouth   Adolphe A Gilly 6 Feb 1871
                        H Gilly 27 Jul 1874
                        Jules P Gilly 1 Sep 1874
Disc 27 Sep 1875

Delhi   Calvin H Moore 15 Jun 1873
                        Ronald M Kincaid 28 Dec 1874
                        George Slattery 25 Oct 1875
                        Franklin P McLemore 10 Nov 1875
                        William W Murphy 28 Mar 1879
                        Sarah M Watts 11 Nov 1884

Crew Lake   Thomas Lang 23 Feb 1875
Disc 27 Sep 1875

Charlieville   Charles M Noble 17 May 1877

Goshen   James G Draughon 23 Jun 1884

Boughton   Thomas W Chapman 14 Sep 1886
                        Henrietta F Nichols 18 Nov 1887
                        Isaac W Choat 10 Aug 1888
                        Kate Choat 26 Mar 1892

Mangham	Nathaniel C Vickers 25 Nov 1890 Mary J Powe 27 Oct 1891
Archibald	James B Archibald Jr 14 Jul 1891

SABINE PARISH

Fort Jessup	Theodore Beck 19 Mar 1872 Joseph L Barbee 1 Jul 1874 James N Draughon 23 Nov 1882 Leslie Barbee 21 Apr 1884 William H Barbee 3 Dep 1888
Many Courthouse	William B Stille 22 Apr 1870 Robert B Stille 14 Sep 1875 John B Vendegar 22 Aug 1879
Mill Creek	Samuel T Sibley 23 Oct 1874 Franklin D Self 20 Apr 1875 Jesse P Leach 8 Nov 1875 John A Leach 9 Sep 1889 A C Leach 8 Dec 1890
Darnell's Gin	John Honeycutt 15 Feb 1875 Mrs. Clio A Tuggle 23 Mar 1875 William W Webb 28 Jan 1886 Charles B Darnell 25 Sep 1888
Columbus	John J M Godwin 4 Apr 1876
Negreet	A J Montgomery 7 May 1877
East Pendleton	Daniel P Gandy 23 Jul 1877
Bellemont	Calvin Hardin 12 Aug 1878
San Patricio	Robert G Barron 16 Aug 1878
Lula	James Jackson 29 May 1879 Irwin T Harrell 16 Sep 1879

	A S Robertson 20 May 1881
	Robert L Pollard 15 Jun 1881
Garden	John M Speights 24 Jan 1881
Disc 18 Apr 1881	
Bruce	George E Boles 21 Nov 1881
Disc 19 Jan 1883	
Pleasant Hill	Irwin T Harrell 30 Mar 1882
Bayou Sue	William C Maines 3 Jun 1884
Grover	Elbert M Miles 20 Aug 1885
	Mrs. Julia B Miles 28 Feb 1887
	Moses H Speights 10 May 1887
Disc 9 Mar 1888	
Toro	Moses S Anthony 6 Oct 1885
Prospect	John M Sandell 28 oct 1885
	James E Lee 1 Feb 1886
Disc 8 Jan 1891	
Cedar Grove	Stephen H Westbrook 4 Apr 1887
Mitchell	Jackson L Mitchell 6 Feb 1888
	John B Fuller 23 Oct 1889
	George W Harper 3 Jan 1891
	Albert W Morgan 15 Oct 1891
Royalty	William H Farmer 31 Jul 1888
Rolly	Charles W Adredge 7 Nov 1888
	Meredith M Peters 2 May 1890
Quirk	William Bolton 23 Nov 1889
Belmont	Lewis A Traylor 2 Dec 1889
	George W Heard 28 Jan 1891

	George W Heard 21 Mar 1892
Tynes	Silas A Ricks 30 Jan 1890 William S Tynes 6 Mar 1891
Hatcher	George W Hatcher 19 May 1890
McShan Disc 23 May 1891	George W McShan 30 Jul 1890
Speicher	Winston S Farrar 27 May 1891
Corleyville	William D Hall 13 Jul 1891 Jackson S Corley 6 Jan 1892
Darthula	Serena E Clower 14 Sep 1892
Umber	Fleming Tynes 15 Sep 1892

ST. BERNARD PARISH

Drew's Station Disc 3 may 1875	Francisco Arista 15 Jun 1871
St. Bernard Courthouse	Mrs. Martha A Van Ruff 27 Jun 1871 Christian D Armstrong 11 Mar 1882
La Chinche	William E Wigginton 10 May 1880 John B Mestre 11 Aug 1880 Mrs. Sarah A Woodruff 20 Sep 1880
Disc 3 Aug 1882	
Hopedale	Mrs. Sarah A Woodruff 3 Aug 1882 Katie N Woodruff 2 Mar 1887
Arabi	Arthur J Padrou 25 Aug 1882 Victor Estopinal 5 Jul 1888 Albert Nunez 12 Feb 1889 Albert Nunez 6 Jan 1891 (Pres & Sen)

Reggio	William J Barrett 18 Aug 1884 Arthur Acosta 9 Sep 1885 Leon Nunez 4 Jan 1890
Shell Beach Disc 15 Jul 1886	Jules B Olivier 29 Sep 1884 Antonio Juan 23 Oct 1884
Violet	Alex Latil 21 Nov 1890 Adolphe Hena 4 Sep 1891

ST. CHARLES PARISH

Allemand's	Junius F Williams 13 Dec 1872 Walter Gillespie 20 Mar 1875 Alena M Kincade 11 Oct 1876 Wesley W Wall 13 Mar 1878 Felix Roux 7 Oct 1878 (Illegible entry) Miss Mary Roux 25 Oct 1881 Mrs. Mary Hopkins 21 Nov 1881
Boutte	Joseph B Friedman 6 Aug 1872 Hicks L Young 8 Jul 1886
St. Charles Courthouse	Jacob J Burbank 28 Apr 1873 Marcellus Vallas 13 Jul 1875 John W Innes 8 Aug 1878 Max Gugenheim 27 Jan 1879 (Illegible entry)
Luling	Joseph B Friedman 3 Jan 1878 John W Blanton 22 Mar 1878 Daniel Blum 9 Aug 1880 Joseph Reichenburg 15 Nov 1880 Charles Kluger 28 Mar 1881 Max J Chapsky 20 May 1881 Charles Gassen 5 Apr 1887
Hahnville	Thomas C Madere 14 May 1880

	John Bennett Hinton 20 Mar 1882
	Joseph H Carew 23 Jan 1883
	Abraham Katz 3 Mar 1887
Sarpy	Leon Sarpy 29 Apr 1886
	John Trigre 9 Oct 1889
Elkinsville	John B Walton 21 Nov 1889
Ama	Octave Chenet 27 Apr 1891
	Abraham Strauss 13 Feb 1892

ST. HELENA PARISH

Arcola	John W Leonard 20 Nov 1865
Darlington	S D Heap 13 May 1872
	Louis M Pipkin 20 Aug 1877
	Barnabas H Pipkin 12 Apr 1886
Dennis Mills	John P Merrick 4 Jan 1872
	John Bickham 11 Jan 1875
	John R Hatfield 19 Feb 1875
	Eldridge D Harrell 17 Oct 1877
	Isaac Odom 26 Nov 1877
Disc 7 Mar 1878	
Reest 9 Aug 1878	Enos W Fenn 9 Aug 1878
	Eldridge D Harrell 3 May 1880
Greensburg	James W Cole 15 Mar 1871
Courthouse	William D Floyd 12 Feb 1879
	William A Gill 3 Mar 1879
	Charles M Sitman 17 Dec 1880
	Jonathan A Addison 22 Apr 1881
	Margaret R Wellendon 10 Oct 1881
	Pierce Phillips 4 Jun 1889
Hog Branch	Mrs. Lydia Underwood 25 Jan 1869
Disc 25 Jun 1875	

Pine Grove	William Fletcher 6 Dec 1872
	James P Watson 25 Jun 1875
	William H Miller 13 May 1884
	George W Watson 3 Dec 1884
	Alexander M Hathord 9 May 1888
	James P Watson 28 May 1888
Sunny Hill	Peter Brumfield 23 Nov 1871
	Calvin H Dyson 2 Mar 1884
Tangipahoa	Johnson E Yerkes 25 Oct 1869
Grangeville	James M Odom 8 Dec 1879
Lookout	John D Adcock 11 Dec 1879
	Thomas W Gill 30 Apr 1886
	John B Nettles 22 Dec 1891
Liverpool	Barnham D Rand 3 May 1880
Chipola	Orlando L Collins 22 Jan 1882
Mayer	John D Mayer 15 Jun 1886
Mount Pelier	John M Wilson 22 Jun 1888
	Doctor S Killian 30 Oct 1890
Harvell's Mills	William C Harvell 10 Jul 1888
Hurstville	James A Carruth 9 Apr 1892
Denis Mills	Albert L Odom 7 Sep 1892

ST. JAMES PARISH

Convent Courthouse	Joseph W Shade 1 Feb 1873
	George E Bouee 11 Jan 1875
	Joseph P Landry 24 Aug 1877
	Joseph N Gordain 2 Mar 1887
	Charles Lachapelle 4 Jun 1889

Long View	Alice Melancon 12 May 1871
	Louis J Bourgeois 16 Aug 1875
Disc 20 Oct 1876	
Reest 31 Jan 1877	F P Schexnader 31 Jan 1877
Disc 2 Mar 1877	
Reest 29 Nov 1881	Joseph A Bourgeois 29 Nov 1881
	Theophile F Laiche 29 Aug 1882
St. James	Louis F Fazende 9 Apr 1873
	John J Clayton 18 May 1874
	Adam Travis 27 Apr 1875
	Octave Pourrier 16 Jun 1877
	Arthur J Billon 12 Jan 1882
	Elphege J Pertuit 6 Jun 1887
	Leopold J Peyret 14 Sep 1889
	Paul Billon 27 Jun 1890
St. Patrick	Elphege Poche 5 Dec 1872
	Eraphemon Hebert 18 Jun 1877
	Auguste F Kroll 5 Dec 1889
	Louis J Bouregois 21 Mar 1890
Welcome	B Henry Elfer 14 May 1872
	Auguste Bertaut 12 Feb 1874
	Hugues Serre Jr 13 Sep 1874
	Joseph Cohn Jr 14 Feb 1879
	(Illegible entry)
	Pierre Cagnolatte 11 Nov 1886
	Marie L Gaines 12 Apr 1892
Whitehall	James Roman 1 Mar 1875
	Charles Lachapello 27 Jan 1876
	Benjamin Cohen 7 Apr 1876
Disc 19 Jun 1876	
Central	Charles D Lowenstrom 30 Nov 1881
	Jean A Bourgeois 11 Nov 1884
	Pamelia Bourgeois 20 Nov 1884

Vacherie	Jacob Block 28 Oct 1881
	Armand Johnson 3 Sep 1885
	Pierre A Donaldson 1 Oct 1885
	Louis R Webre 22 Jul 1886
Hester	George C Phillips 23 Nov 1885
	Emmanuel Kahn 27 Jun 1888
Lauderdale	Eugene B Laplace 21 Jan 1889
Union	Henry Thalsheimer 15 Nov 1889
	Jean B Lesaicherre 2 Jan 1892
Paulina	Joseph B Greig 5 Aug 1891
	Florian Brignac 13 Feb 1892
Lutcher	John Faxon 11 Sep 1891
	Daniel H McEwen 10 Oct 1891
	John L Thompkins 29 Mar 1892
Oubre	Thelesmar Oubre 12 Jan 1892

ST. JOHN THE BAPTIST PARISH

Bonnet Carre	Charles Lasseigne 10 Nov 1870
	Jean A Curry 2 Apr 1885
	Mrs. Louisa Hart 30 Apr 1886
De Sair Station	Frederick Bredemeier 25 Mar 1872
	George Huber 19 Mar 1874
	Henry Zollinger 6 Apr 1874
	Hugo J Walther 18 Oct 1875
Disc 17 Apr 1876	
Edgard	Maximillian Bionel 28 Feb 1872
	Optime Rodrique 16 Feb 1881
	Louis Aubert 11 May 1886
	Louis R Webre 25 May 1886
	Emile Bernard 28 Jun 1889
	Jules Joseph 11 Feb 1891

Frenier Disc 15 Apr 1878 Reest 6 Apr 1880	John R Hunter 29 Oct 1877 Mauriel Gannon 6 Apr 1880
Lucy	Agricole B Huguet 2 May 1884 Pierre St. Pierre 5 Mar 1888
Mount Airy	James J Bourgeois 25 Sep 1884
Wallace	Alovon Granier 27 Sep 1886
Eugenia	Henry L Sabourin 26 Sep 1887 Basil Laplace 2 Apr 1891
Ruddock	Leonidas West 12 Nov 1891
Laplace	Basil Laplace 12 Oct 1892

ST. LANDRY PARISH

Arnaudville Disc 17 Apr 1874 Reest 22 Jun 1874	Adeline Durio 13 May 1870 Thules Guilbeau 22 Jun 1874 Emile C Rogers 5 Feb 1875
Bayou Boeuf	Barnabas S Gay 23 May 1868 Barnabas S Gay 10 May 1875
Bayou Chicot	Mrs. Martha A Haas 22 Mar 1871
Big Cane	Leopold Coudchaux 12 Mar 1873 Warren F Jackson 25 Mar 1878 Lewis G Sloane 8 Mar 1888 Elizabeth Sloane 2 Jul 1891
Churchville	William M Nelson 28 Feb 1873 Charlton W Havard 5 Jan 1874 John M Sherrouse 18 Jun 1874 Henry Moulaison 10 Apr 1876

                        Joseph Gibbs 12 Jun 1877
                        Oglesby S Smith 13 Aug 1877
                        Joseph Gibbs 10 Jan 1879
                        J S Morris 14 Oct 1880
                        William C Gordon Jr 7 Aug 1882

Dunbarton   John W Harvey 17 Mar 1873
Disc 16 Jan 1874
Reest 12 Jul 1877   Isaac F Littell 12 Jul 1877
                        James Leake Sr 11 Feb 1878
Disc 12 Dec 1878

Faquetique   Joseph Chenier 5 May 1873
Disc 15 Dec 1873   Joseph Fabacher 18 Jun 1873
Reest 7 Feb 1880   Edward Dardean 17 Feb 1880
Disc 18 Nov 1880

Grand Coteau   Alexander H Castille 22 Mar 1871
                        Mrs. Lizzie D Smith 1 Aug 1889
                        Angello H Grimer 24 Jul 1890

Leonville   Jules D Alfrey 3 Jun 1872
Disc 25 Aug 1875
Reest 6 May 1878   Lawrence Carrere 6 May 1878
                        Joseph N Robin 15 May 1879
                        Pierre Mistick 9 Dec 1879
                        Adolphe Dupuis 19 Mar 1883
                        Adolphe Dupuis Jr 18 Apr 1883
                        Joseph N Robin 30 Apr 1886

Mermenton   Jules Castel 7 Apr 1873
                        Paul Castel 10 Jun 1873
                        Jean Castex 3 Sep 1874
                        Victorian Maignaud 2 Aug 1875

Opelousas   Paul J Lefebure 30 Jan 1872
                        C Donato 1 Jun 1876
                        C Mayo 11 Dec 1876
                        Charles M Thompson 22 Jan 1877 (Pres & Sen)
                        Charles M Thompson 20 Jan 1879 (Pres & Sen)

	Louis Desmarias 15 Sep 1879 (Pres)
	Louis Desmarias 13 Jan 1880 (Pres & Sen)
Disc 30 Jun 1880	
Reest 1 Jul 1880	Louis Desmarias 1 Jul 1880 (Pres & Sen)
	Louis Desmarias 3 Aug 1882 (Pres & Sen)
	Cecile Bailey 12 Aug 1886 (Pres)
	Cecile Bailey 29 Dec 1886 (Pres & Sen)
Plaquemine Broulee	Dallas B Hayes 18 Jan 1872
	George J Rose 18 Jan 1873
	Colbert W Foreman 15 Aug 1873
	Edmund L Harman 27 Apr 1885
Prudhomme	Spotswood H Sanders 15 Apr 1873
	Theodore C Chachere 18 May 1875
	Etienne Staff 25 May 1880
	J O Brunson 8 Feb 1881
	Raymond Chachere 9 Nov 1881
	Etienne Staff 27 Dec 1881
St. Peter's	Frederick Millspaugh 3 Feb 1869
	George W Wilson Jr 31 Jun 1874
	Daniel B Hudson 3 Feb 1876
	William C Scott 2 Jan 1878
	Randolph W Foster 14 Jan 1879
Ville Platte	Oscar Dantean 28 Feb 1872
	Mrs. Octavia Mouilland 22 Aug 1879
	Fremont Fuselier 13 May 1892
Washington	Edward P Goodwin 6 May 1872 (Pres & Sen)
	Henry Woodworth 6 Mar 1876
	Jacob Plousky 24 Jan 1881
	Charles E Nash 15 Feb 1882
	Edward P Goodwin 1 May 1882
	Frank G Ulrick 5 Mar 1883
	Lewis D Prescott 10 Nov 1885
	Francis L Brown 10 Jun 1885
	Jacob Plousky 6 Feb 1890

Fabacher	Joseph Fabacher 11 Jun 1873
	Jenon Huber 12 Mar 1878
Church Point	Jules David 29 Sep 1873
	(Illegible entry)
	P L Guidry 9 Aug 1881
Petite Prairie	Thomas A Hicks 17 Nov 1873
	Evander W Sylvester 12 Feb 1875
	Louis L Andre 6 Jul 1875
	William L McHenry 8 Aug 1876
	George M Perkins 13 May 1879
Disc 8 Jul 1879	
Boreta	Susan I Young 23 Feb 1883
Porte Barre	David P Laizan 13 Mar 1878
Bayou Currant	Henry Skipworth 13 Mar 1878
	Samuel H Faulkner 5 Dec 1879
	Bram A Richards 18 Aug 1881
Pouppeville	Joseph D Bernard 24 Oct 1878
Paris	Alein Vidrine 19 Sep 1879
Disc 17 May 1880	
Turkey Creek	Archibald McPhatton 26 Sep 1879
Science Hill	Abraham W Carroll 26 Sep 1879
	Esther S Brewer 29 Jul 1880
	William H Welch 16 Jan 1883
	John Parrott 19 Oct 1888
Plaisance	Jean Jumere 26 Sep 1879
Disc 16 Dec 1879	
Reest 24 Feb 1881	(Illegible entry)
	Will Evans 19 Mar 1887
Chataignier	Bertha Geullet 20 Nov 1879

Esther Wood Disc 18 Sep 1882	Joseph Ray 3 May 1881 Eugene D Ray 10 May 1882
Range	Joseph D Bernard 20 May 1881 Nicholas Young 26 Jan 1882 Alphonse Duclos 5 Jan 1886
Goudreauville Disc 14 Nov 1881	Samuel Ellinger 3 Oct 1881
Barbreck	Henry M Payne 12 Dec 1881
Garland	Edmund C Quirk 18 Aug 1882 John P Savant 9 Apr 1890 Edmund C Quirk 3 May 1890
Elba	William C Gordon 29 Dec 1882 William C Gordon Jr 24 Jan 1883 Eugene C Richard 19 Jan 1889
Atchafalaya	John A Hayden 5 Jan 1883 Johana H Levy 6 Sep 1883
Morrow Disc 11 Jun 1884 Reest 16 Mar 1888	Ernest Morrow Sr 12 Jun 1883 Fielding E Bell 16 Mar 1888 Warren G Jackson 30 Mar 1888
Goshen Disc 14 Feb 1884	Louis O Guidry 7 Sep 1883
Bearer	Agustus Richmond 28 Sep 1883 William T Morris 26 May 1886
Bossman	Laurent J Bossman 21 Nov 1883 Jacque Siffert 30 Apr 1886
Cartville	Samuel Cart 6 Feb 1884

Rosa Disc 21 Apr 1887 Reest 6 Jun 1889	Joseph F Taurnois 18 Jan 1886 Daniel D Hudspeth 6 Jun 1889 William C Scott 28 Nov 1890
Notleyville	Notley C Devilliers 3 May 1886 William C Johnson 3 Jan 1889 Villier C Devilliers 19 Apr 1890
Schamber	Louis F Schamber 24 Apr 1888
Palmetto	Wesley Budden 28 Apr 1888
Seeleyville	Rodolph C Setting 8 Jun 1888
Pot Cone Disc 13 Feb 1891	Emile Gaubert 31 Aug 1888
Melville	Lyman J Dodge 16 Jan 1889
Shuteston	Edgar Boudreau 19 Aug 1890
Opelousas	Henry Bloch 26 Mar 1891 (Pres) Jules L Chachere 17 Dec 1891 (Pres & Sen)
Frozard	Agricole C Olivier 14 Jul 1891
Pearceville	John H Pearce 1 Aug 1891
Mamou	Augustine Lehay 14 Aug 1891
Belair Cove Disc 12 Feb 1892	Erteluce T Lafleur 11 Sep 1891

ST. MARTIN PARISH

Breaux Bridge	Cyprian Melancon 5 Oct 1890 Elodie Comcan 4 Aug 1885 John A Delhomme 26 Feb 1892

St. Martinville Courthouse	Charles Neven 28 Jul 1873 (Illegible entry) Adolphe Bienvenu 7 Sep 1876 Charles Broussard 28 Jul 1885 Felix Bienvenu 18 May 1889
Laplace	Frederick This 14 Jul 1873 Andre Lastrapes 2 Feb 1880 Amelia Lastrapes 4 Feb 1886 Mrs. Marie Lastrapes 1 Feb 1888
Bayou Chine	Joseph Mendoza 7 Mar 1876 Anatole J Perret 8 Oct 1877
Grand Rivere Disc 17 Jan 1881	Joseph W Allen 24 Aug 1880
Barbreck	Anthony J Bercier 18 Nov 1881
Newton Disc 20 Apr 1887	Charles S Babin Jr 25 Jan 1886
Patin	Joseph A Patin 2 Oct 1889
Cades	Aladin Broussard 28 Jul 1885
Deshotels	Henry H Deshotels 20 Apr 1892

ST. MARY PARISH

Baldwin Disc (No date) Reest 17 Oct 1881	Mrs. Jane S Roberts 27 Jan 1870 John T B Labau 17 Oct 1881 Gustave C Francis 24 Oct 1882 Edward Dasher 7 May 1884 Walter S Borah 12 Jun 1884 Josie Carr 10 Jul 1885 Mrs. Ann Stansbury 19 Feb 1887 Walter S Borah 5 Nov 1889

Brashear	Charles Miller 12 Apr 1870
	Charles Miller 15 Jun 1875 (Pres & Sen)
Centreville	Paul Cheval 9 Aug 1871
	Abram H Cooke 13 Oct 1874
	Paul Cheval 19 Jan 1875
	August B Etienne 21 Feb 1878
Cypremont	O Pecot 29 Apr 1872
	Octave Stouff 8 Nov 1875
	Charles C Hardy 21 Aug 1888
Franklin Courthouse	Abraham Davis 3 Jun 1872
	Washington B Smott 18 Jan 1880
	Abraham Davis 21 Mar 1881
	Abraham Davis 16 Jan 1883 (Pres & Sen)
	James Todd 14 Feb 1887 (Pres & Sen)
	George B Shepherd 11 Apr 1887 (Pres & Sen)
	George B Shepherd 16 Jan 1888 (Pres & Sen)
	Emile H Cornay 30 Apr 1890 (Pres & Sen)
Jeanerette	William F Hudson 19 Oct 1865
	Alex W Edgar 23 Sep 1873
Pattersonville	George W Kern 9 Sep 1870
	Timothy Davis 3 May 1882
Charenton	Mrs. Marguerite C Bienvenu 8 Jul 1873
Le Teche	Mrs. Jane S Roberts 18 May 1875
	Mrs. Emma E Seeley 13 Jan 1876
	Mrs. Jane S Roberts 18 Jul 1876
	John T B Labau 21 Mar 1881
Grand Woods	Robert Gooch 16 Aug 1875
	John Bartells 13 Apr 1876
Disc 20 Apr 1877	
Morgan City	Charles Miller 15 Feb 1876 (Pres & Sen)

	Charles Miller 3 Mar 1880 (Pres & Sen)
	O F Woodcock 19 Jan 1882 (Pres & Sen)
	Neil Sinclair 4 Feb 1884 (Pres & Sen)
	Neil Sinclair 1 Jul 1884
	Jacques Lehman 16 Oct 1884
	Henry M Mayo 18 Nov 1884
	Felix M Tucker 30 Aug 1890
North Bend Disc 8 Oct 1879	S J Swenson 1 Jul 1879
Glencoe	Spencer B Roane 2 Jul 1877 (Illegible entry) Joseph D C Brown 2 Jun 1881 Moses S Alexander 27 Dec 1883 Addie A Gordy 8 Feb 1886 Moses S Alexander 30 Aug 1890
Irish Bend Disc 31 Dec 1878 Reest 30 Oct 1885	Edward M Johnson 1 May 1878 Alexander K Sterling 30 Oct 1885 Ralph E Hine 15 Feb 1889
Berwick	Elias S Batner 19 May 1879 William S Cary 8 Apr 1880 Webster Radler 5 Oct 1883 Isaac Reinauer 12 Dec 1883 Mrs. Henrietta Rosenbaum 12 Jan 1888
Grand Cote	Augustus T Caillouet 13 Oct 1879 William T Weeks 11 Jan 1882
Amelia	Joseph S DeLucky 19 Mar 1880 Felix Thibodeaux 22 Jul 1885 Joseph S DeLucky 6 Nov 1889
Achen Disc 25 Jun 1883	E N Ratier 28 Jan 1881 Domingue Rodrigue 26 Jul 1881 James Gasper 25 Aug 1881

Bartels	James J Inneranty 22 May 1880
	Gradenijo J Young 23 Feb 1882
	Louis Levy 21 May 1883
	Gradenijo J Young 14 Jun 1883
	Joseph J Inneranty 20 Dec 1883
	William W Weightman 22 Jan 1887
	Herman L Bidstrop 4 Apr 1887
	Isaac Mayer 2 Apr 1890
Foster	Roswell W Trowbridge 1 Apr 1881
	Gustave Schmulen 26 Sep 1884
	Joseph Van Brook 23 Oct 1885
	Joseph E Munson 4 Feb 1886
	Adolphe D Lacy 22 Dec 1886
	George F Leminger 15 Jun 1889
	Seymour P Gagnet 3 Jun 1890
	J D Capron 19 Nov 1891
	Joseph Washington 11 Mar 1892
Scally	Michel Schmulen 9 Oct 1884
	John Markham 5 Jun 1885
Disc 19 Nov 1885	
Louisa	Jules M Burguieres 3 Aug 1885
Patterson	Timothy Davis 16 Dec 1887
Ramos	John J Greenwood 4 Apr 1888
	Ernest W Dreibholz 8 Mar 1892
Winsted	Samuel H Kinchire 19 Feb 1889
Rhodes	John J Greenwood 2 Aug 1890

ST. TAMMANY PARISH

Covington	Mrs. Anna M Dumas 18 Nov 1872
	Charles Heintz 1 Jun 1885
	William W Johnson 18 Jun 1889

Madisonville	Washington H R Haugen 8 Jan 1872
	Henry B Baughman 23 Oct 1877
	Thomas Badneaux 12 Sep 1878
	John R Haas 23 Jun 1881
	Bernard Goldat 20 Nov 1882
Mandeville	Wyndham R Nixon 26 May 1871
	William C Morgan 26 Aug 1874
	Mrs. Jane Angelina Mugnier 5 Feb 1877
	Louise Alvarez 9 Dec 1885
	William W Johnson 17 Dec 1890
	(Illegible entry)
	Frank Ribava 10 Oct 1891
	Louise Alvarez 23 Feb 1892
Bonfonca	S Block 6 Oct 1875
	John Frederick 2 Mar 1876
	N Levy 11 Sep 1884
Disc 27 May 1885	
Bayou Lacomb	Charles Aubry de Isle-Roux 6 Oct 1875
	Walter C Ernest 17 Jan 1881
	Joseph H Black 27 Aug 1881
	Euphrasie Cousin 11 Nov 1891
Pearl River	Friday N Porter 6 Oct 1875
	Emily J Welsh 7 Jun 1888
	Henry J McGehee 20 Mar 1891
	Aline M Lagrone 3 Feb 1892
English Lookout	George M Brown 16 Dec 1878
	Mrs. Amantheus P Joyner 13 Jan 1879
	Angelo V Ward 20 Jun 1882
	Daniel L Green 10 Sep 1885
Tchefuncta	George R Deichman 26 Feb 1879
	J M Core 13 Nov 1882
Disc 1 Mar 1883	
Halloo	Joseph A Stafford 20 May 1880

Halloo	Joseph A Stafford 20 May 1880
	George L Peavance 30 Mar 1881
	Cyrus W Gillin 25 Aug 1882
	Emily J Welsh 10 Sep 1883
Violin	Samuel R Wilson 7 Jun 1880
	Bannat Bourn 21 Oct 1881
	Margarett Magee 27 May 1886
	Samuel R Wilson 16 Feb 1891
Talisheek	Jesse M Abney 19 Jul 1880
	Frederick Matthies 2 Jan 1883
Sun	John G Mizell 14 Sep 1882
Slidell	Jacob F Hufft 7 Jan 1884
Lewisburg Disc 3 Mar 1885	Jules Herbelin 1 Sep 1884
Abita Springs	Thomas H McAvoy 20 Dec 1887
	Alfred A Cooley 22 Jul 1891
Florenville	John A Orr 22 May 1888
Pearlville	Friday N Porter Jr 7 Jul 1888
Delphi Disc 8 Sep 1891	William H Shaw 14 Aug 1890
Guthrie	John J McHarron 14 Aug 1891
Chinchuba	E V Lebreton 25 Nov 1891
	Hyacinthe C Mignot 10 Dec 1891
Thomasville	Edward B Thomas 1 Mar 1892
Verger	Paul Verger 14 Mar 1892

TANGIPAHOA PARISH

Amite City Courthouse	William H Wilder 15 Jan 1866
	George W Bell 23 Apr 1875
	M H Hankstow 5 Jul 1876
	James B Cason 22 Nov 1876
	Archibald A Alsworth 18 Sep 1879
	James B Cason 20 Jan 1881
	John N Alsworth 20 Jun 1883
	Guy C Kemp 17 Mar 1879
Hammond	Henry C Mooney 11 Sep 1868
	Miss Mary E Fitch 3 Dec 1890
	Mrs. Mary E Watson 26 Jun 1891
Independence	Hillary K George 14 Dec 1871
	Henry Saal Jr 16 Dec 1873
	Darling B Cason 19 Apr 1875
	Robert L Cloud 3 Apr 1876
	John C Albin 19 Jan 1879
Ponchatoula	Michael Biegel 19 Dec 1866
	Thomas M Ferry 5 Nov 1875
	Michael Biegel 23 May 1876
	Mrs. Katherine Biegel 20 Oct 1876
	James Tucker 25 Feb 1878
	Robert Benefield 8 Mar 1881
	George A Biegel 25 Oct 1881
	Millard F Tucker 16 Dec 1885
	Thomas M Akens 12 Jan 1889
	Caroline Biegel 20 May 1889
Tickfaw	Henry Watts 7 Aug 1871
	James S Gatlin 19 Jan 1875
Disc 3 Mar 1877	
Reest 17 Dec 1877	William A House 17 Dec 1877
Disc 8 Aug 1878	
Reest 9 Feb 1880	William A Welby 9 Feb 1880
	Morris Bankston 2 May 1884
	Willie C Ogilvie 10 Sep 1884

	John W Bradley 18 Mar 1885
	Mary P Gatlin 27 Nov 1885
	Lillie O Kinchen 12 Feb 1887
	John Albecht 17 Mar 1888
Disc 7 Dec 188	
Reest 28 Dec 1888	William L Wright 28 Dec 1888
Welch's Bridge	James D Welch 5 Aug 1872
Disc 24 Sep 1875	
Pass Manchac	James M Alexander 9 Jun 1873
Disc 8 Apr 1880	
Tangipahoa	Johnson E Yerkes 25 Oct 1869
	G W Wheat 3 Sep 1874
	Charles H Hyde 12 Jan 1875
	John Paris Wall 23 May 1876
	Richard C Eubanks 3 May 1877
Sunny Hill	Calvin H Dyson 2 Mar 1874
	George W Dyson 3 Sep 1874
	James O Magee 9 Jul 1880
Arcola	Alfred Rhody 22 Dec 1874
	Isaac N Wands 22 Jan 1883
Chappeau Pela	Thomas Garaky 2 Jul 1877
Liverpool	Levi R Stark 22 Sep 1879
	Burnam D Rand 3 May 1880
Peace Grove	Richard H Scaries 9 Jun 1880
Moss	Leonard W Strader 14 Nov 1881
Disc 30 Jan 1883	
Kentwood	William G Hall 29 Feb 1888
	Leroy S Stanford 2 Aug 1889
	Samuel L Broyles 10 Dec 1890

Husser Mill	Hyppolite L Husser 17 Jul 1888
Murdock	James D Brock 31 Jul 1888
Roseland	George L Sharretts 13 Jun 1889 J R Richard 14 May 1891 (Order rescinded 14 May 1891) George L Sharretts 14 May 1891
Katie	Katie Cooper 25 Oct 1889
Breland	William G Breland 6 Sep 1890 Salissa E Pierce 28 May 1891
Bailey	Caldwell H Bailey 18 Oct 1890
Gessen	Gallus M Aneran 15 Nov 1892

TENSAS PARISH

Buck Ridge Disc 14 Apr 1874 Reest 22 Jun 1874 Disc 9 Jan 1877	Edward Lake 22 Jan 1872 Thomas Q Munce 22 Jun 1874
Hard Times Landing	Henry P Bell 14 Apr 1873 Samuel W Wren 21 May 1874 Henry C Bridge 12 Oct 1874 Jacob R Groves 1 Oct 1877 Daniel Morris 2 Dec 1878
St. Joseph Courthouse	Charles E Bowman 16 Jan 1871 Henry F Shaifer 11 Jan 1875 Miss Jennie Parr 30 Dec 1878 James Curry 20 Oct 1881 Albert Boudurant 24 Dec 1883
Waterproof	Benjamin F Bonney 19 Oct 1871 Lewis Cossel 5 Jan 1884 Hamilton McCullough Jr 27 Mar 1874

	Michael Marron 2 Oct 1874
	William H Griffith 17 Oct 1876
	Napoleon B Hunter 13 Dec 1878
	Calvin H Kinney 26 Dec 1882
	William F Reilly 14 Aug 1883
	S W Green 26 Sep 1884
	Miles Bonney 22 May 1885
	William F Bonney 11 Mar 1887
	Mark Andrews 28 Jun 1889
Mound Bayou Disc 9 Aug 1887	R B Lynch 22 Jun 1874
New Carthage Disc 6 Nov 1877 Reest 18 Dec 1877	Daniel Andrews 3 Aug 1874 Stanton B Pittman 18 Dec 1877 Clarence S James 22 Aug 1879 Lucien D James 1 Aug 1881
Point Pleasant	Ernest Turner 17 May 1877 M L Merchant 7 Mar 1882 Archibald Bland 3 Jul 1882 John S Campbell 19 Dec 1890 Samuel Marks 18 May 1891
Highland	William F Reilly 20 Jun 1879 Harrison C Miller 18 Jun 1883
Argent	Joseph P Porter 3 Jul 1879 William M Seaman 5 Mar 1886 Berthold B Lehmann 16 Jan 1880
New Light	William W Cooley 7 Jan 1880 Daniel F Myers 13 Sep 1883
Ashwood	John A Quackenboss 5 Apr 1880 John B O'Kelley 13 Feb 1883
Newellton	Charles Michelson 6 May 1880 Edward T Newell 9 Jun 1880

	Julius Morris 10 Mar 1881
	Louis Buckner 29 Sep 1884
Goldman	Emmanuel Levy 4 May 1886
	Nathan Levy 26 May 1886
	William M Seaman 30 Apr 1891
Dickard	Andrew J Gibon Sr 4 Aug 1886
Stellia	Pliny W Smith 23 Nov 1889
Ettringham	John B Barry 9 Dec 1891

TERREBONNE PARISH

Ardoyne Disc 17 Nov 1873	Henry V J Cooke 3 Jun 1872
Chacachoula	Leonard P Lasseigne 7 Apr 1873
	Jules D Echaus 1 Feb 1875
	R P Fleming 30 Jul 1880
	Richard S McMahon 8 Nov 1880
	Numa F Boudreaux 17 Jul 1890
Houma Courthouse	James L Belden 18 May 1870
	Mrs. Louisa Verdella 1 Jul 1873
	Mrs. Josephone Sherburn 16 Feb 1877
	M C B Mason 25 May 1891
	John B Budd 2 Oct 1882
	John B Budd 14 Feb 1884 (Pres & Sen)
	Isham Pollard 16 Jun 1884 (Pres & Sen)
	Caroline Wagner 10 Jul 1885
	Morley H Wallis 18 Mar 1889
	Morley H Wallis 1 Oct 1890 (Pres & Sen)
Live Oak	Monarch Littman 13 May 1872
	Henry C Balch 2 Mar 1874
	James D Wilson 14 Feb 1877
Disc 8 Jan 1879	
Reest 30 Jan 1879	James Lunny 30 Jan 1879

	Mrs. Emma Lunny 24 Feb 1879
	James D Wilson 24 Mar 1881
Terrebonne	Henry B Holcombe Jr 26 Aug 1872
	Henry Schlesinger 8 Aug 1873
	James Toler 19 Jun 1874
	Henry M Johnson 24 Jul 1874
	Benjamin D Johnson 1 Nov 1879
	Julius D Machade 16 Oct 1880
	Benjamin D Johnson 11 May 1881
	Thomas Beary 14 May 1883
	F W Smith Jr 26 Dec 1883
Tigerville	William Price 13 Nov 1871
	Rufus E Rose 16 Apr 1875
	Aristide E P Albert 12 Apr 1876
	William M Moody 4 Aug 1876
	John B Moody 19 Apr 1888
Point Farm	Peter P Flynn 31 Mar 1875
Disc 13 Nov 1876	
Jewell	Lillie Bascle 13 Mar 1875
Disc 27 Sep 1875	
Belle Grove	Thomas J Dannis 1 May 1878
Disc 10 Jun 1878	
St. Eloi	Armand St. Martin 18 Dec 1879
Disc 20 Oct 1880	
Ellendale	William Ritter 1 Mar 1882
Landoak	E S Rochel 1 Aug 1882
	J C Jackson 4 Sep 1881
Disc 27 Nov 1882	
Dulac	James D Wilson 22 Jan 1883
	A J Davidson 21 May 1885
	Louise Robichaux 7 May 1887

	Alphonse Z Boudreaux 18 Jan 1888
	Frank Lotsinger 18 Apr 1888
Lacache	Arthur Leblanc 7 Jan 1884
	Pierre S Malbroux 11 Jan 1886
	Ludger Guidry 22 Dec 1886
	Mollie Concannon 17 Dec 1887
	Alcide C Lasseigne 27 Nov 1888
Disc 29 Aug 1889	
Schriever	Edward H Chapman 8 May 1885
	George C Marshall 29 Sep 1886
	Cleophas A Toups 1 Apr 1887
	John T Moore 21 Jan 1892
Montegut	Eugene Fields 22 Jul 1885
Disc 15 Sep 1888	
Gibson	John B Moody 12 Jul 1888
	John B Moody 15 Sep 1888
Theriot	Armand St. Martin 21 Aug 1891

UNION PARISH

Downsville	Wesley B Anderson 31 Mar 1873
	William J Brewster 10 Nov 1873
	Wesley B Anderson 5 Jan 1874
	Perry K Smith 17 Jul 1876
	Curtis T Hines 17 Oct 1876
	W B Ethridge 18 Oct 1877
Disc 3 Sep 1879	
Reest 17 Nov 1879	Edward S Pipes 17 Nov 1879
	Charles J Hammons 14 Aug 1882
	Delana P Hicks 13 Sep 1883
	Colwell C Hester 18 Aug 1884
	Thomas P Ford 10 Jul 1886
	James M Hamilton 5 Oct 1887
Farmerville	James C Trimble 17 Oct 1867

Courthouse	William C Carr 10 May 1875
	Isaac Shuster 30 Jan 1878
Lone Well	James H McBroom 20 Nov 1867
Disc 17 Dec 1884	
Marion	John J Loper 4 Oct 1869
	George F Clark 4 Feb 1874
	Benjamin F George 4 Jun 1879
	John W Hopkins 9 Feb 1880
	Jasper H Rourk 19 Apr 1880
	B T Hopkins 7 Mar 1881
	Jasper H Rourk 4 May 1881
	E L Powell 22 Mar 1890
	James L Hopkins 9 Jun 1890
	Jasper H Rourk 11 Jun 1892
Meridian	John B Robinson 2 Jun 1873
Disc 21 Aug 1876	
Ouachita City	William Parks 2 May 1872
	Ollio B Steele 28 May 1877
	James O Barr 1 Dec 1879
	Oliver P Smith 30 Jan 1880
	R S Swan 29 Sep 1880
	John A Peak 21 Jun 1881
	Charles E Pratt 14 Sep 1889
	Celestia Newman 28 Aug 1890
	Edna F Clark 14 Feb 1891
Shiloh	William G Simmons 4 Feb 1873
	J J Booles 3 Jan 1875
	Joseph W Heard 2 Jan 1885
Spearsville	James M Post 6 Jan 1873
	Basil J Hayes 27 Mar 1874
	Robert W Goyne 18 Nov 1878
	John C Cole 29 Jul 1886
Union Cross Roads	Mrs. Dettie A Goldsby 5 Oct 1868

Mars Hill Disc 7 Feb 1877	Samuel G Stozier 20 Jan 1874
Oakland	Mrs. Dettie A Goldsby 6 Apr 1874 Joseph H Seale 8 Feb 1875 Thomas H McFadin 15 Dec 1881 George E Murphy 22 Apr 1892
Moseley's Bluff	Richard S Ashcroft 17 Mar 1875 Marion W Raley 10 May 1881 Henry E Moseley 2 Mar 1882 Richard S Ashcroft 6 Mar 1882 Henry E Moseley 6 Jan 1883 Richard S Ashcroft 28 Sep 1883 Henry E Moseley 22 Jun 1886
Cherry Ridge	William E Davis 11 Jun 1875
Bethel Springs	James B Huff 4 Dec 1877 Alfred J Ward 19 Feb 1879
Alabama Disc 5 Sep 1882	Lewis G Campbell 3 Jan 1878
D'Arbonne	Eli Rugg 22 Mar 1880 James M Pardue 23 Dec 1880 John S Bransford 27 Mar 1886 James M Pardue 28 May 1891 William P Turner 4 Dec 1891
Walnut Lane	Sallie C Sellers 23 Jul 1880 Sarah A Sellers 26 May 1886
Port Union Disc 15 Feb 1882	William P Smith 8 Nov 1880
Conway	Ezra B Bilberry 19 Apr 1881
Raleigh	Henry T White 13 Nov 1883

Disc 20 Feb 1885	
Farmerville	Isaac Shuster 25 Sep 1886
Colson's Disc 22 Sep 1887 Reest 15 Jul 1889	Francis M Roane 12 Mar 1887 Jacob L B Caver 15 Jul 1889 Shadrack J Wall 5 Apr 1892
Weldon	Jordan Jones 20 Nov 1889
Deglaze	Samuel B Reppond 14 Jun 1890
Point	Jessie P Reilly 14 Aug 1891

VERMILION PARISH

Abbeville	George E Lyons 4 Feb 1873 Joseph T Labit 29 Mar 1875 Ophelius Bourque 10 Jul 1885 Joseph T Labit 4 Jun 1889
Grand Chenier	James B Rogers 1 Mar 1871
Grand Marais	Desire Delcambre 6 Jul 1880
Indian Bayou	William Shepherd 7 Mar 1879 Martin Sarver 9 Dec 1879 Esaphania Hoffpauir 5 Mar 1891
Tiger Bend	Alexander N Gass 18 Dec 1879
Perry	Alfred Baudoin 16 Mar 1887 (Illegible entry) John T Hamblett 24 Oct 1889
Ramsey	Martin Bagley 28 Jan 1884
Gregg	Celeste A Monisset 16 May 1884 Homer Leman 2 Feb 1886

	Lucius Leblanc 1 Dec 1886
	Desire Delcambre 9 Mar 1888
Peigneur Disc 31 Mar 1890	Nicholas Broussard 18 Apr 1886
Shell Beach	Eugene Deschamps Jr 20 Dec 1887
Theall	Joseph Theall 6 Mar 1888
Milton	Desire O Broussard 24 Sep 1890 Milton R Cushman 6 Jan 1892
Tortue Disc 15 Aug 1891	Donat Mouseaux 21 Nov 1890 William G Lounsberry 11 Jun 1891
Henry	William M Conerly 25 Nov 1890

WASHINGTON PARISH

Franklinton Courthouse	William H Jones 4 Dec 1872 Mrs. Nannie Buckham 30 Mar 1881 W W Babington 17 May 1881 Thomas M Babington 10 Nov 1881
Palestine	Young P Bankston 25 Aug 1871 David H Stringfield 7 Mar 1877 Emma Applefield 14 Apr 1880 Edward Myles 16 Nov 1881 Edward W Dykes 9 Jan 1883 Henry A Goings 4 Apr 1887
Shady Grove	William A Daniel 18 Dec 1871 William G Stovall 3 Dec 1875 Robert Daniel 28 Nov 1886 Thomas P Fornea 30 Apr 1887 L Poole 29 Dec 1890 Samuel W Wilkes 5 Apr 1892

Thomas Mill	Stephen S Thomas 11 Jun 1878
	Stephen S Thomas 3 Jul 1888
Lee's Creek	Martin G Williams 5 Dec 1879
Balltown	Julia S Ball 21 Aug 1884
Sunny Hill	James O Magee 9 Jul 1880
Gorman	Uriah V Brumfield 18 May 1887
Mount Herman	Elbert W Ott 12 Jun 1888
Magee	H G Magee 16 Jun 1888
Mount Point	Walter L Smith 17 Jun 1888
Robertson Disc 9 Dec 1891	Alonzo L Brown 7 Jul 1888
Enon	Eldridge Magee 11 Feb 1889
Zona	Eldridge Magee 14 Feb 1889
	Margaret A Magee 30 Mar 1891
Whittington Disc 2 Mar 1892	Wesley W Whittington 9 Dec 1889
Popeville	Alexander C Pope 9 Jun 1890
	James McSchilling 7 Jan 1892
Myles Disc 2 Apr 1892	Edward Myles 19 Aug 1890
Booth	John E Ball 1 Apr 1892
Bogalousa	James G Rester 6 Aug 1892
Faliah	Sandy D Bullock 28 Sep 1892

McDougall	Myford McDougall 21 Oct 1892

WEBSTER PARISH

Cotton Valley	George W Martin 13 Oct 1871 Sidney R Bryan 6 Nov 1878 Hattie Collins 24 Dec 1884 Nancy C Wattis 15 Jul 1886 James D Middlebrooks 20 Jan 1889 Harry L Parham 8 May 1890 Elizabeth Mouzingo 15 Apr 1891 Hattie Collins 12 Feb 1892
Minden Courthouse	James D Harper 3 Jun 1870 George W Morrow 8 Feb 1875 James C Wilkins 16 Aug 1875 John C Chaffe 31 Jul 1877 William T Nuckolls 18 May 1889
Buckhorn Disc 15 Sep 1879 Reest 14 Oct 1879	John Adams Mims 15 Feb 1867 David J Mims 26 Apr 1875 John W Hutchens 14 Oct 1879 Martha A Mims 11 Jul 1881 John W Hutchens 4 Sep 1883
Shongaloo Disc 14 Jul 1881 Reest 10 Aug 1881	Thomas H McEacham 18 Apr 1878 W M Harrison 10 Aug 1881 George W Patten 17 Jan 1888
Dorcheate	Jackson Sikes 14 May 1878 Jesse F Sikes 15 Nov 1881 Rebecca C Boydston 20 Dec 1881 William H Manley 11 Jan 1884 J O Martin 27 Apr 1885 William J Benthall 8 Jun 1885 Jesse F Sikes 20 Mar 1886
Sikes Ferry	Martha F Sikes 11 Nov 1879

	Thomas L Cox 13 Jul 1888
	Benjamin F Smith 21 Dec 1888
	Benjamin F Sikes 1 Dec 1890
	William J Waggoner 31 Jul 1891
Martinsville	Timothy Oakley 20 Nov 1879
Timothea	Timothy Oakley 5 Jan 1880
Sarepta	John M Moore 16 Jul 1883
	James J Allen 24 Nov 1884
Taylor	Lawrence A Taylor 10 Sep 1883
Lanesville	Reuben A Brittian 6 Mar 1884
	Sylvanus M Kemie 21 Jul 1884
	Rufus F Lane 27 Apr 1885
	John W Wilson 18 May 1886
	Rufus F Lane 8 Jun 1886
	B J McLemore 21 Jul 1886
	John W Wilkinson 22 Jan 1887
	Fannie E McLemore 23 Nov 1889
Brushwood	John J Ellington 11 Jun 1884
	Edward J Kennon 27 Apr 1885
	Charles C Cheshire 11 Jan 1886
Doyline	Henry C Doyle 29 Aug 1884
	Thomas J Jackson 10 Sep 1888
Pleasanton	Albert P Edwards 28 Sep 1885
Dubberly	Charles C Cheshire 26 Mar 1887
Langston	Robert Langston 4 Apr 1887
Milton	James M Caldwell 6 Aug 1888
	James Smith 22 Aug 1888
Disc 19 Oct 1888	

Hearn	James W Bickenou 17 Jan 1891
McGinty	Fleming L McCoy 29 Jun 1891 John T Martinsdale 21 Dec 1891
Clifford	William B Stevens 8 Aug 1892
Yellow Pine	Harris S Matthews 10 Aug 1892
Velma	William H Nichols 22 Oct 1892

WEST BATON ROUGE PARISH

Brusly Landing Disc 6 Apr 1874 Rest 31 Jul 1875	Joseph E Caire 22 Jul 1872 Henry C Bernard 31 Jul 1875 John E Babin 31 Jul 1876 Joseph E Caire 31 Jan 1883 Edwin O Gwin 21 Jan 1889 John E Babin 11 Feb 1889 Charles S Burns 22 May 1884
Labdell's Store Disc 12 Sep 1873	Archibald H Lamon 20 Nov 1871
West Baton Rouge Courthouse	Philip Bauer 19 Apr 1872
Glenwood Disc 20 May 1874	Abraham Levy 24 Oct 1873
Allain	W Shannon Woods 5 Mar 1875 Cornelius J Barrow 31 Jul 1876
Hermitage	Francis E Trudeau 12 Apr 1877 Hermes E Trudeau 8 Apr 1880 Louis Villemez 21 Jan 1889
Grossman's Landing	Jacob Grossman 26 Apr 1879

	E Kaufman 3 Feb 1882
Port Allen	Cornelius J Barrow 24 Apr 1875
	William W Bauer 11 Jun 1889
	George D Cole 1 Sep 1890
	Henry G Parker 2 Nov 1891
Arbroth	S L Hereford 11 Oct 1880
	Theodore J Reames 24 Oct 1880
Labdell	James L Labdell 18 Nov 1880
	James L Labdell 8 Aug 1883
	Edward F Phillips 27 Feb 1886
	Thomas Jones 6 Dec 1889
Devall	George W Hamilton 17 Apr 1882
Sinclair Landing	Charles S Burns 19 Aug 1892

WEST FELICIANA PARISH

Bayou Tunica	William A Williams 2 Feb 1869
	John J Winn 1 Jul 1874
St. Francisville Courthouse	James H Stephens 1 Apr 1872
	Joseph R Watson 4 Sep 1876
	James H Stephens 27 Sep 1876
	John S Dulo 15 Dec 1876
	John S Dulo 20 Mar 1877
	James H Stephens 2 Jul 1877
	H A Banq 22 Oct 1877
	H A Binning 26 Oct 1877
	James H Stephens 6 Mar 1878
	John H Wooster 8 Dec 1879
Angola	(Illegible entry)
	Claude M Acklen 19 Dec 1877
Disc 3 Jan 1879	
Reest 10 Aug 1882	Isidore Lemle 10 Aug 1882
	Samuel Jacobs 26 Dec 1882

	Samuel L James 28 Nov 1883
Bayou Sara	John S Wooster 4 Feb 1880
	J Oscar Howard 24 Jul 1882
	Warren S Gay 15 Jan 1884 (Pres & Sen)
	Warren S Gay 4 Jul 1884
	J Oscar Howell 2 Jan 1885
	John S Wooster 28 Sep 1885
	Francis M Mumford 15 Jul 1886
	Francis M Mumford 28 Feb 1889 (Pres & Sen)
Miles Disc 16 Nov 1882	Charles S Miles 10 Aug 1882
Row Landing Disc 20 Apr 1887	Harmon W Jones 6 Feb 1884
Woods Disc 21 Apr 1887	Walter Woods 30 Dec 1885
Ratcliff	John H Clack 14 Mar 1888
Laurel Hill	Charles H Argne 25 Jun 1889
Converse	Edward W Converse 11 Mar 1890

WINN PARISH

Atlanta	Mrs. Emily E Peace 20 May 1873
	Mrs. Addie Lecois 27 May 1881
	George C Lewis 28 Feb 1882
	Mrs. A Lewis 9 Mar 1883
	George C Lewis 3 Apr 1882
Flat Creek	Samuel J Harper 3 Jul 1872
	George W Fletcher 12 Dec 1873
	William Fletcher 29 Jan 1874
	Hugh M Naughton 1 Jul 1874
	George W Fletcher Jr 5 Oct 1875

Gansville Disc 3 Mar 1875 Reest 21 Jun 1875	William M Moffett 20 Jan 1873 James E Bain 21 Jun 1875 George L Stinson 7 Apr 1879 Mrs. Lee J Wilkinson 10 Jul 1888
Montgomery	George A Matthews 24 Jul 1867
Newport	Levi Banks 3 Jun 1872 William B Everett 18 Jun 1877 John H Morris 28 May 1881 William L Mayes 15 Mar 1888 John H Morris 1 Mar 1890
Pine Ridge Disc 4 Aug 1875 Reest 28 Sep 1875	James P Readheimer 23 Jun 1871 John W Snelling 28 Sep 1875 Smallwood D Clifton 20 Dec 1887 Simna A Clifton 29 Aug 1888 John D Meadows 23 Nov 1889
St. Maurice Disc 29 oct 1874 Reest 11 Jan 1875	Conrad Starks 12 Jun 1871 William A Strong 11 Jan 1875 H M Prothro 20 Nov 1877 Jessie H Hickman 20 Aug 1878 Mrs. Sarah M Sims 10 Oct 1881 Charles L Boulle 12 Jul 1882 Henry T Carr 11 Nov 1884 Elisha J Gamble 28 Jan 1886
Winfield Courthouse	Austin C Banks 14 Mar 1872 J Meade Jennings 26 Apr 1875 David F Dunn 5 Mar 1883
Hickory Valley	Amos M Casty 22 Jun 1874
Hermitage	John C Landreau 10 Jul 1867 Jacques Deplaigne 19 Feb 1875 John C Landreau 23 Mar 1875

	E Trudeau 12 Apr 1877
Beech Creek	Lewis N Holmes 31 Mar 1879
	G M Tippen 23 Aug 1880
Disc 8 Nov 1880	
Gaar's Mills	Pinkney E Grisham 12 May 1879
Sills	Sarah E James 13 May 1881
	James L Dark 17 Jun 1884
	John M Jones 13 Dec 1886
	Alexander P Collins 17 Jul 1890
Cold Water	Thomas E Thompson 7 Aug 1882
	Ambrose M Bryant 22 Oct 1883
Cold Teagle	Emma Teagle 20 Feb 1884
Disc 5 Apr 1884	
Millsborough	John J Dickinson 13 Jun 1884
Couley	Charles J Phillips 3 Sep 1885
	Nancy J Everett 29 Oct 1890
Killen	George W Killen 10 Nov 1885
Disc 21 Apr 1887	
Bertrand	David B Williams 16 Mar 1886
	W B Mask 4 Dec 1890
	Nathan D Morris 29 Dec 1890
	Roxey Ray 17 Dec 1891
	Finis E Fullerton 17 Dec 1891
Tunica	Spencer M Smith 16 Mar 1886
Carthage	Edward Eagles Jr 15 Sep 1886
Red Hill	James J Holmes 26 Aug 1887
	Abraham L Wright 12 Jan 1892

Wattsville	Delaney M Bryant 25 Jun 1889
	James Carter 13 Jan 1891
Walls	James R Sikes 15 Jul 1889
Hurricane	Osy M L Barnes 20 Jul 1889
	Theodore L Jones 13 Aug 1890
Disc 15 May 1891	
Wheeling	William J Robbins 30 Jan 1890
Disc 6 Aug 1890	
Hudson	J E Gaar Sr 17 Oct 1890
Disc 6 May 1892	
Mount Zion	Susie W Harris 5 Mar 1891
	Elisha Crew 28 Jun 1892

VERNON PARISH

Burr's Ferry	John M Liles 1 Jul 1873
	Charles B Burr 24 Apr 1876
	James C Roberts 13 Feb 1879
	John M Liles 18 Dec 1882
	Lewis A Perkins 14 Oct 1884
	James C Roebuck 15 Jul 1886
	Thomas C Wingate 24 Oct 1889
Leesville	Isaac O Winfree 22 Aug 1873
	Cora A Bolgiano 20 Nov 1889
Walnut Hill	Jessie E Collins 10 Nov 1873
	(Illegible entry)
Disc 13 Oct 1879	
Reest 5 Dec 1879	Samuel C Sweat 5 Dec 1879
	Samuel Roberts 19 Jan 1880
	Thomas H Bedsole 3 Sep 1885
	James G Hagan 20 Apr 1891
	John Ford 3 Mar 1892
	James S Derrough 29 Mar 1892

Black Land Cottage Disc 21 Jun 1880	Cavil Bray 22 Dec 1873
Anacoco	John J Kirk 28 Sep 1875
Loretta	John A Lovett 8 Dec 1879 T M Cain 17 Aug 1881 Edward Cain 3 Nov 1881
Disc 21 Jun 1882 Reest 5 Jul 1888	Ethelbert L Cannon 1 Feb 1883
Toleda	William R Shehan 26 Jan 1880 John K Foster 31 May 1890
Elmwood	Nathaniel S Williams 26 Mar 1880
Caney	Thomas Richardson 22 Jun 1880
Carmel Disc 2 Feb 1882	Aplin E Chitty 13 Sep 1881
Almadane	Daniel R Wright 3 May 1882 John C Knight 19 May 1886
Hardshell	Christopher C Hunt 10 Mar 1884 James W Brumfield 15 Mar 1886
Dido	John J Weldon 14 Jul 1886 John F Sirmons 2 Dec 1889
Sandy Creek	Young C Palmer 3 Nov 1886
Hicks	James J Hicks 18 May 1887 John M Newman 11 Jul 1887 Daniel Johnson 4 Aug 1888
Cora	Michael Smith 17 Dec 1887
Davis Mills	John C Davis 10 Apr 1888

Disc 6 May 1892

Slab Town	James S Roberts 5 Nov 1887
Tilley	Thomas N Tilley 21 Nov 1890
Smithville	Jeremiah Smith 11 Apr 1891
Adaline	Wayne L German 18 Apr 1891
Cottonwood	Isaac W Midkiff 5 Jun 1891
Rosebud	Thomas S Knight 5 Jun 1891
Simpson	William A Jackson 29 Apr 1891
Burr Ferry	James C Cavanaugh 5 Mar 1892
Conrad	Napoleon B Johnson 19 Mar 1892

LINCOLN PARISH

Vienna
Elihu A Fulford 2 Jul 1874
Ainsley H Mayfield 20 May 1875
Silas K Scott 30 Jan 1879
W J Pollard 27 Sep 1883
Nanimus Debony 21 Jan 1884
Robert G Jackson 17 Mar 1884
Mrs. S E Stone 27 Mar 1885
Lewis D Golson 11 Sep 1886

Greensborough
Miss Mattie Greene 22 Feb 1875
Mrs. Mattie Wright 12 Nov 1876

Disc 25 Feb 1879

Walnut Creek
John W Williams 30 Sep 1875
James W Williams 8 Oct 1877
George W Braswell 27 Jan 1880

Disc 5 May 1884

D'Arbonne	Sidney S Caricker 4 May 1876
	Jasper M Colvin 17 Sep 1877
Douglas	Laura Colbert 6 Apr 1877
	Wesley W Hinton 14 Oct 1878
	Mrs. Eliza E Stuckley 31 Jan 1880
	Wesley W Hinton 14 Jun 1881
Feasterville	Jasper M Colvin 11 Apr 1878
Disc 11 Nov 1878	
Reest 12 Apr 1880	Jasper M Colvin 12 Apr 1880
Disc 1 Dec 1880	
Redwine	Benjamin F Smith 5 Aug 1878
Woodville	Will Gaillatt 22 May 1874
Bonner	Joseph Bernstein 19 May 1879
	Samuel Russell 9 Aug 1881
	John W Williams 8 Aug 1883
	William G Nelson 7 Jan 1884
Bell	Lorenzo Bell 23 Nov 1880
Disc 14 Feb 1887	
Roan	Wesley W Hinton 10 Oct 1883
	Larkin H Stedman 20 Aug 1884
Averett	Nathaniel G Tippit 28 Nov 1883
	Charles E Averett 26 Apr 1886
	Barton M Carter 11 Jul 1887
Ruston	James O Colvin 15 Jan 1884
	Mrs. R M Burton 15 Jun 1889
	William H H Mullin 2 Jan 1890
	William H H Mullin 8 Oct 1891 (Pres & Sen)
Sibley	Eugene F Warren 12 Feb 1884
Simsboro	Edward R Braswell 27 Feb 1884

	George W Braswell 15 Jan 1891
Hico	John S Cox 6 Aug 1884 John E Tucker 12 Mar 1890 John L Williams 9 Apr 1890
Vining Mills	James E Vining 6 Aug 1884 William B Morgan 8 Mar 1887 James A Clifton 26 Mar 1890 Stephen Fautheree 24 Dec 1891
Knowles	George W Knowles 15 Sep 1884 George W Knowles 28 Jun 1886
Allen Greene Disc 21 Jan 1886	Hulvatus H Howard 30 Sep 1884
Colvin Disc 8 Mar 1887	James O Sutton 11 Nov 1884
Douglas	Lazare Davis 17 Jul 1886
Unionville	John A Colvin 20 Jun 1887
Cedarton	Harbin R Davis 21 Jul 1887
Choudrant	Larkin H Stedman 17 May 1890
Sumpter	Sumpter D Rhinehart 13 Mar 1891

WEST CARROLL PARISH

Kilbourno	William J Killbourn 13 Nov 1879 Amos R Strong 13 May 1887 Thomas A Keys 22 Aug 1889 John W Billington 29 Nov 1889 Thomas W Jay 16 Feb 1891
Oak Grove	George R Faith 20 Jun 1880 Mary A Leonard 27 Jul 1881

	Hiram J Cheatham 5 Oct 1883
	Jason U Johnson 16 Nov 1891
	Samuel M Aiken 13 May 1892
Floyd	William H Parker 17 May 1881
	Simeon Taylor Jackson 19 Jun 1882
	Mrs. Catherine Alley 19 Oct 1885
Caledonia Disc 8 Mar 1887	Simon Witkouski 23 Jan 1873
Forest	Simeon T Jackson 1 Mar 1888

ACADIA PARISH

Cartville	Samuel Cart 6 Feb 1884
	Savinien Cart 10 Jul 1890
	Louis Cart 22 Oct 1891
Church Point	P L Guidry 9 Aug 1881
Fabacher	Zenon Huber 12 Mar 1878
	Joseph Kops 22 Apr 1890
	Calvin Heath 31 Dec 1890
	Zenon Huber 16 Apr 1891
Mermenton	Victorin Meignaud 12 Aug 1875
	Jean Catex 15 May 1890
Prudhomme	Theodore C Chachere 16 Jul 1886
Plaquemine Brulee	Edmund L Harman 27 Apr 1885
	Edgar Barousse 1 Mar 1890
Rayne	Alphonse Duclos 5 Jan 1886
	A C Poulet 18 Nov 1889
	Michael D Coleman 23 Nov 1889
	Alphonse Duclos 1 Mar 1890
Crowleyville	Andrew D Tomlinson 21 Apr 1887

Crowley	Jack Frankel 14 May 1887
	James A Williams 20 Jun 1889
Millersville	Denis Miller 18 May 1887
	Leon Viterbo 3 Nov 1890
Duson	Joseph G Bertrand 24 Oct 1887
Schamber	Louis F Schamber 24 Apr 1888
Disc 25 Jan 1889	
Regan	John Regan 15 Jul 1888
	Thomas D Schrock 25 Jun 1890
Thrailkill	William F Thrailkill 13 Jul 1888
Basile	Frank E Garrould 25 Jan 1889
Estherwood	Thomas C Lewis 2 Oct 1889
	J J Aulds 11 Mar 1890
	Samuel H Goldberg 12 Mar 1892
Echo	Henry A Abney 20 Aug 1890
	Avery Tobey 25 Oct 1890
	James E Andrus 23 Oct 1891
Disc 29 Feb 1892	
Canal	Joseph H Fabacher 30 Aug 1890
Redtop	James A McMillan 25 Aug 1891
Ebenezer	Charles W Faulk 11 Sep 1891
Miller	Isaac G Jarvis 17 Feb 1892
Branch	Edgar Barousse 12 Nov 1892

Index

Abel
  John P, 164
Abell
  Edward C, 201
  Frederick N, 202
Aber
  W C, 38
  William C, 96
Abney
  Henry A, 290
  Jesse M, 264
Abraham
  Simon, 214, 233
Abramovich
  Raduslav G, 234
Abraugh
  John H, 244
Abribat
  Gustave Jr, 214
Achee
  Anatole A, 128
Acklen
  Claude M, 280
Acosta
  Arthur, 248
Adair
  James M, 96, 97, 179, 183
Adam
  Octave W, 214
Adams
  Adrian E, 53, 117
  Howell C, 33, 90
  Isaac R, 183, 188
  Robert W, 56
  Rosanner P, 145
  Wiley B, 91
Adcock
  John D, 250
Addison
  D, 16
  Eugene J, 144
  John D, 225
  Jonathan A, 249
Adema
  Victor, 234
Adger
  Joseph E, 165
Adkins
  John H, 6, 24
Adler
  Eugene, 201
Adredge
  Charles W, 246
Agee
  Joseph S, 219
Ager
  William, 138
Aiken
  George R, 182
  Samuel M, 289
  William M, 170, 181, 182
Aillet
  Ursin, 23
Airey
  Mollie, 225
  Thomas H, 55
Akenhead
  James, 65, 134
  William, 17, 64
Akens
  Thomas M, 265
Akers
  Thomas M, 115
Akins
  William, 10
Alaucis
  Lavis, 51
Albadnao
  Marius, 30
Albert
  Antoine P, 234
  Aristide E P, 270
Albin
  John C, 265
Albrecht
  John, 266
Alexander
  Abel A, 144
  A B, 164
  Charles H, 56
  Hugh, 6
  James M, 151, 266
  Moses S, 261
  Mrs. Esther, 161
  R J, 194
  William, 99
Alford
  Abram A, 235
  Haywood, 21, 22
  J, 56
Alfrey
  Jules D, 254
Allain
  Emile S, 108
Alleman
  Narcisse, 84
Allen
  Alvin T, 233
  Ananias, 7
  Charles G, 210
  Charles H, 63, 131
  James J, 278
  John R, 217
  Joseph W, 259
  Josiah F, 88
  J T, 110
  Miss R, 97
  Mrs. A E, 186
  Mrs. Jane F, 215
  Philip, 104
  Samuel, 74, 145
  Shakespeare, 137
  William M, 12,

Index

104, 194
Alley
  Alonzo L, 140
  Mrs. Catherine, 289
Allfrey
  Jules D, 135
Alling
  William, 116
Allison
  James H, 7
Allums
  Benjamin S, 80
Alston
  Louis M, 218, 219
  Macayah T J, 44
  Robert H, 104, 194
  William K, 219
Alsworth
  Archibald A, 265
  John N, 265
Altemus
  Jacob W, 209
Alvarez
  Louise, 263
Ambrose
  Robert E, 197
Amsden
  Francis B, 238
  Mary, 238
Anders
  Thomas J, 211
Anderson
  Asa, 35
  Benjamin F, 98
  F, 52
  Jesse A, 188
  Louis W, 161
  M, 65
  Robert D, 200
  Thomas G, 216
  Wesley B, 141, 271

  William D, 99, 188
Anderton
  George P, 233
Andre
  J L, 112
  Louis L, 256
Andrews
  Daniel, 268
  Jacob W, 74, 146
  James, 182
  John W, 53
  Mark, 268
  Marquis D L, 187
Andrus
  James E, 290
Andues
  Shivene S, 173
Aneran
  Gallus M, 267
Angelloz
  Emile, 214
  Oscar, 214
Ansley
  Sterling, 104
Anthony
  Moses S, 246
Applefield
  Emma, 275
Applewhite
  Isaac, 17
Arceaux
  Francis H, 55
Archer
  Henry, 142
Archibald
  James B Jr, 245
Ard
  James F, 75, 146
Arden
  Daniel D, 240
Ardrey
  James M, 14

Argne
  Charles H, 281
Arista
  Francisco, 128, 247
Ariste
  Francisco, 23
Arkenhead
  Gertrude A, 159
  Walker, 159
  Walter, 85
Arlington
  Robert, 236
Armant
  John V, 64, 131
Armelin
  Aristion, 19
Armigate
  L W, 156
Armistead
  William W, 164
Armour
  Francis W, 77, 79, 88
Armstrong
  Augustus, 128
  Christian D, 247
Arnold
  John W, 76
  Levi, 115
Arrington
  B B, 204
Arsenaux
  Hubert, 84
Arthur
  Solomon, 127
Artiste
  Francisco, 62, 128
Ashcroft
  Richard S, 273
Ashley
  Marion W, 76
Atkins

Index

Albert L, 188
Benjamin T, 120
James W, 166
Joseph D, 166
Will S, 242
Attlesey
  Jeff D, 219
Aubert
  Louis, 252
Aubery
  Charles, 84
Aubry
  Charles, 158
Aulds
  J J, 290
Aurst
  Henry A, 57
Ausley
  Charles W, 226
Austen
  David, 148
  David A, 76
  Davis, 24
  William A, 37
Austin
  Sterling C, 181
  Sterling T, 96
Autrau
  Auguste G, 132
Autrey
  John, 141
Auvray
  Peter P, 49
Averett
  Charles E, 287
  John W, 165
Aycock
  R J, 194
  T Lafayette, 194
Ayer
  Gorcham P, 122
  Gordham P, 57

Babcock
  Lucie K, 179
Babin
  Alphonse, 208
  Charles S Jr, 259
  John E, 279
  Louis S, 109
Babington
  Ellen J, 146
  Robert, 146
  Robert A, 51
  Thomas M, 275
  W W, 275
Baccarat
  Elie, 158
Bacon
  Thomas S, 124
Badger
  Algernon, 227
  Wallace, 8
Badneaux
  Thomas, 263
Badon
  Jeremiah, 13
Baehl
  Joseph, 198, 200
Bagley
  John M, 177
  Martin, 274
Bailey
  Caldwell H, 267
  Cecile, 255
  Champion P, 147
  James M, 123, 235
  James O, 193
  J H, 216
  J Oscar, 192
  Miss Eunice, 237
  Thomas C, 235
  Walter, 59, 125
  William, 108
Bain

James E, 150, 282
Baird
  Bythol H, 55
  Lucy, 166
Baker
  Alexander S, 162
  Isaac L, 98
  James T, 188
  John, 5, 40
  Mary E, 221
  Miss Lucy J, 98
  Percy, 165
  Robert H, 161
  Stephen F, 44
Balch
  Henry C, 269
Baldridge
  J W, 204
Baldwin
  Jeremiah J, 118, 151
  John, 61
Ball
  Julia S, 276
  Michael, 117
Ballow
  John E, 276
  Thomas H, 232
Banks
  Austin C, 150, 282
  C, 81
  Levi, 150, 282
  Levy, 178
Bankston
  Hilliard J, 80
  Morris, 265
  Young P, 147, 275
Bannerman
  Mary E, 187
Banq
  H A, 280
Barbarot

Index

Claude F V, 57, 122
Barbe
  Chancy, 92
  Charles, 92
  Charvey, 172
Barbee
  Joseph L, 245
  L, 127
  Leslie, 245
  William H, 127, 245
Barberot
  Claude V F, 232
Barbin
  Francois B, 31
Barbour
  P H, 11
Barbury
  William, 63
Bard
  Lazarus L, 5
Barfield
  Levi, 48
Bargas
  James E, 109
  Joseph E, 209
Barilleaux
  Ferdinand, 83
Barker
  Alexander, 214
  Martha J, 203
  R R, 42
  Samuel, 53
  William H, 16
Barksdale
  Allen, 86, 162
Barnes
  Osy M L, 284
  Pleasant, 120
  Seth, 75, 147
Barnett

James F, 101
Barnette
  James T, 190
Barnidge
  Lewis, 126
  Lewis Q, 238
Barousse
  Edgar, 289, 290
Barr
  James O, 146
  James O E, 272
  John S, 72
  Samuel E, 143
Barrett
  Edward J, 126, 237, 238
  John M, 205
  John T, 49
  Mary A, 238
  William J, 248
Barringer
  Henry V, 102
Barron
  James L, 163
  Llewellyn G, 223
  Robert G, 245
  Thomas C, 241
Barrow
  Charles D, 41, 100
  Cornelius J, 279, 280
  Joseph W, 175
Barry
  James, 108
  John B, 269
  John C, 32
  Sylvester J, 65, 135
Bartells
  John, 260
Barthet
  F, 30
  Joseph A, 207

Bartholemy
  Felix R, 181
Bartlett
  Abel, 10
  Henry, 73
Barton
  J D, 8
Bascle
  Lillie, 270
Baskin
  Adolphus D, 202
  James C, 202
  P C, 202
Bassett
  Jules, 157
  William H, 17, 19, 30, 31
  William H Jr, 85
Bastion
  Washington, 12
Bates
  Paschal P, 78
Bath
  Hyman, 125, 238
Batner
  Elias S, 261
Batte
  William S, 58
Battison
  William, 20
Baudoin
  Alfred, 274
Bauer
  Philip, 147, 279
  William W, 280
Baugh
  Edward H, 90
Baughman
  Henry B, 263
  Henry G, 187
Baughmann
  Henry Y, 35, 93

Index

Baumfield
  George, 23
Baxley
  Jesse, 204
Baygents
  George W, 35
  Jeorge W, 93
Bayley
  James M, 14, 58
Bayliss
  James K, 25, 32
  John A, 71
Baynard
  Thomas H W, 53, 70, 117
Beacham
  Henry, 73
Bear
  Mrs. Sussanne, 106
Beard
  Benjamin F, 188
  Edward J, 80
  James A, 44
  Joseph H, 33, 90, 168
  Michael, 98, 184
  Michael J, 186
  Mrs. Effie M, 186
  William F, 221
Beary
  Thomas, 270
Beasley
  Jeff T, 116, 218
  Reubin M, 183
Beason
  Benjamin A, 22, 74
Beauchamp
  Stephen O, 199
Beaurais
  Willis, 157
Beauvais
  Narcisse, 13

Beck
  Charles, 61, 127
  George W, 188
  Theodore, 127, 245
Beckett
  James W, 190
Beckhaur
  M J, 101
Becnel
  Maxmillian, 132
  Sosthene, 132
Bedford
  George C, 1
  Madison, 220
Bedsole
  Thomas H, 284
Beene
  William, 41
Beer
  Rudolphe, 133
Belden
  James K, 12, 55
  James L, 140, 269
Bell
  Clarence, 200
  Fielding E, 257
  George H, 3
  George W, 265
  Guy H, 17, 65
  Henry P, 140, 267
  John M, 23, 46, 106
  Lorenzo, 287
  Mrs. Sarah A, 221
  Samuel, 66
  Walter T, 236
  W L, 170
Bellew
  Thomas, 47
Benedict
  Lewis, 52
Benefield

  Robert, 265
Benham
  George C, 95
  Mrs. Carrie F, 182
  William G, 182
Bennefield
  Robert K W, 215, 216
Bennett
  Charles, 61
  George M, 241
  James B, 208
  James M, 94, 178
  J Yates, 50
  Mary D, 178
  William J, 63, 130
Benoist
  Charles F, 10, 55
  Victor L, 119
  Victor S, 222
Benson
  Charles R, 179
Benthall
  William J, 277
Bentley
  William J, 160
Benton
  Robert, 52, 114
Berand
  Thomas L, 160
Berbin
  Charles, 132
Bercier
  Anthony J, 259
Bernard
  Emile, 252
  Henry C, 279
  Ignace, 212
  Joseph D, 136, 256, 257
  Romain U, 213
Bernstein

Index

Joseph, 287
Maurice, 150
Philip, 149
Berrett
   Joseph D, 208
Berson
   Boyd W, 74
Berstein
   Joseph, 209
Bertaut
   Auguste, 251
Berthoud
   William B, 211
Bertrand
   Gustave, 113
   Joseph G, 213, 290
Besse
   Charles A, 29
   Pierre H, 84
Bethard
   George W, 185
   Mary V, 185
Bettis
   Scott, 116, 218
Betton
   Joseph R, 48
Bevan
   George B, 99
Beyusdorfer
   Michael, 193
Bickenou
   James W, 279
Bickham
   Alexander C, 146
   John, 23, 249
Bicknell
   Frank D, 171
Bidstrop
   Herman L, 262
Biegel
   Caroline, 265
   George A, 265
Michael, 151, 265
Mrs. Katherine, 265
Bienvenu
   Adolphe, 259
   Delphan Jr, 157
   Felix, 259
   Mrs. Marguerite C, 138, 260
   Robert S, 237
Bihm
   Milton L, 171
Bilberry
   Ezra B, 273
Biller
   Thomas C, 70
Billes
   Joseph, 204
Billington
   John W, 288
Billon
   Arthur J, 251
   Paul, 251
Bingham
   William R, 150
Binion
   Robert L, 243
Binning
   H A, 280
Binow
   John Randolph, 187
Bionel
   Maximillian, 252
Bioron
   John D, 50
Biosat
   Eugene R, 124
Biosatt
   Eugene R, 59
Biossat
   Eugene R, 124
Henry A, 239, 240
Birard
   Achille, 18
Bird
   Vallen J, 71
Bishop
   Charles, 13
   Elbert, 194
   John, 36, 95
Bissett
   Simon, 58
Biven
   Samuel, 175
Bivens
   Albert W, 182
Black
   Isaac, 139
   Joseph H, 263
   Thomas C, 7
Blackburn
   Jasper, 100
Blackman
   Marion C, 186
Blackmon
   Zachariah, 104, 195
Blackshear
   David A, 44
Blackwood
   Thomas M, 163
Blake
   John P, 96
Blakston
   Pleasant M, 3
Blanc
   Henry, 133
Blanchard
   Arthur D, 84
   B P, 121
   A G, 11
   Gustave, 30
   S F, 45

Index

Sulia, 83
Bland
  Archibald, 268
Blanks
  Frederick A, 34
  Robert A, 34
Blankston
  Simeon C, 20
Blanton
  John W, 248
Bleason
  D, 51
Bledsoe
  Mrs. Flora F, 201
Bloch
  Henry, 258
  Moise, 68
Block
  Archibald, 9, 49
  Herman, 108
  Jacob, 252
  Joseph, 181
  S, 263
Blocker
  William C, 171
Blonin
  Joseph D, 1
Blouin
  Leon, 64
Blouk
  Henry, 197
Blount
  James A, 16
Bluestein
  S, 239
Blum
  Daniel, 248
  Samuel, 125
Blume
  John H, 163
  Mrs. Rebecca E, 164

Boggs
  Henry J, 168
  William B, 166, 168
Bogguss
  Robert D, 11
Boles
  George E, 246
Bolgiano
  Cora A, 284
Bolin
  Leonidas C, 190
Bollenhagen
  J, 4
  Jacob, 26, 34
Bollinger
  James M, 213
Bolls
  Jasper G, 220
Bolton
  Sallie E, 177
  William, 246
Bond
  Benjamin W, 85
  Howard B, 140
  James K, 161
  Mrs. Mary A, 161
  Richard, 1
  William E, 111
  William F, 76, 77
Bondreaux
  Gustave, 214
Bonds
  James Sr, 224
  Solomon, 17
  William H, 224
Boney
  Green L, 116, 218
Bonnemaison
  Dominique, 212
  Jacques, 113, 212
Bonner

  Allen D, 5
  James B, 8
  Mrs. Sallie, 202
  Thomas H, 14
Bonnett
  Augustin F, 161
  J, 31
Bonney
  Benjamin F, 140, 267
  Miles, 268
  William F, 268
Bonnin
  Octave P, 136
Bony
  William J, 33
Booles
  J J, 272
Boon
  Curtis, 80
  William F, 78, 88
Booter
  William R, 1
Booth
  Andrew B, 105, 197
  James, 162
  James B, 80
  John W, 233
  Winnie, 197
Boozman
  S, 119, 221
Borah
  Walter S, 259
Bordelon
  Gervais A, 86, 159, 160
  Hilaire, 11
  Remie, 160
Bordes
  Paul V, 233
Boreland

Peter, 151, 203
Boring
   Mrs. Etta V, 189
Borzant
   John, 227
Bosley
   Andy, 241
   James R, 55, 119
Bossier
   Onezime, 64
Bossman
   Laurent J, 257
Boston
   Alexander, 120
Boswell
   Berry, 224
   Silas W, 220
Bosworth
   William, 56, 121
Bouderant
   Albert, 267
Boudreau
   Edgar, 258
Boudreaux
   Alphonse Z, 271
   Amede, 141
   Gustave, 113
   Louis, 113
   Numa F, 269
Bouee
   George E, 250
Bougere
   Frank, 192
Bougeret
   Alphonse, 64
Boulet
   David H, 81, 149
   Thomas J, 149
Boulle
   Charles L, 282
Bourdells
   Jean, 122

Bouregois
   Louis J, 251
Bourg
   Aubin, 71
   Ely R, 113
   Hilaire, 84
   Trasimond, 147
Bourgeois
   Anatole B, 157
   Cyprien, 29
   Filebert, 215
   James J, 253
   Jean A, 251
   Joseph A, 251
   Louis J, 251
   Magloire, 83, 157
   Pamelia, 251
Bourgoin
   Charles J, 140
Bourn
   Bannat, 264
Bourque
   Ophelius, 274
Boutte
   Elias, 206
Bower
   Henry P, 223
Bowers
   Isaac T, 145
Bowes
   Robert, 231
Bowman
   Calvin D Jr, 215
   Charles E, 140, 267
   Charles O, 185
   Frank J, 98, 185
   Henrietta E, 185
   Joseph H D, 5
   Mrs. Alice, 206
   William H, 70, 139
Boyce
   Henry A, 125

   John, 11
Boyd
   Henry, 20
   James A, 34, 93
Boydston
   Rebecca C, 277
Boyer
   Alonzo L, 86, 160
   Jacques A, 160
   James A, 86, 160
Boyes
   John H, 31
Boykin
   A B, 189
Boyle
   William, 234
Bozeman
   Dan, 32
   Daniel, 25
   William G Jr, 59
Bozone
   William A, 177
Bradford
   Daniel, 234
Bradley
   J, 47
   James W, 143
   John W, 266
Bradon
   Francois, 133
Bradshaw
   Benjamin, 75
Brady
   Alfred G, 233
   D, 123
   George W, 144
   Thomas, 191
Brainerd
   William A, 121
Brame
   John T, 58
Branch

Index

John, 127
Brand
   Henry C, 156
   Joseph A, 158
Brandin
   Leopold P, 178
Branon
   Joseph S, 75
Bransford
   John S, 273
Brantley
   Robert, 205
Brashear
   Charles D, 31
   Richmond J, 24, 53, 116
   Robert B, 68
   Thomas T, 68, 137
Braswell
   Blake W, 163
   Edward R, 287
   George W, 286, 288
Bray
   Cavil, 285
Breaux
   Arvillien, 9
   Eugene, 9
   Joseph, 9
Breckenridge
   Christopher G, 105
   Marcus P, 62
Breda
   J Emile, 223
Bredemeier
   Frederick, 252
   Fred K, 132
Breland
   William G, 176, 267
Bres
   John B Jr, 72
Brewer
   Aaron H, 54
   Esther S, 256
Brewster
   James, 31, 86, 230
   William J, 271
Brian
   Iley M, 205
Brice
   John C, 162
   Martha V, 164
   William, 162
Bridgeford
   William, 71
Bridger
   John James, 164
Bridges
   Barney W, 99
   Harry S, 176
   Henry C, 267
   L P, 120, 223
   Thomas D, 129
   William H, 217
Brigham
   J L, 22
Bright
   William H, 52
Brignac
   Forian, 252
   Henry, 114, 215
Brilliot
   Rene, 213
Bringier
   Louis A, 156
Britain
   Benjamin F, 243
Brittian
   Reuben A, 278
Broadus
   E, 62
   Thomas E, 128
Broadwell
   Jacob B, 224
Brock
   Albert C, 244
   James D, 267
Brodnax
   Benjamin H, 221
Brodway
   Thomas J, 178
Bronson
   Edward, 142
Brooke
   John C, 119
Brooks
   Dexter, 23
   James R, 54
   John A, 188
   John T, 14, 57
   Joseph K, 208
   J T, 124
   Mrs. Louise W, 74, 146
   Pervis, 117
   Thomas F, 71, 140
   Thomas W, 188
   William, 13
   William B, 167
Brosset
   Oliver, 119
Brou
   A J Numa, 128
Broussard
   Aladan, 187
   Aladin, 206, 259
   Charles, 259
   Desire O, 275
   Jerisan, 92, 172
   Louis D, 128
   Louis F, 194
   Nicholas, 275
   Octave S, 157
   Valsaint, 50, 112
Brown

Index

Alexander G, 68
Alonzo L, 276
Charles C, 47
Charles R W, 184
Coleman, 4, 37
Corydon C, 200
David C, 146, 228
Edward G, 130
F B, 198
Francis L, 255
George M, 263
George W, 123
Guion J L, 150
Henry M, 177
Henry S, 49, 109
James C, 71
James H, 78, 88
John T, 106
John W, 220
Jonathan, 111
Joseph C, 242
Joseph D C, 261
J R, 243
Leroy, 98
Lindsey L, 239
Moses, 44
Richmond W, 218
Robert H, 112, 244
S C, 181
William F, 94
William H, 163
William V, 78
William W, 189
William Z, 36
Browning
  Harmon, 184
  James J, 100
Broyles
  Samuel L, 266
Bru
  Ulysse, 141
Bruce

George W, 204
Josiah, 151
William G, 184
Brugier
  Amedee C, 105
Brumby
  Robert H, 95
Brumfield
  Charles, 114
  James W, 285
  Peter, 131, 250
  Uriah V, 276
  William, 22, 74,
    75, 146
Brunet
  Peter, 207
  Remistine, 207
Bruno
  Theobold, 131
Brunson
  J O, 255
Bryan
  Henry M, 230
  James L, 210, 229
  John L, 144, 229
  John T, 73
  Joseph, 19
  M L, 152, 187
  Sidney R, 277
  Waid A, 210
Bryant
  Ambrose M, 283
  Delaney M, 284
  John A, 68
Bryson
  Samuel, 168
Buchanan
  James H, 17
  William B, 38
Buck
  Henry E H, 44, 104
  John J, 10

John L, 21
Samuel H, 227
Buckelew
  William B, 203
Buckham
  Mrs. Nannie, 275
Buckley
  D W, 14
Buckner
  Eli T, 80, 87
  Louis, 269
  Meredith, 80
Budd
  John B, 269
Budden
  Wesley, 258
Buford
  James, 48
Bugel
  Michael, 115
Buie
  John, 97
Bulger
  W G, 151
Bullard
  C A, 227
  Charles A, 11, 55
Bulliard
  Edmund, 18, 66
  Etienne, 18
  Valsai, 67
Bullock
  Samuel C, 148
  Sandy D, 276
Bunch
  William O, 191
Buras
  Louis P, 233
Burbank
  Jacob A, 129
  Jacob J, 248
Burd

Index

Henry, 16
Burel
  Pierre, 16
Burges
  Calcott F, 237
Burguieres
  Jules M, 262
Burke
  James T, 205
  John, 9
  Mary A, 223
Burnett
  Albert, 176
  R H, 6
  William L, 45
Burns
  Charles S, 279, 280
  A H, 89, 165
  James M, 101
Burnside
  Janie C, 226
  Robert, 32
  Roseaner T, 226
Burr
  Gilman B, 61, 127
Burrell
  Charles B, 284
Burrill
  George C, 192
Burris
  James M, 74
Burton
  Mrs. R M, 287
  Robert Y, 130
  William, 60
  William L, 41
Bush
  George I A, 49, 108
  George J A, 208
  James S, 41
Bushee

A T, 84
Butler
  James E, 144, 228
  John, 234
  Sarah A, 234
  Stephen, 5, 39, 40
  Thomas B, 35, 177
  Thomas F, 196
  Thomas M, 187
  W W, 146
Butterfield
  Ralph, 42
Buvens
  Henry J, 243
Bynum
  Wade H, 60
Byrne
  Joseph, 199
Byron
  William H, 73
Cabeen
  James H, 165
Cabry
  Ernest E, 48
Cade
  Charles T, 206
  John W, 146, 230
  Stephen M, 178, 229
Cagburn
  James E, 194
Cagnolatte
  Pierre, 251
Caillouet
  Augustus T, 261
Cain
  Edward, 285
  James O E, 161
  T M, 285
Caire
  J, 147
  Joseph E, 279

Caldwell
  James B, 145
  James M, 278
  W J, 95
Calhoun
  George A, 140
  James A, 69, 139
  Lucius M, 230
  Mrs. Eliza S, 139
  Nathan, 193
Call
  Orrin, 178
Callahan
  Michael, 40
Callaway
  Robert C, 206
Callegari
  Louis F, 159
Callegory
  Serge, 159
Callery
  Ernest, 109, 207
Calligan
  John, 106, 199
  Joseph T, 17
Calmer
  Joseph, 20
Calvert
  John D, 38, 97
Calvit
  Tacitus G, 60
Calwell
  James, 54
Campbell
  Albert G, 192
  Benjamin, 52, 186
  Benjamin C, 227
  Fountain L, 192
  A J, 229
  John A, 44
  John S, 268
  Lewis G, 273

Index

Mrs. Kate L, 201
Robert H, 61
Seaborn M, 192
William C, 171
Canier
  Joseph M Jr, 66
Cann
  T J, 142
Cannon
  Ethelbert L, 174, 285
  James D, 38
  Maurice, 15
Capers
  Hickson, 225
Cappel
  Joseph, 85, 159
Cappell
  Joseph, 30
Capron
  J D, 262
Carathers
  David A, 100
Carew
  Joseph H, 249
Caricker
  Sidney S, 287
Carl
  James, 105
Carlton
  John S, 41, 101
Carmody
  Patrick, 170
Carmouche
  Desire N, 157
  Pierre, 83
Carnal
  Reuben H, 238
Carnes
  William J, 34, 92
Carpenter
  Robert L, 218, 219

Carr
  Abraham A, 228
  B, 55
  Benjamin F, 173
  Cornelius E, 100
  David, 79
  Henry T, 282
  James S, 44
  John M, 116
  Josie, 259
  Mrs. Ann Stansbury, 259
  R T, 194
  Stansbury, 259
  W B, 120
  William C, 141, 143, 272
Carrere
  Lawrence, 254
Carroll
  Abraham W, 256
  John, 74
  William R, 196
Carruth
  Aleck C, 124
  James A, 250
Carruthers
  David A J, 189
Carrville
  Octavia, 208
Carson
  James T, 163
  Robert A, 76
  Theodore A, 164
Carstarphen
  Robert L, 167
Carstle
  Cullen M, 47
Cart
  Louis, 289
  Samuel, 257, 289
  Savinien, 289

Carter
  Barton M, 287
  Benjamin E, 184
  Henry, 77
  Hiram, 50
  James, 284
  John H, 184
  Joseph C, 48
  Lewis E, 32
  Miss Easther, 130
  Patrick H, 96, 183
  Sarah, 97
  A V, 224
  Warren H, 215
  Wellington W, 63
  Wiley E, 194
  William A, 46, 47
  William N, 168
Cartwright
  Thomas, 42
Cary
  Joshua B, 19, 67
  William S, 261
  W S, 67
Casey
  John A, 88
  Mrs. Anne, 141
  Zadock, 236
Cashell
  Edward G, 142
Cashie
  Auguste, 137
Casmer
  Isaac, 3, 24, 25
Cason
  Darling B, 265
  James B, 265
Castel
  John, 135
  Jules, 135, 254
  Paul, 135, 254
Castex

Jean, 254
Castille
   Alexander H, 135, 254
Castle
   Nathan D, 216
Casty
   Amos M, 282
Catchings
   F Silas, 220
Cater
   C W, 194
Catex
   Jean, 289
Cathcart
   Joseph, 57, 122, 232
Catliff
   Richard A, 25
Causey
   John P, 222
   Mrs. Mary L, 199
Cavanaugh
   James C, 286
   John C, 60, 126
Caver
   Jacob L B, 274
   T, 84
Cavileer
   James, 117
Cawthon
   Josiah D, 170
Cazeaux
   Pierre, 21
Cazey
   John W, 107
Chacher
   Alexander B, 135
Chachere
   Constant, 65
   Jules L, 258
   Raymond, 255
   Theodore, 65, 135
   Theodore C, 255, 289
Chaffe
   John C, 277
Chaffin
   Nathan S, 34
Chafin
   Winburn L, 161
Chaix
   Emilie, 9
   Francois, 15, 62
Chaler
   Peter Oscar, 56
Chalmers
   William, 44
Chamberlain
   Samuel E, 139
Chambers
   John C, 47
Chambliss
   Thomas J, 3, 21
Chance
   Samuel J, 63, 129
Chandler
   James, 88
   Thomas J, 204
Chaney
   B J, 8
   C R, 199
   Jackson M, 8
   William F, 107
Chapdre
   Arc, 16
Chaplin
   Chichester Jr, 26, 61
Chapman
   Edward H, 271
   Samuel D, 199
   Thomas W, 244
Chapsky
   Max J, 248
Chargois
   John H, 113
Charlet
   Alphonse, 29
Charpantier
   Charles M, 18
Chase
   Valentine, 137
Chassaugnac
   Jacintha, 212
Chatham
   Cunningham C, 194
Chaze
   Emile, 85
Cheatham
   Hiram J, 289
   H J, 181
   James A, 145, 229
Chellete
   John L, 204
Chemier
   Joseph, 136
Chenet
   Octave, 249
Chenier
   Joseph, 171, 175, 254
Cherry
   William P, 187
   William R, 97
Cheshire
   Charles C, 278
Chesnut
   Thomas, 9
Cheval
   Paul, 137, 260
Chevalier
   William, 77
   William N, 78
Chick

Index

Randolph, 46, 106
Childress
  Paris, 15
Chitty
  Aplin E, 285
Choat
  Isaac W, 244
  Kate, 244
Chopin
  Lamay, 225
Christian
  James C, 164
  James M, 33, 90
  John G, 91
Christianson
  James, 235
Cientat
  Henri, 206
Cinnel
  F B, 157
Clack
  John H, 281
Clark
  Alice, 213
  Amos, 73
  Daniel Jr, 2
  Edna F, 272
  George F, 272
  James T, 225
  Jesse B, 18, 65, 135
  John, 224
  Joseph, 18
  Kenneth M, 239
  Samuel, 120
  Stephen T, 3, 38
  William L, 54, 118
  William M, 225
Clarke
  Michael M, 13
Claudet
  Auguste, 214

Clauss
  George W, 57
Clayton
  Emily S, 217
  John J, 131, 251
  John M, 193
Clegg
  Judge R, 165
Clement
  Alfred H, 207
  Eych, 173
Clemmans
  William, 58
Cleneary
  Benjamin B, 216
Cleveland
  Charles C, 240
Clifton
  James A, 288
  Simna A, 282
  Smallwood D, 282
Cline
  Orville H, 201
Clopton
  William, 85
  William H, 31
Cloud
  Jeremiah H, 11
  Robert L, 265
  Samuel G, 27, 47, 107
Clower
  Elbert, 23
  Serena E, 247
Coates
  Joseph P, 178
  Martin B, 217
Cobb
  William, 23
Cochran
  Robert A, 2, 30
Cocke

  Richard T, 19
Cockerham
  Jackson E, 187
  Martha, 97, 183
  Moses A, 163
Cockfield
  Angelo P, 226
Coco
  Edward D, 161
Codukes
  John, 239
  Mrs. R D, 239
Cofield
  John C, 129
Coggins
  John G, 69
Cogullin
  Louis Jr, 139
Cogullon
  Louis, 69
Cohen
  Benjamin, 251
Cohn
  Herman H, 197
  Hyppolite L, 198
  Joseph Jr, 251
  Julian J, 197
  Samuel, 119
Coker
  Thomas C, 110
Colbert
  Laura, 287
  Mrs. L E, 209
  William B, 162
Colby
  Joseph N, 38
Cole
  Abner, 289
  George D, 280
  James, 92, 171, 174
  James W, 130, 249

Index

John C, 272
John D, 72
John R, 92
Randall, 155
Ransom T, 169, 170
Richard, 150
Robert, 130
Thomas S, 103
Coleman
  Absolam, 17
  Isaac, 86
  Michael D, 289
  William C, 184
Colfield
  John C, 62
Collier
  F S, 150
Collingsworth
  William, 15, 16
Collins
  Albert F, 191
  Alexander P, 283
  Emilie, 83
  Hattie, 277
  James, 68
  James E, 203
  Jeptha R, 178
  Jesse E, 241
  Jessie E, 284
  Mary J, 210
  Moses, 39, 97
  Orlando L, 250
  Philip L, 242
  Ransom W, 38
  William E, 87
Colombo
  E, 58
Colomer
  Josi, 138
  Colorner
  No first name, 68

Colton
  Ethan, 68
Colvin
  James O, 287
  Jasper M, 287
  Jeptha, 21, 72
  John A, 288
  Thomas, 71, 76
  Thomas B, 110
Comcan
  Elodie, 258
Comeau
  Pierre D, 212
Complin
  Tilghman G, 14
Compton
  T G, 90
  Thomas W, 14
  Tilghman G, 135
  William T S, 26, 70
  William W, 119
Comstock
  Joseph W, 237
Concannon
  Mollie, 271
Condon
  James, 128
  Miss Abigail, 117
Conerly
  William M, 275
Connell
  Elias F, 89, 165, 166
  E R, 169
Connelly
  Frank, 237
Conner
  Wesley, 102
Conrad
  E L D, 197
  Ethel, 234

Leonidas, 64
Continent
  Joseph D, 207
Contini
  Daniel J, 17
Converse
  Edward W, 281
Conway
  Augustus, 103
  John M, 106
Cook
  D P, 143
  Edward B, 55
  James E, 86
  James Jr, 186
  John, 18
  Sanders B, 93
  Thomas, 24
Cooke
  Abram H, 260
  Henry V J, 141, 269
  Thomas, 49
  William B, 32
  William B., 90
Cooley
  Alfred A, 264
  William W, 268
Coombs
  Richardson, 78
Coon
  Levis A, 230
Coons
  Jacob A, 73
  Temple C, 53
Cooper
  Jackson J, 41
  James C, 54, 241
  Katie, 267
  Leslie A, 107
  Shelby D, 204
  William N, 186

Index

Copeland
  James C, 201
Copes
  William C, 5, 40
Corbette
  Jackson S, 87, 163
Corbitt
  Mrs. Nancy H, 203
Corde
  Louis, 158
Cordilt
  Joseph, 202
Core
  J M, 263
Corley
  Jackson S, 247
  James M, 225
Cornay
  Arma, 19
  Emile H, 260
Cornwell
  Benjamin G, 236
Corry
  James W, 188
Cortez
  Daniel, 129
Cossel
  Lewis, 267
Cottingham
  Thomas C, 108
Cottrell
  William, 66, 135
Couch
  Thomas J, 37
Coudchaux
  Leopold P, 253
Couedin
  G, 57
Courcelle
  Leon C, 231
Courcelli
  Leon C, 122

Courlay
  John E, 106
Courtney
  David Hampton, 41
  John W, 114
  Marshall W, 200
Cousin
  Euphrasie, 263
Couvillon
  Gregory O, 160
  Pierre, 206
Covington
  John A, 228
Coward
  Hardy, 26, 34
  Needham, 27, 34
Cowart
  William J, 117
Cox
  Charles W, 207
  John S, 288
  M J, 165
  Mrs. Missouri, 110
  Philip S, 29
  Richard H, 161
  Thomas L, 278
Coy
  Philip Le, 1
Coyle
  Walter F, 160
  Walter T, 236
Craft
  Thomas R, 130
Craig
  James P, 52
  Joseph A, 182
  Joseph M, 191
  Nancy, 52
  Presley H, 11
  William A, 198
Crain
  James, 9

Cramer
  William C, 84, 157
Crane
  Benjamin P, 106
  Robert A, 14
  Samuel P, 194
  Thomas I, 30
Crawford
  E A, 88, 162
  Govener B, 163
  Thomas, 88, 162
Cree
  Georgiana, 227
Creed
  William N, 204
Cretini
  Auguste, 214
Crew
  Elisha J, 284
Crews
  Robert W, 187
Crocker
  Peter H, 91
Croocks
  Philip S, 38
Crook
  James M, 107
Crooks
  Philip, 185
Croom
  Calvin S, 90
  Mrs. Margaret A, 90, 169
  William H B, 90, 169
Cross
  Edward, 113
  John S, 194
  Mrs. Selina J, 113
Crouchet
  Henry, 212
Crow

Index

Robert A, 99
Temple W, 98
Crowell
  James, 108
  Miss Rosanna, 108
Crowson
  Elijah G, 67
Crowther
  George H, 232
  Olivia, 232
Croxton
  Giles M, 53
Crutcher
  William C, 41, 100
Cuhn
  Bonhome, 94
Culbertson
  Green, 40, 99
  John, 104
Cullen
  Mrs. Lydia, 110
Cuney
  Samuel E, 151
Cunningham
  John H, 41, 100
Cureton
  William H, 14
Currier
  Nathaniel S, 77
Curry
  James, 267
  Jean A, 252
  Mrs. Florence, 185
Curtis
  Antonio, 167
  Bennet A, 19
  Henry, 54
  Mrs. Jennie, 214
Cushman
  Milton R, 275
Custis
  Thomas C, 203

Custman
  John F, 7
Cuthbert
  Forbes, 128
Cutrer
  Joseph, 22
Dagrie
  Gilbert, 6
Daigre
  Aristides, 45
  Joseph A, 105
  Joseph H, 45
Daily
  William W, 236
Daire
  Marcel, 65, 135
Dakin
  Thomas P, 238
Dalcour
  Lazard D, 234
  Leonard, 234
Dale
  Samuel L, 187
  William, 43, 102
Dalferes
  W D, 158
Dalsuet
  Jules A, 85
Daly
  James R, 68
Dameron
  John F, 191
Damerson
  John F, 103, 192
Dancy
  Charles K, 218
Dangerfield
  S Prentiss, 116
Daniel
  John W, 136
  Joseph J, 221
  Robert H, 275

  William A, 147, 275
Daniels
  William, 227
Dannis
  Thomas J, 270
Dantean
  Oscar F, 255
Darby
  Ernest H, 206
  William A, 71
Dardean
  Edward, 254
  Oscar, 135
Dark
  James L, 283
Darling
  Nathan, 55, 61
Darmond
  Gideon, 63
  J G, 106
Darnell
  Charles B, 245
Dasher
  Edward, 259
Daughters
  James M, 3
Daunoy
  Darestan D, 234
Daunt
  William G, 133
Davenport
  James W, 70
  Josiah D, 221
  J W, 26
  Thomas, 88
David
  J Johnson, 198
  Jules, 256
Davidson
  Andrew M, 215
  E M, 114

Index

Isaac J, 199
A J, 270
James A, 215
John, 103
John F, 173, 174
John H, 52
John T, 176
Laclair P, 135
Lewis L, 222
T G, 15
Davis
   Abraham, 138, 260
   Allen J, 39
   Andrew, 238
   Andrew J, 96
   Charles H, 24
   DeWitt, 96
   Elisha K, 39, 81, 148
   Flournoy B, 183
   Harbin R, 288
   Henry J, 195
   Jack R, 213
   James S, 110
   John, 65
   John C, 285
   John S, 93, 177
   Johnson, 209
   Lazare, 288
   Nathan M, 92, 177
   Robert E, 77, 110
   Robert H, 168
   Thomas H, 156
   Thomas V, 35
   Timothy, 260, 262
   William D, 95
   William E, 273
   William H, 156
   William J, 44
   William L, 162, 174
   William R, 175
   William V, 156
   Zephaniah B, 71, 72
Dawson
   Alonzo H, 190
   John B, 12
   William Y, 189
Day
   Lemuel P, 147, 148
   Leonard P, 123
   Milton, 20
   Sanders P, 40
Dayries
   Celeste, 235
   Leon B, 57, 235
Dean
   Handsford, 54
   James T, 230
   Rufus M, 203
Dear
   Louis F, 198
   Miss Hattie L, 216
Dearing
   George W, 197
DeBellvue
   Oscar B, 159
Deblanc
   Denis, 222
Debony
   Nanimus, 286
Deck
   Burton P, 79
Decker
   Seth, 130
Decuiors
   Louis, 64
DeCuir
   Charles, 152
Decuir
   Charles, 205
   H W, 134
Dees
   Willoughby J H, 26
DeFrance
   Parke W, 152, 244
Dehon
   Auguste, 207, 208
   Jules, 208
   Louis, 208
Deichman
   George R, 263
De Isle-Roux
   Charles Aubry, 263
Dejarlais
   Louis A, 29
Delacerde
   Edmond, 225
Delahoussaye
   Aritide, 66
   Mrs. Sidonie, 138
De Lancieville
   (no first name), 16
Delcambre
   Desire, 274, 275
   Michael, 206
Delery
   Charles, 72
Delhomme
   John A, 258
De Llano
   Manuel, 143
DeLucky
   Joseph S, 261
   Stephen, 68, 132, 137
   Thomas S, 158
Demanade
   Paul, 213
Demary
   Nicholas, 79
Demorvello
   Zenon, 14
Dempsey
   Cornelius G, 188

Denham
  William W, 222
Dennesse
  Thomas, 232
Dennis
  Charles, 122
  Thomas C, 232
  William, 63
  William Jr, 63
Dennison
  No first name, 68
Denoyer
  Lazin, 64
Denson
  James M, 79
  Thomas S, 160
Deplaigne
  Jacques, 282
Deplantier
  Alberie, 62
Derivas
  Archibald D, 160
Derosier
  Adolphe, 92
Derouen
  Delino, 92, 172, 174
  Theodore A, 206
Derrough
  James S, 284
DeSarodeire
  Randolph, 105
Desbois
  Dominique, 30
Deschamps
  Eugene Jr, 275
Desessants
  Helaire, 135
Deshotels
  Henry H, 259
Deslonde
  P G, 207

Desloriches
  Numa, 222
Deslouches
  Belus, 55, 119
Desmarias
  Louis, 255
DeSobry
  Louis, 8
Desouge
  Urene, 217
Desrayaux
  Jules, 60
DeValcourt
  John, 18
Devalcourt
  John, 67
  Theodore, 66
Devilliers
  Notley C, 258
  Villier C, 258
Devlicux
  Bernardin L, 224
Deweese
  George P, 117
Dewess
  Mrs. Harriet, 194
Dezendorf
  James T, 241
Dickey
  John F, 7
Dickinson
  John, 283
Dicks
  Matthew, 20
Dickson
  James W, 171
  Palmer, 171
Didier
  Jules E, 160
  Mrs. Clara Frank, 160
Dinkgrave

  Miss Nicettie M, 144, 145
  Mrs. Nicettie M, 229
Disch
  William G, 202
Dixon
  Abel, 141
  Jared S, 226
  J M, 194
  John A, 241
Dobbs
  William H, 16
Dobyns
  Benjamin F, 42, 102
Dodge
  Lyman J, 258
Doiron
  Onesime, 75
Dollehide
  Richard H, 36, 95
Domingelo
  Van, 58
Dominiques
  John, 9
Donaldson
  Pierre A, 252
Donato
  C, 254
Doninique
  A, 83
Doniphan
  Miss Amelia K, 97
Donley
  Mrs. Ellen, 168
Donnam
  Andrew, 94
Donnan
  Andrew, 180
Doremus
  Peter, 13, 17

Index

Doresiett
  Daniel, 67
Dorman
  Miss Martha, 163
  Wiley M, 163
Dormas
  Amedre, 30
  Jean Pride, 159
Dorsey
  George M, 48
  George W, 107
  Grafton, 54
Dortch
  Elaine S, 166
  Nathaniel C, 24
  Nathaniel E, 53
Dosher
  Edward, 184, 235
Dossat
  Rudolph H, 158
Dosson
  Michael H, 3
Doty
  Edward, 4
Doucet
  Louis, 171
Dougherty
  Benajah, 8
  James C, 70
Douglass
  Joseph S, 140
  William R, 32
Doval
  Henry, 29
Dowden
  Abraham R, 224
  John A, 177
  Kent M, 97
  Mrs. Sarah E, 97
  S G, 224
Doyal
  Henry, 83

Doyle
  Henry C, 278
  Henry G, 9
  H G, 9
  Lewis, 198
  Simeon R, 78
Dozier
  James A, 71, 142
  Mrs. Harriett R, 142
Draghan
  Benjamin F, 16
Draghon
  George R, 104
Draifouse
  Joshua, 91
Drailouse
  Joshua, 33
Drake
  J P, 102
  Leona, 178
  Reuben, 5, 56
  William A, 40
Draughan
  Sheppard B, 16
Draughn
  James W, 95
Draughon
  James G, 244
  James N, 245
Draughton
  James M, 37
  Robert H, 46
Dreuen
  Fenelon, 180
Drew
  Larche C, 230
Dreyfous
  Felix, 201
Dreyfus
  Albert, 182
  Emanuel, 177

Emile, 209
M, 182
Driebholz
  Ernest W, 262
Drury
  Francois, 69
Druz
  Oscar A, 208
Dubourg
  Jean D, 16
Ducas
  Elie, 214
  Theophile, 214
Duchesne
  Alexander, 93
Duclos
  Alphonse, 257, 289
Duff
  Leonidas B, 243
Duffell
  Henry E, 155
Dufilno
  Leon, 125
Dufresne
  Pierre L, 48
Dugan
  Charles, 213
Dugas
  Francis O, 66, 134
  Oscar, 158
  St. Clair, 205
Duke
  Bailey C, 31
  James M, 32
  Mayo S, 239
Dulo
  John S, 280
Dumarest
  J J, 10
Dumartrait
  Francois M, 66
Dumas

Index

Mrs. Anna M, 262
Dunbar
   Henry S, 135, 136
Duncan
   Henry, 50
   Oliver S, 156
Dundas
   James J, 218
Duniai
   Mrs. Anna M, 138
Dunn
   Christopher C, 203
   David F, 282
   A J, 205
   James W, 177
   John R, 11
   John W, 219
   Milton A, 204
   Samuel C, 2
   William B, 52
   William T, 173
Dunnam
   Jacob W, 34
Dunning
   Sophie R, 232
Dunvern
   Francis M, 218
Dunwoody
   Robert J, 218
Duplantier
   Fergus, 6
Dupre
   Adolphus, 119
   Charles, 223
   Pierre, 133
Dupuis
   Adolphe, 254
   Adolphe Jr, 254
Dupuy
   Charles E, 109, 207
   Charles F, 49
   Gustave, 132

Henry, 85, 159
Durand
   A, 1
   E P, 207
   Nelson, 2, 31
   Pierre A, 31, 85, 159
   Pierre E, 158
Durbin
   Levi, 217
Durie
   Mrs. Azilie, 134
Durio
   Adeline, 134, 253
Dustmann
   Herman, 233
Dutch
   Charles L, 139
Dutell
   Charles, 67
Duty
   Littleton M, 40
   Wiley, 40
Duval
   James H L, 118
Duvall
   Charles, 124
   Hawkins, 54
   William H, 1, 31
Dwight
   John A, 19, 68
Dwingelow
   C Van, 58
Dyer
   Albert S, 113, 212
   Dickson H, 39, 40
   William, 54, 117
   William Sr., 241
Dyess
   James P, 79
   Joshua, 56
Dykes

Edward W, 275
Dymond
   John, 233
Dyson
   Calvin H, 250, 266
   George W, 75, 151, 266
Eady
   Elijah S, 130
Eagles
   Edward Jr, 283
Eames
   David W, 228
Earle
   Henry T, 47
   Zachariah T Jr, 209
Earnest
   John D, 159, 161
Easeley
   Drew M, 217
Eastbarn
   Joseph R, 15
Easterley
   John B Jr, 215
Easterly
   John B, 105
Easton
   H B, 18
   Ransom, 18
Eastwood
   Elisha, 84
Eaton
   Stephen M, 227
Eccles
   James W, 197
Echaus
   Jules D, 269
Eddleman
   John J, 180
   William H, 180
Edgar
   Alexander W, 205

Alex W, 260
Clarkson, 18
Edgeworth
　John A, 93
　Lizzie T, 93
Edington
　James B, 36, 94
Edmunds
　Samuel, 33
Edrington
　Thomas S, 64
Edwards
　Acy, 10
　Albert P, 278
　Benjamin F, 159
　Edmund H, 149
　Edmund W, 81
　James, 72
　James M, 159
　Thomas G, 199
Effingham
　Lawrence, 233
Egan
　Eugene, 18
Elder
　David J, 77
　Irvin F, 167
　Moses, 230
　Thomas D, 170
Eldred
　William R, 240
Eldridge
　Lewis, 79, 80, 87
Elender
　Jacob A, 180
　Mary A, 180
Elfer
　B Henry, 132, 251
Elkes
　Robert M, 34
Ellinger
　Samuel, 257

Ellington
　John J, 278
Ellis
　E P, 22
　F P, 46
　James, 176
　John H, 216
　Richard M, 130
　Stephen, 74
　Thomas P, 220
Ellison
　Robert, 136
Elliston
　Robert, 92
Ellsworth
　J, 57
Elmore
　James P, 51
Elstner
　John C, 243
Elston
　James W, 167
　Joseph W, 167
Embrey
　Joel, 77, 110
Emonet
　Michael, 66, 135
　Mrs. Mary F, 135
Encolade
　Pascal, 232
　Paschal, 122
Enete
　Clement, 58, 123
　Clementine, 123, 235
　Emile, 185
Engman
　Edward J, 233
Enlow
　James A, 101
Ennemoser
　Julius, 229

Ennes
　Alphonse, 208
Ennesmoser
　Julius, 112
Enright
　John, 185
　Mrs. Laura R, 185
Enswiler
　G W, 53
Epperson
　Robert J, 67, 133
Eppes
　Ballard F, 25, 32
Erbelding
　Frederick, 180
Ernest
　James M, 69
　Joseph W, 139
　Walter C, 263
Escoubas
　Adolphe, 92
Escude
　Alphonse J, 160
Eskew
　George W, 189
Esmond
　William, 46
Esnard
　J R, 133
Estess
　James, 177
Estopinal
　Victor, 247
Etheridge
　William M, 231
Ethridge
　George L, 203
　W B, 271
Etienne
　August B, 260
Etler
　Edward, 40

Index

Ettredge
  Richard C, 196
Eubank
  Wilson E, 26
Eubanks
  Richard C, 266
  Thomas, 63
Evans
  Bettie W, 191
  Lula M, 176
  Marion E, 149
  Will, 256
Everett
  George, 72
  John, 85, 158
  Nancy J, 283
  William B, 282
Ewell
  John, 136
  Joseph K, 31, 85
  William E, 85
Ewing
  Elijah, 50, 79
Extorge
  Albert, 213
Eymard
  B, 213
Fabacher
  Joseph, 136, 254, 256
  Joseph H, 290
Faber
  Henry, 112
Fairchild
  Edward J, 174, 176
  Edwin F M, 174
  Samuel A, 92, 172
Faith
  George R, 288
Falgout
  Onesime, 214
Fanly
  William, 104
Fant
  Fielding, 6
Fargue
  William F, 175
Farley
  William E, 166
Farmer
  Archibald A, 243
  Enoch, 95, 181
  William H, 246
Farquhar
  Henry C, 172
Farrar
  Thomas G, 59
  Winston S, 247
Farrelly
  Bernard, 148
  Charles, 148
Farris
  Edom L, 3
Fass
  Nathan, 184
Fasterling
  Anna, 231
  Bernard, 231
Faulke
  David, 73
Faulkner
  Charles W, 290
  Samuel H, 256
Fauntleroy
  T R, 208
Fautheree
  Stephen, 288
Fawcett
  John D, 211
Faxon
  John, 252
Fay
  Charles, 9, 48
  E G, 108

Fazende
  Louis F, 251
Fazinde
  Louis F, 132
Felder
  Baxter, 51, 114
  David, 10
  Jesse J, 51
  Otis, 51
  Rufus K, 114
Fell
  Harry F, 218
  John E, 117
Fenn
  Enos W, 249
Fenwick
  Charles H, 140
Feray
  Eugene, 30, 84
Ferguson
  John F, 44
Ferinas
  Archibald, 31
Ferrand
  Alfred, 35
  Emile V, 178
Ferraud
  Alfred, 94
Ferren
  Thomas B, 172
Ferrin
  M, 85
Ferris
  David S, 239
  M, 123
Ferry
  Eli, 24
  Elihu, 36
  Thomas M, 265
Fetche
  Henry A, 201
Fettus

Index

Henry J, 232
Fields
    Eugene, 271
Filhiol
    John B, 21, 72
    Roland M, 229
Finlay
    Daniel, 39, 96
Finney
    Ludger M, 235
Fischel
    Alfred L, 219
    Edward M, 220
    Maximillian, 218
Fisher
    Augustus, 58, 123
    Jacob, 14, 58
    Matthew M, 226
    Miers, 5
Fitch
    Grove S, 73, 144
    Miss Mary E, 265
    Thomas A, 52
Fitzgerald
    F E, 120
    James G, 35
Flagg
    O J, 129
Flanner
    Thomas J, 226
Fleming
    Ezekial, 64
    R P, 269
Flemming
    George, 165
    Thomas S, 166, 169
    T L, 91
Fletcher
    Eleazer, 38, 97
    George W, 281
    George W Jr., 281

William, 131, 250, 281
Flinn
    C A, 227
Flournoy
    William, 32
Flowers
    Robert W, 184
Floyd
    Henry M, 116, 218
    S C, 37
    William D, 249
Flunacher
    Joseph H, 199
Flynn
    Peter J, 3, 36
    Peter P, 270
Foney
    John T, 32
Fonteley
    Miss Artemise G, 83
Fontenelle
    Joseph, 235
Fontenette
    Ernest, 133
Forbes
    Andrew J, 68
Ford
    David, 22
    E L, 195
    George W, 175
    Henry A, 2
    James F, 101, 188
    John, 284
    Joseph D, 84
    Nellie E, 195
    Noah, 54
    Stephen S, 183
    Thomas P, 271
Foreman
    Annie, 199

Colbert W, 255
Forman
    Charles H, 70
    Oscar H, 197
    William, 17
Fornea
    Thomas P, 275
Forsyth
    Thomas W, 26
Forsythe
    James, 98, 184
Fortier
    A B, 234
    Eugene J, 212
Foster
    Dennis M, 172
    James, 121
    John K, 285
    L B, 41
    Randolph W, 255
Fournet
    J B, 213
    Valsin A, 18, 66
Fourny
    James, 138
Fowler
    A C, 13
    F H, 116, 218
Fox
    G Raymond, 232
    Simon, 95
Francis
    Gustave C, 259
    Richard W, 140
Frank
    David, 143
Frankel
    Jack, 290
Franks
    Doctor, 41
Frasier
    William G, 24

Index

Frazar
  Moses E, 174
Frazer
  John, 98
Frazier
  Moses L, 206
  William G, 52
Frederick
  Amidie, 155
  John, 263
Freeman
  Richard W, 224
  Z T, 215
Frellsen
  Henri, 4
French
  Josiah, 67
  Thomas B, 237
Fridge
  Benjamin F, 198
  John R, 217
Friedman
  Joseph B, 129, 248
Frierson
  David J, 195
  Robert B, 44, 195
Frisler
  Matilda C, 187
Fristas
  Robert, 3
Frost
  James W, 115
Fudge
  James, 79
Fulford
  E C, 210
  Elihu A, 286
Fulgaar
  Caspar H, 185
Fuller
  James H, 111
  John B, 246

John M, 101
William, 204, 229
Fullerton
  Finis E, 283
Fullford
  Mrs. Mary King, 113
Funk
  Michael, 176
Fuqua
  William T, 85
Furniss
  Samuel M, 166
  Samuel N, 77
Fusalier
  Fergus, 18
Fuselier
  Fremont, 255
Gaar
  J E Sr, 284
Gagne
  Edward O, 29
Gagnet
  Seymour, 262
Gague
  Joseph A, 71
Gaidry
  Octave, 175
Gaillard
  Jules, 67
Gaillatt
  Will, 287
Gaines
  Marie L, 251
Galbert
  Thomas J, 181
Gallian
  William P, 102
Gallien
  Louis, 55
Galloway
  James B, 219

Galvin
  John, 3
Gambill
  John F, 78, 89
Gamble
  Elisha J, 282
  John B, 43, 103
Gamblin
  John S, 169
Gandy
  Daniel P, 245
Gannon
  Mauriel, 253
Ganthreaux
  Joseph G R, 158
Garaky
  Thomas, 266
Garand
  Marcellin, 17, 65
Gard
  S F, 113, 213
Gardner
  Alvan N, 113
  John L, 171
Garland
  Alexander N, 190
  William J, 190
Garlande
  E H, 60
Garrett
  Alfred M, 194
  Eden G, 21
  Isaiah, 229
  James, 21
  Jonathan, 22
Garrould
  Frank E, 290
Gary
  Barney S, 134
Gasoley
  John, 69
Gasper

Index

James, 261
Gass
  Alexander N, 274
Gassen
  Charles, 248
Gassin
  Antoine, 129
Gates
  Cyrus H, 167
  William J, 51
Gathright
  P, 68
Gatlin
  James S, 265
  Mary P, 266
  Thomas W, 7
Gaubert
  Emile, 258
Gaude
  Joachim, 113, 214
Gause
  George H, 129
Gauthier
  Charles J E, 29
  Francois X, 29
  L L, 160
Gautreaux
  P Alcide, 156
Gay
  Barnabas S, 253
  Julian P, 243
  Stephen, 22
  Warren S, 235, 281
Gayden
  Iverson G, 200
Gayle
  Caleb O, 130
  Christopher W, 217
  Clinton O, 167
  Julian P, 151
  William H, 73, 144
Gee

Sack P, 5
Geiseler
  W L, 212
Geismer
  Charles, 157
Gelphin
  Charles L, 219
Genin
  F, 18
Gentran
  Auguste, 83
George
  Benjamin F, 272
  Charles H, 114, 150
  Hillary K, 151, 265
  James H, 63, 130
  Lorense, 150
  Wiley P, 32, 33
  William L, 226
George W L, 241
Germain
  Presley, 22, 74
  Thomas, 15
German
  Wayne L, 286
Germany
  Major J, 217
Geullet
  Bertha, 256
Gheens
  Joseph P, 214
Gibbs
  Hiram, 80, 87
  Jasper, 40
  Joseph, 254
Gibon
  Andrew J Sr., 269
Gibson
  D P, 93
  John, 76
  Jordan, 238, 239

Obadiah D, 108
Giffen
  Adam, 18
Gigleux
  Ernest, 137
Gilbert
  Charles H, 49
  Daniel C, 201
  Edward, 73
  James, 24, 49
  Miss Josephine R, 107
  Nathan, 17, 65
  Warren W, 184
Gilchrist
  David, 22
Gilcooly
  Barney, 50
Gill
  Hardy C, 174
  Thomas W, 250
  Vinklen H, 170
  William A, 249
  William B, 41
Gillcrease
  Elisha W, 150
Gillespie
  Walter, 248
Gillin
  Cyrus W, 264
Gilloly
  Barney, 112
Gilly
  Adolphe A, 151, 244
  H, 244
  Jules P, 244
Gilmer
  George E, 167
  William L, 225
Gilmore
  Henry E, 232

Index

Gilson
  George G, 140
Girod
  Theophilis, 48
Givens
  John H, 162
Gladney
  Thomas R, 171
Glass
  F A, 178
Glasscock
  Hillery S, 215
  William J, 42
Glasspool
  Charles, 92
Glaze
  Patrick H, 2
Glenn
  Samuel Jr, 37
Glover
  J G, 196
  John F, 45
Glucksman
  Alexander, 126
Godley
  Jesse C, 40
Godwin
  Augustus C A, 61
  John J M, 127, 245
Goff
  James C, 162
  John R, 22
  Joseph M, 111, 210
  Mrs. Carrie, 162
  Robert T, 162
Goffaly
  Charles, 232
Gogreve
  Harman H, 49, 111
Goings
  Henry A, 275
Goldat
  Bernard, 263
Goldberg
  Samuel H, 290
Goldenberg
  Jacobs, 213
Goldsby
  Mrs. Dettie A, 143, 272, 273
Golson
  Lewis D, 286
Gonsoulin
  Adrien, 152, 205
Gonzales
  Joseph Jr, 157
Gooch
  John S, 32
  Robert, 260
  William D, 195
Goode
  William H, 149
Goodrich
  Henry, 36, 95
Goodwin
  Duncan C, 59
  Edward P, 255
  Edward W, 136
Gordain
  Joseph N, 250
Gordan
  Alexander C, 157
  George A, 41
Gordano
  Frank, 232
Gordon
  Alexander C, 157
  Jefferson W, 237
  John, 44
  John L, 94
  John S, 37
  William C, 257
  William C Jr, 254, 257
Gordy
  Addie A, 261
Gorman
  Clement W, 172
  Jonathan K, 131
Gorton
  Francis A, 70
  Joseph, 26, 70
  Lewis, 2
Gorum
  Joseph M, 226
Goss
  George W, 44
Gosserand
  Joseph P, 236
Goudchaux
  Leopold, 134
Goudrau
  Joseph, 157
Gouesen
  Emil, 34
Gould
  John A, 127
Gowers
  Leonard Z T, 215
Goyne
  Joseph R, 142
  Robert W, 272
Goynes
  Wiley W, 60
Grace
  Major J, 94
Gradnight
  Hylaire, 2
Graffenreid
  William L, 146, 228
Graham
  Andrew S, 140
  Henry R, 75
Grandchamp
  E, 204

Index

Granier
 Alovon, 253
Grant
 Francis M, 145, 229
 Israel I, 228
 John G, 232
 Poas A, 204
Grappe
 Francis L, 223
 Lucious O C, 243
Graves
 John F, 183
 Tarleton W, 38
Gray
 Benjamin H, 220
 James, 81, 149
 John F, 86
 Mamie K, 227
 W H, 86
Grayden
 Govan D, 167
Grayson
 Andrew J, 26
 James S, 73, 145
 John F, 80
 Wiley B, 47
Green
 Allen, 111
 Daniel L, 263
 George W, 42
 G H, 192
 Henry L, 39, 97
 James A, 54
 John G, 12
 Maggie E, 227
 Mary A, 227
 S W, 268
 Thomas M, 199
 Thomas O, 193
Greene
 Alexander, 40

Alexander C, 46
Allen, 209
Charles S, 79, 89
Miss Mattie, 286
William L, 209
Greenhill
 Sam J, 32
Greenlee
 James A, 107
Greenwell
 Robert W, 46, 105
 Washington, 45
Greenwood
 John J, 112, 262
 John S, 182
 Newton S, 118
 Wiliam J, 68
Greer
 J J, 98
Gregory
 Samuel, 178
 Thomas, 224, 225
Greig
 Joseph B, 252
Gremillion
 F M, 160
 John R, 31, 86
 Valerien, 31
Grenes
 Christian, 51
Grey
 James D, 199
Griffin
 Edwin R, 198
 James T, 158, 159
 Louis M, 201
 Mrs. Effa S, 159
 Wesley T, 48, 74
 William D, 80, 87
Griffing
 Zack, 220
Griffith

Isaac, 173
John H, 164
William, 98
William H, 268
Griggs
 James M, 210, 229
Grigsby
 Joseph, 164
Grimer
 Angello H, 254
Grinage
 Richardson, 71
Gringoy
 Andrew, 1, 29, 83
Grisham
 James, 22, 76
 Pinkney E, 283
Grogan
 John R, 238
Grooms
 Elijah, 40
Grossman
 Jacob, 279
Grounds
 Frederick T, 168
Groves
 Jacob R, 267
Grow
 Miss Mary I, 203
Gubert
 Auguste, 69
Guerin
 Francis J, 237
Guerineau
 Jean J, 85
Guffey
 Henry M, 93
Gugenheim
 Max, 248
Guice
 Jesse, 42
Guidry

Index

Joseph D, 84
Jules, 213
Louis O, 257
Ludger, 271
P L, 256, 289
Guilbeau
   Thules, 253
Guilfoux
   Carmelite C, 205
Guillard
   Jules, 19
Guillebert
   Constant, 31, 85
Guiu
   Manuel, 191
Gullatt
   William, 210
Gurin
   John, 48
Guthrie
   Sheldon Jr, 213
Guyard
   Robert P, 51
Guyol
   Adolph, 16, 64
Gwin
   Edwin O, 279
   George A, 107
Haas
   Alexander M, 160
   Felix, 213
   Henry, 178
   Isaac L, 34
   John R, 263
   Mrs. Marth A, 253
   Mrs. Martha A, 134
Hackett
   D, 6
   Orton, 105
Haden
   Robert S, 44

Hadley
   William H, 222
   William P G, 59
Hadnot
   Mrs. Lavina A, 205
Hadwin
   William D, 149
Hagaman
   Abraham, 46, 106
Hagan
   Edward H, 205
   James G, 284
Hagar
   John, 34
Haggard
   Martin L, 108
Hailes
   Thomas D, 12, 25, 43
Hale
   Charles C, 169
   James M, 171
Haleran
   Michael, 232
Hall
   Charles F, 182
   David, 94
   Harrison, 212
   John E, 44, 103
   Leander M, 100
   Mrs. Rebecca, 148
   Ransom, 98, 184
   Robert, 44
   William D, 247
   William G, 266
Halley
   John B, 122
Halsey
   Benjamin F Jr, 50
Hamblett
   John T, 274
Hamilton

A, 18
Alexander, 73
Alexander G, 228
George W, 280
J A, 203
James I, 175
James M, 271
John A, 58, 124, 240
John D, 142
John H, 206
John I, 65
Miss Virginia, 204
Mrs. Annie C, 228
William E, 78, 89
William S, 23
Hamlin
   Robert H, 182, 183
Hammer
   Charles W, 165
   Charlie W, 164
   Lorenzo, 164
Hammett
   George, 12, 55
Hammock
   Wilson H, 72
Hammons
   Charles J, 271
Hanchey
   William C, 179
Handy
   Samuel W, 222
Hanes
   Emma M, 168
   Shep B, 184
Hankstow
   M H, 265
Hanley
   Henry, 219
Hanlon
   Edward W, 237
Hanna

Index

William J, 34, 35, 93
Hanson
  Richard T, 155
Haralson
  B, 6
Harang
  Thophile, 214
Harard
  Augustus D, 239
Hardardt
  Frank, 112
Hardaway
  R F, 100, 188
Hardin
  Calvin H, 245
  John, 169
Hardonier
  Albert G, 62
Hardy
  Charles A, 34, 92
  Charles C, 260
  Jules, 18
  Nero S, 144
  Robert, 87, 162
  Robert M, 221
Hargis
  Joseph F G, 99
  Quincy A, 81
  William B, 4
Hargrave
  John G, 110
Hargrove
  James A, 111
  James H, 77
  John B, 177
  Reuben, 77
  William R, 240
Harkins
  William B, 223
Harman
  Edmund L, 255, 289
Harmon
  Judson, 19
Harp
  George H, 170
Harper
  Albert L, 101, 189
  George W, 246
  James D, 152, 277
  John W, 189
  Samuel J, 150, 281
Harppe
  Anchel, 36
Harrell
  Eldridge D, 249
  Irwin T, 195, 245, 246
  A J, 163
  James O, 231
  John P, 163
  Samuel S, 8
  S P, 169
Harrington
  Washington, 177
Harris
  Allen, 5, 39
  Charles C, 228
  Datus W, 100, 189
  Edward J, 226
  Harkwell H, 37
  James, 228
  James L, 114, 215
  Jarret, 93
  M A, 163
  Richard H, 185
  Solomon, 192
Harrison
  E, 71
  Edward P, 118
  George M, 118, 221
  James T, 11
John R R, 169
John W, 242
P, 51, 162
Susie W, 284
W M, 277
Hart
  Benjamin Jr, 22
  Clabourn, 22
  Garland S, 44
  H W, 133
  John D, 191, 193
  Mrs. Louisa, 252
  Simon M, 55
  Squire E, 150
Harten
  Fred Von, 49
Hartiens
  Adolph, 240
Harvell
  William C, 250
Harvey
  Frank H, 95
  James A, 203
  John, 36, 95
  John W, 136, 254
  Thomas, 81
  William A, 75
Harvill
  George H, 204
Haskell
  J A, 206
  Joseph C, 206
  W H, 172
Haspie
  L, 122
Hass
  Samuel, 85
Hatch
  Charles T, 108
  Frank T, 91
  Joseph T, 60, 125, 240

320

Index

Mrs. Emma P, 244
Hatcher
  George W, 247
Hatfield
  John R, 249
Hathord
  Alexander M, 250
Haugen
  Washington H R, 139, 263
Haughton
  Milus W, 167, 169
Havard
  Charlton W, 253
Hawkins
  A, 52
  John A, 91
  R, 65
  Walter E, 242
Hawley
  Orestis K, 125
Hawthorn
  A, 47
Hayden
  H, 63
  John A, 257
Hayes
  Basil J, 272
  Bernard M, 240
  Dallas B, 135, 255
  Eugene C, 161
  James W, 143
  John R, 241
Haynes
  Bythell, 46
  Dennis E, 150
  F B, 88, 165
  Henry, 20
  W H, 46
Haynie
  James E, 143
Hays

Henry, 179
  Orasamus, 135
  Xanthus D, 200
Hayward
  Harry, 235
Haywood
  Alonzo P, 89
Head
  Addie, 165
  Annie, 228
  James K, 210
  Walter A, 231
Headen
  B B, 20
  Eli, 20, 69
Headrick
  William J, 194
Healy
  William W, 89
Heap
  Samuel D, 129
  S D, 249
Heard
  George W, 173, 246, 247
  Henry P, 66
  James B, 163
  James R, 80
  John F, 133
  John W, 186
  Joseph, 6
  Joseph W, 272
  Thomas J, 86, 160
Hearick
  Sam C W, 59
Hearn
  Stephen M, 210
Hearne
  Asa H, 78, 89
  Elvin C, 169
  Thomas J, 168
Hearrington

John C, 170
Heath
  Calvin, 289
  Henry H, 47
  Isaac C, 48, 107
  John T, 17
  William H, 197
Hebert
  Adolphe, 49
  Alexander P, 172
  Charles, 208
  Eraphemon, 251
  Euphemon, 132
  Jean Eli, 8
  Joseph A, 218
  Joseph S, 215
  Joseph T, 84
  Julia M, 218
  Leon, 208
  Oscar F, 157
  Pierre A, 173
  Placido, 92
  Thomas, 207
Hedrick
  William A, 180
Heffner
  William, 90
Heintz
  Charles, 262
Heller
  August, 235
Hellinger
  Joseph, 175
Helluin
  Edgar P, 158
  Pierre F, 1, 29
Helmich
  Alexander L, 230
Heminis
  Mrs. Mary L, 211
Hemkin
  Barnard, 21

Hemler
John A Jr, 243
Hemphill
Tilman, 80
Hempstead
Orlando H, 109
Hena
Adolphe A, 248
Henchert
Conrad, 111
Henderson
John F C, 14
Lewis, 142
Miss Ann L, 125
Robert M, 59, 125
Hendrick
Robert C, 53
Hennigan
Michael, 204
Henning
John T, 175
Henry
F A, 107
Francis, 188
Harriet I, 179
John H, 226
John M, 189
Samuel P, 152, 179
Stewart L, 111
Henson
D C, 63
Herbeg
Josephine, 168
Miss Henrietta, 290
Herbelin
Jules, 264
Hereford
S L, 280
Herrick
George W, 231
Herring
F D, 217
John R, 124
John S, 94
J R, 59
Robert J, 37
Herron
Joseph R, 230, 231
Hester
Charles H, 103
Colwell C, 271
Elias P, 41
Nathan H, 179
Robert S, 126
Hetherwick
Clarence, 161
Jefferson, 161
Hewitt
J E, 196
Hewson
David C, 74
Hibbler
I E, 119
Hickman
George W, 151, 204
Jessie H, 282
Hicks
Delana P, 271
James J, 285
Thomas A, 256
Higgins
John, 185
Higguson
Frederick, 156
Hightower
E Herbert, 163
Higman
John B, 222
Hildenbrand
Ava H, 211
Hill
Edward L, 210
Edwin Lawrence,
94
John, 103, 175
John G, 71
William T, 215
Hilliard
John M, 54, 118
Hilllman
Hercules, 3
Hillman
Hercules, 35
Hills
Thomas C, 155, 156
Thomas E, 83
Himel
William, 83
Hinchen
Alexander W, 216
Andrew F, 216
Annie T, 216
Hine
Ralph E, 261
Hines
Benjamin F, 53
Curtis T, 271
James, 60
John James, 162
Mattie A, 177
William H, 177
Hingle
Mrs. Abigail H, 231
Hinkley
Hargnin, 30
Hinson
Henry, 96, 181
Hinton
John Bennett, 249
Miss Minerva, 111
Wesley W, 209, 287
Hirsch

Index

Martin, 222
Hitchcock
  Henry H, 113
Hobbs
  Sallie S, 169
Hobby
  Barnabas M, 156, 157
Hodgeon
  Michael W, 88
Hodnett
  William H, 203
Hoffpauir
  Elijah, 213
  Esaphania, 274
Hogan
  Thomas, 95
  William, 75
Holbrook
  Frederick R, 182
Holcombe
  Henry B Jr, 270
Holder
  Jesse J, 108
Holland
  A, 86
  Allen, 128, 162
Holley
  John, 79, 88
Holliday
  James A, 71
Hollingsworth
  Jacob B, 145
  James C, 3, 35
  J Y, 6, 26, 69
  William R, 224
Holloway
  John, 15
  John M, 78
Holmes
  B A, 103
  Henry B, 144

James J, 283
John L, 168
Lewis N, 283
Holstein
  Mary A, 185
  R E, 185
Honeycutt
  John, 128, 245
Hood
  Chapman, 96
  Mrs. Martha A, 210
  Whitfield, 210
Hooper
  Churchile A, 59
  Churchill A, 125
  Jess, 7
  Jesse W, 15
  Leslie A, 199
  Thomas, 15
  Thomas B, 59
  Thomas S, 192
Hopkins
  Albert L, 97
  B T, 272
  Daniel R, 11
  D R, 11
  James I, 272
  John W, 272
  Joseph, 125
  Mrs. Mary, 248
  Mrs. Mary J, 142
Horgan
  Daniel B, 240
Hornsby
  William K, 140
Horton
  Eugene F, 168
  Solomon S, 46
Hosea
  John S, 160
Hough

Robert, 102
Hougham
  John, 217
House
  John, 108
  Thomas L, 171
  William A, 265
Houston
  Edith A, 238
  James M, 149
Howard
  Eugene, 111
  Harting P, 16
  Hulvatus H, 288
  J Oscar, 281
  William R, 161
Howe
  A P, 42
Howell
  James Oscar, 199
  J Oscar, 281
  Joseph, 90
  Rufus K, 24
  Sarah K, 201
Howle
  Epaphedilius, 67
  Epephedilius, 138
Huber
  George, 252
  Jenon, 256
Hubert
  F Eugene, 235
  Zenon, 289
Huckabay
  George W, 170
  Harold H, 170
Huddleston
  Isaac, 60
Hudgins
  Benjamin K, 47
Hudson
  Daniel B, 159, 161,

Index

255
James, 8, 46
John E Jr, 215, 217
John E Sr, 215
Mrs. Laura F, 161
William F, 138, 260
Hudspeth
  Daniel D, 258
Huesman
  Charles F, 159
Huested
  William T, 162
Huey
  James III, 73, 144
  John Jr, 76
  Mason, 73
  Mrs. Catherine, 144
Huff
  James B, 273
Huffman
  Benjamin Jr, 185
Hufft
  Jacob F, 264
Hughes
  Isaac, 33, 90
  Samuel B, 16
  William C, 168
  William J, 89
Huguet
  Agricole B, 253
Hull
  Thomas W, 91
Humble
  George W, 202
  Jacob, 172
  Thomas J, 35, 92, 228, 231
Hummell
  Richard J, 198
  Theresa M, 198

Humphreys
  David George, 220
Humphries
  Benjamin N, 177
Hundley
  Aurelius S, 94, 177
  Dabney M, 34
Hunsicker
  Henry, 32, 90
Hunster
  Mrs. Susan J, 106
  Susan H, 148
Hunt
  Christopher C, 285
  Newcomb, 9
Hunter
  John A, 196, 243
  John R, 253
  Napoleon B, 268
Hurst
  James M, 123
  Theodore M, 138
Husser
  Hyppolite L, 267
Hutchens
  John W, 277
Hutchins
  Anthony W, 207
Hutchinson
  William, 243
Hutchison
  John O, 216
Hyams
  Henry M, 224
Hyde
  Charles H, 266
  E, 4
Hyland
  Thomas A, 220
Ilar
  William C, 48
Imboden

James, 182
Impson
  Benjamin F, 74
  C, 51
  Joseph A, 197
Inge
  Haley J, 70
  R Albert, 219
Inneranty
  James J, 262
  Joseph J, 262
Innes
  John W, 248
Irvine
  Gordon H, 11
  John A, 11
Irwin
  Gordon H, 10
  Mary E, 204
Isabell
  John B, 13, 17
Israel
  Gustave, 155
  Joseph, 106, 199
Ivey
  Walter E, 171
Ivins
  Joseph T, 170
Ivy
  Peter W, 243
  William T, 243
Jackson
  Andrew, 208
  Edward, 182
  George, 186
  Isaac R, 65, 134
  James, 195, 245
  James H, 174, 176
  J C, 270
  John H, 109
  Joseph H, 174
  J Taylor, 180

Index

Miss E J, 130
Miss Lucinda, 173
Robert, 130
Robert G, 286
Simeon T, 289
Simeon Taylor, 289
Susie S, 194
Thomas J, 278
Thomas M, 218
Warren F, 134, 253
Warren G, 257
William, 173
William A, 65, 286
Zachariah M, 110
Jacobs
  Samuel, 280
  Thornton F, 169
Jacquet
  Felix, 206
Jacquin
  Virginia C, 211
James
  Alice, 219
  Clarence S, 268
  John, 145
  Lucien D, 268
  Samuel L, 281
  Sarah E, 283
  William C, 125
Janney
  John, 38
Jarvis
  Isaac G, 290
Jassap
  Josephine J, 202
Jaumes
  Francois, 29, 83
Jay
  Thomas W, 288
Jeanerett
  John W, 19

Jeanfreaux
  A F, 234
Jeansonne
  Traville E, 161
Jeffrey
  Edward S, 116
Jeffries
  A, 202
Jenkins
  James D, 90
  Willis, 56
Jennings
  J Meade, 282
  Peter E, 49, 109
  William M, 47, 107
Jernigan
  Joseph, 169
Jewell
  Alva W, 170
  Joseph, 13, 57
  Washington, 13
Joel
  E M, 116
Joffrion
  Francois M, 160
Johns
  Joshua, 43
Johnson
  Armand, 252
  August, 174
  Benjamin D, 270
  Benjamin F, 33, 91
  Daniel, 285
  Edward M, 261
  Elmer J, 175
  Henry, 98
  Henry M, 226, 270
  Isaac C, 159
  James B, 58, 123
  Jason U, 289
  J Eugene, 240
  Josiah, 34, 91

  Lawford, 121
  Mary L, 199
  Mrs. Matilda, 121
  Napoleon B, 286
  Nettie L, 230
  Obey, 240
  Samuel, 205
  Vandice, 234
  William C, 177, 258
  William W, 262, 263
Johnston
  James H, 49
  Theodore, 49
Joiner
  George W, 141
Joinville
  Doiron, 147
Jolesaint
  Joseph Jr, 109, 207
Jolessaint
  Lewis, 128
Joly
  Ami M, 112, 211
  Joseph G, 155
Jones
  Andrew, 216
  Charles D, 170
  F A Jr, 184
  Harmon W, 281
  Harrison C, 38
  Ira, 219
  Isaac C, 35
  James, 45
  James H, 78, 162
  James L, 71, 142
  James M, 89, 226
  James W, 88
  J G, 168
  John C, 76
  John M, 283

Index

John R B, 54
Jordan, 274
J Welch, 46
Lafayette, 53
Martha J, 203
Miss D A, 148
Oliver C, 243
Robert L, 181
Spicer, 84, 157
Theodore L, 284
Thomas, 280
Thomas H, 5, 40, 115, 215
Thomas M, 54, 118
William A, 162
William H, 146, 275
William P, 11
William R, 3
William S, 210
Jordan
  E E, 224
  Enoch G, 155, 156
  John T, 225
  A W, 194
  William H, 104, 224
  William T, 54
Joseph
  Jules, 252
Joyner
  Eugene L, 196
  Marion R, 223
  Mrs. Amantheus P, 263
Juan
  Antonio, 248
Judice
  Alcide, 213
Juge
  P Emile Jr, 158
Jumere

Jean, 256
Kahn
  Emmanuel, 252
  Nicholas, 218
Kaisser
  Charles, 78
Kalord
  Walter G, 102
Kalow
  Walter G, 191
Kantrowitz
  M, 214
Karner
  William J, 233
Karr
  Henry L, 50
Katz
  Abraham, 249
Kaufman
  E, 280
Kaufmann
  Isadore, 219
Kay
  Charles S, 233
Keating
  Charles W, 90
Keenan
  Edward F, 187
  Hugh, 39, 96
Keene
  Richard T, 96, 181
Kees
  John M, 186
Keith
  Commodore P, 186
  Henry T, 171
  Perry P, 171
Keler
  Philip, 20
Kellar
  Philip, 68
Keller

Alexander N, 222
John G, 179
Kelley
  James R, 46
Kellogg
  Adam, 218
  Adams, 219
Kelly
  Charles, 234
  James A, 71
  Joseph, 54
  L J, 198
Kemie
  Sylvanus M, 278
Kemp
  Guy C, 265
  Hillery, 130
  Thomas D, 64, 130
Kemper
  Enoch B, 50, 112
Kendrick
  F C, 16
  H F, 16
Kenico
  James B, 100
Kennard
  Perry L, 25
  Robert John, 106, 197
Kennedy
  Dawson W, 77, 109
  Gilvary H, 20
  Jesse, 36
  Warren G, 146
Kenner
  Minor, 112
Kenney
  Benjamin G, 120
Kennon
  Edward J, 278
Kenny

Index

Lawrence R, 24
Kent
  Amos, 6, 7
  Frederic M, 8
  Giles W, 200
  Isaac N, 36
  Joseph T, 173
  Seaborn B, 200
Kenton
  James D, 197
  Joseph D, 197
Kenyon
  Nelson, 85
Keogh
  James, 46
Ker
  William H, 12
Kern
  George W, 138, 260
Kerr
  James D, 21
  John, 45
Kett
  Thomas P, 219
Key
  Landry A, 5, 40
  Philip B, 1
Keys
  Thomas A, 288
Kibbe
  Alfred, 36
  Charles, 2, 30
Kibbs
  William, 79
Kiblinger
  A E, 200
  Elijah C, 106, 200
Kidd
  William E, 211
  William J, 56, 81
Kiernan
  Jacob P, 116
Kijean
  Evariste, 17
Kilbourn
  Mrs. Frances, 108
Kile
  Jacob, 224
Kilgore
  Robert, 41
  Robert L, 4
Killbourn
  William J, 288
Killen
  George W, 283
Killgore
  G A, 226
  Robert, 100
Killian
  Doctor S, 250
  Joseph, 63, 131
Killingsworth
  D, 151
Kilos
  John C, 155
Kimball
  Benjamin W, 31
  Charles Y, 20
  Thomas H, 1
  Zachariah, 85
Kimbro
  Thomas B, 161
Kimbrough
  George M, 222
Kimpel
  David, 221
Kincade
  Alena M, 248
Kincaid
  Ronald M, 244
Kinchen
  Lillie O, 266
Kincher
  Oren M, 115
Kinchire
  Samuel H, 262
King
  Alfred P, 79, 87
  Edmond, 5
  John H, 189
  Washington W, 189
  William L, 162
Kingrey
  Joseph Jr, 174
  Joseph S, 225
  Samson R, 174
Kingsburg
  John L, 123
  Samuel M, 123
Kingsbury
  John S, 235
Kingsley
  Charles, 165
  Joseph S, 241
Kinney
  Calvin H, 268
Kinsey
  W H, 228
Kipes
  James E, 187
Kirk
  George Van, 95
  Ignatius, 2, 31
  Isaiah, 61, 126
  J, 2
  J J B, 124
  John J, 285
  Joseph B, 166
  Joseph J B, 165
  T C, 124
Kirkland
  No first name, 42
Kirkman
  J B, 172

Index

Kirkpatrick
   Mrs. Martha, 100
   Samuel, 99
Kirkwood
   John B, 145
Kiser
   Daniel C, 47
Kitterlin
   D J, 125
Kleinpeter
   Mrs. Cecelia L, 233
   Sebastian L, 198
Kluger
   Charles, 248
Knight
   Henry A, 173
   John C, 285
   Thomas S, 286
   Zachary T, 141
Knobloch
   F Adolph, 113
Knott
   John C, 72
   John E Jr, 224
Knowles
   George W, 288
Knox
   Miss Georgia, 101, 189
   Robert, 54
Kobleur
   D, 138
Koehn
   William J, 238
Koerber
   Paul, 212
Kops
   Joseph, 289
Koranson
   Joseph C, 129
Kostmayer
   John G, 185
Kraemer
   E, 214
   George W, 130
   Mrs. Margaret, 215
Krantz
   John Jr, 211
Kroll
   Auguste F, 251
Krouse
   Francis O, 99
Kuntrel
   D S, 149
Kussman
   William, 129
Labadie
   L T, 30
Labarre
   Charles, 212
Labau
   John T B, 259, 260
Labdell
   James A, 23
   James L, 280
Labit
   Joseph T, 274
LaBranch
   Alcice, 62
   Octave, 62
Lacey
   August M, 46
   Josiah H, 81, 148
Lachapelle
   Charles, 250
Lachapello
   Charles, 251
Lacour
   Ambroise, 30
LaCour
   J M Bret, 14
Lacroix
   Eugene H, 215
   Louis, 213
Lacy
   Adolphe D, 262
   James M, 152, 179
   John D, 237
Lafargue
   Adolphe, 31
Lafleur
   Ernest, 175
   Erteluce T, 258
   Joseph D, 174
Laforest
   Antoine, 10
LaForest
   Thibodeaux, 10
Lafreyre
   Joseph, 155
Lagrone
   Aline M, 263
Laiche
   Theophile F, 251
Laird
   David J, 44
Laizan
   David P, 256
LaJeune
   Eli, 23
Lake
   Edward, 140, 267
Laman
   Honore V, 29
Lamb
   Henry J, 11
   Henry S, 55
Lambright
   Benjamin F, 101
   Benjamin J, 40
Lamereaux
   Jules, 203
Lamon
   Archibald H, 147, 279

Index

Lampite
  Joseph A, 222
Lancaster
  Ryal A, 100
  Ryal L, 40
Landaman
  John, 22
Landers
  James B, 144
Landiman
  Rudolph, 155
Landreau
  John, 123, 147, 235
  John C, 282
Landreut
  Auguste C, 214
Landry
  Alphonse, 133
  Dorselie, 109, 207
  Dorvill A, 205
  Elizer, 49
  Hercule, 156
  Jean B, 157
  Joseph, 64
  Joseph Jr, 16
  Joseph P, 250
  Joseph Sr, 16
  Jules, 29, 83
  Lenfray T, 23
  Marcelin, 134
  Onezipher, 137
  Pierre, 83, 155
  Terince J, 1
  Vincent Paul, 83
Lane
  Rufus F, 278
Lang
  Mrs. Mary, 211
  Thomas, 244
Lange
  Leon, 146, 229
Langford
  J M, 94
Langley
  James P, 49
  Sevrin, 175
Langlier
  E, 10
Langston
  Robert, 190, 278
Lanier
  Lewis, 72
Lanius
  Jacob, 39
LaNone
  John C, 45
Lansdell
  Walter T, 160
Laplace
  Basic, 253
  Basil, 253
  Eugene B, 252
Larase
  James T, 208
Lard
  Absolom E, 148
Laremore
  Wilson L, 197
Larkin
  John E, 72
  Michael W, 78
Larose
  James O, 109
  J O, 207
Larrasan
  John, 109
Lartiges
  Armand, 57
Laspeyre
  John, 137
Lasseigne
  Alcide C, 271
  Charles, 132, 252
  Leonard P, 141, 269
Lassiter
  Campbell, 142
  Wiley D, 196
Lastrapes
  Alfred H, 134
  Amelia, 259
  Andre, 259
  Mrs. Marie, 259
Lataste
  Victor, 19
Lathrop
  Andrew W, 71
Latil
  Alex, 248
Latiolais
  Felix C, 213
Laudoner
  Aaron, 202
Laurents
  Felix, 172
Lavigne
  George B, 217
Law
  James, 199
Lawes
  Samuel E, 137
Lawhon
  George W, 163
Lawless
  Matthew, 147
Lawrence
  Henry C, 221
Lawson
  Alexander, 9
Lawton
  Amos, 37, 94
Lea
  Alexander, 22
  David G, 22
  Jefferson, 51, 114
  Miss Martha Ann,

Index

114
Leach
  A C, 245
  Henry, 74, 115
  Jesse P, 245
  John A, 245
Leake
  James Sr, 254
Lear
  Theodore, 84
Leatherman
  F M, 229
  T M, 145
Leavel
  Thomas J, 221
  Thomas O, 118, 221
Lebesque
  Flavius, 66
Lebeuf
  Nevil, 212
LeBlanc
  Andre, 1
Leblanc
  Arthur, 271
LeBlanc
  Charles, 48
  Deminie, 83
Leblanc
  Lucius, 275
LeBlanc
  Marcellin, 214
  Maxile, 8, 49
  Nicholas, 158
  Rosemand, 79
  Rosemond, 50
Leboeuf
  Edouard, 64
LeBoeuf
  Norbert, 180
Lebourgeois
  Octave, 217

Lebreton
  E V, 264
Leckie
  Charles, 14
Lecler
  Francis, 212
Lecois
  Mrs. Addie, 281
Lecomte
  Elizabeth, 211
Lecour
  Amboise, 2
  Ambroise, 2
Ledbetter
  James W, 3
Lederer
  Simon, 233
Ledoux
  Osite, 180
  Ozette, 176
Lee
  Edward, 2
  Francis, 13
  Hanson, 87
  H W, 108
  James E, 246
  Jesse, 138
  John, 4
  Maria Agnes, 172
Lees
  William, 1
Lefebure
  Paul J, 135, 254
Lefort
  Francis, 1
  Louis, 155
Leftwich
  Delimer C, 216
  Thomas L, 217
Legare
  John Cecile, 155
Leggett

J B, 123
Legrand
  Robert W, 32
Legrase
  Rosemond, 3, 38
Lehay
  Augustine, 258
Lehmann
  Berthold, 191
  Berthold B, 268
  Isaac, 137
  Jacques, 261
  Karl, 192, 193
Lehmanowsky
  Edward C, 20, 68
Leigh
  Mrs. Azema, 86, 160
LeJeune
  Eli, 75
Leman
  Homer, 274
Leminger
  George F, 262
Lemle
  Isaac, 192
  Isadore, 192
  Isidore, 280
Lemoin
  Clovis, 125
Lemoine
  Avit, 159
  Oscar, 159
Lemon
  James J, 205
  John R, 46
  William H, 148
Lemonin
  Arthur F, 203
Lennard
  Isaac L, 101
Leonard

Index

John W, 131, 249
J S, 66, 133
L L, 116
Mary A, 288
Lepine
  Evariste A, 76, 113
Leroy
  Charles, 120
Lesaicherre
  Jean B, 252
Lesesune
  Amades, 214
Leveque
  Mary J, 172
Levier
  George W, 219
Levy
  Abraham, 106, 200, 279
  Daniel, 124
  Emmanuel, 269
  Henry, 60
  Johana H, 257
  Leon, 157
  Lewis, 6
  Louis, 262
  M, 15
  Mrs. Sue, 232
  N, 263
  Nathan, 269
  Robert, 232
Lewis
  Charles, 10
  Chauncey, 107, 201
  George C, 87, 163, 281
  Isaac L, 181
  John S, 148
  Mrs. A, 281
  Soloman, 130
  Thomas C, 22, 290
  William, 182
  William L, 25
  William T, 102, 191
Liddell
  Mrs. Annie C, 244
Lignon
  Joseph F, 51
Ligon
  Lemuel T, 107, 200
Liles
  John M, 153, 284
Lilly
  Nathaniel J, 120
Lindsay
  John C, 193
Lindsey
  Burkett B, 101
  Hugh N, 57
  Thad, 183
Linkins
  John H, 104
Linn
  F, 78
Linossier
  Claudius, 30, 84
Linson
  William J, 167
Lipscomb
  Thomas D, 201
Lisso
  Samuel M, 242
Littell
  Isaac F, 254
Little
  Hardy, 216
  William A, 155
Littlejohn
  Angus C, 157, 158
  William, 32
Littman
  Monarch, 141, 269
Livingston
  Aaron, 53
  Emanuel, 186
  S S, 46
Lockett
  James M, 162
Lockhart
  John B, 52, 115
Loeb
  Henry, 155
  Michael, 86
Loey
  John E, 100
Loflin
  L P, 45
Lofton
  John C, 88, 165
Logan
  Samuel W, 62
Lombard
  Mrs. Rebecca S, 177
Long
  Miss Marg V, 88
  Mrs. Mary, 112
  William F, 220
Looney
  Benjamin F, 78, 89
  Robert J, 77
Loper
  John J, 142, 272
Lopez
  Gustave, 45
  John, 58
Loret
  Adolphe, 29
  Frank, 83
Lorio
  Peter E, 50, 113
Lorrain
  Louis, 173
Lothrop

Index

Mrs. Flora F, 201
Lotsinger
  Frank, 271
Loud
  George B, 109
Loudon
  James M, 198
Louiat
  Leonce M, 208
Lounsberry
  William G, 275
Loutret
  P, 69
Louviere
  Octave, 206
Love
  Albert C, 156
  Claiborn S, 78
  Leander E, 116
  Mycajah, 52
  S E, 53
  Thomas M, 167
Lovelace
  George W, 3
  Micajah H, 116
  Miss Sallie E, 97, 185
Lovell
  Lavenia J, 203
  Lavenia Jane, 125, 237
Lovellette
  Augustus P, 100
Lovett
  John A, 285
Low
  John B, 149
Lowe
  Mary A, 179
Lowell
  Charles W, 121
Lowenstrom
  Charles D, 251
Lowery
  Thomas, 142
Lowrey
  George M, 41
  George W, 99, 188
Loze
  Felix H, 2
Lucar
  General L, 170
Lucas
  Coleman H, 218
  E A, 149
  John G, 219
  William, 145
  William A, 80, 86
Luce
  Jonathan N, 187
Lucious
  Samuel G, 61
Luckner
  Robert, 125
Lucky
  Lewis J, 163
Lunny
  James, 269
  Mrs. Emma, 270
Lupe
  James M, 71, 142
Lyles
  Cordelia, 239
  Hiram C, 173
  Thomas, 166
Lyman
  Francis J, 40
Lynch
  John, 96
  R B, 268
  Richard B, 70
  William F, 70
Lyons
  David A, 34, 172
  Franklin S, 156
  George E, 144, 274
  John Jr, 17, 64, 134
  Joseph, 121, 227
  Patrick, 122, 231
  Thomas, 232
  William, 34
Machade
  Julius D, 270
Mackenzie
  George, 16
Mackie
  Willington A, 11
Macouchy
  William, 72
Madden
  Abraham, 73
  Abram, 145
  Thomas H, 201
  William, 5
Maddry
  James H, 190
Madere
  Adolphe, 132
  Thomas C, 248
Mading
  Jerome B, 77
Maes
  Benoni, 207
Magamaud
  Victor, 135
Magee
  David A, 74
  Eldridge, 276
  H G, 276
  James O, 266, 276
  Margaret A, 276
  Margarett, 264
  Mrs. E A, 74, 146
  Thomas H, 138
Magoun
  Cyrus S, 43, 102

Mahaffy
  John D, 196
  Mollie A, 196
Maignaud
  Victorian, 254
Mailhiot
  Elisee E, 29
Maines
  William C, 246
Mains
  W W, 237
Major
  Albin, 235
  Arcade, 237
  Joseph D, 237
  Veronegas, 58
  Veronique, 58, 124
Majors
  Thomas J, 218
Malachowsky
  Joseph, 238
Malagarie
  Lognerd, 212
Malancon
  Edmund O, 29
Malbroux
  Pierre S, 271
Malhiot
  Elisee E, 1
Mallett
  Isaac W Jr, 226
  Louis V, 240
Mallory
  Wesley, 19
Malone
  George T, 54, 118
Mandeville
  Henry D, 38
Manheim
  Heyman, 224
Manley
  William, 101

  William H, 277
Mann
  Thomas A, 37
  Thomas M, 95
  Thomas W, 181
Manning
  Simon, 5, 12, 39
  Thornton D, 143
  William R, 188
Mansfield
  Lott, 156
Manti
  Mignet, 243
Maraist
  Auguste, 66
Marburg
  William, 73
Marbury
  William, 20, 69
Marcalle
  John, 11, 55
Marciacoje
  Jean Louis, 57
Mardis
  Abner R, 184
  Alonzo F, 184
Mareno
  C H, 212
Margenis
  John, 52
Margot
  Benjamin, 211
Marin
  Victor, 29
Marinovich
  Antoine, 222
Marion
  Francis J, 49
Maritz
  Leopold, 97
Markham
  Hugh, 36

  John, 262
  William, 75
Marks
  Louis, 193
  Mrs. Theresa M, 158
  Samuel, 268
Marner
  M M, 239
Marnist
  Auguste, 133
Marrero
  Louis H, 212
Marron
  Michael, 268
Marsalis
  Benjamin F, 189
Marschalk
  Francis, 42
Marsh
  George W, 65
Marshall
  Francis W, 125, 237
  George B, 125
  George C, 271
  A Pearcy, 140
  William Branch, 31, 85, 158
Martin
  Augustus, 78
  Austin, 141
  C G, 68
  George W, 152, 277
  James W, 38
  J J, 216
  J O, 277
  John W, 44, 104
  Leon, 57
  L L, 216
  Miss Lou, 100

Index

M T, 213
William A, 89,
　165, 166, 167
Martinsdale
　John T, 279
Marvin
　Mrs. Ruth A, 97
　Schuyler, 97
Marx
　Jonas, 191
Marye
　Robert V, 25, 32
Mascaline
　Lena, 216
Mask
　W B, 283
Mason
　Calvin Jr, 118
　John P, 70
　John T, 117
　John W, 53
　M C B, 269
Massingale
　Joseph P, 44
　Warren J, 44
Massingill
　Leon C, 181
Massy
　Pool P, 42, 99
Mather
　Samuel, 44
Matta
　Andrew, 198
　John H Jr, 208
Matthews
　Burrell H, 79
　Charles B, 141
　Edward, 95
　Frederic W, 140
　George A, 150,
　　203, 282
　Harris S, 279

　Thomas B, 38
Matthies
　Frederick, 264
Mauk
　Daniel F, 47
Maury
　Anatole A, 233
Maxey
　William H, 189
Maxwell
　Friend S, 218
May
　Frank, 146
　Joseph A, 13
Mayer
　Bernhardt, 239
　David, 116
　George L, 85, 159
　Isaac, 262
　John D, 250
　Maxey, 235
Mayes
　William L, 282
Mayfield
　Ainsley H, 286
Mayo
　C, 254
　Henry M, 261
　Oren, 3, 38
Mazilly
　Louis E, 173
McAllen
　Henry, 61
McAllister
　James M, 120
McAvoy
　Thomas H, 264
McBride
　Robert W, 214
McBroom
　James H, 143, 272
McBurton

　William D, 72
McCabe
　John H, 185
McCain
　Henry A, 203
　John J, 203
　Robert, 95
　Robert M, 36
McCall
　Henry, 157
McCallson
　William, 117
McCallum
　L W, 94
McCandless
　David, 37, 95
McCarroll
　George W, 95
McCarstle
　Angus, 7, 46
　Nele N, 23
McCarthy
　R, 20
McCarty
　Thomas J, 67
McClellan
　Emma S, 166
McClelland
　John M, 33
McClenagham
　Cunningham, 167
　Miss Mary M, 167
McClendon
　Francis J, 229
　Samuel W, 72, 141
McClure
　David F, 91
McCollister
　Isham N, 127
McCook
　Granberry, 56
　James M H, 224,

Index

McCord
  Ambrose O, 118, 225
  Miss Mary E, 221
McCormick
  Ferdinand M, 210
  George W, 230
  John M, 45
  Joseph, 45, 105
  Thomas, 35, 93
  Willis H, 231
McCornas
  Josias H, 42
McCoy
  Fleming L, 279
  Thomas L, 207
McCrae
  Duncan A, 94
McCray
  William J, 165
McCrory
  Thomas, 65, 134
McCullough
  Hamilton Jr, 267
  William M, 182
McCutcheon
  James W, 62, 128
  Samuel, 62
McDade
  Luther E, 167
McDaniel
  Elizabeth, 222
  John W, 119
  Samuel S, 99
McDonald
  Fadra A, 209
  John W, 55, 85
  Robert K, 26
  Stephen, 43
  William, 73, 216
  William C, 111, 209
  William D, 74
McDonato
  Robert, 12
McDougall
  Myford, 277
McDowell
  John, 80
  John T, 110, 209
McEacham
  Thomas H, 277
McEachern
  Dan, 24
McEmery
  Paul, 21
McEnery
  James, 31
McEwen
  Daniel H, 252
McFadin
  Thomas H, 273
McFall
  J D, 152
McFarlain
  Andrew D, 174
McFarland
  Arthur, 40, 99
  John W, 190
McGaha
  John, 75
McGahey
  Daniel R, 48
McGehee
  Henry J, 263
McGinty
  Elisha K, 81, 148
  Henry R, 242
McGoldrick
  John R, 242
McGowen
  Joseph A, 221
McGraw
  Thomas G, 242
McGregor
  Alexander J, 197
McGuire
  Joseph F, 72
McGunnegle
  Robert, 133
McHarron
  John J, 264
McHatton
  Robert E, 57, 121
McHenry
  William L, 256
McIlie
  Richard M, 182
McIntosh
  William, 104
McIver
  Archibald, 63
McJilton
  Miche, 30
McKain
  William E, 220
McKaskle
  James P, 210
McKay
  L, 16
McKee
  William A, 111, 210
McKeithen
  Archibald J, 177, 179
McKelvy
  David S, 95
McKenley
  Sam E, 79
McKenna
  Arthion, 106
  Mrs. Sarah, 106
  William, 91, 169
McKie

335

Index

Harrison, 63
McKiernan
  Jacob P, 117
McKinney
  Miss Iva H, 240
  William M, 63
McKnight
  William E, 233
McLain
  Kenneth, 146
McLanahan
  John A, 12, 56
McLean
  Hector H, 52
  John O, 57
McLeary
  Hector H, 25
McLemore
  B J, 278
  Fannie E, 278
  Franklin P, 244
  Sterling G, 61, 127
McLeroy
  Francis M, 110, 111
McMahon
  David, 4
  Isaac, 4
  James E, 174
  Richard S, 269
McManus
  John L, 199
McMeans
  A C, 220
McMichael
  Stouton E, 183
McMillan
  Duncan B, 44, 104
  James A, 290
McNamar
  William, 206
McNeeley
  William B, 237
McNeil
  A T, 20
McPhatton
  Archibald, 256
McQuatters
  Joseph J, 186
McQueen
  William H, 12
McSchilling
  James, 276
McShan
  George W, 247
McVey
  Frank, 173
  W H, 218
  Willis H, 202
McVicker
  Duncan B, 73
McWhiney
  Thomas E, 195
Meacom
  Hardy, 39
Mead
  James W, 122
Meadows
  Isaac S, 173
  John D, 282
  Olney W, 189
Mearns
  William D, 172
Meeker
  Joseph H, 239
  Moses L, 6
Meers
  William, 92
Meignaud
  Victorin, 289
Melancon
  Alice, 132, 251
  Cyprian, 132, 133, 258

Jean B S, 112
Marcel, 112
Paul, 123
Victor, 64
Victor L, 131
Melchior
  August, 212
Melchoir
  August, 113
  Viviana, 212
Melder
  Felix Van, 240
  Henry L, 240
Melton
  William, 16
Melwick
  Ezekial P, 176
Mendoza
  Joseph, 259
Menes
  F S, 229
Meng
  Harry G, 191
Mercer
  D D, 71
  J A, 116
Merchant
  M L, 268
  Washington B, 227
Meredith
  Asa, 177
  John H, 4
  John J, 35, 93
  Marquis L, 177
  Thomas, 35, 93
Merle
  A, 69
Merrick
  David T, 236, 237
  John P, 130, 249
Merrill
  Mrs. A, 109

Index

Merrit
  Jonathan, 48
Merritt
  Jerome, 198
  John B, 198
  Mrs. Cecelia L, 233
  William H, 216
Mestre
  John B, 247
Metoyer
  Alain L, 223
Meuer
  Andrew, 117
Meunet
  George A, 158
Mevers
  Bernard, 232
Meyer
  Bernard D, 238
  Herman, 142
  Mrs. Bridget, 108
  William, 172
Meynard
  John, 67
Michael
  M S, 235
Michelson
  Charles, 268
Mickosson
  S T, 220
Middlebrooks
  James D, 277
Midkiff
  Isaac W, 286
Migeat
  John, 138
Mignot
  Hyacinthe C, 264
Miles
  Charles S, 281
  Elbert M, 246
  Mrs. Julia B, 246
  Pleasant L, 187
  Wyatt S, 205
Millard
  Nathaniel P, 133
Miller
  Alcide, 179
  Amaziah R, 90
  Charles, 137, 260, 261
  Charles F, 215
  Daniel H, 45, 208
  Denis, 290
  D F, 102
  Francis D, 8
  Frederick F, 215
  Garrand W, 43
  George W, 38
  Harrison C, 268
  Henry W, 83
  Hugh, 190
  James W, 39, 98
  John, 95, 181
  John M, 36
  Joseph, 59
  Joseph A, 124
  Joseph D, 191
  Joseph E, 43, 102
  Levi A, 173
  Peter K, 180
  R, 70
  Ralph P, 191
  William, 52
  William D, 139
  William F, 184
  William H, 250
Milling
  James H, 73
Mills
  Frank M, 186
  John Chapman, 66, 134
  Robert H, 79, 144
  William Jr, 124, 237
Millsaps
  Miah, 145
  Thomas F, 229
  Uriah, 229
Millspaugh
  Abraham, 65, 136
  Frederick, 136, 255
Milner
  Abner, 18
  John C, 41
  Oriel R, 110
  William A, 71
Milton
  Michael, 115
Mims
  David J, 277
  James D, 80
  John Adams, 277
  John James, 88
  Larkin M, 176
  Martha A, 277
  Mrs. Martha A, 87
Miner
  Abner D, 133
  Andrew, 220
  Henry D, 156
  William E, 5
Minor
  John S, 83
Minton
  Isaac A, 217
  Thomas W, 20
Minvielle
  Theodore A, 206
Mires
  James, 66, 134
Miscon
  Nathaniel, 76
Mistick

Index

Pierre A, 254
Mitcham
  William, 100
Mitchell
  Francis F, 93
  Jackson L, 246
  William P, 101
  William R, 230
Mix
  Charles, 58
  Charles A, 10
Mixon
  Albert, 179
  Irvin, 111
  V Z, 163
Mizell
  John G, 264
Mobberly
  Samuel H, 181
Mobley
  Jesse, 79
Moffett
  William M, 150, 282
Moffitt
  William J, 129
Mollere
  Camille, 155
  S C, 84
  Silveste C, 158
Monisset
  Celeste A, 274
Monnier
  Auguste, 212
Monno
  Aristede T, 206
Monroe
  Bettie A, 86
  Donald, 171
  George, 120
  James, 80, 86
  Matilda A, 86
  Thomas C, 101
Montamat
  Gabriel, 12
Montfort
  John, 12
Montgomery
  Charles J, 186
  A J, 245
  Joseph E, 184
  Pleasant T, 61
  Solomon, 105
Moody
  John B, 270, 271
  Thomas O, 70
  William M, 141, 270
Mooney
  Henry C, 115, 150, 265
  Michael H, 137
Moore
  Arthur S, 91
  Calvin H, 95, 180, 244
  James M, 9, 50
  Jethro, 145, 229, 230
  John M, 278
  John T, 271
  Loretta A, 231
  Martha A E, 173
  Matthew M, 104, 194
  Mrs. Maria, 90
  Nathaniel, 5
  Robert B, 165
  Thomas J, 165
  William T, 202
  William Y, 149
Mooring
  Edward R, 171
Mora
  August, 137
Moraine
  Victor, 13
Morales
  Alexander, 129
Morand
  Rufin J B, 122, 232
Moreland
  Howard J, 184
  William C, 42, 100
Morgan
  Albert W, 246
  Charles, 58, 59, 139
  Daniel, 8, 105, 197
  Davis A, 130
  Dempsey D, 243
  George A, 53
  John L, 139
  William B, 110, 288
  William C, 263
Moritz
  Bernard, 185
  Leopold, 185
Morris
  Jesse, 127
  Joel L, 101
  Joel S, 188
  John, 134
  John E, 145
  John H, 282
  J S, 254
  Julius, 269
  Nathan D, 203, 283
  Thomas M, 97
  William J, 241
  William L, 231
  William T, 257
Morrison
  Alexander, 93, 177
  Amos, 211

Daniel, 267
Morrow
  Ernest Sr, 257
  George W, 277
  Joseph H, 72
Mortimer
  Ewen, 236
Morton
  Frank, 193
  Mrs. Kettie, 193
Mosby
  Benjamin C, 103
  William B, 103
Moseley
  George M, 243
  Henry E, 273
  John C, 162
  Thomas M, 217
Moses
  Thomas A, 205
Mosley
  John C, 87
Moss
  Charles E Jr, 95
  John R, 166
  Joseph E, 34
  Oliver R, 92, 172
Mouilland
  Mrs. Octavia, 255
Moulaison
  Henry, 253
Moulton
  William A, 117
Mourain
  Victor, 57
Mouseaux
  Donato, 275
Mouser
  Emanuel, 181
Mouzingo
  Elizabeth A, 277
Moylan

John, 112
Moyse
  Leon, 102
Mudgett
  William S, 243
Muggah
  David R, 67, 138
  James, 68
Mugnier
  Mrs. Jane Angelina, 263
Mullin
  William H H, 287
Mullins
  Miss Mahala, 130
Mumford
  Charles H, 203
  Francis M, 281
Munce
  Thomas Q, 267
Munday
  George W, 7
Munson
  Joseph E, 262
  Robert O, 199
Munzesheimer
  Frederick J, 59, 123
Murchisson
  John M, 36
Murdock
  Robert, 140
Murphy
  Elias, 164
  Elias H, 15
  Francis J, 32
  George E, 273
  Jesse, 164
  John L, 202
  Matt A, 195
  Robert C, 226
  Susan A, 196

William W, 244
Murrell
  John, 4, 39
  John Jr, 39
Muso
  Ferdinand L, 17
Musson
  Michael, 56
Myatt
  Alexander, 146, 228, 231
Myers
  Charles, 51
  Columbus C, 179
  Daniel F, 268
  Henry F, 173
Myles
  Edward, 275, 276
  Isaac A, 23, 74
Myrick
  Benjamin, 118
Nabors
  John H, 196
  Mrs. Mary L, 196
Naff
  Henry M, 118
Nall
  John P, 104
Nash
  Charles E, 255
  Charles H, 95, 181
  Gabriel E, 47
  J, 61, 127
  Mrs. Jane E, 141
  Valentine, 127
Naughton
  Hugh M, 281
Naul
  Judson D, 199
Neal
  Ananias, 223
  John B, 93

Index

Neblett
  Robert, 17
  Robert C, 18
Neell
  John M, 8
Neely
  John, 53, 116
Neil
  Elias O, 89
Neilson
  James J, 6
Nelson
  Andrew M, 183
  Hugh L, 65
  John, 168, 171, 243
  John A, 164
  John M, 195
  John T, 159
  Mrs. Kate F, 209
  Paul, 206
  Thomas W, 137
  William C, 236
  William G, 287
  William M, 136, 253
Nettles
  John B, 250
  Thomas, 89
Nettleton
  Charles, 19, 67
Neven
  Alphonse, 113, 212
  Charles, 133, 259
  Jean J, 113
Nevitt
  Arthur S, 57
Newcomb
  Henry L, 182
Newell
  Edward T, 268
  John A, 38
Newhall
  Henry B, 244
Newman
  Celestia, 272
  Fred C, 73
  George R, 3, 36
  H L, 5
  John M, 285
  Samuel B, 224
Newport
  A G, 8, 47
  Robert W, 7
Newson
  Robert J, 39
Newton
  James F, 98
Neyland
  James, 13
Nicholas
  Clovis, 215
  Demary, 19, 67
  Thomas W, 208
Nichols
  Charles E, 116
  Henrietta F, 244
  Joseph, 7
  William H, 279
Nicholson
  Robert, 182
  Wash B, 41
Nicols
  Charles E, 218
Niles
  Joseph R, 50
Nimmo
  Edward L, 19
  Matthew Jr, 19
Nixon
  John C, 230
  Wyndham R, 139, 263
Noble
  Charles M, 244
  Fleming, 4
Nock
  William J, 193
Noel
  W D, 168
Nolly
  John N, 117
Norfleet
  Whitmet P, 238
Norman
  David R, 164
  James M, 190
Normand
  Aurdie P, 30
  Pierre J, 30
Norment
  James, 14
  Whitlock, 186
Norris
  John F, 194
North
  Charles, 141
Norvell
  Thomas, 16
Nosworthy
  John, 71
Nott
  George W, 227
Noyes
  Emeline, 75
  Hiram, 23, 75
Nuckolls
  William T, 277
Nugent
  Benjamin F, 170
  Edmond, 47
  George C, 70
  John R, 47
Nunez
  Albert, 247
  Leon, 248
  Vincent, 24, 61, 62

Index

Nygaard
   James C, 71
Oakley
   Timothy, 278
Oakman
   Robert, 191
O'Brien
   Percy, 137
   Philip, 3
O'Bryan
   Daniel, 9
O'Callaghan
   John, 106
Ochiglevich
   Mrs. Mary, 231
   Peter, 231
O'Connor
   James, 9
   John, 105, 196, 197
Oden
   John D, 161
Odom
   Albert L, 250
   Isaac, 249
   Jacob W, 216
   Jacob Wiley, 63
   James M, 250
   Lafayette W, 115, 216
Odum
   William, 240
O'Ferrell
   Peter H, 193
Ogilvie
   Willie C, 265
O'Kelley
   John B, 268
Oliphant
   Wilford A, 224, 225, 243
Oliver
   Peter G, 36
   William T, 36, 48
Olivier
   Agricole C, 258
   Jules B, 248
   Mary O, 206
O'Neal
   William A, 76
Oneal
   Joseph B, 166
O'Neill
   James B, 167
Onley
   John H, 95
Opdenweyer
   William C, 114, 215
Opelek
   Victor J, 160
Orellon
   Joseph L, 207
Orillion
   Joseph L, 49
O'Rourke
   James, 69, 139
   John, 139
Orr
   Daniel T, 2
   James W, 32, 90
   John A, 264
Orwell
   P H, 98
Ory
   Lesin, 64
Osborn
   Armstrong, 108
Osery
   James Jr, 104
Ott
   Elbert W, 276
Otts
   Joel P, 77
   William P, 110
   Willis B, 76
Otway
   John A, 227
Oubre
   Eugene, 123
   James F, 131
   Leon, 123, 124, 235, 236
   Marcellin, 64, 131
   Thelesmar, 252
Owen
   Benjamin F, 9
   George S, 181, 182
   James, 19
   John J, 117
   William W, 37, 95
Owens
   Bettie W, 241
   Daniel P, 190
   Gidon, 91
   William P, 119
Owings
   Thomas O, 53
   William P, 56
Pace
   Micajah C, 86
Pack
   William C, 37
Packard
   Christopher C, 122
   James B, 103
   No first name, 63
Packwood
   Goerge, 63
Padrou
   Arthur J, 247
Page
   Vincent, 14
   William, 109
Pages
   Charles G, 197
   Juan, 147

Index

Thomas L, 242
Painter
  John P, 169
  John V, 75, 147
Palmer
  Benjamin, 156
  George A, 182
  Young C, 285
Palso
  William, 62
Pardos
  Joseph, 49, 109
Pardue
  James M, 273
Parent
  Charles, 132
Pargas
  Joseph E, 49
Parham
  Beverly B, 192
  Harry L, 277
Parilleaux
  Ferdinand, 30
Park
  William D, 155
Parker
  Benjamin, 92
  Edward, 108, 202
  Eli S, 230
  H C, 184
  Henry G, 280
  James George, 63, 130
  John, 69
  John M G, 121, 227
  Stephen D, 33
  West, 73
  William H, 289
  William L, 196
  William O, 202
Parkham

Peterson G, 38
P G, 43
Parks
  William, 142
  William C, 272
Parnell
  Andrew J, 168
  Benjamin F, 87
  James H, 91, 168
  Thinalder F, 163
Parr
  Miss Jennie, 267
Parrott
  John, 256
  Philip H, 19
Parsons
  Sylvester G, 10
Pascoe
  Alfred H, 211
Paseut
  Francis P, 112
Pate
  Stephen, 12
Patin
  Alphonse J, 66
  Joseph A, 259
Patrick
  W W, 228
Patten
  George W, 277
Paul
  Elizabeth A, 176
  John S, 183
  Michael, 126
  Salathies S, 243
  Samuel, 96
Pavell
  August, 180
  Ferdinand, 180
Pavey
  Francis M, 161
Payer

W W, 142
Payne
  George E, 128
  Henry M, 257
  Nicholas R, 74
  Philip, 40
Peace
  Mrs. Emily, 150
  Mrs. Emily E, 281
Peacock
  James S, 47
Peak
  John A, 272
Pearce
  Alonson G, 2, 30, 31
  Clint, 159
  John H, 258
Pearse
  Rovell, 7
Pearson
  Thomas, 23, 75
Peavance
  George L, 264
Pecanty
  Mrs. Elizabeth, 193
Pecard
  Joseph, 156
Peck
  Amy L, 185
  Ruluff W, 61
Pecot
  O, 138, 260
Peevy
  Charles A, 230
Peignot
  Pierre, 30
Peniston
  Samuel, 6
Penn
  Alexander G, 56
  Martin G, 23

Pennill
  Henry, 139
Pennington
  Levi, 109
  Pinkney A, 215
  Robert O, 130
Penny
  Oren L, 242
Pennybaker
  Amedis J, 108
  Amides J, 202
Pepper
  William, 63
Percy
  Hampton D, 155, 157
  Robert D, 4
Perkins
  Allen J, 172
  Eli A, 34, 175
  Fredericka A, 176
  Fredericka G, 175
  George M, 256
  Henry C, 161
  Ivan A, 176
  James, 34
  James K, 172
  John, 6
  Lewis A, 284
  Mrs. Emeline D, 94, 178
  Reed, 17
  William F, 175
Perot
  Leopold, 222
  Solon B, 119, 222
Perret
  Anatole J, 259
  Edgard C, 64
  Emile, 137
Perrilliat
  Armand, 132
Perrin
  Frederick Jr, 139
  Ignace, 211
Perrot
  E Edgard, 132
Perry
  Charles D, 195
  Elihu, 53
  James M, 36
  Michael, 146, 230
  Norman J, 173
  Robert, 9, 50
  Sandford, 7
  William I, 65
Pertuit
  Elphege J, 251
Peterkin
  George A, 221
  Jesse A, 118, 221
Peters
  Anastase, 196
  Meredith M, 246
Peterson
  Lillian, 209
  Rodin C, 238
Pettery
  Daniel H, 77
Pettis
  Edmund B, 53, 117
Petty
  Don G, 225
Pevoto
  Joseph B, 180
Peyret
  Leopold J, 251
Peyton
  William B, 103
  William C, 45, 104
Phelps
  Charles A, 107
  R A, 117
Phillips
  Charles J, 283
  Edward F, 236, 280
  George C, 252
  Isaac S, 13
  J A, 76
  John M, 13
  Littleton A, 73
  Marshall P, 236
  Mrs. Eugenia, 192
  Noah, 78
  Pierce, 249
  Rufus, 39
  William B, 151
  William L, 100, 188
Piccard
  Leon, 156
Pickell
  Miss Nancy, 143
  Washington J, 142
Pickens
  David G, 4, 38
  Montezuma L, 120
Pickett
  Christianna L, 176
  James C, 55
  John, 166, 167
  Samuel M, 146
Picot
  Antoine A, 66
  Octave A, 137
  Peter, 19
Pierce
  Oliver A, 109
  Salissa E, 267
Pierson
  David, 149
  Frank J, 243
Pignido
  John B, 233
Pike
  George A, 45, 197

Pillet
  Archibald H, 148
Pinard
  Aristides, 233
Pinatado
  Eudaldo G, 84
Pinaud
  N Aristides, 234
Pinn
  Alexander G, 13
  M V, 20
Pinson
  John H, 35, 93
Pintado
  Eudaldo G, 157
  Facuna E, 157
  Facunda E, 84
  Mrs. Johanna W R, 157, 158
  Vincent T, 84
Pintardo
  Eudaldo G, 30
Pior
  Allen S B, 86
Piper
  Ruffin, 123
Pipes
  Edgar F, 191
  Edward S, 271
  Uriah C, 110
  William, 143
Pipkin
  Barnabas H, 249
  Barnabus H, 63, 129
  Louis M, 249
Pirot
  Remy, 11
Pittman
  Stanton B, 268
Plantevignes
  John J, 123

  Justin, 235
Platt
  David B, 89
  Edwin M, 166
Plauche
  Jean V, 161
  J J A, 223
Pleasants
  Robert G, 142
Plousky
  Jacob, 255
  Jacobs, 255
Poche
  Elphege, 131, 132, 251
Poer
  William B H, 71, 141
Polansky
  John, 95, 96
Pollard
  Isham, 269
  Robert L, 195, 246
  W J, 286
Pond
  Mary, 200
  Olivia A, 200
Pool
  Thomas W, 41
Poole
  Albert W, 8, 46, 47, 106
  Howard M, 200
  J B P, 46
  L, 275
  Maria R, 106, 200
  Samuel C, 175
Pooley
  Thomas B, 67
Pope
  Alexander C, 276
Porche

  Arthur, 123, 236
  Louis V, 123
Porter
  Chaunay Charles, 49
  David, 227
  Friday N, 263
  Friday N Jr, 264
  John A, 216
  Joseph P, 268
Portier
  Pierre, 141
Posey
  Frank E, 207
  Frank M, 207
  John, 65
Post
  Arthur L, 140
  James M, 142, 143, 272
Postlethwaite
  William D, 219
Poston
  John B, 195
Potash
  Bernard, 232
  Joseph, 235
Potter
  Alfred, 24
Potts
  Paul M, 196
  William A L, 139
Poughel
  Josephina, 180
Poulet
  A C, 289
Pourcian
  Alphonse, 236
  Cyrille, 236
  Lavinien, 13
  Mrs. Matilda, 236
Pourrier

Octave, 251
Powe
   Mary J, 245
Powell
   Belitha, 117
   E L, 272
   Horace B, 179
   Jeremiah, 42, 58
   John A, 135
   Lucas, 54
   Miss Mary E, 110
   Mordacai, 15
   M Shelby, 181
   Stephen M, 200
Powers
   Charles, 176
   John B, 105
   John S, 197
Powlis
   Jasper, 25
Prather
   John M, 45, 104
   Wesley G, 169
   William R, 165
Pratt
   Charles E, 272
   David C, 5
   Frank B, 221
Preifus
   Emanuel, 93
Prentice
   T M, 3
Prescott
   J B, 36
   Lewis D, 255
Presler
   Miss Beneta, 128
Presley
   Hosea, 11
Pressburg
   Benjamin E, 239
Pressler
   Herman F C, 112
Prestidge
   J M, 41
Prestridge
   J M, 101
Preusch
   George F, 234
Prevatt
   Stonewall J, 220
Prevost
   Clet, 19
   Nicholas L, 19
   Paul, 68, 138
Prevost Jr
   First name illegible, 67
Prewitt
   James B, 106
Price
   George W, 41, 100
   Louisa C, 71, 140
   Ralph, 27, 47
   Thomas, 63
   William, 88, 141, 270
   William Ralph, 201
Prichard
   Drury M, 97
   John S, 138
   Thomas B, 97
Priche
   Victorin, 29
Prickard
   Lewis C, 179
Pritchard
   Jeremiah, 8
Proctor
   Jesse D, 99
Prothro
   Alfred B, 87
   H M, 282
   William B, 81
Prout
   Edward, 30, 84
Provost
   Clet, 67
Prude
   John T, 195
Prudhomme
   Paul, 145
   Victorin, 226
Pruyn
   Robert H, 197
Puckett
   Franklin F, 198
   Gustavus A, 145
   J William, 231
   Samuel M, 229
Puckette
   Charles J, 55
Puffpower
   John H, 136
Pugh
   Heloise L, 231
   James A, 53
   John B, 105
   William T, 53, 116
Pullen
   James T, 52
Pullin
   Edward, 191
   James, 102, 190
Purley
   Mrs. M, 130
Purvis
   William C, 36, 94
Pyborn
   Dennis M, 210
Pyron
   Andrew J, 68, 137
Quackenboss
   John A, 268
Quarles
   Hugh C, 167

Samuel, 44
Quays
  Philip D, 182, 183
Quenu
  Charles Jr, 147
Quinlan
  Patrick, 103
Quinn
  Micajah P, 76, 110
Quirk
  Edmund C, 257
Rablais
  Evarist, 2
Rabon
  Hodge, 164
Raborn
  Henry A, 164
  Joseph, 89
Rabun
  Hodge, 87
Rachal
  Gilbert W, 223
Radler
  Webster, 261
Ragan
  Aaron V, 149
Ragland
  Zachariah, 40
Raiford
  William H, 145
Rainey
  A, 104
  James W, 108, 201
Rains
  John J, 120, 121, 223
  John W, 166
Raley
  Marion W, 273
Ramsey
  James A, 201
  John, 141

R C, 201
Ranaldson
  William B, 46
Rand
  Barham D, 250
  Burnam D, 266
Randolph
  Benjamin H, 240
  Isaac, 5, 12
  Jacob F, 50
  William, 60, 126
Randon
  Peter, 14
  Shaw N, 2, 30
Rano
  Thomas, 15
Rash
  Willis P, 118
Rashiet
  Morris, 119
Ratcliff
  Allen D, 3
  D F, 95
  Matthew, 242
Rathbern
  Philamon, 5
Rathburn
  Lysander, 77
Ratier
  E N, 261
Ratliff
  James P, 195
Raven
  R, 101
Rawlings
  Z H, 24
Ray
  B W, 31
  Eugene D, 257
  James R Jr, 31
  James S, 72, 119
  James W, 205

Joseph, 257
  Robert Jr, 229
  Roxey, 283
Rayburn
  Albert, 106, 200
  William, 138
Rea
  Richard N, 181
Read
  W, 51
Readenheimer
  Lawrence, 163
Readheimer
  James P, 149, 282
Reading
  Asa A, 11
Reagan
  George W, 236
  Samuel E, 230
Reames
  Theodore J, 280
Reathinner
  James P, 222
Rebouche
  Joseph, 30
Recoulley
  Peter, 178
Reddick
  Henry B, 211
  Noah, 186
Redditt
  William C, 34, 93
  William E, 228
Redmond
  James F, 182
Redriques
  Ignace, 176
Reed
  Eliza J, 163
  John, 65
  Thomas, 135
Rees

Henry, 67
Reese
   Daniel H, 113, 172
   George W, 11
Regan
   John, 290
Reichenburg
   Joseph, 248
Reichman
   Red, 219
Reid
   Francis M, 217
Reilly
   George J, 199
   Jessie P, 274
   William F, 268
Reily
   James C, 222
   William H, 12
Reinauer
   Isaac C, 261
Reisor
   Andrew L, 169
Reiting
   Mrs. Sarah C, 129
Renoudet
   Pierre L, 133
Rentz
   James, 150
Reppond
   Samuel B, 274
Rester
   James G, 276
Reuss
   George B, 155
Revillion
   Joachim, 50
Rey
   James Jr, 1
Reynolds
   Fielding, 39
   John H, 125

Rhinehart
   Sumpter D, 288
Rhodes
   Asa H, 32
   George, 96, 181
   John T, 239
   Miss Mary J, 97
   Thomas B, 96
Rhody
   Aldred, 151
   Alfred, 266
Rhorer
   James M, 204
Rhoton
   Albert C, 96, 181
Ribava
   Frank, 263
Rice
   Harvey L, 176
   Henry H, 34
Rich
   Thomas P, 14
Richard
   Edgar, 132
   Eugene C, 257
   Joseph Jr, 207
   J R, 267
   Oscar, 209
   Pierre, 131
   Thomas E, 183
Richards
   Bram A, 256
   James, 43
Richardson
   Charles, 36
   David R, 21
   F D, 19
   George W, 172
   Jacob H, 201
   James C, 73
   James S, 219
   John B, 36

   Lewis, 238
   Matthew, 69
   Mrs. Iowa T, 204
   Oliver, 88
   Richard C, 109
   Samuel L, 203
   Sarah J, 204
   Thomas, 285
   Wesley B, 204
   William P, 220
Richmond
   Agustus, 257
   Robert, 35
Richy
   Joseph, 236
Rickinston
   G, 20
Ricks
   Petty H, 195
   Silas A, 247
Rico
   M C, 38
Ricord
   Fabian, 2
Riddell
   John L, 121
Riddick
   Edgar L, 173
Ridge
   John, 129
Riggs
   Mrs. Mary L, 168
   William A, 133
Riley
   John N, 121
   Mrs. Mary E, 148
Ring
   George H, 206
Ringgold
   Charles W, 121, 227
   Jacob H, 184

Index

Mrs. Hamoline B, 124
Riser
   Adam, 81, 111, 209
   Adams, 148
Ritter
   William, 270
Rivers
   Douglas L, 194
   James S, 129
   John C J, 234
Rivette
   P H, 9
Rizan
   Omer, 29
Roach
   Richard, 8
Roane
   Francis M, 274
   Spencer B, 261
Robb
   Felix, 4, 38
   Frederick, 155
   William E, 97, 183
Robbins
   William J, 284
Roberson
   George W, 229
   William, 105
Robert
   A, 14
   Daniel, 14
   Leonidas A, 14
Roberts
   Caroline C, 240
   Eunice B, 238
   Francis, 6, 45
   A G, 200
   George A, 225
   George S, 64, 130
   George W, 172
   James C, 284
   James S, 286
   Jesse Eaton, 198
   John H, 174
   Mrs. Jane S, 138, 259, 260
   Norton R, 237
   Samuel, 284
   William F, 93
Robertson
   Andrew B, 216
   D H, 20
   Franklin C, 136
   A S, 246
   William, 115
Robichaux
   Louise, 270
Robin
   Joseph N, 254
Robinett
   J J, 100
Robinson
   Elisha, 15
   Hubbard F, 42
   James G, 99
   James J, 182
   Jefferson D, 160
   Jerome B, 86
   John B, 143, 272
   John L, 69
   Joseph T, 11
   Lee E, 174
   Mrs. Mary, 111
   Nathaniel E, 76
   Oliver B, 76
   Rufus R, 238
Robison
   Benjamin, 98
Robson
   William V, 170
Roche
   James S, 109, 207
   William L, 207
Rochel
   E S, 270
Rock
   Herman, 48
Rockwood
   Curtis, 21
   John T, 21, 70, 71
Rodgers
   James B, 144
   John, 124
Rodrigue
   Domingue, 261
Rodrique
   Optime, 252
Roe
   William, 60, 125
Roebuck
   James C, 284
Rogers
   Alen, 20
   Chapel H, 230
   C P, 61
   Emile C, 253
   Henry, 143
   James B, 274
   James C, 87
   James J, 4
   John L, 25
   Miss Lizzie, 138
   Robert M, 81
   William C, 166
   William H, 73
   William L, 26
   William S, 60
Rolling
   Joseph L, 156
Roman
   James, 251
Ronaldson
   James D, 45
   Luther R, 45

Index

Ronatoson
  James A, 7
Rongelot
  Alfred, 140
Ronnsville
  David W, 7
Rose
  George J, 135, 255
  Gus, 126
  Rufus E, 270
Rosenbaum
  Mrs. Henrietta, 261
Rosengrants
  Abiel, 137
Rosenthal
  Henrietta, 194
  Moses, 126, 239
  Raphael, 192
Ross
  David T, 8
  James B, 13
  James C, 53
  John W, 40
Roth
  Jacob, 133
  Michael, 90, 168
  Valrey, 9
Roubien
  Oscar, 10
Roubreu
  Robert B, 223
Roughman
  John, 52, 115
Round
  W S, 15
Rounsevelt
  Alvin N, 89, 165
Rourk
  Jasper H, 272
Roussaue
  John, 133
Roussel
  Louis A, 112
Routh
  Francis, 13, 58
  John, 70
Routon
  Marcus S, 35
Roux
  Felix, 248
  Miss Mary, 248
Row
  James H, 8
  Micajah Jr, 148
  Samuel H, 8
  Windsor, 236
Rowland
  William L, 142
Roy
  Pierre A, 124
Ruddock
  James, 20
Rudisill
  W, 36
Rugan
  Aaron C, 81
Rugg
  Eli, 273
Ruggles
  James, 3
Rule
  William J, 36
Rummell
  James M, 149
Rush
  Christian, 102
  Peter, 32
Rushing
  Warren, 74
Rusk
  James B, 2, 3
Russ
  Edward K, 227
  Sterling E, 195
  Sterling E Jr, 226
Russell
  Augustus D, 146, 228
  Leonard C, 243
  Samuel, 287
Rutland
  Thomas B, 21, 72
Rutsell
  Samuel D, 56
Ruys
  James, 80
Ryan
  John, 130
Ryant
  John N, 86
Rykoski
  John, 112
Ryland
  John E, 241
  Montillion J, 86, 159
  Philip, 60
Rymer
  Richard A, 230
Saal
  Henry Jr, 265
Sabourin
  Henry L, 253
Sachise
  Theodore C, 145
Sadler
  Benjamin F, 138
Safford
  D T, 125
Salassi
  Charles F, 155
  Dennis F, 114
  Joseph, 52, 114
Salles
  William, 217
Salvant

Index

Alfred D, 57, 122
Sambre
  Auguste, 17, 65
  Ramy, 119
Sampite
  J A, 119
Sanaux
  Antoine P, 21, 69
Sanches
  Amelia, 223
Sancier
  Gisard F, 85
Sandborn
  Lemuel, 233
Sandell
  John M, 246
Sanderneau
  John, 108
Sanders
  Jabez, 40
  Jabezo, 5
  James B, 228
  John R, 227
  Nathaniel, 60
  Spotswood H, 136, 255
  Willia H, 228
  Willis H, 228
Sandford
  Durrett B, 74
Sandidge
  Richard S, 78
Sanopaurae
  Mayre, 10
Sarpy
  Leon, 249
  Oscar B, 122, 232
Sartorias
  Jacob, 52
  Philip S, 52
Sartorius
  Philip, 116

Sarver
  Martin, 274
Sary
  Henry B, 1
Satterfield
  William E, 236
Saulnier
  Aristedes, 30
Saunier
  Oliver, 112
Savant
  John P, 257
Savoie
  Jules B, 234
Savoy
  Clairville J, 158
Saxon
  Benjamin B, 172
Sayers
  William M, 196
Scarborough
  Noah V, 120
  William P, 242
Scaries
  Richard H, 266
Schamber
  Louis F, 258, 290
Schardt
  Jacob S, 220
Schauf
  Justus H, 191
Schayot
  Leonard, 235
Scheen
  Herman F, 163
  John H, 87, 163
Scheens
  John Henry, 80
Schenk
  Alois, 216
  Joseph Alois, 115
Schexnader

F P, 251
Schexnayder
  Fulgence P, 206
Schiele
  Jacob, 191
Schinkoth
  Frederick W, 174
Schleicher
  Adolph, 194
  Frederick, 194
Schlesenger
  Albert, 232
Schlesinger
  Henry, 270
Schmidt
  E F, 111
  Frederick G, 57, 121
Schmulen
  Gustave, 212, 262
  Michel, 262
Schneider
  William H, 95
Schockley
  Theodore F, 137
  Theodore W, 67
Schoonmaker
  S H, 196
Schreiner
  Clemens, 201
Schrock
  Thomas D, 290
Schroeder
  Miss Helen H, 103
Schrote
  Henry, 121
Schuster
  Bartold B, 229
Scivieque
  Joseph, 114
Scofield
  William D, 103,

Index

191
Scogin
  Albert G, 33
Scott
  Elijah, 54, 118
  Henry A, 241
  Henry M, 202
  James H, 192
  John J, 89, 165
  Mitchell J, 104, 195
  Robert, 129
  Robert E, 195
  Samuel C, 43, 102
  Silas K, 286
  Terance L, 134
  W H, 59
  William C, 161, 255, 258
  William S, 200
Scribner
  Abram H, 73
Scruggs
  Samuel O, 55
  S O, 119
Seagrave
  George N, 67
Seale
  Jacob C, 24
  James H, 26
  Joseph H, 273
Seaman
  Clinton F, 102
  John C, 103, 191
  Vinton F, 191
  William M, 268, 269
Sean
  Stephen M, 11, 55
Seaton
  John, 25, 53
Seay

  Abram B, 27, 47
Sebastian
  Charles W, 201
  William W, 91, 169
See
  Jesse, 68
Seeley
  Mrs. Emma E, 260
Seiler
  Miss Lilly, 177
Selby
  Thomas B, 242
Self
  Elijah, 61, 127
  Franklin D, 245
  John W, 227
Sellers
  Sallie C, 273
  Sarah A, 273
Semon
  William H, 75
Sempe
  John, 33
Semple
  James S, 182
Sentell
  George W, 78, 88
  Washington, 33
  William M, 88
Serenne
  Firmin, 159
Sero
  John D W, 223
Serre
  Hugues Sr, 251
Sers
  Abel C, 55, 119
  Charles, 55
  Ernest, 222
Setting
  Rodolph C, 258

Settoon
  Burton L, 182
  Young, 10
Sewall
  Charles A, 12
  Charles L, 25
Sewell
  Asbury C, 81
Seymour
  Frank M, 209
Shackleford
  William F, 151
Shade
  Joseph W, 131, 250
Shaifer
  Henry F, 267
Shane
  Lemuel J B, 65
Sharitt
  Joseph L, 60, 125
Sharpe
  Daniel, 15
Sharretts
  George L, 267
Shaul
  August M, 58
Shaw
  Charles M, 241
  Edward P, 237
  Hiram, 87
  William H, 264
  William L, 190
Shawl
  August M, 14
Shean
  Julius, 149
Shearer
  Charles E, 181
  Peter, 44
Shehan
  William R, 285
Shehee

Index

A B, 162
Sheldon
　Seth, 25
　William A, 24
Shelton
　William B, 60
Shenard
　Henry W, 77
Shepherd
　George B, 260
　James R, 141
　Sylvanus, 141
　William, 274
Sheppard
　Daniel H, 87
　H, 80
　James W, 98
Sherburn
　Mrs. Josephone, 269
Sheridan
　James L, 195
Sherman
　Charles T, 74
Sherrard
　William A, 101
Sherrouse
　John M, 253
Shilling
　Michael W, 74
Shillings
　John, 212
Shively
　Joseph H, 172
Shlenker
　Isaac, 97
Sholars
　Randle D, 110
Shows
　John P, 110
　Stephen J, 211
Shroder

S H, 114
Shuster
　Isaac, 272
　Isaac C, 274
Sibley
　Gabriel G, 114
　Isaac F, 88
　Richard A, 22
　Robert F, 22, 61, 75
　Rufus, 166
　Samuel T, 245
　William R, 167
Sickels
　William C, 137
Siess
　Anger, 241
　David, 85, 159
Siffert
　Jacque, 257
Sikes
　Benjamin F, 278
　Jackson, 41, 99, 277
　James R, 284
　Jesse F, 277
　Martha F, 277
　Willis G, 196
Sillard
　Silas, 4, 37
Silliman
　William, 7
Simmons
　Charles P, 137
　J, 17
　Joe W, 152, 244
　John F, 44
　John W, 187
　Joseph M, 74, 147
　Solomon, 34, 91
　A T, 23
　Thomas R, 170

William G, 142, 272
William W, 22
Simms
　Ruben H, 201
　Sylvester D, 51
Simon
　Adam, 165
　Selegman, 57, 121
Simons
　William H, 238
　William M, 240
Simpson
　Charles, 125
　David A, 200
　George D, 200
　Samuel F, 134
　S F, 213
　Thomas S, 53
Simrall
　Bell, 235
Sims
　George W, 164, 190
　Mrs. Sarah A, 282
　Thomas S, 104
Sinclair
　Neil, 261
Singletary
　Benjamin, 51
　Bernice, 216
Singleton
　Seth B, 171
Sirmons
　John F, 285
Sitman
　Charles M, 249
Sitting
　Mrs. Scolastie, 136
Sizemore
　Epoline, 177
Skillman

Index

Ewell H, 198
Skipworth
  Henry, 256
  Henry Jr, 201
  John K, 192
  Wyndham R, 200
Skipwowrth
  Henry Sr, 199
Slack
  Charles W, 109
  Harry J, 208, 209
Slater
  William M, 38
Slaton
  H C, 111
Slattery
  George, 244
Sledge
  John A, 163, 224, 242
Slemons
  Robert S, 186
  R Smith, 177
Slider
  Charles R, 116
Sligh
  George B, 79
Sloan
  Hamilton, 43
Sloane
  Elizabeth, 253
  Lewis G, 253
Slocum
  David, 22
  Samuel E, 146
Slover
  Mrs. Mary M, 210
Smacker
  Thomas S, 63
Smalley
  Abner, 6
Smallwood
  Walter W, 121
Smart
  Titus J, 210
Smith
  Alexander, 197
  Alexander C, 197
  Allan, 9
  Ann E, 187, 224
  Archibald, 241
  Archie D, 236
  Benjamin A, 17
  Benjamin F, 210, 278, 287
  Bruce, 106
  Charles, 160
  Charles B, 17
  Charles T, 168
  Claiborne M, 142
  David A, 240
  E, 15
  Edward, 122
  Edward F, 234
  E G, 90
  Elizabeth, 185
  Elizabeth P, 187
  Frank E, 131
  Frank H, 193
  F W Jr, 270
  George, 20
  George C, 59, 125
  George W, 14
  Henry R, 116
  Hiram S, 210
  James, 48, 186, 278
  James A, 41
  James H, 71
  James M, 76, 110
  Jeremiah, 286
  Jesse P, 100
  John A, 150
  John E, 138
  John Edes, 69
  John F, 65
  Joseph, 74
  Julius, 67
  M, 63
  Mary M, 151, 203
  Michael, 285
  Miss Fanny C, 238
  Mrs. Bruce, 106
  Mrs. Lizzie D, 254
  Mrs. Mary F, 177
  Mrs. Sibby A, 148
  Nicholas H, 71
  Oglesby S, 254
  Oliver P, 272
  Perry K, 271
  Pliny W, 269
  Polk, 192
  Solomon, 55
  Spencer M, 283
  Walter L, 276
  William, 19, 119
  William A, 149, 194
  William B, 40, 100
  William F, 122, 232
  William Jose W, 219
  William L, 110
  William P, 273
  Windsor, 66, 136
Smott
  Washington B, 260
Snead
  Hugh G, 192
  Julius, 152
  T T, 225
Sneed
  Hugh G, 103
Snelling
  John W, 282

Index

Snodgrass
  Amanda, 205
Snowden
  Lowell Howell, 2
Snyder
  Caleb H, 202, 203
  Emma E, 185
  Robert H, 70, 140
Snypp
  Mrs. Ava H, 211
Soape
  James C, 169
Sockard
  Ezekial F, 78
Soflin
  James, 51
Sojourner
  Stephen N, 184
Solis
  Victor M, 122
Sorelle
  James H, 239
Soulier
  Edward E, 206
  Edward S, 241
Sowry
  A J, 2
Spann
  Henry T, 97
  William D, 97
Spaulding
  Alanson, 79, 143
Spearman
  B F, 103
  John B, 170
  William, 229
  William C, 170
Speight
  Moses K, 127
  W R D, 11
Speights
  John M, 246
  Moses H, 246
Spence
  John A, 92
  William E, 185
Spencer
  Stanislau F, 242
Spilker
  William G, 104, 194
Spiller
  Blass, 15, 63
  George W, 217
  Levi, 114, 215, 216
  Philip, 105
Spires
  John, 192
Spivey
  Moses, 77, 110
Sprawls
  Samuel, 80, 87
  William L, 163
Spring
  M, 20
  William, 69
Spurlin
  Albert W, 77, 88
Spurlock
  Mary P, 159
Squires
  George W, 10
Squyres
  Wiley M, 39, 96
  William H, 210
Stack
  Charles W, 207
Staff
  Etienne, 255
Stafford
  David, 186
  Joseph A, 263, 264
Stall
  Bernhard H, 164
Stallcup
  John W, 169
  Laura, 169
Stallings
  William B, 204
St. Amant
  F A, 227
  Joseph, 156
Stamper
  Mrs. C, 111
  Nathaniel, 224
  Nathaniel A, 195
Stanberry
  Thomas B, 68
Standfield
  James D, 176
Staneart
  Charles W, 174
Stanford
  Leroy S, 266
Stanton
  Aaron, 192
Stapleton
  John, 39
Starbrough
  David, 5
Stark
  Levi R, 266
Starks
  Conrad, 149, 282
Starnes
  Edward B, 114
  Frederick, 15
  Purnell F, 115
Starns
  Adolphus, 217
  Edwin B, 51
Starr
  Burlin, 217
Starring
  A P, 11
Stathing

Index

Miss Laura, 111
St. Dezier
   A, 207
St. Dizine
   Joseph, 109
Steadman
   Charles G, 200
   Mary S, 200, 201
Stedman
   Larkin H, 287, 288
Steeg
   Aaron, 106
Steele
   James C, 230
   Ollio B, 272
   Sue, 165
   Thomas J, 196
Stephens
   Hiram P, 204
   James H, 148, 280
   John H, 56
   Joseph H, 225
   Lawrence E, 61
   Leonard W, 223
Sterling
   Alexander K, 261
Stevens
   Charles H, 32, 33
   Chris, 192
   J H, 76
   Mica P, 33
   Mrs. Fanny C, 238
   William, 126
   William B, 279
Steward
   John M, 37
Stewart
   Charles R, 42
   Charles S, 63, 129
   James, 70, 139
   James W, 51
   John M, 95

   William B, 223, 242
   William D, 226
   William L, 122
Stewman
   Benjamin W, 89
St. Germain
   Jules, 58, 123
Stickney
   Robert, 44
Stille
   Robert B, 245
   William B, 127, 245
Stilley
   F, 57
Stillman
   Ezra J, 105, 197
Stills
   Robert B, 61
Stingel
   Henry, 109
Stinson
   George L, 282
   William, 32, 78
St. Julien
   Edmond, 213
   J G, 112
St. Martin
   Armand, 270, 271
   Noel, 62
Stockett
   Mrs. Lucy E, 235
Stockley
   Joseph H, 233
Stockwell
   William, 45
Stokes
   David H, 38, 42
   James L, 4
Stone
   Birkett, 62

   James A, 219
   Mrs. Sallie E, 185
   Mrs. S E, 286
Storens
   Belesaire, 225
Storer
   James, 175
Stott
   Joseph A, 200
Stouff
   Octave, 260
Stovall
   Jeremiah J, 211
   William G, 275
Stozier
   Samuel G, 273
St. Pierre
   Pierre, 253
Strack
   Julius, 234
Strader
   Leonard W, 266
Stratham
   Pleasant B, 74
   Sherwood C, 23
Strauss
   Abraham, 249
Streagall
   Ruben N, 186
Strickland
   R, 63
Stringer
   Margaret M, 199
Stringfield
   David H, 275
Strong
   Amos R, 288
   William A, 282
Strother
   James N, 175
   Joseph T, 58, 123
Stroube

Index

William H, 180
Stroud
   Miss Katie E, 166
Stuart
   J M, 4
   Robert S, 46
   William L, 18
Stubbs
   Franklin, 147
Stuckey
   Anderson M, 230
   William, 33
Stuckley
   Mrs. Eliza, 287
Sturlese
   Emanuel, 179
Sturlise
   Lorenzo, 144
Suddath
   Edwina, 223
Sugg
   Luther M, 67, 133
Sullivan
   John, 217
   John H, 126, 238
Summers
   Mrs. Emma V, 140
Sumrall
   James, 43
Supple
   Jeremiah, 108
Suttles
   James C, 179
Sutton
   James O, 288
   John E, 112
   Shadrack P, 80
Swafford
   Thomas F, 60
   Thomas T, 126
Swain
   John D, 12

John W, 58
Swan
   R S, 272
Swann
   John J, 126
   Joseph W, 241
Swartz
   Edward G, 231
Sweat
   Leonard C, 60
   Robert, 240
   Samuel C, 284
Swenson
   S J, 261
Swift
   Joe S, 179
Swords
   Henry L, 84
Sylvester
   Evander W, 256
Syon
   Thomas S, 33
Taber
   John W, 120
Tagliaferro
   Fidel N, 233, 234
Tait
   Mrs. Mary E, 164
Talbert
   James J, 89
   James T, 78
Talbot
   Milton A, 189
   Paul T, 189
Talbott
   John, 7
Taliafero
   James, 3
Talley
   Enoch B, 69, 138
   Mrs. Emilia, 138
Talliaferro

Robert W, 121
Tanner
   Mrs. A M, 117
   William H, 117
Tate
   Jesse C, 217
Tatum
   Austin, 59
   Joel Jr, 144
   John H, 110
   Seth, 41
Taurnois
   Joseph F, 258
Taylor
   Edward, 208
   Edward W, 17
   F H, 180
   F H G, 181
   Francis M, 186
   Franklin, 41, 99
   Frank T, 190
   Henry J, 89
   James C, 41, 99, 100, 188
   James L, 89
   James S, 46
   John, 18
   John N, 125
   Jonathan C, 192
   Joseph, 188
   Knowles D, 89
   Lawrence A, 164, 278
   Nancy E, 192
   Warren J, 200
   William, 61
   William B, 194
   William R, 62
   William V, 183, 187
Teagle
   Emma, 283

Tebbe
  Henry, 111
  John Henry, 111
  Langdon C, 111, 211
Tegard
  John, 108
Temple
  John, 21, 73, 117
Tennent
  Henry, 9
  William, 115
Teray
  Edward, 137
Terel
  E, 20
Terrell
  Elijah M, 19
Terrill
  William E, 7
Terry
  Eugene A, 242
  Sandford R, 51
  Thomas C, 20, 69
Tew
  William W, 3
Thacher
  John, 73
Thacker
  John, 145
Thalsheimer
  Henry, 252
Thatcher
  William, 25, 32
Theall
  Joseph, 275
Thelcok
  W Frank, 155
Thenet
  Alexandre, 66
Theriot
  Jean B E, 131

Thibodeaux
  Charles G, 50, 113
  Felix, 158, 261
  Pascal E, 158
This
  Frederick, 259
Thomas
  Albert H, 104
  Edward B, 264
  Elias G, 189
  G B, 152, 242
  John, 38
  John J, 78
  Joseph N, 184, 185, 186
  Joseph W, 98
  Malachi B, 93, 178
  Nathaniel W, 219
  Newport, 242
  Simon, 93
  Stephen S, 276
  William, 23
  William P, 50
Thomason
  H S, 48
  John D, 48, 108
Thompkins
  Francis Y, 3
  John L, 252
Thompson
  Andrew J, 65, 183
  A B, 38, 97
  B J, 11
  Carter, 96
  Charles H, 90
  Charles M, 254
  Charlotte, 212
  H A, 126
  Henry B, 204
  Hezekiah, 107, 129
  Hugh B, 173
  Jethro, 174

  Joseph, 229
  Joseph J, 208
  A Judson, 182
  M C, 96
  M H, 183
  Peter G, 87
  Robert E, 100, 189
  Sarah A, 111
  Thomas E, 283
  William, 144
  William H, 160
  William T, 99
Thorne
  John D, 133
Thornhill
  F M, 177
Thornton
  Atlas M, 189
Thorp
  William A, 25
Thorpe
  Thomas B, 6, 42
  William A, 43, 103
Thrailkill
  William F, 290
Thurmand
  C G, 40
Thurmond
  Catlet G, 80
Thus
  Fred, 134
Tildon
  Stephen, 8
  Stephen D, 46
Tiller
  Thomas B, 1, 31
Tilley
  Thomas N, 286
Tillotson
  Shabael, 1, 29
Tilly
  E E, 128

Index

Timon
  Alonzo N, 243
  A N, 224
Tinney
  Edward B, 129
Tippen
  G M, 283
Tippit
  Nathaniel G, 287
Tirquit
  James Eugene, 236
  James Eugene Jr, 236
  Numa, 236
Tisdale
  Lucius E, 244
Titus
  John S, 57
  Louis F, 119
Tobey
  Avery, 290
Todd
  A, 68
  James, 260
  John N, 37
Tolbert
  M T, 191
Toler
  James, 270
  Patrick H, 59
Tomkins
  Francis J, 6
  Francis Y, 21
  Jackson B, 37
Tomlinson
  Andrew D, 289
Tompkins
  Jackson B, 94
  Thomas B, 87
Tonas
  Joseph, 58
Tooley
  Henry, 43
  John F, 102, 191
Toon
  Clara, 159
Torras
  Joseph, 123
Toups
  Cleophas A, 271
Tournier
  E, 112, 211
Tousely
  Reuben, 2
Touzanne
  Onesime, 15, 62
Townsend
  Isaac, 45
  William C, 161
  William L, 16
  William S, 62
Trager
  Louis, 102
Trahan
  Geolfide, 84
  Joseph, 212
Trask
  Charles B, 46
Travis
  Adam, 251
Traylor
  John, 142
  Lewis A, 246
Treadwell
  William H, 120, 223, 242
Trebb
  Jesse, 72, 142
Trice
  John T, 148
Trichell
  Omer, 224
  Septime, 225
Trigre
  John, 249
  Ovide, 132
Trimble
  James C, 142, 271
Tripaquier
  Jules B, 128
Trospher
  James M, 170
Trott
  George S, 40
Trouard
  Prosper, 229
Trousdale
  David B, 71
Trowbridge
  Roswell W, 262
Troxler
  Luis W, 49
Trudeau
  E, 283
  F C, 235
  Francis E, 279
  George N, 59
  Hermes E, 279
  Lewis H, 58, 59
  Louis H, 147
Truly
  Joseph C, 127
Trust
  Mrs. Mary, 131
Tubre
  H O, 85
Tucker
  A F, 91, 168
  Felix M, 261
  Isadore A, 196
  James, 51, 115, 265
  John D, 56
  John E, 288
  Millard F, 265
  Robert W, 198

Index

W, 225
William P B, 163
Tufts
   Anthony W, 208
Tuggle
   Mrs. Clio A, 245
Turead
   Benjamin, 156
Turner
   Archey C R, 175
   Ernest, 268
   James, 52, 115
   James M, 72
   John A, 88, 165
   Jones B, 138
   Lewis P, 37
   Louis F, 178
   Sarah E, 178
   William P, 273
Turnley
   William H, 4, 38
Turpin
   F W, 221
   James M, 220
Tusler
   Mrs. Matilda, 191
Twitchell
   Marshall H, 87
Tynes
   Fleming, 247
   William S, 247
Tyson
   John H, 42
Ulrich
   William B, 102
Ulrick
   Frank G, 255
Underwood
   Mrs. Lydia, 130, 249
   W C, 92
Upshaw

William W, 152
W W, 87
Usher
   John D, 184, 191
Vail
   Alfred B, 137
Valditaro
   Michael, 92
Valence
   Thomas S, 212
Valery
   Marcelle, 14
Valet
   Armand C, 66
Vallas
   Marcellus, 248
Van Brook
   Joseph, 262
Van Cook
   Mrs. Maria, 110
Van Ruff
   Daniel, 128
   Mrs. Marth A, 128
   Mrs. Martha A, 247
Vansickle
   Reuben, 46
Vargas
   Joseph F, 120, 223
Vaughan
   Thomas M, 165
Vaughn
   Robert T, 100
Veasey
   Valsin, 79
Veers
   John W, 107
Veird
   Stanley N, 63
Venable
   Charles J, 151
Vendegar

John B, 245
Verbois
   Emile D, 208
   Thomas R, 177
Verdella
   Mrs. Louisa, 269
Verger
   Paul, 264
Vering
   Henry, 112
Vernon
   Bettie W E, 191
   Frank D, 164
   John S, 88
Verrel
   Nicholas, 133
Verret
   Albert C, 207
Viallon
   Paul A, 207
Vickers
   H F, 151
   Nathaniel C, 245
Vickner
   Celestin, 132
Vidrine
   Alein, 256
   Yves, 65, 135
Vignes
   Joseph G, 235
Villemez
   Louis, 279
Vincent
   John A, 174
   Nathaniel, 175
Vining
   James E, 288
Vinson
   Gideon B, 133
Virille
   Aorian, 19
Viterbo

Index

Leon, 290
Vives
  Edward, 158
Vogel
  Philip, 67
Voizin
  Ernest, 233
Von Karsten
  Frederick B, 112
Voorhies
  William L, 2
Vowell
  Hamilton G, 227
Wachter
  Lawrence, 128
Waddell
  Emma, 204
Waddill
  Abel, 6
  George A, 220
  Hugh T, 6, 45
Wade
  Absolom, 149
  Benjamin T, 191
  Charles A, 190
  James F, 72
  M A, 161
  Mrs. Elizabeth, 177
Wadworth
  Melchi, 69
Waggoner
  William J, 278
Wagner
  Caroline, 269
Wailes
  George B, 42
Waites
  Thomas D, 25
Wakefield
  Samuel, 152
  Terence, 120
Wales

William P, 126
Walet
  Eugene H, 206
Walker
  Delos G, 70
  Emily, 67
  George, 51
  George H, 81
  George Jr, 115
  George L, 227
  Henry, 121, 227
  Henry J, 206
  Hiram, 43
  James B, 195
  Jeptha F, 195
  John L, 149
  Joseph, 128
  Joseph H, 146, 229
  P A, 6
  Robert, 15
  Sophia, 210
  Timothy J, 19, 67
  Vincent, 5
  William, 204
  William W, 140
Wall
  Drury W, 51
  John H, 10
  John P, 131
  John Paris, 266
  Shadrack J, 274
  Wesley W, 248
Wallace
  Caesar, 32
  Cezaire, 78
  James Y, 226
  Milas H, 56
  Thomas B, 188
Waller
  James Thomas, 190
Wallis
  H M, 140

John B, 72
Morley H, 269
William, 135
Walsh
  Eugene, 211
  Joseph, 8
Walsworth
  Henry C, 210
  William F, 210
Walters
  H D, 203
  Robert B, 186
Walther
  Hugo J, 252
Walton
  George L, 192
  John B, 249
  William G, 191, 192
Wammach
  Henry, 52
Wands
  Isaac N, 266
Ward
  Alfred J, 189, 273
  Angelo V, 263
  Frederick W, 46
  James, 40
  John C, 27
  Joseph P, 38
  Leroy S, 48
  Timothy C, 31
  William H, 220
Warner
  Franklin L, 20
Warnock
  James E, 54, 118
Warren
  Daniel R, 23
  Elbert H, 163
  Elbert N, 79
  Eugene F, 287

Index

John G, 188
William B, 77
Washington
  John A, 102, 191
  Joseph, 262
  Josiah G, 137
Waterhouse
  John, 61
Waterman
  Melzar, 115
  Miss Hattie V A, 115
Waters
  William H, 187
Watker
  E O, 171
Watkins
  Caleb B, 21
  Edward L, 126, 238
  Francis P, 117
  Henry B, 72
  Henry P, 73
  Presley, 242
Watson
  Arthur C, 239
  Edmund C, 18
  George W, 250
  G W, 215
  Hugh, 185
  James M, 37, 94, 199
  James P, 250
  Joseph R, 280
  Lewis, 114
  Matthew, 25
  Michael, 7, 45
  Mrs. Mary E, 265
  Oliver C, 203
  William, 139
Watt
  George, 116, 218
William F, 221
Wattis
  Nancy C, 277
Watts
  Henry, 151, 265
  Jacob J, 51, 115
  Sarah M, 244
Weaks
  Pinckney B, 169
Weaver
  Dudley H, 215
  Eliza J, 225
  Henry W, 225
Webb
  Francis, 129
  James A, 178
  Thomas J, 178
  William, 6
  William J, 179
  William R, 186
  William W, 245
Webber
  Sanford, 216
Weber
  Benoni, 180
  Emile L, 155
Webre
  Jean, 30
  Louis R, 252
Webster
  James S, 197
  J S, 168
Weeks
  James C, 56, 81, 149
  Jeptha, 127
  William T, 206, 261
Weems
  Charles C, 240
Weightman
  Roger C, 219
William W, 262
Weil
  Benjamin, 130
  Benjamin F, 64
  Louis, 84
  Mary Ann, 130
  Simon, 241
Weilenman
  Conrad, 187
Weinburg
  Morris, 239
Weiss
  Fred, 197
  Frederick, 215
  Frederick B, 115
Welby
  William A, 265
Welch
  Augustus T, 42
  James D, 151, 266
  James T, 193
  A T, 43, 102
  William H, 256
Welden
  John H, 107, 129
Weldon
  John J, 285
Wellendon
  Margaret R, 249
Wells
  Andrew J, 126
  E M, 58
  Levi, 124, 126, 238
  Miss Bessie G, 239
  Montfort, 238
  William F, 87
Welsh
  Coleman D, 173, 174
  Emily J, 263, 264
Weltz
  J B, 16

Index

Wemple
  Jacob D, 25, 43
Werner
  Albert, 233
Wesler
  Philip, 193
Westbrook
  George W, 222
  Leonidas B, 253
  Stephen H, 246
Westbury
  John O, 77
Wester
  Zachary, 242
Westfield
  Richard, 121, 231
Westmoreland
  William, 10, 50
Whatley
  Phineas, 98, 185
  Uriah T, 183
  William R, 185
Wheadon
  Thomas C, 239, 240
Wheat
  G W, 266
  Hezekiah, 130
  Washington, 63
Wheaton
  Richard J, 145
Whetstone
  Roger, 118
White
  Henry T, 273
  James C, 184
  James Clay, 98
  James T, 143
  John A Jr, 199
  Jonathan C, 10, 50
  Lewis, 31
  Mannsell Jr, 234
  Millard F, 235
  N, 58
  A Sidney, 234
  Victoria L, 194
Whited
  Samuel M, 229
Whitford
  K, 36
Whiting
  Horace G, 1, 29
Whitley
  Clarence E, 162
Whitlock
  Allen, 6
Whitlow
  Grindy C, 163
Whitney
  Albert R, 140
Whitson
  Enoch B, 26, 71
Whitted
  Richard C, 87
Whitten
  James C, 44, 104
Whittington
  Jasper B, 168
  Wesley W, 276
  Wiley D, 117
Whittlesby
  Luther H, 233
Whittmore
  George W, 50
Whitworth
  Joseph S, 137
Wicker
  M, 148
Wiese
  Jochim, 233
Wiggington
  James B, 184
Wiggins
  Moses, 3, 37
Wigginton
  James B, 98
  William E, 247
Wightman
  Leonidas H, 91
Wilbanks
  William B, 96
Wilborn
  Thomas A, 99, 188
Wilbsaw
  Garrard M, 34
Wilcocks
  George, 175
Wilcox
  Bayliss L, 19
Wildblood
  Samuel, 74
Wilder
  Jeremiah J, 81, 149, 150
  Josie, 230
  Samuel H, 150
  William H, 51, 114, 129, 151, 265
Wiley
  John, 23
  Stuart, 202
Wilhite
  Philemon, 72, 141
Wilkenson
  Thomas, 47
Wilkes
  Samuel W, 275
Wilkins
  James C, 277
  Robert S, 65
Wilkinson
  John W, 278
  Miss Mary A, 87
  Mrs. Lee J, 282
  William G, 155

Index

Willard
  Guy B, 8
Willcox
  Thomas R, 94
William
  Stephen D, 239
Williams
  Andrew J, 188
  Archibald H, 14
  Bradford J, 232
  Burrell, 203
  Charles, 38
  Charles C, 113, 213
  David B, 283
  E, 15
  Edward F, 101, 189
  Granville W, 42, 102
  Henry A, 173
  James, 110
  James A, 290
  James W, 286
  John B, 100, 190
  John L, 288
  John Routh, 43
  John W, 286, 287
  Joseph W, 25, 52
  J R, 239
  Julius A, 221
  Junius F, 129, 248
  Martin G, 276
  Mrs. Mary M, 239
  Napoleon B, 163
  Nathaniel S, 285
  Obediah W, 152, 243
  Peter A B, 15
  R B, 149
  Richard B, 226
  Stephen, 94, 178
  Whitfield, 80, 86
Wiley W, 87, 120
William A, 54, 148, 280
William R, 213
Wilson, 110, 209
Williamson
  Mrs. Eliza A, 175
Willis
  Americanus, 100
  John W, 47
  Thomas, 234
Wilson
  Albert, 46
  Alexander, 23, 75
  Clem, 149
  Frank, 101
  George W Jr., 255
  G V, 239
  Hiram, 4
  Hubert, 67
  James D, 269, 270
  John L, 219
  John M, 250
  John W, 278
  Joseph C, 57, 121
  Joseph E, 9
  Samuel R, 264
  Walton, 189
  William D, 114
  William G, 58
Wimbish
  Charles B, 167
Winder
  George G, 242
Windham
  Stephen, 23
Wineberg
  Moses, 35
Wineburg
  Moses, 93
Winegeart
  William, 241
Winfield
  John T, 86, 162
Winfree
  Isaac O, 153, 284
Winfrey
  Mrs. Mary A B C, 110, 111
Wingate
  Laban, 173
  Thomas C, 284
  Thomas E, 175
Winkler
  William B, 202
Winnie
  John J, 280
Winters
  Stephen, 23
Wire
  David G, 232
  J B, 232
Wischusen
  Diedrich, 122, 231
Wise
  David, 70, 140
  Giles L, 101
  John J, 41
  Mrs. Elizabeth A, 99
  N, 189
Wiseman
  John C, 145
Withan
  David, 233
Witherow
  Joseph, 218
Witkouski
  Julius, 182
  Simon, 94, 180, 289
Witter
  James A, 100
Wolf

Index

Benedict, 147
Gustave, 147
Louis, 106
Wolfe
  Benedict, 76
Wolfson
  Jacob A, 55, 119
  Joseph N, 223
Womack
  Jacob G, 186
Wood
  Aaron S, 145
  A B, 146
  Gillian, 16
  John R, 146
  Miss Doxia A, 144
  Samuel J, 55
Woodcock
  O F, 261
Woodland
  F W, 71
  Gabriella, 219
Woodridge
  James, 47
  John R, 38
  Thomas A, 47, 107
Woodruff
  James B Jr, 165
  Katie N, 247
  Mrs. Sarah A, 247
  Thomas W, 89, 136, 165
Woodry
  John A, 116
Woods
  Walter, 281
  W Shannon, 279
Woodson
  Thomas H, 67
Woodward
  Abishai, 8
  John E, 141

Miss Maria Ann, 106
  Sheperd, 21
Woodworth
  Henry, 255
Woodwrd
  Mrs. S, 140
Wooster
  John H, 280
  John S, 281
  N J, 137
Wooten
  Lycurgus H, 179
Word
  Mrs. Cymantha, 202
  Thomas W, 107, 202
Worster
  Frank O, 185
Worthy
  Willis W, 200
Wouton
  Thomas K, 134
Wren
  Samuel W, 267
Wright
  Abraham L, 283
  Bennett W, 118, 221
  Daniel R, 285
  Edward B, 174
  George W, 244
  Henry B, 172
  Henry C, 220
  Isaac H, 16, 63
  James W, 5
  John B, 143
  John E, 93
  John O, 135
  Mrs. Mattie, 286
  Robert D, 11, 56

William L, 233, 266
Wusthoff
  Julius, 131
Wyatt
  Rolla W, 96, 181
Yancey
  Edwin W, 39, 96, 183
  Israel P, 67
  Langston, 187
  S T, 187
  Stephen T, 203
Yarborough
  Arthur, 78
Yarbrough
  Joshua, 22
Yates
  John T, 152, 241
Yeager
  Samuel B, 193
Yerkes
  Johnson E, 131, 250, 266
York
  Sylvester, 140
  Zebulon, 42
Yost
  Sarah Y, 40
Yoste
  John W, 220
Young
  Alfred M, 25, 53
  Ezekial, 102
  Ezekiel, 43
  George M, 230
  George W, 54
  Gradenijo J, 262
  Henry C, 45, 105
  Hicks L, 248
  Nicholas, 257
  Susan I, 256

Index

    William M, 175
    William R, 230
Zeigler
    Nicholas L, 144
Zills
    Marcus P, 50
Zim
    Lewis, 14, 59
    Lewis Jr, 108
    Lewis W Jr, 202
Zimmerman
    Wilmer H, 50, 111
Zinco
    Henry, 197
Zollinger
    Henry, 252
Zuzak
    Sigmon, 193

www.ingramcontent.com/pod-product-compliance
Lightning Source LLC
Chambersburg PA
CBHW060939230426
43665CB00015B/1999